FROM
LITTLE ROCK
TO
BOSTON

FROM
LITTLE ROCK
TO
BOSTON
The History of
School
Desegregation

George R. Metcalf

Contributions to the Study of Education, Number 8

GREENWOOD PRESS
Westport, Connecticut • London, England

Library of Congress Cataloging in Publication Data

Metcalf, George R., 1914-
    From Little Rock to Boston.

    (Contributions to the study of education, ISSN 0196-
707X ; no. 8)
    Bibliography: p.
    Includes index.
    1. School integration—United States—History.
I. Title   II. Series.
LC214.2.M46   1983   370.19'342   82-15581
ISBN: 0-313-23470-1 (lib. bdg.)

Library of Congress Catalog Card Number: 82-15581
ISBN: 0-313-23470-1
ISSN: 0196-707X

First published in 1983

Greenwood Press
A division of Congressional Information Service, Inc.
88 Post Road West
Westport, Connecticut 06881

Printed in the United States of America

10 9 8 7 6 5 4 3 2 1

Copyright Acknowledgment

We are grateful to the authors and publishers for permission to reprint excerpts from *Bring Us
Together,* copyright © 1971 by Leon E. Panetta and Peter Gall (Philadelphia: J. B. Lippincott,
1971) and Harper & Row, Publishers, Inc.

To the consecrated men and women,
living and dead, who courageously
led the battle against school
segregation, often against
insurmountable prejudice

CONTENTS

PREFACE

My motivation for writing about school desegregation stems from my firm belief that the only way to achieve racial integration is through racial togetherness. It is transparent folly to attack bias in housing or employment or education in the absence of togetherness.

With this conviction I determined to point up the aphorism by writing a history of school desegregation that would describe the struggle to join white and black in the same classroom. This effort, I reasoned, would hopefully inspire Americans to acknowledge the need for making integration as much a part of the national school fabric as segregation had once been.

In my opinion, this can only be accomplished by men and women who press relentlessly for desegregation, who recognize and admit that all children—majority and minority—possess the same rights, one no more and no less than another.

It is important not to forget that government also plays a vital role. As this book demonstrates, a weak President and a docile Congress can delay, if not arrest, the best laid plans of dedicated citizens and render their efforts futile. Those who forsake their constitutional oath to support and defend justice and equality must be driven from office.

So many individuals helped to assemble the material for this volume during the five years of its production, yet I can only recognize those who made major contributions.

At the outset, it was Kenneth Clark, the noted psychologist, who encouraged me to write a history of school desegregation, emphasizing in particular, the negative impact of the Nixon Administration.

Representative Leon E. Panetta, (D-Calif.), Ruby Martin, head of HEW's Office for Civil Rights in the final year of the Johnson Administration,

Clarence Mitchell, Washington representative of the NAACP and Peter Milius, of the *Washington Post*, provided useful background for the initial chapters.

The two chapters on Ferndale and Detroit's *Bradley* v. *Milliken* would have been rather impossible without the spontaneous assistance of the Chief Librarian of the *Detroit News*, Ruth P. Braun, and her successor, Betty W. Havlena. They kindly opened their files of dates and happenings from which I later secured printouts at the Syracuse University Library.

Background for the *Keyes* was graciously provided by Mrs. Martha Radetsky of Denver, who had meticulously gathered information from the *Denver Post* over the months preceding the litigation.

Chapters on *Adams* v. *Richardson, Brown III* and Esch-Byrd-Eagleton-Biden could not have come to fruition without the extraordinary assistance of Joseph L. Rauh, Jr., and Elliot Lichtman, of Rauh, Silard and Lichtman, of Washington, D.C., the famed civil rights firm. The two men allowed me the free use of their files, explained the intricacies of the lawsuits and were exceedingly patient with this layman.

In the book's preparation I was especially fortunate to be located across the street from the U.S. District Court for the Northern District of New York, in Auburn, New York. Justice Edmund Port, assisted by Mary O'Connor, took time from their busy schedules on many occasions to locate federal citations.

Finally, to Meyer Weinberg, Director of the Horace Mann Bond Center for Equal Education, and William Taylor, Director of the Center for National Policy Review, I owe my ultimate gratitude for bringing this manuscript to the attention of Dr. James T. Sabin, Vice-President, Editorial, of Greenwood Press, who authorized its publication.

FROM
LITTLE ROCK
TO
BOSTON

1

IN THE BEGINNING

I am convinced that the use of governmental power to break up the remnants of the American caste system is the most pressing public issue of this generation. . . . My fear is that we may fail, largely because of the inadequacies of our governmental system.

Gary Orfield, November, 1968.[1]

On May 17, 1954, a torpid nation learned that the United States Supreme Court had outlawed statutory segregation in the public school system. A unanimous decision in *Brown* v. *Board of Education* proclaimed that "in the field of public education the doctrine of 'separate but equal' has no place."[2] Yet, fully a decade later, in the eleven states of the Old Confederacy, where black children and white children had been forced by law to attend separate schools, only a handful of black students—1.17 percent of the black enrollment—now attended school with whites.[3]

It was not that the cause of civil rights had cooled. In the interim, Congress passed the first civil rights act in eighty years, establishing the U.S. Commission on Civil Rights as well as a civil rights unit in the Justice Department to aid minorities. The inertia centered in the White House where the President neglected to accept the *Brown* decision or call for its implementation. Dwight D. Eisenhower never embraced school integration and was merely discharging his constitutional duty in 1957 when he ordered Federal troops to uphold the law against Gov. Orval Faubus's effort to halt school integration in Little Rock. His successor, John F. Kennedy, did little more initially. Like Eisenhower, he had no desire to confront Southern Congressmen over such an emotional issue. They headed too many congressional committees for that. So like F.D.R., when badgered to enact a Federal antilynching law in the 1930s, the President said as little as possible.

By the spring of 1962, however, history was forcing his hand. Martin Luther King, Jr., backed by nonviolent forces, vowed to demonstrate in Birmingham, Alabama, until segregation in the city's downtown snack bars, public facilities, and stores ended. To quell the disturbances, police used fire hoses and police dogs, carting off blacks by the thousands to hastily erected stockades—all before a national television audience.

In the ensuing uproar, Kennedy finally reacted. He summoned to the White House prominent individuals in the fields of labor, industry, the church, and other professions. By the following February, he was ready to send Congress the most comprehensive civil rights proposal in the nation's history, covering such disparate subjects as public accommodations and school integration. "A hell of a lot of things were thrown in to demonstrate the comprehensiveness of the proposal," a Kennedy civil rights aide, Lee White, later recalled.[4]

Among the items "thrown in" was Title VI which permitted but did not require the Federal government to cut off financial assistance in cases of racial discrimination. Rejecting this discretionary mandate, Roy Wilkins, of the Leadership Conference on Civil Rights, a pivotal group of the nation's major civil rights organizations, told the House Judiciary Subcommittee, "We feel that unless it is made mandatory, all sorts of discretion will be exercised."[5] However, the President felt otherwise. He considered the word *mandatory* excessive, just the sort of verbiage that would antagonize undecided members of the Congress whose alienation would surely defeat the legislation. Moreover Kennedy reasoned that the desegregation problem could best be solved by the Attorney General, not the Secretary of HEW.

Despite this conviction, the majority in Congress eventually turned to mandatory language, while insisting on a prohibition in Section IV of the measure that desegregation to overcome racial imbalance be barred. In that form, the revised bill went to the House floor on November 20, just two days before the President's assassination in Dallas.

That event provoked a new mood in the capital. The conviction took root that only by enacting a strong civil rights program could his martyrdom be vindicated. In addition, the elevation of Lyndon Baines Johnson to the presidency placed in office one of the most dynamic figures in American politics, utterly dedicated to passing Kennedy's legislation. He assured civil rights leaders that they had his unyielding support, and saw to it that Congress did not mistake his mood. "We put up a tough fight," one frustrated Southern opponent confided to Clarence Mitchell, Washington Bureau Director for the NAACP, but "President Johnson is just putting too much pressure on us."[6]

Despite victory in the House, the Senate refused to be rushed and Southerners began a filibuster which droned on for seventy-five days, mostly covering the subject of housing discrimination. In view of the broad effect Title VI would eventually have on school integration, debators said remarkably little on the subject. As Gary Orfield, a school desegregation expert wrote, the provisions were "expected to have little impact on school desegregation because of the minor importance of Federal money in most districts" and because "the Justice Department saw the Office of Education [in HEW] as playing a minor role, one in proportion to its puny role in most local school systems."[7]

Senate Majority Whip Hubert H. Humphrey, the Administration floor manager during the debate, agreed precisely with this interpretation. "If anyone can be against that, he can be against Mother's Day," he declared disarmingly. "How can one justify discrimination in the use of Federal funds and Federal programs?"[8] Such verbal nostrums did not calm the anger of Senator Robert Byrd, of West Virginia, who saw in Title VI a weapon to attack Northern de facto segregation and the neighborhood school, but doubted that the restrictions in Title IV against the assignment of students "to overcome racial balance" would extend to Title VI. Humphrey again tried to soothe with dulcet words. In the first place, he told Byrd, there was the constitutional guideline to fall back on. While it "prohibits segregation," he said, it does not require integration.[9]

In retrospect, it is surprising that Humphrey could still the fears that Title VI aroused. Only Albert Gore, a Tennessee Democrat, foresaw (and acted upon that realization) the extent to which Title VI could move control of the Southern school systems from the state capitals to HEW. His motion to strike out Title VI went down to an overwhelming defeat of 69 to 25, demonstrating that amid arguments over the issue of public accommodations, the question of school desegregation hardly caused a ripple.

Not so in HEW. Within hours of the signing of the Civil Rights Act on July 2, 1964, department officials gathered in the office of Francis Keppel, the Commissioner of Education, to discuss its impact. It was a surprising development, for they had had nothing to do with writing Title VI and had even expressed opposition to mandatory provisions. Indeed, so certain had HEW Assistant Secretary James M. Quigley been that Title VI would fall under segregationist fire that he considered it no more than a "loss leader."[10] Consequently, when the Department finally had to act, its mood was toward leniency. School systems would be approved by simply signing a letter of compliance.

Fortunately, in the battle against segregation, this somnolence did not extend to all Washington agencies. The U.S. Civil Rights Commission, for one, wanted Federal aid pumped into those schools whose officials submitted specific plans for immediate desegregation.

Between these two positions—one soft, one hard—stood the Justice Department, in charge, at White House insistence, of coordinating suggestions for Title VI guidelines. Lawyers for the Department had figured prominently in drafting the legislation and now demanded the new regulations embody the Humphrey commitment, plus a recognition that school districts that complied with court orders on desegregation should not lose Federal aid. They feared nothing would excite congressional passions more quickly than a display of bureaucratic opposition to "Congressional intent." A policy debate ensued for six months over what course to follow. The primary question centered on the interpretation of Section VI, giving the Federal government the authority to withhold school aid. Lee White, who was now Johnson's assistant, in trying to unify the different factions saw it as "an exceedingly potent weapon" which "ought to be used with tremendous care because it was so damn dangerous."[11] He agreed with the President who said the regulation should be "as fair and invincible to attack as possible,"[12] and the guideposts Johnson eventually approved on December 3, 1964, incorporated Justice's thinking which lawyer White approved. "Had HEW been permitted to draft its own regulations," Orfield later wrote, "much of the revolutionary force of the law would undoubtedly have been lost through narrow interpretations by the department's legal staff and operating agency heads."[13]

On New Year's Eve, 1964, scurrying clerks at HEW's Office of Education mailed piles of instructions and compliance forms to more than 25,000 school districts and state education offices and to more than 2,600 institutions of higher learning. It was the beginning of a new chapter in the nation's effort to desegregate public schools. Up to that moment, the only ultimatum for desegregation had been the High Court's "deliberate speed" order of 1955 in *Brown II* and that had integrated less than 2 percent of the South's black children in a period of ten years.[14] The new guidelines that went into effect on January 3, 1965, explained in broad terms what HEW would expect before approving plans. Desegregation of the lowest grades would have to begin at once; gerrymandering of school district was out; freedoom to choose the student's school was in. Offenders would have their funds terminated. Compliance was relatively simple. School districts could either desegregate voluntarily, which in light of the "massive resistance" of the previous decade, few did; they could accept a court order; or they could merely send in written assurance of compliance. These "paper compliances," as they became known, were originally designed to cover only districts that had been desegregated, but they soon provided escapes for totally segregated districts.

Nevertheless, Southern educators were apprehensive from the beginning over living under the bureaucratic gun. The new regulations prevented state education officers from using Federal school funds for either current or new programs until Commissioner of Education Keppel approved the district's compliance with Title VI. As long as Federal spending amounted to only a few million dollars annually, the threat of withholding funds caused little concern, but on April 11, 1965, President Johnson signed the Elementary and Secondary Education Act, releasing more than $1 billion for the education of children in low-income families.

Keppel was jubilant. Writing HEW Secretary Anthony T. Celebrezze, he said Johnson's action "makes possible a new approach in handling civil rights problems in education. Title VI can become less of a negative threat and more of a condition necessary to progress in the future," but to accomplish this, he went on, Southern educators would have to stop thinking "their political leaders [could prevent] the abandonment of the dual school system."[15] Unfortunately, the Secretary was the wrong man to carry Keppel's torch. In the Department, he had built a reputation for wanting "to stay clear of controversy," presumably because his eventual appointment to a seat on the Federal Court of Appeals in the Sixth Circuit could have been blocked by a public embroilment.[16]

So it fell to the Commissioner to take charge of the early school struggles over Title VI, assisted by a thirty-five-year-old lawyer, David Seeley, who had begun compiling possible actions as soon as Johnson signed the statute. When HEW's Office of Education encountered difficulty in establishing standards for different situations, Seeley asked Professor G. W. Foster, Jr., of the University of Wisconsin Law School, to assemble a group of law professors versed in civil rights who could correlate HEW's enforcement criteria with decisions handed down by the Southern Federal Judiciary.

In time, Southern educators who came to Washington seeking advice and counsel met this ad hoc group and discussed plans they hoped to incorporate in their districts. Foster and company informed each visitor that their advice had no "official status" and did not bind the Office of Education, but "it reflects the thinking of the officials charged with the responsibility for enforcement of Title VI."[17] Extensive negotiations invariably followed, and to add to the confusion, pressures from outside interests could upset whatever compromises the professors and the school parties drew up. As Keppel put it, "On the one side is the danger of requiring . . . so much desegregation so rapidly that the educators and leaders of the Deep South who want to accomplish desegregation will be either thrown out of office or unable to move forward. On the other side is the danger that civil rights groups and other branches of the government will protest that the Federal establishment is ducking the issue and permitting inconceivable delays in desegregation."[18]

Yet, with all these handicaps, the number of black children attending desegregated schools in the eleven Southern states tripled during 1965-66. Great credit must go to Seeley for this transformation. To be sure, he was abrasive, but it required a tough individual to turn the bureaucratic wheels. "Thirty-five million people," he declared, "had to be brought into it and convinced for the routine case."[19]

Despite his effort, the spring of 1965 saw distress signals rising from those civil rights groups that had actively campaigned for the landmark legislation of 1964. They found the Title VI guidelines too weak. The Department's approval of a growing number of Southern free-choice plans especially upset them. Such action, NAACP's Roy Wilkins warned, would only "place the burden of initiating changes not on school boards . . . but on their victims, Negro parents and pupils."[20] He argued in a letter to Keppel on May 13, 1965, that Title VI was in danger of becoming "another in the succession of cruel hoaxes practiced on the American Negro citizen."[21]

When such admonitions went unheeded, civil rights forces decided to work through the courts to tighten the legal definition of segregation. During the summer of 1965, the NAACP Legal Defense and Educational Fund, the so-called Inc. Fund, and the American Friends Service Committee combined resources in a school desegregation task force. Its primary aim was the protection of black families allegedly victimized by HEW's freedom-of-choice alternative. Yet the task force could do little so long as U.S. District Courts in the South insisted, as they then did, on permitting freedom-of-choice as one method of desegregation, provided good faith could be shown. For its part, the Office of Education, with an eye to Congress, concluded that it could go no further, while Southern property owners, taking advantage of the economic leverage they held, resorted to outright coercion to keep black children out of white schools. The melancholy letter of a distraught black mother, reported by the Southern Regional Council, echoed the story:

Dear Sir:

We had 26 acres of cotton last year, and this year the man we live with told my husband that he couldn't use him this year. he gave all the people crops but us . . . so we have two childrens in the white school, and we do feel and believe that is the reason he didn't give us a crop. we have 11 childrens to support. And nothing around here to make a living. and I am asking you if you know where i can write will you please send the address.[22]

In hindsight, had the white South been more manipulative with its freedom-of-choice options to its segregated ends, the regulatory force of Title VI might have been blunted. It was only when the Federal circuit courts, prodded by civil rights groups, began to see that freedom of choice was a camouflage for no choice that the judges finally lowered the boom.

Oddly, however, it was not below the Mason-Dixon line, but in Chicago that HEW received its severest challenge during 1965. Keppel had attempted to hold back $30 million in school aid after the city's Coordinating Council of Community Organization charged the school board with violation of Title VI. When Mayor Richard Daley heard that his city's public school system was charged with "probable non-compliance," he hit the ceiling. Having neglected to make a thorough investigation, neither Keppel nor his assistants could document the case. "The Department had absolutely no evidence whatever," an HEW insider later admitted.[23] Daley complained personally to the President, and Johnson responded by sending HEW Undersecretary Wilbur T. Cohen to smooth the school superintendent's ruffled feathers and to order the restoration of funds. What began as a test of HEW's determination to enforce Title VI, presumably in the South, ended as a setback with devastating results. It seriously damaged the civil rights cause by demonstrating that even as strong an advocate as Lyndon Johnson would bow to political pressure if the stakes were high enough. Moreover, it abruptly awakened those black and white civil rights leaders who had mistakenly thought their struggles were safely out of the immediate political arena. Indeed, HEW's effort to enforce Title VI came to a temporary halt, and only direct orders from John Gardner, who had replaced Celebrezze as HEW Secretary in July, put some new life into the enforcement attempt.

In contrast to Celebrezze, Gardner (later to head Common Cause) was a political neophyte. For twenty years before going to Washington, he had lived in the educational ivory tower of the Carnegie Corporation, hardly a stout recommendation for undertaking the thorny civil rights struggles. Yet, Johnson had recognized in this moral man a tough fiber that would stand up to attack and give the Department more credibility than it enjoyed under Celebrezze.

Ultimately, Chicago convinced Gardner that school desegregation could not be achieved without taking a more rigid stand on Title VI. In late 1965, he named Harold Howe, II, Commissioner of Education. A former superintendent of schools in Scarsdale, New York, Howe made no bones about his opposition to school segregation and quickly became the Department's standard bearer on Capitol Hill.

To fortify their joint dedication, Gardner and Howe issued new regulations on March 7, 1966, calling for complete unification by 1967. Close to 5,000 districts in the seventeen Southern and Border states were told to submit letters of compliance by April 15 or face the loss of Federal aid. For the most part, the order fell on deaf ears since no school district up to then had been denied aid for noncompliance. In Georgia, for instance, fewer than one-tenth of the districts complied. When the Office of Education called a meeting in Birmingham, Alabama, to explain the guidelines, a reporter for the *Los Angeles Times* overheard one school official taunt an HEW representative, "Where'd you leave your carpetbags, you dirty Commies?"[24]

By the end of April, scarcely more than 60 percent of the school systems had filed compliance forms. Partly to mollify this opposition, and partly to satisfy the civil right advocates who resented the Southern intransigence, the Office of Education extended the compliance date to May 6 and ordered that payment of Federal funds on new projects be deferred in districts that had not filed by that date. Still, more than 250 districts refused to comply.

In the meantime, Southern members of Congress were becoming inflamed by Washington's intrusion in their affairs. On May 2, eighteen senators from the Old Confederacy complained to Lyndon Johnson. Their letter, written by Georgia's respected Richard Russell, and labelled a "Most Solemn Petition," vigorously protested the "bureaucratic imposition of the guidelines."[25] Johnson, they argued, had served too long as a senator and

Majority Leader not to understand their feelings, but their erstwhile colleague remained unmoved. Although he never replied publicly, Johnson reportedly told Russell the guidelines did not prohibit free-choice plans, which the Southerners approved, nor did they "require racial balance or busing."[26] To his own staff, he was even more direct. According to Douglas Carter, his in-residence expert on education, the President passed along the word, "When you see those civil rights people, you tell them they are going to have to put on sneakers to stay ahead of Lyndon Johnson on civil rights."[27]

In the House, too, the mood changed markedly. On May 4, 1966, Rep. John Fogarty (D-R.I.), the esteemed chairman of the House Appropriations Subcommittee, asked that all spending for civil rights be consolidated into one office "for a much more efficient and effective program."[28] Up to then, the Office of Education, the Public Health Service, and the Welfare Administration—HEW's three pillars—had operated separate offices of "equal opportunity" to cope with civil rights problems. Despite a reference to "efficiency," the underlying thought came through: consolidation would remove HEW's enforcement program from Howe and place it in the hands of Peter Libassi, Gardner's special assistant for civil rights. There, the activity could be more closely monitored. To Fogarty, it seemed an ideal solution to the House's rising temper, but in the face of HEW opposition, Fogarty neglected to press the point. Instead, the committee vented its annoyance on Howe's Office of Education by ordering him to hold full hearings before terminating Federal funds. Worse still, it cut HEW's inadequate compliance staff from 348 to 278.

Surprisingly, in view of growing Southern hostility and growing congressional pressure, when schools opened in the fall of 1966, the dual system showed visible cracks. On September 12, for example, the *Wall Street Journal* revealed that Federal funds had been withdrawn from thirty-nine of the most stubborn districts, steps to end aid undertaken in sixty-four others, and similar action contemplated in forty-seven more.[29] The Deep South still qualified as the greatest offender with 95 percent of the black pupils attending segregated schools. The chief obstacle to further progress lay in its determination to continue free-choice, hoping to gain HEW approval.

In the beginning, a sympathetic Federal Judiciary aided their efforts. However, on March 29, 1967, the Fifth Circuit Court of Appeals assumed a different stance. Sitting en banc in the case of *U.S.* v. *Jefferson County Board of Education*, the justices directed the states of Alabama, Florida, Georgia, Louisiana, Mississippi, and Texas, all within its jurisdiction, to take whatever affirmative action was necessary to create a "unitary school system in which there are no Negro schools and no white schools—just schools." Complained the court, taking aim at freedom of choice, "The only school desegregation plan that meets constitutional standards is one that works." Moreover, it went out of its way to sanction HEW's controversial guidelines, saying the "applicable standard is essentially the HEW formulae."[30]

The NAACP was ecstatic, calling it the most significant school desegregation opinion since *Brown*, and HEW registered its joy by flashing word that free-choice would no longer satisfy the guidelines without proof of workability.

Again, reverberations were felt in Congress. This time, the House Appropriations Subcommittee would not be put off, as in the previous year. Chairman Daniel Flood (D-Pa.), who had replaced Fogarty after the latter's untimely death in January, was furious that civil rights enforcement had not been centralized. Threateningly, he asked Gardner when he planned to "correct the 'failure.'" The Secretary's reply, Flood intimated, would undoubtedly "assist the Subcommittee in its consideration of the 1968 budget," a warning Gardner could hardly mistake.[31] On May 9, 1967, Gardner informed Flood that the "groundwork" for centralization had been laid and "we are prepared to make the additional changes necessary to accomplish the reorganization recommended by the Committee."[32]

Nor was the House alone in attacking the Secretary. In the spring of 1967, Sen. Russell again attempted to halt desegregation by proposing an amendment to the 1967 aid bill funding the Elementary and Secondary Education Act. It would prohibit HEW from withholding money from a noncomplying district during the school year. Such a proposition, if enacted, would neutralize Title VI, and jeopardize the enforcement program. To prevent this, a group of Northern senators, who supported desegregation, prevailed upon Gardner to write a letter to Senator Wayne Morse, chairman of the Education Subcommittee, saying he would not terminate funds unless the school had been notified by March 1 of the previous school year that the possibility of a fund cut-off existed. This satisfied the Southerners and gave HEW a needed respite.

A year later, as it had in the *Jefferson County* decision the Federal judiciary opened the way to new advances. On May 27, 1968, in *Green* v. *County School Board of New Kent County*, the U.S. Supreme Court declared the time for "deliberate speed" had run out, that the only acceptable desegregation plans were those that promised "realistically to work [and] realistically to work *now*." Justice William J. Brennan, Jr., author of the opinion, took pains to italicize the *now*. The court also sharpened the restrictions on Southern free-choice plans by circumscribing their admissibility. "In desegregating a dual system of public education," wrote Brennan, "a plan utilizing 'freedom-of-choice' is not an end in itself." Then, quoting Judge Sobeloff, of the Fifth Circuit, he reiterated, " 'Freedom-of-choice' is not a sacred talisman; it is only a means, a constitutionally required end—the abolition of the system of segregation and its effects. If the means prove effective, it is acceptable, but if it fails to undo segregation, other means must be used to achieve this end."[33] Now the highest court in the land had declared such plans had to be proven effective.

In response, angry Southern whites quickly formed an organization to halt the elimination of free-choice plans, going so far as to close some of their schools. Gov. Lurleen Wallace, of Alabama, substituting for husband George who could not succeed himself, spoke for thousands of segregationists, when she declared with Jacksonian finality, "They have made their decision, now let them enforce it."[34]

In the House of Representatives, Southern members went to work on Northern colleagues, emphasizing the similarity between the Northern neighborhood school and the free-choice classroom in the South. Each represented an isolated entity the white majority could control as though *Brown* had never occurred. If it was the South's lot to lose "free-choice," the North would be next with the abolition of the neighborhood concept.

"What has been visited upon certain areas of the country is about to spread throughout the nation," warned Rep. Jamie Whitten (D-Miss.).[35] As part of his effort to involve the North in a campaign to halt Southern desegregation, Whitten had introduced two amendments to the 1964 Civil Rights Act, hoping to gut Title VI.

The first, Section 409, would prohibit the use of Federal funds for "forced busing of students," and excuse them from attending any high school or "particular school" against their parents' wish. The second, Section 410, would outlaw "forced busing" as a quid pro quo for receiving Federal funds by any state, school district, or school.

Sensing the fact that Whitten was gaining strength among Northern moderates, Congressman Edward R. Roybal, a liberal Democrat from California, took the floor on June 26, 1968, to point out that Section 0.5 of the Mississippi Code makes it "unlawful for any member of the white or Caucasian race to attend any school of high school level or below . . . which is also attended by a member or members of the colored or Negro race, [and violators] shall . . . be fined . . . or imprisoned in the county jail . . . or both."[36]

In light of that, he asked, "What does Mississippi have to show, as its contribution toward ending racial discrimination in the United States? The answer is virtually nothing. Approximately, four out of one hundred Negro students in Mississippi are permitted to attend school with white children, provided they can stand the hostility within the community, and provided their parents can withstand economic pressures, harassment and intimidation."[37]

When the amendments passed the House with a vote of 139 to 109, civil rights advocates were aghast. Like Rep. Jeffery Cohelan (D-Calif.), they wondered how the membership could "in one month vote for open housing or equal voting rights or for other civil rights and now vote for restrictive provisions to tie the hand of the Federal administrators in encouraging integration?"[38]

Watching what had happened in the House, Richard Russell, of Georgia, mounted a similar campaign in the Senate to pass the Whitten amendments intact, but liberal members of the Appropriations Committee refused to be bowled over. In the ensuing debate, however, Section 409 was broadened to include elementary as well as secondary students, but with the qualifying clause, "in order to overcome racial balance," which in effect nullified the thrust of the Whitten Amendment because "overcoming racial balance" was already forbidden by the language of Section IV. To blunt the Whitten thrust still further, senators changed Section 410 to require the same HEW effort against segregation in the North as in the South. Since the North had not been judged guilty of de jure segregation, this could only be viewed as an attack on de facto segregation. Again, however, this was forbidden by Section IV if it involved action to overcome racial balance, and what de facto segregation did not include questions of racial balance?

Nevertheless, on September 4 the Senate approved the revised Whitten amendments only to have the original House versions reinstated by a Senate-House conference committee. It seemed that Whitten was about to win, but in one of those inscrutable legislative turnabouts, the House undid its own handiwork when not enough Whitten supporters attended the session. "We had the votes," agonized John Flynt, Georgia's congressman, "if the people had been there."[39] Into the opening, left by the Whitten defeat, marched Rep. Cohelan, offering a motion that the Senate's weaker language now be restored. The result, a 175 to 167 victory for Northern liberals, obtained Senate acceptance for a second time.

While these inconclusive forays against school desegregation were played out in Congress, an unforeseen movement of the greatest consequence was taking shape in HEW. In working to desegregate the Southern schools, department guidelines had been at times ahead, at times behind, but never far removed from court implementations. As Peter Milius of the *Washington Post* saw it:

HEW played a kind of legal leapfrog with its guidelines. A district judge in one part of the South would hand down an opinion more advanced in one respect or another than those his brethren were then issuing. HEW would seize on the opinion and slip it into the guidelines, spreading it across the South as a whole as if it were gospel, or more important, perhaps, as if it had already been tested and upheld in a court of appeals. Then, to complete the circle, as the guidelines became better known, they in turn began to be cited by judges. The department would borrow from the courts, then the courts would borrow back, and each time the law would be ratcheted ahead a little.[40]

Inside HEW, the chief advocate of the "leapfrog" theory was now a thirty-five-year-old black lawyer named Ruby Martin, Arkansas-born and educated at Fisk University and the Howard University Law School. Like Libassi, she had worked for the U.S. Commission on Civil Rights before coming to HEW in May, 1965. When, two years later, HEW's entire civil rights program was centered in the Office for Civil Rights, she became head of education in the operations division. In Johnson's final year, events quickly propelled her upward. First, Gardner left the cabinet in April to head the nascent National Urban Coalition, taking Libassi with him. Then, when Under Secretary Cohen took Gardner's place, he gave Mrs. Martin carte blanche to enforce Title VI. "She scared all the old stodgy Office of Education types and hangers on. She demanded performance," an aide recalls.[41] No one took more delight in using the *Green* decision to rout free-choice. When white officials refused to give black requests equal consideration with white demands, she reacted furiously. Why, in a pluralistic society, she asked, should white invariably come first? Why should black children be bused to white schools and not vice versa? Why should black teachers invariably be penalized when schools were closed or consolidated?

In the nine months of the Johnson interregnum, Ruby Martin accomplished something few blacks have achieved in this country. Using her official position, she successfully challenged the Southern white power structure, forcing one school board after another to desegregate. In the process of upending a society that had been three and a half centuries in the making, she unwittingly paved the way for a Northern presidential demagogue to promise a halt to HEW's assault if he could capture the Old Confederacy and gain the White House.

Notes

1. Gary Orfield, *The Reconstruction of Southern Education* (New York: John Wiley & Sons, 1969).

2. *Brown* v. *Board of Education*, 347 U.S. 483 (1954).

3. Glenda Bartley, "Full Circle of Failure," Part I, *Lawlessness and Disorder—Fourteen Years of Failure in Southern School Desegregation* (Atlanta: Southern Regional Council, 1968), p. 1.

4. Orfield, *Southern Education*, p. 35.

5. U.S., Congress, House, Judiciary Subcommittee, No. 5, 88th Cong. 1st Sess. Serial No. 4, pt. 3, July 25, 1963, p. 2161.

6. Clarence Mitchell, "The Warren Court and Congress: A Civil Rights Partnership," *Nebraska Law Review* 48, no. 1 (1968): 99 n.21.

7. Orfield, *Southern Education*, p. 40.

8. U.S., Congress, Senate, *Congressional Record*, 88th Cong., 2d Sess., 1964, 110, pt. 5: 6543.

9. Ibid., p. 22337.

10. Orfield, *Southern Education*, p. 60.

11. Ibid., p. 74.

12. Ibid., p. 73.

13. Ibid., p. 75.

14. *Brown* v. *Board of Education*, 349 U.S. 294 (1955).

15. Orfield, *Southern Education*, p. 94.

16. Leon E. Panetta and Peter Gall, *Bring Us Together* (Philadelphia: J. B. Lippincott Company, 1971), p. 34.

17. G. W. Foster, Jr., "Title VI: Southern Education Faces the Facts," *Saturday Review*, March 20, 1965, p. 60.

18. Memorandum from Commissioner Keppel to Secretary Celebrezze, April 13, 1965.

19. Orfield, *Southern Education*, p. 116.

20. Letter from Roy Wilkins to Keppel, May 13, 1965.

21. Ibid.

22. *Special Report: School Desegregation 1966: The Slow Undoing* (Atlanta: Southern Regional Council, 1966), appendix, p. 40.

23. Orfield, *Southern Education*, p. 183.

24. *Special Report: School Desegregation 1966*, p. 10.

25. Ibid., p. 15.

26. Ibid., p. 16.

27. Panetta and Gall, *Bring Us Together*, p. 45.

28. William Steif, "The New Look in Civil Rights Enforcement" *Southern Education Report*, September, 1967: 3.

29. James C. Tanner, "Segregation's Price," *Wall Street Journal*, September 12, 1966, p. 1.

30. *U.S.* v. *Jefferson County Board of Education*, 372 F.2D 836 (5th Cir. 1966) *aff'd en banc*, 380 F. 2D 385 (1967).

31. Steif, "New Look in Civil Rights," p. 4.

32. Ibid.

33. *Green* v. *Board of Education of New Kent County*, 391 U.S., at 438-40 (1968).

34. Bartley, "Full Circle of Failure," p. 15.

35. Robert E. Anderson, Jr., "The Congress, the Courts and the National Will," Part II *Lawlessness and Disorder—Fourteen Years of Failure in Southern School Desegregation* (Atlanta: Southern Regional Council, 1968), p. 20.

36. "School Desegregation Guidelines—Action Taken by the 90th Congress, *Congressional Digest* 48, no. 2 (February, 1969): 59.

37. Ibid.

38. Ibid., p. 51.

39. Anderson, "The Congress, the Courts and the National Will," p. 22.

40. Monograph furnished author by Peter Milius of the *Washington Post*.

41. Panetta and Gall, *Bring Us Together*, p. 53.

2

FOR A MESS OF POTTAGE

> If we don't do this, we are in effect saying, "Well, you'll get your
> constitutional rights a little later on; we can't be in too great a
> hurry about this."
>
> Attorney General Ramsey Clark, January 6, 1969.[1]

When Lyndon Johnson announced on March 31, 1968, that he would not
seek reelection, his most likely successor was thought to be Hubert
Humphrey, the Democratic Vice-President. A former senator from
Minnesota, Humphrey had burst upon the national scene two decades
before at the Democratic national convention when he sponsored and successfully fought for a strong civil rights plank.

Although he won in 1964 as Johnson's running mate, the white South
could not forget his pushing through the Senate, the same year, the hated
Civil Rights law whose Title VI had caused them such pain. Consequently,
below the Mason-Dixon line, Humphrey had few friends.

As an alternative, there was the redoubtable Alabaman, George C.
Wallace, who cried "segregation now, segregation tomorrow and segregation forever," and thereby enjoyed grass roots support, both North and
South, among the nation's bigots, but without a recognized following in
either major party, Wallace came through as a spoiler.

That such impediments existed convinced Southern Republican leaders
that a GOP candidate who would go easy on Title VI could actually carry
the South. Early in 1968, members of the Southern State Republican Chairmen's Association, chosen from Alabama, Arkansas, Florida, Georgia,
Kentucky, Louisiana, Mississippi, the Carolinas, Tennessee, Texas, and
Virginia, decided to act. Their effort was aided by the conservative tide that
already had overtaken the Grand Old Party. Describing this phenomenon,
Kevin Phillips, a young lawyer and political pundit, saw it as an "emerging
Republican majority" developing among the middle and lower-middle
classes of the South and West.[2]

Along with this shifting political sentiment, the Southern GOP drew
encouragement from the fact that its voting strength at the national convention had jumped from 19 to 26.7 percent since Eisenhower's 1952 nomi-

nation in Chicago. The South's 356 convention votes were now more than half the number required for nomination.[3] Their delivery to the choice of the Association could very well sew up the nomination, particularly if that candidate had viable political connections in the North.

To fill this requirement, Nelson A. Rockefeller, of New York, for one, came to mind. An early liberal, the governor had turned sharply right to curry favor with the conservatives. However, he remained, in Southern eyes, a fallen Humpty-Dumpty, with no chance of sealing the cracks. Southerners, especially Republican Southerners, refused to accept the New Yorker's transformation, his public statements and support for the Vietnam War notwithstanding.

Ronald Reagan, of California, a second possibility, aroused greater interest. Something of a political Adonis, an ex-actor, his formal entry to the Republican fold had taken place in the final days of the Goldwater disaster of 1964. Over national television, he momentarily stirred the faithful, facing sure defeat, by leading the cheers for less governmental interference and lower taxes. It evoked an immediate response with more than half a million dollars tumbling into the Republican treasury.

Six months later, Reagan was being touted for governor, a feat he accomplished in the fall of 1966, defeating Pat Brown by almost a million votes. His attractiveness as a vote getter, his emphasis on frugality combined with a dislike for welfare programs, and his opposition to civil rights made Reagan an immediate favorite in the South. Unfortunately for Reagan, the very qualities that endeared him there worked against him in the more liberal and more Democratic North. Reluctantly, the Association decided to seek a third candidate.

As it turned out, the only national figure with sufficient "balance" was Richard Nixon who stood in the middle of the political mainstream. Like the pendulum on a metronome, he had no difficulty swinging from right to left and vice versa. At one time, his message deploring the enforcement of Title VI cheered the conservative South; at another, a word applauding integration reassured Northern liberals. Partisans in each camp, having heard what they wanted to hear, took little note of his words to their opponents. That Nixon could live easily with this dichotomy goes far to explain his early success as well as his eventual downfall.

After a meteoric rise in Congress and two terms as Eisenhower's Vice-President, Nixon narrowly lost the presidency to John Kennedy in 1960. What remained of his political reputation vanished two years later when Pat Brown trounced him in California's gubernatorial race. In the aftermath, he moved to New York City, joined the Wall Street firm of Mudge, Stern, Baldwin, and Todd, and to all outward appearances, wiped his hands of politics.

Then came the Goldwater debacle and the gradual eclipse of Lyndon Johnson, as American opinion turned against the Vietnam War. By 1966, the probability of a switch in administrations was so apparent to an experienced eye like Nixon's that winning the Republican nomination and becoming President appeared synonymous. He was well aware that other men had lost once and tried again. He began to assist Republican candidates from one end of the country to the other, praising them, raising money for their campaign treasuries, and in the process, gaining their I.O.U.'s to be cashed in 1968. Thus, he was able to build an organization whose ideology was conservative and whose loyalty to him was total.

In view of this effort, it is little wonder that the Southern GOP chairmen sought a commitment from Nixon, giving him their backing in exchange for opposition to Title VI. All agreed that the one man to put it together was arch conservative Strom Thurmond, the U.S. senator from South Carolina. He had been a prominent regional politician since his election to the governorship twenty-two years before, and was widely known for his intense opposition to civil rights, even bolting the 1948 Democratic National Convention over the issue. In that year, he became the Dixiecrat nominee for President, taking South Carolina, Alabama, Mississippi, and Louisiana from Harry Truman.

Yet, something in the man's style, his candor, his unequivocal hatred of Communism captured the Southern imagination quite apart from any party consideration. Indeed, he was elected to the Senate in 1954 as a write-in candidate, and in three successive elections, won by margins as high as nine to one.[4] Eventually, announcing that the Democrats were "leading the evolution of our nation to a socialistic dictatorship," Thurmond joined the Republican party in 1964.[5]

Consequently, when Nixon met Thurmond in Atlanta on June 1, 1968, much depended upon the outcome. Nixon knew what Thurmond wanted to hear and was careful to speak in that vein. Impressed, the Southerner agreed to take Nixon under his wing.[6]

By August, as Republican delegates gathered in Miami, most observers were conceding the nomination to the ex-Californian. So certain was Nixon of the outcome that he remained 1,200 miles away, quietly writing his acceptance speech, unaware that Southern delegates, previously committed to his standard, were edging toward Reagan. The desertion had followed the rumor that Nixon was planning to select a Northern liberal for his running mate. Thurmond instinctively knew that regardless of regional and ideological appeal, his candidate's support with Dixie delegates would rapidly vanish if that happened. He telephoned a warning to Nixon who immediately flew to Miami to reassure the wavering Southerners on school desegregation and the selection of a Vice-President.

One after another, the Southern delegations visited Nixon headquarters. It was not "proper," the candidate told them, "for judges to act as local school boards."[7] As to the Vice-Presidency, he professed sympathy for their apprehension, and emphasized his position by exclaiming to enthusiastic clapping, "There is one final thing. I am not going to take, I can assure you, anybody that is going to divide the party."[8] In political terms, this served to redline such Northern potentials as Senator Percy, of Illinois; Senator Case, of New Jersey; and Mayor Lindsay, of New York. To win the nomination, Nixon had now excised his political independence.

The first concession quickly followed. The Nixon entourage agreed to support Spiro Agnew, Maryland's young governor, for Vice-President. This was the man who had alienated state blacks the preceding March after Martin Luther King's assassination by calling out the National Guard to quell rioting. Originally, Agnew seemed to champion minority rights by insisting on black participation in his administration and signing into law an open housing act, but the severity with which he met the uprising was bound to warm Southern hearts.

One of the first to speak out was Jackie Robinson, the ex-Brooklyn Dodger, who said he would now support any Democrat in November and accused Nixon of being part of a "racist" ticket. If Southerners could hold "veto-power" over the naming of the Vice-President, he declared, they could hold the same power over national policy should Nixon win.[9]

In mid-September, the capitulation that Robinson feared took place. During a televised commentary on school desegregation, emanating from Charlotte, N.C., Nixon said it was "going too far" to make the Federal government and the Federal courts responsible for enforcing the *Brown* decision of 1954. Referring to Title VI, he said he was opposed to withholding Federal funds from school districts because of what some Federal administrator or bureaucrat might determine was best for that district. "In my view, that kind of activity should be very scrupulously examined and in many cases should be rescinded,"[10] a proposition the *Washington Post* promptly tagged a "formula for disorder."[11]

So dismayed was Massachusetts' Republican Senator Edward W. Brooke that he promptly flew to Cleveland to confer with the GOP candidate. The only black in the Senate, Brooke feared Nixon would lose thousands of black votes by retreating on school desegregation.

By then, however, Nixon was more concerned by the possibility of Southern defection to George Wallace than what his words on school desegregation might cost him in the North. "The way things are now going," commented columnist Roscoe Drummond, "Wallace, more than Humphrey, is the main threat to Nixon's election."[12]

Within days, however, both Nixon and Wallace stumbled badly, while Humphrey got to his feet and sprinted, producing one of the most dramatic races in American political history. On election day, pollster Lou Harris labelled the outcome "too close to call" with Humphrey a nose ahead.[13] The projection proved too sanguine. Nixon won 302 electoral votes to 191 for Humphrey, and 45 for Wallace, but the popular vote gave Nixon a margin of less than 500,000 out of 73 million votes cast. Although Nixon lost Louisiana, Mississippi, Alabama, and Georgia to Wallace, the fact that he took Florida, the Carolinas, Tennessee, and Virginia, totaling fifty-eight votes, saved him from losing a majority in the Electoral College.

Not surprisingly, Strom Thurmond lost no time telling friends that changes would now occur in Washington. According to a December 19 dispatch in *State*, Columbia, South Carolina's highly influential daily newspaper, the senator called on Southern school districts to ignore HEW's desegregation demands and await the taking of office of the Nixon Administration. He even recommended the "slow stall" for Dixie educators who were being pressed by HEW to adopt acceptable civil rights compliance programs, telling them that Robert Finch, the new President's choice to head HEW, would support the desegregation policy outlined by Nixon.[14]

Fearful of such machinations, Johnson's outgoing Attorney General, Ramsey Clark, the man who had done his best to cooperate with HEW in enforcing civil rights legislation, warned Fred Graham, of the *New York Times*, of "tragic" consequences if Nixon softened the school "guidelines." Clark referred to the immense progress in school desegregation in the Deep South during the final Johnson years, rising from 1 percent in 1964 to 20 percent in 1968 through enforcement of the 1964 Civil Rights Act. "The progress that has been made," he confided to Graham, "is very substantial. It should have been more. It must be more substantial in the future."[15]

The anomaly of what was happening came to a head on January 20, 1969, when Richard Nixon mounted the inaugural platform to announce unblushingly to his countrymen, "No man can be fully free while his neighbor is not. To go forward at all is to go forward together. This means black and white together, as one nation, not two. The laws have caught up with our conscience. What remains is to give life to what is the law: to insure at last that as all are born equal in dignity before God, all are born in dignity before man."[16]

Notes

1. Fred P. Graham, *New York Times*, January 7, 1969, p. 1.
2. Lewis Chester, Godfrey Hodgson, and Bruce Page, *An American Melodrama, The Presidential Campaign of 1968* (New York: Viking Press, 1969), pp. 616, 627.
3. Ibid., p. 189.
4. Wayne King, *New York Times*, July 26, 1977.
5. Ibid.
6. Chester, Hodgson, and Page, *American Melodrama*, p. 447.
7. *New York Times*, August 7, 1968.
8. Chester, Hodgson, and Page, *American Melodrama*, p. 462.
9. *Washington Post*, August 12, 1968.
10. *New York Times*, September 13, 1968.
11. Editorial, *Washington Post*, September 14, 1968.
12. Roscoe Drummond, *Washington Post*, September 18, 1968.
13. Chester, Hodgson, and Page, *American Melodrama*, p. 749.
14. Lee Bandy, *Columbia (S.C.) State*, December 19, 1968.
15. Graham, *New York Times*, January 7, 1969.
16. Richard M. Nixon, Inaugural Address, January 20, 1969.

3

THE KALEIDOSCOPIC
MR. FINCH

Officials of a new Administration will not have to check their consciences at the door, or leave their powers of independent judgment at home.

Richard M. Nixon, September 19, 1968.

On the office wall of Clarence Mitchell, former head of the NAACP Washington Bureau, hangs a framed letter which reads:

Office of the Vice President
Washington
September 19, 1957

Dear Clarence:

This is just a note to thank you for your telegram of August 30, commenting on the passage of the Civil Rights Law.

I share your disappointment that the bill in its final form was not as strong as we would have liked. The very fact, however, that the Congress has at last taken some constructive action in this field is a significant victory for the causes in which we are all interested.

With every good wish,

Sincerely,

/s/Dick Nixon
Richard Nixon

Written as it was slightly more than a decade before Nixon's elevation to the White House, its message suggests he had once been a firm advocate of strong civil rights legislation.

In 1957, he saw the need for vigorous support among Northern liberals if the White House was to become his in 1960. Likewise, in 1968, with the mounting agitation against further civil rights legislation, his political instincts sent him marching in the opposite direction. While, to be sure, this amounts to an oversimplification, it basically explains Nixon's ability to adopt both sides of an issue as though they were not in conflict.

Thus, it is hardly surprising that upon becoming President, he selected as head of HEW a person who could look askance at consistency. Nixon had known Robert Hutchinson Finch, California's Lieutenant-Governor, aged forty-three, for more than twenty years, most of the time as confidant. In 1960, he had managed the President's unsuccessful campaign and attributed the Republican defeat to "big city machines in the North."[1]

To document Finch's precise views on civil rights, given his political flexibility, was rather impossible. Prior to taking office, for example, he promised "constant and steady pressure" against segregation, labelling the Federal guidelines the "teeth" of the school desegregation program.[2] Yet, Nixon was barely elected before Finch was telling friends, "It is perfectly clear that we hardly owe our election to the Negro community" which, he said, allowed him to act "without any hint of political obligation."[3] Based on the record, the President-elect was sending into the trenches a man with questionable dedication to the battle ahead. As one member of the House commented, "I don't think he's all steamed up (morally) about ending desegregation. I think he feels it's primarily his job to do it."[4] Finch as much as admitted the uncertainty. He told a reporter prior to taking office, "I know this could be a political minefield. Any number of people warned me to take something safer like Interior or to take Justice because the Attorney General traditionally is a presidential adviser. They reminded me that with jobs like those, you are farther above the salt than HEW and you draw less fire. But HEW is where the action is. It's the toughest and the most challenging."[5] Little wonder that seven secretaries had presided over HEW in its seventeen years compared with seventeen in the Department of Agriculture's 108-year history and why Sen. Ribicoff (D-Conn.), himself a former HEW Secretary, had told Finch before the latter joined HEW that it was a "dead-end job."[6] Finch went ahead anyway, never quite understanding, as it turned out, the job was basically administrative, not political, and that being a politician, he would prove a poor choice to withstand Southern pressures if they involved Nixon's future.

Even inside HEW Finch was forewarned. Ruby Martin, the departing head of the Office for Civil Rights, handed him a confidential ten-page memorandum urging him to stand firm against softening the school guidelines:

If the policy were reversed, hundreds of school officials who have already moved into compliance would be forced to reconsider their decision. . . . Many school districts would be forced by local pressures to resegregate their schools by reinstituting a freedom-of-choice plan. The reopening of the issue by a shift in Federal policy would drag the race issue back into school board meetings, PTA meetings, the classroom and local elections. A shift in Federal policy would significantly undercut the leadership of moderate Southern white educators, businessmen and political leaders, and would even more significantly weaken the leadership of moderate Negroes in the South who have kept the faith in the goal of integration and equal educational opportunity.[7]

To her, Finch was a decent sort of fellow who was simply over his head, unable to face the scouring of school integration. After three weeks, despite the bait of a higher salary and greater responsibility, she left.[8]

Now the full weight of the battle fell on Finch. Hardly had he taken office when the first crisis arose. As one of his predecessor's final acts, Secretary Wilbur Cohen sent word to Congress in December, 1968, that five Southern school districts—three in the Carolinas and two in Mississippi—were in violation of Title VI of the Civil Rights Act and would lose their Federal aid on January 29. With time running out, officials from Martin County in North Carolina, one of the recalcitrant districts, descended on the capital to test the fiber of the new Administration, to see whether the department would wilt in the face of political pressure.

What transpired was the first demonstration that Finch did not fully control his own fief. Without his being consulted, executive assistant L. Patrick Gray went ahead and hinted strongly to the press that Finch would reverse Cohen's decision. Gray was immediately challenged within the Department. Leon Panetta, soon to take over from Ruby Martin as chief of the Office of Civil Rights; Jack Veneman, the future Under Secretary; and Michael Kahl, a Veneman aide, suggested that Finch terminate the funds, and then, as a peace offering to the five districts, dispatch special negotiative teams from HEW to draw up desegregation plans acceptable to the Department. The operation would have to be completed within thirty days for the districts to get back their lost funds. Although Finch warmed to the approach, as late as Wednesday, January 29, the day he had to announce his decision, he was still undecided. An aide described him as "busting his buttons to come up with something that's equitable."[9] When he finally agreed to the moratorium (now sixty days by White House order), the South was delighted. Strom Thurmond told the press he was "encouraged." It "assures the American people," he said knowingly, "that the policies of this Administration on school desegregation guidelines will be consistent with President Nixon's statements during the campaign."[10] Now, despite the fact that Panetta, Veneman, Kahl, and company had helped Finch through what the *Washington Post* called a "welter of conflicting pressures and advice,"[11] their compromise demonstrated that political pressure paid off and could undo the procedural compliance that had been studiously cultivated from 1964 on.

The Leadership Conference on Civil Rights branded it a "pay-off" to Thurmond.[12] Roy Wilkins, executive director of the National Association for the Advancement of Colored People (NAACP), angrily declared, "The districts in question do not need another 60 days since they have been dodging compliance with the law for more than 14 years. The NAACP will do everything it can to have the Finch position reversed and to prevent it from setting a precedent."[13] The director-counsel of the NAACP Legal Defense and Educational Fund, Jack Greenberg, termed the Finch decision "disastrous." It would "harden the resolve of school officials to continue their efforts to evade the law," he said.[14]

On Washington's Capitol Hill, sentiment among Democratic liberals in the House was also critical. A Democratic Study Group, claiming to speak for over 125 members, sent a letter to the President scoring "the special treatment" Finch had sanctioned for the five school districts.[15]

Yet, nothing that was said against the Secretary's decision compared in content with the statement by Ralph Magill, the controversial, but articulate publisher of the *Atlanta Constitution*. Entitling his column "Listen, Please, Secretary Finch—," it appeared on February 4, only hours after Magill's sudden demise. He had been worried over the consequences of any slowdown in the desegregation process, particularly if it meant the retention of freedom-of-choice patterns. "The freedom-of-choice plan sounds good," he informed Finch, "but freedom-of-choice as it relates to public schools in the South, more especially the small rural town South, all too frequently is a complete *non sequitur*. In some systems, for example, there have been charges of crass intimidation. In others, reports are made of private visits by persons who smile, but say rather grimly, 'You don't want to send your children to the white school? Do you? I don't think they would be happy there. . . . It might not be safe'. " To Magill, freedom of choice, even should it satisfy the judiciary or HEW, placed the badge of inferiority on the black school. "The all-white, or almost all-white, school has a large, well-fitted-out band, a good gymnasium, and a reasonably good curriculum," he informed the Secretary. "The all-white, or almost all-white, school will have state accreditation. The all-Negro school will have no band, no gymnasium, and will not be accredited." In view of this, he went on, "It will be the greatest tragedy with the most foreboding consequences if public school officials are allowed to perpetuate dual systems," ending with the declaration, "You may be assured, Sir, that the freedom-of-choice plan is, in fact, neither real freedom nor a choice. It is discrimination."[16] The appeal so touched Finch, in the aftermath of Magill's death, that he put political considerations temporarily aside and declared it was "neither legally nor morally defensible to 'turn back the clock' and to accept as public policy so-called 'freedom of choice' plans which do not bring about effective school desegregation."[17] It ranked as the Secretary's finest hour, especially since the previous day he had appointed Dr. James E. Allen, Jr., U.S. Commissioner of Education, to succeed the controversial Howe. Allen, the ex-head of the New York State public school system, was, like Howe, a staunch believer in school integration and had struggled endlessly to desegregate the Empire State's school system. "I don't know of any issue in this century," he wrote, "which seems to me to be more important than for us to remove the conditions of prejudice and discrimination that have characterized so much of our society in the last 100 or 200 or 300 years."[18] When Finch followed this by naming James Farmer assistant secretary of HEW, the criticism reached even higher decibels. Farmer, a black, had led the Congress of Racial Equality (CORE) in the fiery days of the early 1960s and was jailed on several occasions for taking part in Freedom Marches. If in addition to his appointment, one counted the fact that Panetta, a known liberal, had become head of the Office of Civil Rights (OCR) and that Jack Veneman, to whom school desegregation was a "normal" obligation,[19] now served as Under Secretary, an inescapable conclusion emerged: Finch sided with the forces against segregation. Had he continued to lean on these assistants, bowing to his own instincts, the history of this extraordinary year would require rewriting.

Unfortunately, Finch would no more escape the political infighting that swirled around him than a moth could disregard a bright light. Having compromised on his first test, he now faced another crisis. Seven more Southern school districts—one each in Arkansas, Georgia, Mississippi, and Tennessee and three in South Carolina—were scheduled to have their Federal aid terminated. Word began to circulate that the Secretary was pliable. "Christ," he confided to Panetta, "I'm getting requests from every goddamn school district in the South to meet with me."[20]

Fearing the worst, Panetta advised Finch to cut off three of the most flagrant violators. "Maybe one way to stop the flow," he said, "is to terminate . . . without the sixty-day business."[21] That convinced the Secretary, and he ordered the Federal money withdrawn, stating the cut-off was final, with no sixty-day grace period as granted two weeks earlier.

Finch's new acerbity aroused liberal cheers and conservative jeers alike. The New York Times, which had been critical of his previous compromise, saw now a new direction. The Nixon Administration was moving "emphatically . . . to dispel doubts about its intention to enforce the public school desegregation laws and guidelines."[22] Again, Human Events saw a different result. "Whatever the Finch gang intends to do," it said editorially, "it seems to be putting an end to any 'southern strategy' for the GOP. Thus the belief grows that the biggest headache Nixon may be faced with in the future is his good friend, the politically ambitious Robert Finch."[23]

What neither publication seemed to comprehend was Finch's incredible capacity to alter stance as the situation required. Having created the impression of a no-nonsense administrator, foursquare behind the law and the guidelines, the Secretary proceeded to undo it all.

First, he approved an interview with the editors of *U.S. News and World Report* in which he outlined his ideas on school desegregation. His statements read like a manual of Southern complaints on the subject: confusion over the guidelines, opposition to busing, emphasis on quality education rather than integration, and forbearance over freedom of choice. He told the editors that because of the "variation in language" among acts of Congress, court decisions, and desegregation guidelines conceived by his predecessors, he would have difficulty "breaking up clear-cut cases of dual school systems." He was against moving pupils about just to obtain a "salt and pepper effect," thus rejecting the need for busing to integrate the schools. "The greatest problem we've got in the elementary and secondary schools in this country," he said, "is not to get so hung up on these other struggles as to let the quality of education in the public school system erode and erode and erode." He was asked, "Are you saying that separate but really equal schools are acceptable?" This was the heart of the freedom-of-choice argument. If schools were equal in the dual system, then measured by the quality of education, it did not matter whether the races remained separate. In which case, *Brown* would not apply. Finch answered, "It's almost 99 percent unlikely, but it's possible."[24]

Once more, the Department was shaken by what Finch said. "It's the pressure," one well-placed official told Peter Milius of the *Washington Post*, "from Thurmond, from Tower [Texas Sen. John C. Tower-R] from all the Southern Republican state chairmen, from Dent [Harry S. Dent, GOP aide] in the White House. These people feel they stuck their necks out in the campaign. It paid off for Nixon. Now they want to see something indicating there has been a change. Finch is a political person, and all the political pressure is coming from one side now."[25]

HEW figures revealed what was happening. Nine months before in June, 1968, there had been 412 school districts refusing to submit desegregation plans that the Department could approve and either they suffered a fund cut-off or were in the process of being cut off. That figure now stood at 582, an increase of 41 percent. Moreover, heartened by HEW's indecision, an increasing number of Southern schools were withdrawing previously filed desegregation plans. It was this development that prompted Ruby Martin to complain bitterly that desegregation had been "set back two years," no matter what Finch said or did next. Reading her prediction, one Department official commented, "Ruby's right. Those statements have set us back tremendously. . . . They're just killing us down South. Everybody believes there's going to be a change. As a result, they don't even want to talk to the people in our regional offices. They want to come to Washington. The problem is they can get away with it."[26]

Some measure of the tempest Finch stirred up could be gauged by the way his words were exploited. Sen. Tower had the story inserted in the *Congres-*

sional Record, Southern school superintendents used it to score HEW demands, and all over the South people sent letters to the Department seeking information. The OCR head of information was overwhelmed by the response. In three years, he announced, he had never seen its equal. "We have a backlog of 2,000 letters we have not answered."[27]

While the storm was still raging, Finch gave new evidence of his penchant for waffling under pressure. Chester County in Western Tennessee, one of the three counties affected by his February order, was scheduled for a fund termination on March 15. It was red-neck country which George Wallace carried overwhelmingly the previous November. It was also next to the Eighth Congressional District in which a special election would take place on March 25. Because the Nixon Administration was especially concerned over the outcome, it was a perfect set-up for exerting political pressure on HEW.

Finch's original determination had so "shocked" the school board that superintendent V. M. Plunk wrote Senator Howard H. Baker, Jr., (R-Tenn.) to request one more review. He told how he had integrated part of Chester's black students, and thought that should suffice. In the meantime, HEW emissaries had tried to negotiate a plan that would integrate the entire student body, but had failed on three separate efforts. They simply could not convince Plunk nor his board to switch the black student population in segregated Vincent to a nearby white school.

"This is really hot, Leon," Finch explained to Panetta. "The White House is thinking about nothing else but that congressional race. It's a test of whether the Republicans can effectively challenge the Wallace vote in the South, and we've got to pull all the strings."[28] Late in the afternoon of March 15, only hours before the termination was to take effect, HEW capitulated. Baker would invite Plunk to Washington for a head-to-head encounter with Finch, but to save face, HEW would merely advance the cut-off date.

Four days later, Plunk was in the capital, accompanied by the head of the Chester County School Board. He informed Finch and his aides plus Sen. Baker and his assistants that his Board was prepared to desegregate Vincent after all. Blacks in grades nine to twelve would transfer to white Chester County High School the following September. The problem facing HEW was that Vincent's elementary grades remained untouched and Department guidelines required immediate desegregation unless the district was preponderantly black or construction was necessary to accomplish desegregation. When it was pointed out to Plunk that the black elementary grades could be integrated with the white elementary school, he refused. Such an arrangement, he said, would require the transfer of white pupils to the black school in the center of the black community. Next HEW offered Chester the option of building an addition to the white elementary school. Still, Plunk would not yield. There was only one remaining alternative—to exchange black and white students on a strict schedule. Finch made the offer and after some debate, Plunk agreed to send thirty-five to forty white elementary pupils to the Vincent school for music and chorus, beginning September, 1969, with a promise of total desegregation by 1970.

As the meeting broke up, Baker said to those present, "I want to say to all of you that this is the way these problems must be dealt with—by working together and finding a basis for compromise." He then announced to the press that Finch was restoring the funds to Chester County, but politically it accomplished nothing for the GOP. The Democrat won the congressional seat, the Wallaceite finished second, the Republican third, and the "210 black children in Chester County's Vincent School," observed Panetta, "came in last."[29]

This erosion of HEW policy was further heightened in March when Robert C. Mardian, a conservative California Republican, became the Department's general counsel. Finch did not select him, but he enjoyed White House backing. His raison d'être was to pour salt on the tails of the Department's liberals, and for the niche he was appointed to fill, his credentials were excellent. During the starched Goldwater campaign of 1964, he had been a special field representative for the Republican National Committee in ten western states and four years later had been equally active in getting Nixon elected.

Finch viewed Mardian with some suspicion and asked him to submit his personal views in a memorandum. Thus, Mardian openly stated his conviction that HEW had been too tough on the South. The guidelines exceeded what was called for in the 1964 Civil Rights Act or the recent *Green* case. He further contended that when the High Court said that a school board should "come forward with a plan that promises realistically to work *now*," as it had in *Green*, it meant only to *start* desegregating now.[30] In addition, he told Finch HEW was altogether too arbitrary in its handling of cases in the Deep South. In situations requiring great finesse, where Southern officials were clearly hung up on the race issue, HEW spokesmen had gone out of their way to correct school authorities for saying "nigra" instead of "Negro" even when "they knew that's the only way those people could say it." Finally, Mardian was highly critical of fund cut-offs, especially when the chief victims were black pupils. "Some people take the view that regardless of the consequences you use every weapon at your command to enforce desegregation. I think that's the meat-axe approach. The problem of the schools is to educate the young. That's their duty. Our duty is to attempt to see to it they don't do it in a discriminatory fashion."[31] Nevertheless, HEW's latest addition opposed publicizing any revision of the guidelines. Any such move, he declared, "would be misinterpreted as a basic retreat by the Department."[32]

This was too much for the Secretary and he disavowed the statement as soon as the press got wind of it. Even so, its publication stirred the Leadership Conference to open rebellion. Chairman Roy Wilkins said Mardian should publicly repudiate the report if it did not represent his views. And "if it is true," he went on, "it raises grave questions" about whether he should "serve as HEW general counsel."[33]

His concern was counterbalanced by the optimism of Southern Republican chairmen who had gathered twice in Washington, first on February 17 and again on March 10, to demand their due. Led by Clarke Reed, the Mississippi chieftain, they applauded Mardian's presence at HEW, a step Harry Dent, the President's in-house political adviser, told them "should take care of the school thing."[34] They rejoiced to hear Congressman Rogers Morton, a six-foot-six-inch Kentucky transplant, now representing a Maryland district, and soon to become the GOP's national chairman, speak of togetherness. "We need each other in this business," he emphasized,[35] which according to one Dixie official, was "as far as anyone in Washington has gone so far."[36]

As one incident involving HEW followed another, it became increasingly clear that whatever commitment Finch had originally had to school desegregation, the pressures were tearing him apart. One day he told the officers of the Leadership Conference that "there will be no—repeat, no—erosion of the guidelines—there will be no relaxation of enforcement," and the following day, compromised them to accommodate Chester County.[37]

It was no wonder the *Columbia State*, South Carolina's largest daily, saw in the Nixon program for school desegregation, "a hint here, a vague something there, a shadow glimpsed out of the corner of the eye."[38] In late March, a Federal court ordered twenty-one South Carolina districts to desegregate their schools within thirty days, using HEW technicians to develop permissible plans. School officials were angered by the suddenness of the order, especially since one of the four jurists handing down the ruling was a former law partner of Thurmond. As executed, HEW's proposals called for an end to separate schools in September, 1969, but at the last moment in deference to the Senator, *1969* was crossed out and *1970* pencilled in. Some plans were softened by inserting the word *should* instead of *will*. In others, the transition from segregation to desegregation was to be accomplished without giving black teachers and administrators any assurance their jobs would be there when the process was complete. As Gary Orfield sorrowfully observed, "This was the administration's interpretation of the Supreme Court's directive for the speediest possible elimination of separate schools."[39]

What perhaps hurt HEW most was the rumor that guidelines would be changed. Whether the source of the report was the conservative White House coterie, Southern Republicans with an axe to hone, or simply disgruntled school officials looking for an out to their problems, who could tell? Finch's assurance to the Leadership Conference that there was no truth to the allegation failed to scotch the rumor, and by the first week in April, John Herbers, of the *New York Times*, was describing the "confusion and ambiguity" that had abounded since the Administration took office over "how school desegregation will be enforced."[40]

Baffled by the rising tide of uncertainty, the President called in Finch, Attorney General Mitchell, and his chief domestic adviser, John Ehrlichman, to discuss the problems HEW was encountering. Fearing the Secretary's proclivity for shifting stance, Panetta drew up an unmistakable memorandum on the need to stand firm. With questions and answers, he laid out the story. Why were the guidelines controversial? Because in the South guidelines were a "symbol of harassment by Federal enforcement agents." Their revision was viewed as simply a "softer enforcement of the law." Why should the terminal date for desegregation not be extended, as the Southern officials were demanding? Because only 11 percent of the school districts were in noncompliance and to give them additional time "not received by the other 89 percent could well jeopardize the entire school desegregation program."[41]

Finch prevailed and at the conclusion of the meeting, a communique said, "No change is contemplated now in the existing guidelines."[42] A week later, when asked to elaborate his position, Finch replied, "The guidelines which are in existence are going to be enforced. . . . why is there constant discourse about wavering, I just don't understand it." Only a court ruling could change the guidelines, he added.[43]

The one thing Finch could not do was to keep the political termites from entering the HEW woodwork. On May 19, at the suggestion of Ehrlichman and the President's appointment secretary, H. R. Haldeman, Nixon's trouble shooter, Harry Dent, sent Finch a memo from the Georgia state Republican chairman. It concerned the Washington County school system in east central Georgia where a mere 1 percent of the black student body attended school with whites. Federal aid had been terminated eight days before. Now the chairman was telling Dent that "some very wealthy individuals" had promised "substantial contributions" to the Georgia GOP if the funds could be restored. He had talked with Panetta until he was "blue in the face"; now he wanted Finch to intervene.[44]

To his credit, Finch refused, but there was no silencing the White House clique on the subject of changing guidelines, whether it violated the law, the courts' decisions, or took away the rights of two million black children by denying them an equal education. Title VI was perfectly clear about barring Federal funds to any school district that practiced legal segregation. However, Dent, Bryce Harlow, Nixon's chief aide on congressional relations, Ehrlichman, and the Attorney General went ahead anyway attempting to avoid the traumatic cut-offs and expecting Finch to join forces. The Secretary, sensing what lay ahead, had not acted on six termination orders, although three had been on his desk since April 3 and three more since May 7. The available alternatives to termination, aside from sidestepping the law, were to secure highly unlikely voluntary settlements, abrogate the timetable set down in the guidelines, or turn over HEW's enforcement responsibilities to the Justice Department which could be counted on to work more slowly, especially with Mitchell, the arch exponent of the Southern Strategy, calling the signals.

Gradually, the path to desegregate was becoming a continuing struggle among three forces—the White House, Justice, and HEW—with each determined to have the last word. To HEW's discredit, Finch proved to be no match for the other two. He had no stomach for termination, now that he was experiencing vitriolic criticism. "I've been spending all my goddamn time on this issue and nothing else. I'm tired of it," he confided to Panetta. "Why the hell should we terminate funds at all, and if we do, shouldn't it be after a district fails to comply with a court order? In other words, let Justice move first, with HEW developing the plan, and then if the district fails to implement the plan, have HEW move to terminate."[45] Clearly, Finch wanted to let Mitchell make the decisions he was too hesitant to fashion. Yet, his public stance continued unchanged. The guidelines would not be weakened, he vowed. The 1969 deadline would hold.

At that point, two unexpected events occurred which hardened Finch's resolve for the first time in weeks. He had been advocating since January the selection of Dr. John Knowles as Assistant Secretary for Health. Knowles, who headed Boston's famed Massachusetts General Hospital, was a brilliant medical person with progressive ideas, too progressive, in fact, for the American Medical Association (AMA), which strenuously and openly fought his appointment. On June 19, the President announced during his press conference that he would settle the issue by naming his choice the following week.

Finch was vacationing in California, but immediately on hearing the news, he rushed back to Washington to importune Nixon. Initially, it seemed he had won. A premature HEW report reaching NBC said the appointment was no longer in doubt. Then opposition to Knowles erupted on Capitol Hill. The American Medical Political Action Committee, the AMA's political "arm twister," reminded every senator and representative whom it had bankrolled the previous election of its intense distaste for Knowles. All this took place against the background of a furious controversy over the extension of the income tax surcharge which the Administration eagerly sought. Would the President now trade off Knowles at the cost of jeopardizing his relationship with Finch in order to pick up the conservative votes he needed to pass the legislation? No one understood the dilemma

more clearly than Republican Everett M. Dirksen, the Senate's Minority
Leader. Out of a desire to retain AMA support plus a natural aversion to
Knowles's liberalism, Dirksen put it on the line with the White House: he
would have trouble holding his troops in line should Knowles get the job.
His House counterpart, Gerald R. Ford, was no less troubled, telling a
group of Republican congressmen who asked where he stood, "There must
be a less controversial person for the job."[46] A further embarrassment to the
President was the fact that he had assured Dr. Edward Annis, of Miami, a
former AMA president, that he could have a hand in selecting the Assistant
Secretary of Health. Besides being one of Nixon's largest campaign contri-
butors, Dr. Annis was unalterably opposed to Knowles.

The first indication that the President was having second thoughts about
his commitment to Finch was his invitation to the Secretary to accompany
him on a boat ride down the Potomac with Attorney General Mitchell, top
domestic aide John Ehrlichman, and White House lobbyist Bryce Harlow.
From the moment the five steamed forth on the Presidential yacht *Sequoia*,
the atmosphere was definitely anti-Finch. Not one of the presidential aides
supported the Secretary. Hadn't the time come, the President asked his
intimates, to resolve the Knowles situation? "This has gone on far too long,"
he said looking at Finch who five days before had the appointment in his
pocket. "Let's do something that's constructive, let's do something that is
acceptable." HEW should remain free of congressional controversy.[47]

What could Finch say? For the next twenty-four hours, the Knowles affair
lay cloaked in uncertainty, no one knowing what to expect. Finally after
conferring for forty-five minutes with Nixon, Finch learned he had lost.
Feeling deserted, he angrily stalked out, confiding to Tom Foley, of the *Los
Angeles Times*, the President "will have to find another Secretary," but
team player that he was, he quickly denied having made the statement.[48]

The waves Nixon's action set in motion washed up Pennsylvania Avenue.
In the Senate, Republican Hugh Scott, of Pennsylvania, speaking for the
GOP liberals, warned the President they might revolt if the Administration
insisted on following a domestic program that was more and more con-
servatively tainted. Sadly asked the *Washington Post*, "Is this a fair
measure of what we can expect from the Nixon presidency?" The President
had once been "so full of grand ideas about the role of his cabinet
members," it went on.[49]

It so happened that on the same day that Finch publicly confirmed
Knowles's fall from grace, in another section of the capital, Harry Dent was
informing a group of GOP politicians that the new Administration was
being "organized politically" on Nixon's instructions, that "the door is wide
open in the Oval Office as far as politics is concerned."[50] Moreover, departments, said Dent, were to benefit from this munificence. Each one would
have its political coordinators, "men with the ear of the Secretary, with the

confidence of the Secretary, men who can go anywhere in the department and get things done."

"If you pick up a telephone and call a department," he went on, "you might not get your request handled. You might be talking to some Democrat or some bureaucrat who is planning to spend his life there. But if you follow your procedures through the Republican National Committee and on to the political coordinators, you will get priority consideration. You will get attention because you are a friend and the President knows you helped put him in the White House."[51]

With Dent in the White House and Rep. Morton at Republican National headquarters, conservatives would now occupy the saddle. Those who could say "Yes" to Southern strategy and "No" to school integration were on the way to becoming the GOP power structure.

By the following day when Finch called in the press to announce that Dr. Roger Egeberg, dean of the School of Medicine at the University of Southern California, would take over as Assistant Secretary of Health, he had had time to read the papers and grasp what Dent was saying. Defiant, his pride now injured, he promised Under Secretary Veneman, "I can't lose two in a row."[52]

Would the guidelines be softened, he was asked by reporters. "No," he replied, "There is not going to be any give at all in the 1969 and 1970 deadlines."[53]

Notes

1. *New York Times*, December 12, 1968.

2. *Washington Post*, January 17, 1969.

3. Leon E. Panetta and Peter Gall, *Bring Us Together* (Philadelphia: J. B. Lippincott Company, 1971), p. 73.

4. *Washington Post*, September 21, 1969.

5. William Greider with the reporting assistance of Stuart Auerbach and Peter Milius, *Washington Post*, June 14, 1970.

6. Ibid.

7. James K. Batten, "The Nixonians and School Desegregation," *Southern Education Report* June, 1969, p. 24.

8. Author's conversation with Ruby Martin, Washington, D.C., August 4, 1977.

9. *Washington Post*, January 30, 1969.

10. Ibid.

11. Panetta and Gall, *Bring Us Together*, p. 77.

12. *New York Times*, January 31, 1969.

13. Ibid.

14. Ibid.

15. *Washington Post*, February 4, 1969.

16. *Atlanta Constitution*, February 4, 1969.

17. *New York Times*, February 5, 1969.

18. James E. Allen, Jr., "Integration is Better Education," *Integrated Education*, September-October, 1969.

19. Batten, "The Nixonians and School Desegregation," p. 25.

20. Panetta and Gall, *Bring Us Together*, p. 86.

21. Ibid.

22. *Editorial, New York Times*, February 16, 1969.

23. Panetta and Gall, *Bring Us Together*, p. 87.

24. *U.S. News and World Report*, March 10, 1969.

25. Peter Milius, *Washington Post*, March 16, 1969.

26. Ibid.

27. *New York Times*, March 12, 1969.

28. Panetta and Gall, *Bring Us Together*, p. 117.

29. Ibid., p. 121.

30. Ibid., p. 110.

31. Batten, "The Nixonians and School Desegregation," p. 27.

32. Panetta and Gall, *Bring Us Together*, p. 111.

33. *New York Times*, March 25, 1969.

34. Panetta and Gall, *Bring Us Together*, p. 106.

35. Ibid., p. 108.

36. *Washington Post*, March 21, 1969.

37. Panetta and Gall, *Bring Us Together*, p. 121.

38. John Herbers, "Ambiguous Moves on Desegregation," *New York Times*, April 6, 1969.

39. Gary Orfield, "The Politics of Resegregation," *Saturday Review of Literature*, September 20, 1969, p. 78.

40. Herbers, "Ambiguous Moves on Desegregation."

41. Panetta and Gall, *Bring Us Together*, p. 140.

42. Ibid., p. 143.

43. Ibid., pp. 144-45.

44. Peter Milius, "Nixon Political Aide Intervened on Schools," *Washington Post*, March 15, 1970.

45. Panetta and Gall, *Bring Us Together*, p. 174.

46. *Washington Post*, June 27, 1969.

47. *Washington Post*, June 28, 1969.

48. Panetta and Gall, *Bring Us Together*, p. 205.

49. Editorial, *Washington Post*, June 28, 1969.

50. *Washington Post*, June 28, 1969.

51. Ibid.

52. Panetta and Gall, *Bring Us Together*, p. 207.

53. Ibid., p. 208.

4

JULY 3, 1969

> This Administration is unequivocally committed to the goal of finally ending racial discrimination in schools steadily and speedily, in accordance with the law of the land.
>
> Fitch-Mitchell Memorandum, July 3, 1969.

The Secretary's change of heart had occurred at a time when no one could accurately predict White House intentions. A pall of uncertainty hung over the Oval Office as it had from Inaugural Day. One thing was certain: the President was determined to find a way out of the vexing Southern school maze. As far back as January 12, his speech writer, Ray Price, had begun preparing a statement to clarify the Administration's position, a difficult assignment in view of what was transpiring.

By now, the opening paragraph spoke of "wrestling with the knotty problems" of school desegregation. After an "intensive examination of the system" inherited from the Johnson Administration, "we have concluded that it simply does not work," largely because of a "clutter of anomalies and inconsistencies." The solution, argued Price, was for Nixon to relax the guidelines, to follow the principles laid down by Mardian, a beginning *now*, not a consummation *now*.[1]

Upon seeing it, Panetta cried "sellout"; experience had taught him to expect an irreparable result if he did not move immediately in the opposite direction.[2] When he told Finch of his concern, the Secretary responded by saying, "Leon, the best thing you can do is to point out the weaknesses, draft alternative language. . . ."[3]

First, he decided to test his alter ego in the Department of Justice, Jerris Leonard, Assistant Attorney General for Civil Rights. Leonard had a reputation for upholding civil rights. As Majority Leader of the Wisconsin State Senate, he had sponsored the 1965 open housing law. Only thirty-eight, Leonard belonged to that select group of Young Republicans, all Nixon protégés, whom the President hoped to make U.S. senators in the fall of 1968. Failing this, he rewarded Leonard with a Justice appointment, and the latter, being a professional politician, responded by putting loyalty to the White House first.

"Well, Leon," Leonard replied to Panetta's telephone explanation, "We've got to look at the big picture. . . ."

"I know, that's what I'm worried about," Panetta shot back.

"Well, why don't you make some recommended changes in the text, give them to the Secretary and let's see where we get, okay? And don't worry—everything will work out," he dulcified.[4]

With that solicitation, Panetta called in two HEW lawyers, telling them to write a second memorandum exposing the statutory violations of the Price draft. Copies of the finished document then went to Leonard, HEW Under Secretary Veneman, and Steve Hess, a friendly White House aide.

Following this, Panetta contacted the White House's new assistant on civil rights, Leonard Garment, formerly associated with the Lawyers Committee for Civil Rights under Law, and a significant help in winning victories in the South during the early days of the civil rights revolution. Garment's instincts, Panetta thought, *must* be against weakening the guidelines if only out of a sense of loyalty to the past. Panetta told him he was adamantly against weakening the law, and that Mardian bore primary responsibility for slowing down desegregation because he misinterpreted the *Green* case. When Garment requested a memorandum outlining his views, Panetta gave him a copy of what he had previously circulated within Justice and HEW.

Next day, they met again, this time joined by Price. Carefully, Panetta explained what was involved. "Thousands of districts in the South," he said, "have come into compliance believing that the law would be strongly enforced. . . . if the Administration weakens the guidelines by removing the September deadline, it will not only encourage the recalcitrant districts but undermine the efforts of those that have complied. That's the danger . . . that's the kind of dynamite we're playing with."[5]

Sooner or later, the press was bound to scent this tug-of-war within the Administration. Although Finch had assured reporters there would be no change in the guidelines, on Friday, June 27, 1969, Peter Milius, the *Washington Post's* specialist on school affairs, wrote that Price's draft "would give Southern schools more time to desegregate than current guidelines allow."[6]

The announcement caught the Administration by surprise and panic ensued. Word went out from the White House to button up, but the warning came too late. Governor Winthrop Rockefeller, of Arkansas, a prominent Southern Republican, wired Nixon of his "distress" and asked that he not "break faith with the black community" by easing the guidelines.[7]

It was now clear that an immediate decision was needed to prevent the public clamor from getting out of hand. Statements shuttled back and forth from HEW, to Justice, and on to the White House, where they were compared and rewritten in an effort to gain consensus. Secretary Finch, coming off the high ground of the Knowles debacle, was demonstrating a new firmness against White House and Justice attempts to weaken the guidelines.

Unfortunately for school desegregation, preparation of the drafts remained in the hands of Mardian, Leonard, and Dent—the three men who would predictably put political considerations first. Soon, it became evident that the only hope of saving the guidelines lay in Finch's ability to make peace with Justice.

Until then, based on the record, such cooperation seemed unlikely, but outward appearances were deceptive. True, Mitchell scoffed at the guidelines because they interfered with his Southern Strategy, and true, Finch was determined at that point not to weaken the guidelines, but standing above these two knowns were Mitchell's desire to take over HEW's control of the guidelines and Finch's complementary desire to remove himself from the unpleasant duty of terminating Federal funds. In this context, a quid pro quo was not only possible, it became a desirable trade-off.

By Thursday, July 3, after twelve successive drafts and three additional revisions by the President, the Finch-Mitchell statement was finally released. The first paragraph read like an Independence Day declaration. "This Administration," it proclaimed, "is unequivocally committed to the goal of finally ending racial discrimination in schools, steadily and speedily, in accordance with the law of the land." Thereafter, the language fell away from the high ground. It equivocated, presumably because of last-minute White House instructions. The guidelines would remain firm, yes, as a sop to Finch, but if there were "sound reasons for some limited delay," such as "educational and administrative problems," the districts would be given additional compliance time.[8] In the eyes of the *Washington Daily News*, this was "deliberately calculated to confuse liberals and Southerners alike into believing each had won."[9] Even Jerris Leonard told reporters, at a press briefing, "I can't, in my wildest dreams, tell you how to read it."[10]

On Capitol Hill, Senator Jacob K. Javits (R-N.Y.) called the statement "an invitation to the 800 school districts still to be desegregated, largely in the South, to further defer this long overdue historic change."[11] In Jackson, Mississippi, where the NAACP was holding its annual convention, the contents caused Roy Wilkins to lament, "It's almost enough to make you vomit! This is not a matter of too little, too late, rather this is nothing at all."[12]

Initially, most of the criticism was directed against softening the guidelines. Little was said about Mitchell and the Department of Justice taking from HEW the real power of enforcement. The shift was couched in obscure verbiage. "The 'guidelines'," read the statement, "are administrative regulations promulgated by the Department of Health, Education and Welfare, as an administrative interpretation, not a court interpretation of law. Frequently, the policies of the Department of Justice, which is involved in law suits, and the Department of Health, Education and Welfare, which is involved in voluntary compliance, have been at variance. Thus, we are jointly announcing new coordinated procedures, not new 'guidelines'."[13]

This was clearly a throwback to the days between 1954, the year of the *Brown* decision, and 1964, the year Congress changed the enforcement procedures, when the judiciary enforced the law and school desegregation moved at a snail's pace. The benefit of the shift, the report maintained, was "to minimize the number of cases in which it becomes necessary to employ the particular remedy of a cutoff of Federal funds."[14]

The person with the most to gain by this maneuver was formerly a Wall Street lawyer, known for his expertise in municipal and state bond issues. Until January, 1967, when his firm merged with the Nixon group, John Newton Mitchell, fifty-eight, had barely known the President, nor taken any open interest in elective politics. A single-purpose mentality, inordinate ambition, and an appetite for power brought the two together. When added to this was Mitchell's brilliant talent for organization, the reasons for Nixon's naming him campaign manager in 1968 clearly emerge. Between them, they worked out the so-called Southern Strategy which consisted of folding the South and Southwest into the Republican structure to form a national organization. One young Republican who campaigned with Mitchell described him as "an almost inhuman personality, totally unemotional, [a man with] no warmth at all. You talk with him and you get absolutely no reaction."[15] This conceptual vacuum impressed others as well. "Some would classify him as a liberal, some see him as a conservative," the former co-chairperson of the Citizens for Nixon-Agnew commented. "He's very pragmatic and has no hard-cut ideological viewpoint."[16] With such credentials, making him responsible for school desegregation thrust the fox into the chicken coop to protect the birds.

Surprisingly, Panetta's initial reaction to Mitchell's ascension to power was to admit no change. On the day the Finch-Mitchell statement went public, he informed the press that the "mandatory date" for compliance still held, and as far as he was concerned, "the current guidelines" remained unchanged.[17] Indeed, Panetta went so far as to inform reporters that HEW intended to mail a confirming letter to all school districts and to expect few extensions. Of the 263 districts scheduled for desegregation, there were only a "very, very few," he said, that would qualify.[18]

Meanwhile, the President had left for Key Biscayne, Florida, for the July 4th holiday. He opened the *Washington Post* on the morning of July 4 to find Panetta's promise. Immediately, Nixon instructed John Ehrlichman to telephone Panetta and say, "We're not quite sure this is the right time for that. We sort of feel things should be allowed to settle a while."[19]

However, with what had happened, "things" just would not "settle," not while Southern school superintendents were in doubt about the meaning of Finch-Mitchell, which surfaced just as HEW's steady pressure—the legacy of the Johnson years—was beginning to turn them around. Even in South Carolina, a particular thorn in the Department's side, the new state superintendent had concluded that school desegregation was inevitable, Strom Thurmond or not, and had offered help to local school superintendents. A number of schools had bitten the bullet, and according to one state official, were breaking down racial shibboleths "much more rapidly than . . . had [been] anticipated three years ago or even two years ago."[20] The head of the State University's School Desegregation Consulting Center described the educator's mood as "Let's do it, painful as it is."[21] Because they were doing it, they were beginning to realize that their fears of integration had been exaggerated.

Superintendents who were projecting teacher resignations at levels as high as 25 percent discovered that they had lost only 2 to 3 percent. "What really amazes me," the Center's head reported to Gary Orfield, on tour of Southern state capitals, "is the progress that has been made and what can be made if moderate pressure is maintained."[22] Since the year before, desegregation had doubled and an additional thirty-five plans were to take effect by 1970. Now, the Administration's new policy was shooting holes in that advance, and as reported by James Batten, of the Knight newspapers, Southern school officials learned from Nixon men that "extensions would be available."[23]

Panetta had hoped to reverse this downhill slide by assuring Dixie school superintendents in an HEW missive of departmental firmness, but against White House opposition and a nervous Finch, angered by a new burst of criticism from 1600 Pennsylvania Avenue, he now found himself on hold. Yet, to avoid breaking his pledge, he took the unusual alternative of firing off a memorandum to HEW's regional offices, alerting them to the meaning of the July 3 pronouncement—à la Panetta. "I wish to make clear," he informed them, "that HEW policies on school discrimination remain intact, that there will be strict limitation on any exceptions to the September, 1969, target date for desegregation."[24] While the contents actually had the approval of Panetta's close friend, Under Secretary Veneman, they were hardly designed to calm a jittery White House or an upset HEW Secretary who more than anything craved silence.

How two individuals as politically sophisticated as Panetta and Veneman concluded that unfriendly eyes would not see such a memorandum is hard to imagine. Within days, word drifted back to Washington. Rep. William Brock (R-Tenn.), a strong opponent of desegregation, obtained a copy and made sure the contents were circulated throughout the Administration. In the following furor, any thought of mailing Panetta's letter of explanation to the schools evaporated. The OCR Director was ordered by the Secretary on July 15 not to send it, amid press reports that Panetta's slap down was a new victory for the segregationists.

In the aftermath, the House renewed its effort to enact the Whitten Amendments. Again, as a year earlier, the same restrictions on desegregation were attached to the HEW appropriation bill by a vote of the House Appropriations Committee. As soon as the measure reached the floor, the press wanted to know what HEW intended to do.

Finch remained silent, again wishing to avoid controversy. Even as his aides attempted to prepare an answer while the Secretary travelled through California, he wanted it cleared with the Attorney General. Meanwhile, Rep. Silvio O. Conte (R-Mass.), the leader of the anti-Whitten forces, received assurances from HEW he could expect a written Finch endorsement. It was the kind of confrontation Finch abhorred. He could not please Mitchell if he opposed Whitten and he could not satisfy Conte if he supported it. Not so the Attorney General. He used his office to tell a group of influential House members that the Administration would not interfere. When liberal Republican Congressmen questioned what had happened to the promised statement from Finch, they were told he was in California and presumably unable to draft a statement.

Thus buoyed, the segregationists won another victory, 158 to 141, employing a teller vote (with no record kept) so as not to embarrass any representative.[25]

Notes

1. Leon E. Panetta and Peter Gall, *Bring Us Together* (Philadelphia: J. B. Lippincott Company, 1971), p. 191.

2. Ibid.

3. Ibid., p. 192.

4. Ibid., pp. 192-93.

5. Ibid., p. 195.

6. *Washington Post*, June 27, 1969.

7. *New York Times*, June 28, 1969.

8. *New York Times*, July 4, 1969.

9. *Washington Daily News*, July 4, 1969.

10. *New York Times*, July 4, 1969.

11. Ibid.

12. Ibid.

13. Ibid.

14. Ibid.

15. *New York Times*, December 12, 1968.

16. Ibid.

17. *New York Times*, July 4, 1969.

18. Ibid.

19. Panetta and Gall, *Bring Us Together*, p. 227.

20. Gary Orfield, "The Politics of Resegregation," *Saturday Review of Literature*, September 20, 1969, p. 60.

21. Ibid.

22. Ibid.

23. Ibid.

24. Panetta and Gall, *Bring Us Together*, p. 230.

25. Ibid., p. 247.

5

ALEXANDER v. *HOLMES*

> A retreat from the principles of *Brown* would tell more than
> volumes what this country stands for.
>
> > Jack Greenberg speaking to the Supreme Court in
> > *Alexander* v. *Holmes.*[1]

Although the Whitten episode impacted somewhat on the national conscience, it could not by any measurement equal the impact of the drama
that was about to unfold in Mississippi. On the day Finch-Mitchell was
announced, the U.S. Court of Appeals for the Fifth Circuit, citing the *Green*
decision that freedom of choice was not enough unless it achieved complete
desegregation, ordered thirty Mississippi school districts to end their dual
school systems in time for the September school opening. As a result of the
ruling, HEW assistance teams, working under Dr. Gregory Anrig, chief of
the Division of Equal Education Opportunity, visited each district to
negotiate plans that, by direction of the court, would have to be filled by
August 11 and implemented two weeks later.

Approximately ten days before the filing date, Finch began to feel pressure from the White House asking for a delay. Passage of the Administration's anti-ballistic missile program, it was said, could easily depend upon
the action of its chief proponent, Mississippi's John Cornelius Stennis,
chairman of the Armed Services Committee, who in turn was besieged by
plans from his constituents to halt school integration. Tightly wedged into
this fulcrum, Stennis had an ideal opportunity to demand a quid pro quo.

Stennis resided in Kemper County, on the state's eastern border, a rural
stronghold known for its asperity and dedication to traditional Mississippi
ways. Members of the Lawyers Committee for Civil Rights under Law who
had gone there to try a civil rights case admitted afterwards they were lucky
to escape lynching. For years, the county had been involved in continuous
litigation over desegregation; in fact, it was one of the thirty counties cited
in the circuit order. Up to then, under a nominal freedom-of-choice plan,
only three black pupils (from the same family) had chosen to integrate with
whites.

Fearing disintegration of the state's social fabric if the court's timetable remained unchanged, Stennis warned President Nixon that he might have to return home to aid Mississippi educators. His departure would make Stuart Symington (D-Mo.) the next ranking senator on the Armed Services Committee, temporary chairman, and Symington, as Nixon knew, had been increasingly critical of the vast sums being voted for defense.

Nevertheless, as the deadline neared, it appeared that despite Stennis's threat, the major provisions of the Anrig program would survive. Without reneging on the compliance date, he had skillfully proposed a two-pronged plan to take effect in one or two steps—either by 1969 or 1970—leaving the court to decide. It was hoped this would satisfy Stennis and keep HEW from losing face at a time when so many other plans, negotiated previously, were about to be implemented. Finch, on the basis that the recommendations contained optional features giving the districts additional time to comply, gave his consent and the plans were filed.

These concessions, however, failed to silence either Stennis or the white Mississippians whose children would have to attend school with blacks. In such an atmosphere, with D-Day approaching, all eyes turned to the western White House in San Clemente, California, where the President had holed up with members of his cabinet. At last convinced that Stennis might finally leave Washington to aid his constituents, Nixon went into action. He directed Finch, Mitchell, and Defense Secretary Melvin R. Laird to contact the senator in hopes of finding a compromise, but Stennis, quick to sense his advantage, turned them down. He was determined to humiliate the Administration on the issue of school integration.

So the President raised the white flag. To be more specific, he had Finch raise it for him. So abrupt was the President's decision that even as the plan for surrender was being developed in Washington, uniformed field representatives of HEW and lawyers for Justice and the NAACP Legal Defense Fund were closeted in the Sun and Sand Motel, Biloxi, Mississippi, preparing affidavits to support their case and alerting Title IV technicians of the need to give favorable evidence in court on the feasibility of the desegregation plans.

At the same time, Panetta, Jack Veneman, and Pat Gray were gathered in Finch's office for a briefing. As they talked, the light on the white phone, connecting the Secretary to the White House, suddenly glowed. It was the announcement that Finch had been selected as the sacrificial lamb. After hanging up the phone, he exploded in a rare outburst. "Goddamn it, one of these days I'm going to tell them they can have this job."[2] However, he was too loyal to Richard Nixon and to his only half-acknowledged ambition to do that.

Within twenty-four hours, a letter from the Secretary was on its way to the Chief Judge of the Fifth Circuit asking that the hearing be delayed until December 1 so that HEW could file other plans. Finch argued that the Office of Education had been under "great stress" formulating plans "in approximately three weeks" for a school opening on September 11. "I am gravely concerned," he continued, "that the time allowed for the development of these terminal plans" has been much too short to be "implemented this year. The administrative and logistical difficulties which must be encountered and met in the terribly short space of time remaining, must surely, in my judgement, produce chaos, confusion and a catastrophic educational setback to the 135,700 children, black and white alike, who must look to the 222 schools of these 23 Mississippi districts for their only available educational opportunities."[3] Prior to its dispatch, neither Commissioner Jim Allen nor Greg Anrig, the two officials in the Office of Education most responsible for formulating the desegregation plans, were informed of its contents. As Panetta described it, "The Secretary had publicly repudiated the work of his own employees, had asked for a delay that was not justified by any previous standard, and had let himself be the fall guy for it all. Worst of all, he had committed a symbolic act of retreat on school desegregation which couldn't help but infect all such programs."[4]

Noisy snorts of disbelief greeted Finch's plea when Chief Judge John R. Brown released the contents in Houston. So dismayed was the head of the Justice Department's delegation in Mississippi by this turn of events, his refusal to shift allegiance forced Assistant Attorney General Leonard, himself, to draft the motion for delay. Despite this, the Secretary acted as though he and he alone were responsible. To the media's question, had the President given the order, Finch replied, "If he did, he never communicated to me. I never discussed this case with the President at all. This was my decision. Nobody in the White House or any place else pressured me."[5]

Giving in to the request for a delay, Brown ordered two district judges in the Fifth Circuit to hear the appeal in Jackson the following Monday, August 25, and forward the testimony to the Court of Appeals in New Orleans. The suddenness with which the court responded shook the composure of HEW and Justice. On such short notice, who was there to defend the new policy?

Working to meet the deadline, a conference took place at HEW headquarters in Washington two days prior to the hearing to settle on a substitute plan. Leonard demanded that someone be found to defend the delay. Anrig was no help. "I'm sorry, Mr. Secretary," he told Finch, "But I feel that all those districts could implement the plans we developed this September."[6] Although three of the thirty districts in question faced considerable hardships in complying with immediate desegregation, there were sixteen districts with five schools or less, and three districts that contained only two schools. To ask for a delay in all thirty, as Finch had, notwithstanding these variations, to label the plans in their entirety "a catastrophic educational setback," this simply went too far.

Accordingly, Leonard had to dig down into the Department's regional personnel to get assistance. In this way, he found two allies: Jesse J. Jordan, HEW's regional director for Title IV in Atlanta, and Howard Sullins, an ex-school superintendent based in HEW's regional office in Charlottesville, North Carolina.[7]

As one might anticipate, the Jackson hearing turned farcical. Leonard confessed he was "somewhat embarrassed" by the Administration's action, but held to the idea that delay was necessary, a point that Jordan and Sullins readily confirmed.[8]

For the first time in litigation bearing on school desegregation, Justice and the Legal Defense Fund took opposite sides. For Melvyn Leventhal, LDF attorney, the confrontation struck a bitter memory. He recalled how churlishly Mississippi whites had reacted to Federal District Judge Griffin Bell's freedom-of-choice decision in 1964. In little Durant, with which Leventhal was familiar, bigots had plastered utility poles with a sign reading, "The following are names of parents and/or guardians of children integrating the Durant Public School."[9] The list included thirty-two names, all black, who lost their jobs for exercising the right to integrate.

Now, Leventhal was asking the court to cast the Federal government as a defendant in order to stand with the segregationists. "The U.S. government," he told the jurists, "for the first time has demonstrated that it no longer seeks to represent the rights of Negro children."[10] The court rejected his argument, heard the pleas, approved the government's request for a delay, and forwarded its decision to the U.S. Fifth Circuit Court of Appeals for review.

Meanwhile, as news of the government's sell-out filtered into Washington, Justice lawyers in the capital reacted with shock and anger. Half the staff officers in the Civil Rights Division, about forty, met privately for two and a half hours planning "what action, if appropriate," should be taken.[11] They concluded that for the time being, at least, they would do no more than hand Attorney General Mitchell a list of grievances.

The following Friday, August 29, in a unanimous opinion handed down by Judge Brown, the Fifth Circuit bowed to HEW's request, delaying the desegregation deadline from September 1 to December 1. In doing so, the court insisted that "significant action" be taken to desegregate the schools during the school year September, 1969, to June, 1970.[12] Nettled by the government's dallying, the jurists reminded the Administration that until August 21—the day Attorney General Mitchell filed the motion for delay—there had been no inkling "that the times fixed by the court should be relaxed or extended or that such timetable was unattainable."[13]

So infuriated was Jack Greenberg by this judicial backslide that he openly protested, warning "segregationist school boards across the South will all now be demanding the same treatment."[14] He requested Supreme Court Justice Hugo L. Black to vacate the order. This the Alabaman refused to do, but in denying Greenberg his petition, he accepted partial blame for the impasse, referring back to his part in the 1955 *Brown II* decision with the emphasis on "all deliberate speed." The phrase, he confessed, turned out to be "only a soft euphemism for delay."[15] As long as it stood, Black feared the dual school system would remain. "In my opinion, there is no reason why such a wholesale deprivation of constitutional rights should be tolerated another minute," but "deplorable as it is," he wrote, "I must uphold the court's order which both sides indicate could have the effect of delaying total desegregation of these schools for as long as a year."[16]

Black's ruling cheered the critics of delay. The *Washington Post* editorially called the Administration's record in Mississippi the "latest example of how things are coming unstuck. . . . Doubtless the Administration is onto a surefire thing in the sense that school desegregation has never been what you would call a very popular issue, and it is getting less popular every day." But, anguished the *Post*, it was deplorable what the policy was doing to those trying to promote integration "through the orderly processes of law." The white Southerners "who put their reputation on the line," the lawyers for LDF, and the Justice Department who had persisted "against a rising tide of black and white separatism"—these were the people the *Post* cited who were being sacrificed for a "short-term gain," when they should be regarded as Nixon's "best friends and most worthy allies for the long haul."[17]

A fortnight later, the U.S. Commission on Civil Rights added its criticism. For the first time, the Commission said, the Federal government had requested a slowdown in the desegregation pace. Unanimously, the members identified Finch-Mitchell as a "major retreat," ridiculing its figures which made it appear "full desegregation is just around the corner."[18] Secretary Finch and Attorney General Mitchell had boasted in their July 3 statement that of 4,477 school districts located in the seventeen Southern and Border states that formerly imposed racial segregation by law, 2,994 had desegregated "voluntarily and completely."[19] Commission members disputed the significance of this claim by pointing out that at least 1,018 of the "completely desegregated" districts contained no black students at all.[20]

Coming from a respected body, one chaired by Father Theodore M. Hesburgh, President of Notre Dame University, the judgement particularly upset the White House. The President had appointed the Catholic cleric in one of his first official acts in the mistaken belief that Hesburgh would agree with his interpretation of the Commission's role. Hesburgh had been particularly firm with students who tried to take over the university's administration building in the heady days of the mid-1960s, and his firmness had impressed the President. The fact he could be fully as adamant in dealing with anyone who violated another's civil rights came as a shock to Mr. Nixon.

The criticism stung Finch. On the day after the rebuke, the Secretary appeared before a gathering of black elected officials to counter Hesburgh's critique. Vast strides, he announced, had been made in school integration; in fact, the Nixon Administration was accomplishing more than had occurred in the past fifteen years by working through the courts. Under questioning, however, Finch admitted that much of the progress resulted from Johnson Administration policies. It turned out that only 106 desegregation plans, a mere 2 percent of the total number of schools involved, had been integrated since Inauguration Day.[21]

In late September, still another issue rose up to embarrass the Administration. An article, appearing in the *Jackson Daily News*, written by Charles J. Overby, an ex-member of Sen. Stennis's press staff, publicly lifted the lid on the secret understanding between the White House and the senator, which preceded Mitchell's request for a delay in desegregating the Mississippi schools. The President, when interrogated by the press, admitted some knowledge of the senator's unhappiness, but said, "Anybody who knows Senator Stennis and anybody who knows me, would know that he would be the last person to say, 'Look, if you don't do what I want in Mississippi, I am not going to do what is best for the country.' He did not say that, and under no circumstances, of course, would I have acceded to it."[22] It was a perfect dodge because Finch had already taken full credit, or blame, for the Mississippi imbroglio.

Having leaped agilely over the Stennis pitfall, Nixon took off on what he liked best, an excursion into the philosophical realm: "It seems to me," he continued, "there are two extreme groups. There are those who want instant integration and those who want segregation forever. I believe we need to have a middle course between these two extremes. That is the course on which we are embarked. I think it is correct."[23]

Trying to balance the two, "instant integration" and "segregation forever," a reporter asked, "It is now 15 years since the Supreme Court made its decision. How much longer do you think school segregation should be allowed to exist anywhere in the country?"[24] In view of Mr. Nixon's oft-expressed belief in law and order, the question had explosive potential. He could hardly say that integration, already delayed fifteen years, was "instant," nor that an order of the Supreme Court was not worth following. That would violate his pledge to law and order. So he drifted off into more musing about schools without answering the question. He mentioned two goals, "the goal of desegregated schools without at the same time irreparably damaging the goal of education now for the hundreds of thousands of black and white students who would otherwise be harmed if the move toward desegregation closes their schools."[25]

This goose grease convinced the *Washington Post* that the President had "missed his calling. He should have been an editorial writer. Mr. Nixon seems to know all our professional secrets; he slips with ease into each and every one of those dreadful locutions that are as highminded as they are off the mark and which (we try to think) we only use when the hour is late, the typewriter stuck and the issue layered in fog, mud, and glue. . . ."[26]

Despite the President's best effort to calm the waters, clamor over the Mississippi delay would not die. What critics of the Administration's foot dragging found particularly offensive was Leonard's claim that his office could not enforce total desegregation throughout the South. There were just not enough "bodies" and "people," should the court order it.[27] When the *New York Times* upbraided him for declaring openly he could not enforce court orders, Leonard called a second conference to defend the Administration's policy and to accuse the *Times* of being "picayunish and pusillanimous." To him, critics represented a "lot of people who are frankly running off at the mouth."[28]

Nothing could halt the rush of events that were now about to unfold, not Leonard's pugnacious statements, nor Erwin Griswold, the Solicitor General, who urged the Supreme Court to deny or delay the Legal Defense Fund's September 22 appeal to terminate the "deliberate speed" language of *Brown II.* On October 9, the High Court agreed to hear the appeal, and Griswold, thinking better of his role, assigned Leonard the task of convincing the justices that the Fifth Circuit order should stand.

Litigation of *Beatrice Alexander* v. *Holmes County Board of Education* commenced two weeks later. Mrs. Alexander was a black Mississippian, mother of one of the black children to whom the Holmes County Board of Education refused entrance to a white school. Speaking for the plaintiff, Jack Greenberg, LDF's attorney, said the case would show "whether we go forward or halt." In the years since the 1954 *Brown* decision, "segregation forever" had been replaced by "litigation forever." It is time to end the delay and put the ship of state back on course. "A retreat from the principles of *Brown*," he heatedly stated, "would tell more than many volumes what this country stands for."[29] When Leonard's turn came to refute Greenberg, he became confused under a barrage of questions from the bench. Justice Byron R. White pried from him the admission that the government intended to offer in December plans not unlike those it had wanted held back in September. To his embarrassment, Leonard had no plausible explanation.

Then Justice Black intervened. "You have too many plans," he told the Assistant Attorney General," and not enough action. I ask you why [the plaintiffs] would not be right in asking us to order an end to segregation?

"I think that would be terribly wrong," Leonard answered. "I ask the court not to do something precipitous."[30]

"Precipitous"—that was a word to conjure up memories for Black. He had been a member of the Court since 1937. In 1950, he had participated in one of the early cases involving school integration, *Sweatt* v. *Texas* in which the court ordered the state university to admit a black student to its law school. Then came *Brown I* outlawing legal segregation and a year later *Brown II,* with its interpretative compliance phrase "with all deliberate speed." The court had gone so far in its 1955 decision as to require only a "prompt and reasonable" start toward desegregation, and even softened this command by allowing the schools to set their own desegregation schedules as long as they were established in the "public interest" and "consistent with good faith compliance at the earliest practicable date."[31] The only caveat the court used was a warning that the principle of desegregation be not surrendered "simply because of disagreement" with it.[32]

Understandably, by 1964 when progress was still miniscule, the court's patience had begun to wear thin. Reviewing the experience of Prince Edward County, Virginia, one of the five school systems involved in the original *Brown* litigation, it found that no steps toward desegregation had been taken. 'The time for mere deliberate speed' has run out," the justices fumed, "and that phrase can no longer justify denying these children their constitutional rights to an education afforded by the public schools in other parts of Virginia."[33] Finally, in the spring of 1968, the court pointedly observed in *Green* that a desegregation plan must work *now*.[34] So here was Leonard, a government official sworn to uphold the law, asking the court to confirm a delay that it had previously said would deny "children their constitutional right."[35]

"The frustration has been going on for 15 years," Black exploded, "could anything be precipitous in this field now, after all the time since our order was given?" Leonard sought to unloosen the legal knot that was beginning to enclose him. It was not really fifteen years, he countered, trying to change the time frame, only eighteen months of the requirement for immediate compliance. Such problems as preparing new facilities, arranging new bus schedules, and the like would need to work out regardless of the court's admonition.

"This means one more year," Black interrupted.
"Only for parts of the plan," Leonard responded.
"But it's still another year," Black shot back. 'Why not put it into effect and make arrangements afterwards?"[36]

All that remained was for Greenberg to smooth the mortar around the foundation stone of his original argument. There would be, he admitted, disruption in the school curriculum as a result of immediate action. This would represent loss to the children, but more importantly, they would learn that "the supreme law of the land is binding on all Americans" regardless of class or color.[37]

Six days later, the court handed down its decision. In a unanimous ruling, the first major opinion since President Nixon named Warren E. Burger Chief Justice, the justices reversed the Fifth Circuit. They were angry, they explained, because thousands of Mississippi schoolchildren were still attending segregated schools despite previous court decisions. The time had come to stop quibbling. Like a furious father, determined to chastise his unruly children, the High Court proceeded to set down the disciplinary terms:

(1) The Fifth Circuit must order each school district to convert its system from dual to unitary at once to prevent any pupil from being excluded due to race or color.

(2) In doing so, the Circuit Court would have discretionary power to accept "all or any part" of the original HEW plans submitted on August 11, 1969, that had been delayed by plea of the Justice Department.

(3) To prevent District courts, considered unfriendly to the original *Brown* decision, from interfering with the Court's latest ruling, the Circuit Court would retain jurisdiction at all times.

(4) Whatever revisions or amendments the District courts might allow in any final resolution, nothing was to be done without approval of the Circuit.[38]

In short, as Warren Weaver of the *New York Times* observed, "Its basic message was to integrate now, litigate later."[39] The ruling understandably evoked a mixed response. Greenberg jubilantly exclaimed, "Now that the court has accepted the principle . . . of no further delays . . . we are going to press for such relief in all pending school cases."[40] On the other side, Strom Thurmond dourly contended the Supreme Court had "allowed ideological passion to overcome reason in this tragic ruling. . . . The Nixon Administration stood with the South . . . but the Court has chosen to override both the State of Mississippi and the Justice Department."[41]

The White House did not react immediately. The President preferred not to comment on the fact that the new Chief Justice had joined the remaining members of the Warren Court to bring school segregation to heel. Since Mr. Nixon had equated "instant integration" with "segregation forever" during his September 26 news conference, dubbing both positions "extreme," there was little else he could do.

Notes

1. Leon Panetta and Peter Gall, *Bring Us Together* (Philadelphia: J. B. Lippincott Company, 1971), p. 297.

2. Ibid., p. 254.

3. Ibid., p. 255.

4. Ibid., p. 256.

5. Don Oberdorfer, "Mississippi Schools Deal Denied by President," *Washington Post*, September 27, 1969.

6. Panetta and Gall, *Bring Us Together*, p. 259.

7. Ibid., p. 262.

8. *New York Times*, August 31, 1969.
9. Author's conversation with Melvyn Leventhal, October 26, 1977.
10. *New York Times*, August 31, 1969.
11. *New York Times*, August 27, 1969.
12. *Washington Post*, August 29, 1969.
13. Ibid.
14. Ibid.
15. *Washington Post*, September 6, 1969.
16. Ibid.
17. Editorial, *Washington Post*, August 28, 1969.
18. *New York Times*, September 13, 1969.
19. *New York Times*, July 4, 1969.
20. *New York Times*, September 13, 1969.
21. *New York Times*, September 14, 1969.
22. Oberdorfer, "Mississippi Schools Deal."
23. Ibid.
24. Ibid.
25. Ibid.
26. Editorial, *Washington Post*, October 1, 1969.
27. *New York Times*, September 30, 1969.
28. *New York Times*, October 3, 1969.
29. Panetta and Gall, *Bring Us Together*, p. 297.
30. Ibid., p. 298.
31. *Brown* v. *Board of Education*, 349 U.S. 294 (1955).
32. Ibid.
33. *Griffin* v. *County School Board of Prince Edward County*, 377 U.S. 218 at page 234 (1964).
34. *Green* v. *County School Board of New Kent County*, 391 U.S. 430 (1968).
35. *Griffin* v. *County School Board*.
36. Panetta and Gall, *Bring Us Together*, pp. 298-99.
37. Ibid., p. 299.
38. *Alexander* v. *Holmes*, 396 U.S. 19 (1969).
39. *New York Times*, October 30, 1969.
40. Ibid.
41. *Washington Post*, October 30, 1969.

6

SOUTHERN ANGER FLARES

"My kids ain't riding no buses all over the country just to make the damned Supreme Court happy."

Georgia parent's response to *Alexander* v. *Holmes*.[1]

Looking back to the time frame of *Alexander* v. *Holmes*, it seems incredible that the Nixon Administration should have initially adopted such a benign reaction to the decision. The response was simply atypical, as though suddenly the Southern Strategy had disappeared. The three principal architects—the President, the Attorney General, and the HEW Secretary—were suddenly sweetness and light, bathed in the sunshine of a new day, determined not to cause a constitutional crisis by word or deed.

"The Administration will carry out the mandate of the Court and will enforce the law," the President announced on the day following the decision through his press secretary, Ronald Ziegler.[2] The Attorney General responded with equal frankness. The Justice Department would use "every available resource" to execute the Court rulings "pursuant to the Supreme Court decisions."[3] As for HEW, Secretary Finch promised not to "tolerate any further delays in abolishing the vestiges of the dual system."[4]

Nor was all the euphoria confined to Washington. In the South, where liberal hopes for desegregation had been waning, optimism revived. The director of the Southern Regional Council saw the decision completely undermining "the Nixon argument that in locales where, because of community pressure or administrative difficulty there is likely to be trouble, you don't press for immediate desegregation."[5]

Despite this, the mood of Southern segregationists remained unchanged. Officials of the (White) Citizens Council of America promoted the growth of private schools to replace public instruction and predicted, to Mr. Nixon's distress, that school integration would become "a real issue in 1972," engulfing the entire country, not only the South.[6]

To round out the picture, Jack Greenberg began filing plaintiff suits to supplement the Supreme Court's decision. In almost one hundred courts across the South, the Legal Defense Fund took action to integrate the public school system. "We'll ask immediate integration. We will not wait for the close of the year or even until the end of the semester. Every Southern state will be affected," Greenberg announced. The extent of the effort's success would rest in large part on the ability of the twenty-five Fund lawyers in New York and 250 cooperating Southern attorneys to file motions promptly. Much also depended upon the Fund's ability to overcome its financial deficit, then running at about $250,000. Nevertheless, the executive director moved in, determined to break "the back of Southern school resistance."[7]

Initial reports seemed unexpectedly sanguine. *New York Times* reporter Jon Nordheimer, filing an on-scene story from New Albany, Mississippi, only ten days after *Alexander,* discovered a give-and-take in the mixed classrooms. A white teen-ager confided to him, "They're not as dumb as lots of us figured." Black communication likewise improved. A black girl, asked to state her impressions, replied, "They're not as mean as lots of us thought."[8]

Paul Rilling, HEW's regional civil rights director who supervised desegregation in the South's six states—Mississippi, Alabama, Georgia, Florida, South Carolina, and Tennessee—confirmed Nordheimer's findings by saying from his headquarters in Atlanta, "There has been trouble in individual schools, but on the average, I'd say that many Southerners are learning to their great pleasure that desegregation can work smoothly and without discord with the right kind of leadership."[9]

Unfortunately, the harmony was quite ephemeral. As Rilling himself later conceded, "The strategy of the Deep South segregationists is to bend with pressure, to accept minimal change, to maneuver skillfully, to buy time, to wait until the pressure lets up. The Southern segregationists are willing to lose battle after battle until they ultimately win the war. The tactics may change from Jim Crow to massive resistance, to tokenism and freedom of choice, to neighborhood schools, antibusing, and uniform application of the law, but the end remains the same."[10]

White-dominated school boards, in establishing unitary school systems, reached decisions that often as not infuriated black parents. The insistence on white superiority posed a particularly sensitive issue. Melvyn Leventhal, the Defense Fund's representative in Jackson, Mississippi, found that in one Mississippi high school building, the athletic and scholastic trophies won by blacks were removed upon integration and replaced by white awards. "They change the names of black schools," Leventhal reported to Bruce Galphin, of the *Washington Post*, "to completely erase whatever black characteristics the school might have had."[11] In other ways, too, the anti-black drumfire was maintained. Even though blacks and whites attended the same school, the two races used separate classrooms, going so far on occasion as to occupy opposite sides of the same room. As the system contracted from dual to unitary, those to suffer most were black principals and teachers, the segregated staple prior to *Brown*. The National Education Association found that from 1968 to 1970, a total of 1,072 black educators lost their jobs in six Southern states. At the same time, 5,575 white teachers and administrators got jobs.[12]

The great anomaly was that while the white power structure continued its dominance of the public school system, it lost no time in providing private instruction for its own children. According to the Southern Regional Council, by October, 1969, approximately 300,000 white children attended private schools. Such institutions, said the Council, had increased tenfold in the previous five years, many of which tended to be "not only racist but also right-wing extremist, attracting board members and teachers who are philosophically in accord with anti-democratic values."[13]

In Washington, official action following the *Alexander* decision was desultory after the initial declaration of support. As expected, the Justice Department, having lost its plea for delay, was willing, even eager it seemed, to permit the judiciary to bear the onus. "All we're doing is leaving it up to the courts," Jerris Leonard told Panetta. On November 5, seven days after the High Court had spoken, Justice submitted a court order for the thirty-three segregated districts, leaving the deadline for desegregation to the Fifth Circuit. "It would have been laughable," wrote Panetta, . . . "if it wasn't such a sad default on Justice's responsibility to respond to the Supreme Court."[14]

Again, the judicial club fell. This time, speaking for the Fifth Circuit, Judge Griffin Bell, of Atlanta, Jimmy Carter's future Attorney General, said pointedly, "The burden is now reversed. We read the government's motion, but the only people who can construe the mandate of the Supreme Court are the judges of this court. We are a different branch of government."[15] The court ordered twenty-seven Mississippi districts to desegregate completely by December 31, and because of large student populations and incompleted facilities, three more were granted 1970 terminal dates.

In contrast to the do-nothing attitude that prevailed in Justice, HEW used the *Alexander* decision and the November 6 ruling of the Circuit Court to inject new energy into the desegregation effort. After three days of intra-office sessions, the Office for Civil Rights mailed letters to 112 Southern districts announcing that school negotiations, looking to affirmative action, would begin at once. The largest category affected were the forty-six districts, many with majority black populations, that had remained relatively unchanged since the Civil Rights Act of 1964. Like the Mississippi districts under court order, they would have to desegregate by December 31 or risk losing Federal aid. A second group, thirty-one districts that had long tried to escape court-approved desegregation, received until December 31 to comply or face termination. In neither case did HEW choose to explain why it had waited since 1964 to undertake the discipline.

A final body of thirty-five districts consisted of those who had already submitted acceptable plans to take effect in September, but had reneged. They would be cited immediately for noncompliance or referred to the Justice Department for appropriate action.

As something of a postscript, HEW cited ninety-seven segregated school systems that had lost Federal funds, but could get the order rescinded if, by December 31, they submitted acceptable plans.[16]

Yet HEW's announced intentions were about to be sabotaged by a clandestine body of its own making, known simply as the Ad Hoc Committee. The first meeting of this extraordinary departmental invention took place in Secretary Finch's office on October 24, 1969, just five days before *Alexander*. Ostensibly, it was set up to sort out and accept or reject Title VI desegregation plans. In reality, it was designed to take the heat off the Administration by eliminating conditions that Southern districts found offensive. Pat Gray, Finch's confidant, became chairman; others included Jerris Leonard, from Justice; Jerry Brader, the new Title IV chief, who replaced Dr. Anrig, in HEW's quest for greater pliability; Jesse Jordan, Brader's assistant, whose willingness to testify against his own department's conclusions at Jackson in August had not gone unnoticed; Robert Mardian, HEW General Counsel; and of course, Panetta, OCR head.[17]

"Ad hocking," Panetta recalled, involved the inquisition of Title IV technicians and their plans for desegregation. In the effort to get away from Title VI cutoffs, the Department increasingly depended upon such personnel to pull the teeth of Southern bitterness. The committee soon became the czar of school desegregation by monitoring each plan. Its existence was one of Washington's best kept secrets. Not until January, 1970, did the media scent its trail.[18]

What happened in Orange County, Florida, perfectly illustrated the operation. Although the Fifth Circuit Court of Appeals had ordered the county to desegregate the schools and Title IV experts put together a plan that included busing and complete desegregation, assuring a white majority in each school, the justices never saw the proposal. First, Florida's Senator Edward Gurney paraded various members of the Orange County School Board before sympathetic members of the Ad Hoc Committee. Then Pat Gray and Jerris Leonard, alarmed by the emphasis on busing, withdrew HEW's plan and the Orange School Board presented its own plan to the Federal District Court, inferring it carried the Department's consent. Consequently, freedom of choice was reinstated with black-majority schools as before.[19]

As word spread of a more permissive attitude prevailing in Washington, a significantly greater number of school districts reneged on previous commitments to desegregate. In their effort to disregard the 1964 Civil Rights Act, Southern communities discovered a trump card in busing. Complaints against pairing black and white schools, against closing some and opening others, and against the loss of "quality education" when schools were in a state of flux from segregated to integrated, all had their uses, but nothing so touched the viscera of white parents as the picture of their small children being bused long distances into unknown areas. The fact that legal segregation had compelled black parents to send their children formidable distances to gain a schooling had no bearing. The very word *busing* became a dirty word, a euphemism for the desegregation they hated. Typical was the comment of an angry Georgia white parent who told a visiting *New York Times* reporter a week after *Alexander*, "My kids ain't riding no buses all over the country just to make the damned Supreme Court happy."[20]

In reality, desegregation was reducing the busing mileage. The southeastern regional office of OCR in Atlanta conducted a survey in early 1970 which showed "some reduction" in four of the five states studied. "However, in Tennessee, where the greatest amount of desegregation had occurred, total mileage in the 37 districts covered by the survey decreased by 2 million miles from 1964-65 to 1968-69."[21]

For all the resentment that rose below the Mason-Dixon line in the final months of 1969, the majority of Southerners still knew they could not escape the judgement of the Federal courts. Judge Bell had ordered twenty-seven Mississippi school districts desegregated, and here and there compliance began. Even in Wilkinson County, where blacks outnumbered whites 3½ to 1, two white children from a white student population of 800 entered school with 1,500 blacks. Their parents, a poor couple, were determined they should receive training. "Education," said father Brown, who couldn't qualify for a local factory job because he lacked a high school diploma, "is more important to me than race. Most people around here are prejudiced. They'd rather see their kids grow up ignorant than go to school with the colored." To which his wife added, "Mine's not going to be ignorant. They're getting as much education as I can give 'em."[22]

Much reaction to desegregation depended on demography. In Columbia, a lumbering town of 7,000 with twice as many whites as blacks, constructing a unitary system posed little difficulty. In Yazoo City, with blacks and whites about equally divided, the white business leaders, assisted by the local *Herald*, persuaded white parents to stand behind desegregation. As a result, a mere one hundred out of 1,500 white students failed to attend the public system. Together, Columbia and Yazoo City demonstrated that desegregation had an excellent chance of success whenever whites enjoyed a majority or the community's power structure endorsed the transformation.

In situations that could have proven explosive, trouble was usually averted because Mississippi repealed its compulsory school-attendance law in 1956, two years after *Brown I*, to avoid further judicial entanglements. White youngsters could refuse to attend public school, prompting Charles Evers, Fayette's black mayor, to note sardonically, "Let them grow up ignorant—like we did."[23]

Another straw in the wind was the state's encouragement of private, segregated schools. "Anybody can open a private school in Mississippi, and
there is nothing we can do about it," a *Newsweek* correspondent learned
from a state official.[24] On a visit to Hattiesburg to observe the new phenomenon, James T. Wooten, of the *New York Times,* described dozens of
private schools "blossoming faster than cotton and magnolias from Dixie's
segregationist soil."[25] They popped up in such isolated locations as
abandoned schools and factories, community centers, and church base-
ments. The faculty was recruited from a list of retired teachers, housewives,
and untried college graduates, and paid at least $200 less than public school
teachers in Mississippi, whose annual salaries were already "far below" the
national teacher salary standard.[26]

At times the curricula produced jaundiced results. A young student from
a private academy near Jackson informed Wooten, "We were taught that
Earl Warren is a Communist, that the Supreme Court is under Communist
control and that integration is a plot made up by Communists and Jews."[27]
School tuitions were held deliberately low so as to include as many of the
white children as possible. "We'll take anyone who can pay anything, and
we'll pay the rest," said the top official of the Canton Academy.[28] These so-
called instant academies grew spectacularly because in sixteen of the thirty
districts under court order blacks were in the majority. White parents who
would not send their children to school with black majorities were faced
with two alternatives: either neglect their offspring's education or join the
private school movement. Most white families chose the latter. Sardonically, one school authority noted, "We've had a private school system all
along. But the state supported it. Now we have to find private support for
it."[29]

Back in Washington, the Administration seemed to have learned nothing
from *Alexander* v. *Holmes.* On December 31, 1969, Justice again asked the
Supreme Court to delay desegregation until the fall of 1970. Its request
involved sixteen school districts in six states of the Old Confederacy and
contained a promise to marshal every resource in enforcing the deadline.
The action followed a ruling of the Fifth Circuit on December 1 interpreting
Alexander to permit such a delay, and the quick appeal of black parents,
represented by the Legal Defense Fund.

On January 14, 1970, the High Court expectedly overruled the Fifth Circuit and ordered desegregation to take place not later than February 1. The
lower court, it said, had "misconstrued" *Alexander,* but for the first time, in
action involving school desegregation, the opinion was not unanimous.
Chief Justice Burger and Justice Potter Stewart dissented, saying the Circuit
was "far more familiar" with the problems of each school district.[30]
Southern reaction to the Supreme Court's latest interpretation was
expectedly resentful. "It's time to take your children away from these
people," boomed Senator Sam J. Ervin (D-N.C.) to an audience of 1,000

angry neighbors.[31] Sen. Stennis, eyeing his Northern colleagues, told them he would dare any Presidential candidate two years hence to campaign in Northern and Western states and "say to parents there, I'll do to your schools what we've done to the schools in Mississippi, Alabama and Louisiana if I'm elected President—if they do, they'll be defeated."[32]

For Southern school authorities, the court's abruptness caused great consternation. Examples of frustration abounded. The superintendent of schools in Bessemer, Alabama, for instance, lamented he had "no earthly idea how the school system could be completely mixed by February 1."[33] Meanwhile, sentiment in the North held firm for desegregation—in the South. In an editorial "Damn the Resisters—Full Speed Ahead," the *Washington Post*, of January 20, said, "The court can hardly be called heedlessly impatient. It has simply had all the delay and all the deliberation it could stomach without sacrifice of its authority." The editorialist could not explain Justice rationale which "seems always able to find sympathy for the travail for white citizens who must make a painful adjustment to the ideal of racial equality, yet is rarely able to muster up much feeling for blacks who have had to adjust to inequality for the whole of their lives and seek something better for their children."[34]

In the face of this pressure, would the South now yield? Gains for desegregation could be enormous. In the nearly fifty districts ordered to desegregate, there were more than 500,000 students, about 200,000 of them black. They constituted almost 7 percent of the black pupils in all eleven states of the Deep South, a significant number to desegregate in one sweep of the judicial net.[35] Encouragingly, for the first time, Gov. Robert Scott, of North Carolina, told a news conference the courts clearly wanted immediate school desegregation, and "we might as well get on with it. This state, in my administration, will be a state that will abide by the law."[36] Gov. Robert E. McNair, of neighboring South Carolina, also sounded an optimistic note, "We have run out of time. We have run out of courts."[37]

However, when February 1 passed, so did the "time for truth." While approximately one-fourth of the districts desegregated their schools, the remainder either closed their doors, were boycotted by white students, simply disregarded the court's ultimatum, or obtained reprieves from Federal district judges.

Fearing the political repercussions, the Nixon Administration announced, on the same day the Supreme Court order triggered, that it would establish a cabinet-level committee to ease recalcitrant districts into court-ordered integration "in the least disruptive way." To assist the effort, the government would appoint a body of Southern educators—black and white, Republican and Democratic—who would give advice to school districts "having the most difficulty."[38]

This evidently followed the Nixon pattern of giving the impression of moving one way while actually going another. The chairman was to be

Spiro Agnew, joined by the Attorney General, the Secretary of HEW, and either Daniel Patrick Moynihan or Bryce N. Harlow, top White House advisers, the latter an avowed supporter of Southern conciliation. To top it off, Mardian would add to his position on the Ad Hoc Committee, responsibility for directing the Agnew Committee, a combination that would enable him to finger every plan for Southern education, bowing to the South's racial incrustations, as he declared the preceding month in New Orleans before the Louisiana School Boards Association, "Your most difficult problem is the social one—that of the cultural lag between social mores and the new law. You have the burden of finding an accommodation to the fact of racial prejudice until such time as our customs and our mores catch up to the law."[39]

Notes

1. Georgia parent, *New York Times*, November 3, 1970.
2. *New York Times*, October 31, 1969.
3. Ibid.
4. Ibid.
5. Ibid.
6. Leon E. Panetta and Peter Gall, *Bring Us Together* (Philadelphia: J.B. Lippincott Company, 1971), p. 302.
7. *New York Times*, November 1, 1969.
8. Jon Nordheimer, "South Learning to Live With Desegregation," *New York Times*, November 10, 1969.
9. Ibid.
10. Paul M. Rilling, "Desegregation: The South *Is* Different," *New Republic*, May 16, 1970.
11. Bruce Galphin, "School Battle in South Not Yet Won," *Washington Post*, January 1, 1970.
12. Alex Poinsett, "The Dixie Schools Charade," *Ebony*, August, 1971.
13. *New York Times*, October 19, 1969.
14. Panetta and Gall, *Bring Us Together*, p. 307.
15. Ibid., p. 308.
16. *New York Times*, November 14, 1969.
17. Panetta and Gall, *Bring Us Together*, p. 294.
18. Ibid., p. 295.
19. Ibid., p. 313.
20. *New York Times*, November 3, 1970.
21. Rilling, "Desegregation: The South *Is* Different."
22. *Newsweek*, January 26, 1970, p. 59.
23. James T. Wooten, "A New Day Ends Public Segregated Schools in Mississippi," *New York Times*, January 11, 1970.
24. *Newsweek*, January 26, 1970.
25. Wooten, "A New Day Ends."

26. James T. Wooten, "Private Schools Boom in South," *New York Times*, February 1, 1970.

27. Ibid.

28. *Newsweek*, January 26, 1970.

29. Ibid.

30. *New York Times*, January 15, 1970.

31. *New York Times*, January 16, 1970.

32. Ibid.

33. Ibid.

34. Editorial, *Washington Post*, January 20, 1970.

35. *Washington Post*, February 1, 1970.

36. Ibid.

37. Rilling, "Desegregation: The South *Is* Different."

38. *New York Times*, February 2, 1970.

39. Robert C. Mardian, "School Desegregation," *Integrated Education: Race and Schools*, May-June, 1970.

7

HAYNSWORTH AND
CARSWELL

"They've got the wrong sow by the ear. I don't fetch and carry
when some fat cat calls up and tells me what to do."

Senator William Saxbe, Ohio.[1]

During the presidential campaign of 1968, Richard Nixon vowed to cheer-
ing crowds that as President he would appoint "strict constitutionalist"
judges to the U.S. Supreme Court, persons who strongly believed in law
and order.[2] Even before taking office, it was clear he would be naming a
new Chief Justice, for on June 13, 1968, Earl Warren had requested retirement "at the pleasure of the President."[3] Proceeding to replace him, Lyndon
Johnson nominated his long-time friend and intimate counselor, Abe
Fortas, who was then an Associate Justice and one of the sturdiest pillars of
the Warren edifice. Fortas, a graduate of Yale Law School, had been at age
twenty-nine general counsel of the New Deal's Public Works Administration and at thirty-two an Under Secretary of the Interior, but because of his
attachment to Warren, his nomination set off a bitter fight between Senate
liberals and conservatives. On October 1, by a 45 to 43 vote, the Upper
House refused to invoke cloture on a motion to confirm Fortas, thus
effectively blocking his confirmation. Three days later, Johnson withdrew
the nomination at Fortas's request, and out of respect for the anti-Warren
mood then prevailing, Johnson made no further nominations.

Thus, Nixon took office in January, 1969, knowing one of his first major
decisions would be the appointment of a new Chief Justice. He held back,
however, and by mid-May the position still remained open. In the meantime, a *Life* magazine reporter, working on a tip, discovered that Fortas,
while a member of the court, had accepted a $20,000-a-year contract for life
with Louis Wolfson to advise the Wolfson Family Foundation. He received
his initial payment in January 1966, but then had second thoughts after
Wolfson was indicted for stock manipulation. The fact he returned the
money did not quiet the public outcry against a member of the Supreme

Court engaging in such activity and on May 15, 1969, he resigned his seat, leaving two positions for the President to fill.

A week later, Nixon took the first step by nominating Warren Earl Burger for Chief Justice, calling the sixty-one-year-old judge of the Federal Court of Appeals in Washington a man of "unquestioned integrity throughout his public and private life." History, continued the President, teaches that Chief Justices "have probably had more profound and lasting influence on their times and on the direction of the Nation than most Presidents have had."[4]

The man who was to replace Warren was outwardly, at least, a happy choice. Silver haired, authoritative, robust, he looked the part. Burger was born in St. Paul of Swiss-German Protestant heritage and after spending his early years on a Minnesota farm, worked his way through the University of Minnesota and St. Paul College of Law, graduating *magna cum laude*. By 1953 when President Eisenhower named him Assistant Attorney General in charge of the Justice Department's Civil Division, Burger had practiced law in Minnesota for twenty-two years and argued more than a dozen cases before the Supreme Court.

On the Court of Appeals, to which Eisenhower named him in 1956, he became known as a dissenter—a conservative in a liberal-oriented court, headed by the well-known Chief Judge David E. Bazelon. Burger believed that the Supreme Court had exceeded a prudent limit in protecting the rights of the criminal. He worried about "a society incapable of defending itself—the impotent society,"[5] While his stand on civil rights was considered moderate, Mississippi's conservative James O. Eastland, chairman of the Senate Judiciary, and such other influential conservatives as John McClellan (D-Ark.), Roman L. Hruska, (R-Nebr.), Robert C. Byrd, (D-W.Va.), John Tower (D-Tex.), and J. Strom Thurmond (R-S.C.), all opposed to the court's recent rulings on school desegregation, hailed the appointment. Hearings on his qualifications lasted but three weeks and on June 24, the United States had a new Chief Justice, sworn in by Warren.

Immediately questions arose over whom the President would now appoint to take Fortas's seat. Again Mr. Nixon appeared to be in no hurry. While he said he would move "with all deliberate speed,"[6] it was August 18 before the summer White House in San Clemente announced that Judge Clement Furman Haynsworth, Jr., of South Carolina, would be nominated.

Haynsworth, fifty-six, a native of Greenville, was then Chief Judge of the United States Court of Appeals for the Fourth Circuit, covering the Carolinas, Virginia, West Virginia, and Maryland with headquarters in Richmond. Although a fifth-generation lawyer, enjoying community status, Haynsworth had experienced the economic travail of legal paucity. Indeed, this conflict on young Haynsworth between social respectability and financial pressure produced the nominee's eventual imprimatur. He

attended the Greenville public schools, and after a year in a Rome pre-
paratory school, matriculated at Furman University, a Southern Baptist
college in Greenville, from which he graduated with highest honors. By
1936, he had earned a degree from the Harvard Law School and was back in
Greenville, practicing law in the family firm.

Following a stint in the Pacific as a naval intelligence officer during World
War II, Haynsworth resumed his practice and, on the side, began promoting the industrial growth of Greenville, a city of 75,000 that was described
then as "tough, aggressive and disposed to put aside the amenities should
they become a hindrance to 'progress'."[7] What the young attorney touched
turned to gold. In 1950, he helped form the Carolina Vend-A-Matic with a
$20,000 capitalization. Sixteen years later when the company was merged
with ARA Services, his original investment of $3,000 produced
$437,710.16.

As his practice flourished and his corporate activity increased, he
invested in textiles, insurance, banking, radio and television stations, rail-
roads, hotels, and other industries estimated to be worth slightly under
$1 million.

Totally concentrated as he was on law and business, he never bothered
with politics, choosing to remain a Democrat in name only. However, his
distaste for Adlai Stevenson's liberalism led him in 1952 and 1956 to switch
to Dwight Eisenhower, who responded in 1957 by naming him to the Fourth
Circuit. Seven years later, Haynsworth became its Chief Judge.

The announcement of his nomination to the Supreme Court set off a
wave of comment, some good, some bad, and much speculation as to why
Nixon had chosen him. Southerners were happy, Northerners glum, but
initially confirmation appeared certain. Judiciary Chairman Eastland said
Haynsworth's record was "outstanding,"[8] and the Committee's ranking
member, Everett M. Dirksen, (R-Ill.), saw no problem in getting the
nominee confirmed. Others were not so sure. Senator Jacob Javits (R-N.Y.)
voiced "grave concern" over the appointment,[9] and Roy Wilkins, of the
NAACP, declared, "There would be no more unobtrusive yet deadly way
of negating completely the legislative victories won through the hardest
effort by the nation's minority of black children than for a president to
nominate for the nation's highest court a judge who already had voted for a
racial segregation policy outlawed and made illegal by the Congress."[10]

The chilling prospect of a conservative Southerner on the highest bench
caused Wilkins to exaggerate the judge's anti-school desegregation record.
True, Haynsworth was no civil rights protagonist, but neither was he a segregationist in the mold of many of his Southern colleagues. "We can see,"
said Lawrence E. Walsh, of the American Bar Association, "that in those
areas where the Supreme Court is perhaps moving most rapidly in breaking
new ground, he [Haynsworth] has tended to favor allowing time to pass in

following up or in any way expanding these new precedents."¹¹ That was hardly the position of the segregationist. In *Bowman* v. *County School Board of Charles City County, Virginia*, a 1967 case, for instance, Haynsworth upheld a freedom-of-choice school desegregation plan, but only if the "choice is free in the practical context of its exercise."¹² This preceded the *Green* decision, a year later, in which the Supreme Court abrogated free-choice plans unless they "actually work" to achieve unitary school systems,¹³ and demonstrates a willingness on Haynsworth's part to work in that direction. Moreover, he went on to explain what he meant by "free" by upholding the Federal District Court in an appeal involving the Franklin County Board of Education in eastern North Carolina. In 1965, the Board had adopted a freedom-of-choice plan, but because of violence instigated by the Ku Klux Klan, only 1.5 percent of the black students had become a part of the new system. "Since it clearly appears that the School Board did nothing to relieve the pressures inhibiting the free exercise of the right of choice," wrote Haynsworth, "the District Judge properly required the Board to turn to other measures."¹⁴ This was the reasoning of a strict constructionist, not a segregationist.

In September, 1969, the Senate began reviewing the nominee's credentials, not so much on civil rights as on the fact he had failed to disqualify himself in 1963 litigation involving Deering Milliken and Company, a textile giant, and the Textile Workers Union, an AFL-CIO affiliate. Zealously anti-union, the firm had closed its plant in Darlington, South Carolina, to five hundred workers rather than engage in collective bargaining. Haynsworth, it turned out, cast the deciding vote in a 3 to 2 decision against the Union. Only later was it discovered that the Judge's Carolina Vend-A-Matic, in which he had a one-seventh interest and which constituted about one-half his personal fortune, was grossing at the time of the decision, $100,000 annually from machines at three Deering Milliken plants.

One had to assume that Haynsworth, as the foremost jurist of the Fourth Circuit, knew that Canon 26 of Judicial Ethics Code read: "A judge should abstain from making personal investments in enterprises which are apt to be involved in litigation in the court, and after his accession to the bench, he should not retain such investments previously made longer than a period sufficient to enable him to dispose of them without serious loss."¹⁵ In view of this restriction, why had he not severed his official connection with Vend-A-Matic when he joined the Fourth Circuit in 1957? To make it worse, he had told a Senate subcommittee the previous June, "Of course, when I went on the bench, I resigned from all such business associations I had, directorships and things of that sort."¹⁶

He had done no such thing. Haynsworth held Vend-A-Matic stock for seven years after going on the bench, served as vice-president, collected $12,000 in director fees, pledged his collateral for company loans, and took a hand in promoting sales. He told the Committee that as soon as his owner-ship became public knowledge in December, 1963, he had sold his interest "as quickly as I could."[17] Yet he waited four months, long enough for the Securities and Exchange Commission to approve the company's merger with ARA Services, a move that vastly increased the value of his holdings. There was no allegation on his part that he attempted to sell his shares during the four-month period at a lower return. As to the charge of failing to disqualify himself, Haynsworth could see no violation since, as he pointed out, only 3 percent of Vend-A-Matic's sales were with Deering Milliken.

Further doubt was cast on the Judge's ethical standards by the revelation that in litigation involving the Brunswick Corporation, Haynsworth had voted in favor of Brunswick, but before announcing the decision had pur-chased 1,000 shares of Brunswick stock. When asked for an explanation, the Judge said he "simply did not recall, at the time of the purchase," that the case was unfinished.[18]

Early on, AFL-CIO chieftain George Meany added to Haynsworth's diffi-culties by castigating the Judge's labor decisions. Appearing before the Senate Judiciary Committee, Meany declared the nominee had ruled in seven labor cases and allegedly was antilabor in each. The High Court unanimously reversed him six of the seven, and in the seventh, reversed with only one dissenting vote. To show his concern, Meany assigned forty full-time lobbyists to twist arms in the Senate.

With these disclosures, a feeling of doubt swept the Senate. "If there is a consensus at the moment in the Senate," Senator Edward N. Brooke (R-Mass.) wrote the President, "I think it is the view that Judge Haynsworth is not the distinguished jurist whom the country expected would be nomi-nated."[19] Would the President withdraw the nomination? No. "I have most carefully examined the record," Nixon assured Sen. Scott, the Minority Leader. "There is nothing whatsoever that impeaches the integrity of Judge Haynsworth. There is no question as to his competence as a judge."[20] On October 10, the Senate Judiciary Committee voted 10 to 7 to move the nomination to the floor. An endorsement for Haynsworth followed on October 24 from sixteen past presidents of the American Bar Association (ABA), and the ABA's twelve member Committee on the Federal Judiciary, a group with such strong ties to corporate America, so filled with aging members of the establishment that one ABA critic complained, "You used to have to have prostate trouble to get on the committee."[21]

These benedictions were the high-water mark of the campaign to confirm Haynsworth. Shortly afterward, Senator Margaret Chase Smith, of Maine, Republican Conference Chairman, wrote Mr. Nixon she intended to vote against the nominee. "I felt very strongly against the Fortas nomination for reasons very similar to those on the Haynsworth nomination."[22] Then the assistant to Minority Leader Scott, GOP Senate Whip Robert Griffin, of Michigan, withdrew his previous support of Haynsworth. He had "agonized" over the decision, he told Nixon, but had no alternative but to vote against the nominee.[23] In the wake of these setbacks, the President continued to stand firm, refusing to withdraw the nomination or to "take upon my hands the destruction of a man's whole life, to destroy his reputation, to drive him from the bench and public service."[24] In the meantime, the White House went to work with a vengeance to beat back the opposition. Harry Dent, Nixon's chief political agent, called state and local Republican operatives, telling them to light bonfires under their senators. Among the first to feel the heat was Senator James Pearson, of Kansas, who originally indicated opposition to Haynsworth. However, the hint he might face a primary campaign in 1972 if he continued to oppose Haynsworth and the discovery that all members of the Kansas Supreme Court favored the Southerner nicely adjusted his position. However not every Republican senator reversed gears under White House pressure. Ohio's William Saxbe puffed, "They've got the wrong sow by the ear. I don't fetch and carry when some fat cat calls up and tells me what to do."[25]

The cajoling and the threats continued to the end. While both sides exuded confidence over the outcome, victory eventually depended upon the decisions of eleven publicly uncommitted senators. With ten of their ranks voting "No," Haynsworth went down to defeat 55 to 45. To Dent and company's chagrin, 40 percent of the Senate's Republicans, seventeen out of forty-three, broke with the party. A combination of circumstances produced a defeat the most rabid Haynsworth detractors could not have foreseen in August. First, organized labor violently opposed the nomination. Sen. Hruska, the President's floor manager, called its effort the "main thing" in the outcome.[26] A second consideration was the nominee's moderate view on civil rights which such groups as the NAACP, the National Urban League, and the Leadership Conference on Civil Rights exploited. Sen. Javits, detailing their fears, informed his colleagues that after studying every case in which Haynsworth had stated his views on segregation as a circuit judge, he was convinced the Judge had been "consistently in error, systematically and relentlessly opposed to implementation of the Supreme Court's 1954 desegregation decision [Brown] and consistently sympathetic to every new device for delay of desegregation."[27]

Cogent as these arguments seemed, in the end, ethical considerations swung the uncommitted against Haynsworth. They refused to endorse a man who to them appeared insensitive to the moral demands of the Supreme Court. One of them, Senator Albert Gore (D-Tenn.), whose political survival rested on his support of Haynsworth, stated his reasons for casting a negative vote: "I voted against him because of the danger of the precedent of promoting a judge to the highest court who had persisted in trying cases in which he had a personal interest."[28] In a true sense, the Haynsworth defeat closely paralleled the case of Abe Fortas. A group of conservatives had found Fortas insensitive to the moral tenets of judicial behavior; now a body of liberal senators fell on their prey for the same reason.

At the White House a chastened President expressed disappointment at the outcome, but promised to submit the name of another candidate who would "restore proper balance" to the court. When Congress reconvened, he would nominate an American whose judicial judgement would be "consistent with my commitments to the American people before my election as President a year ago."[29]

For Clement Haynsworth, the man who stood in the middle of the political hurricane, there was crushed pride mixed with relief that "the ordeal of the last two months had ended.[30] At first, he mused whether he "should leave the Court of Appeals and return to private life," but in a few weeks, his equilibrium restored, he decided to retain the post.[31]

On January 19, 1970, the President, through his press secretary, Ronald L. Ziegler, announced the name of his third nominee to the Supreme Court, the man who the White House hoped would "interpret" the law, not "make" it.[32] He was fifty-year-old G. (for George) Harrold Carswell, of Tallahassee, Florida, a member of the Fifth Circuit Court of Appeals. In making the appointment, Nixon again relied heavily on the advice of Attorney General Mitchell, who reportedly went over the judge's record personally and declared, "He's almost too good to be true,"[33] a sentiment readily seconded in the Senate by Georgia's Richard B. Russell, who observed that he could not imagine a "more appropriate appointment."[34]

In point of accomplishment, Carswell did enjoy an enviable record. Born December 22, 1919, at Irwinton, Georgia, he earned a baccalaureate degree from Duke University, 1941, and a law degree from the Walter F. George School of Law at Mercer University in Macon, Georgia, 1948, with time out during World War II for naval service. In 1949, he moved to Tallahassee, joining one of the city's prestigious law firms.

The son of a former Georgia Secretary of State, young Carswell supported Sen. Russell's abortive presidential attempt in 1952 and, like Haynsworth, after the Democratic party nominated Stevenson for a second time in 1956, he switched to Eisenhower, eventually enrolling as a Republican. The President rewarded his protégé by naming him U.S. Attorney for the Northern District of Florida, a heady promotion for a man of thirty-four. Five years later, he appointed Carswell a Federal district judge, the youngest in the nation, and only the previous June, President Nixon had promoted him to the Appeals Court of the Fifth Circuit.

If, prior to his nomination to the Supreme Court, little had been known about the opinions of Clement Haynsworth, still less was known about the latest nominee. Professor Leroy D. Clark, of New York University, who headed the NAACP Legal Defense Fund in Northern Florida during the early 1960s claimed Judge Carswell "invariably handed down improper decisions after creating improper delays and concluded, 'It was my view that of the federal district judges I appeared before Harrold Carswell was clearly the most openly and blatantly segregationist.' "[35]

This tendency to move forward grudgingly, as later evidence revealed, sprang partially from a perverseness to integration, and partially from a conservative bias that stuck to the letter of the law and preferred in the words of Fred P. Graham, of the *New York Times*, not "to move beyond clearly settled precedents to rule in favor of the civil rights position."[36] For instance, a 1968 study by a Yale University doctoral candidate, who analyzed the civil rights decision of thirty-one Federal district judges appointed in the Deep South between 1953 and 1963, found that Carswell placed twenty-third on the basis of rulings favorable to black plaintiffs, and of Carswell's opinions appealed, 60 percent were reversed by a higher court.[37]

The Floridian's nomination had not been in the hands of the Senate Judiciary Committee forty-eight hours before Carswell's past lit up the sky like a Roman candle. It was disclosed that on August 2, 1948, while campaigning for a seat in the Georgia Legislature, he had told an American Legion Chapter at Gordon, Georgia, "Segregation of the races is proper and the only practical and correct way of life in our states. I have always so believed, and I shall always so act."[38] Although he went on CBS to renounce "specifically and categorically" the words themselves and the thought they represent, as "abhorrent," the incident soiled his reputation.[39] The Administration was stunned, for Ziegler, in announcing the nomination, had spoken of a "thorough investigation by the Justice Department," [40] and later had to admit ignorance of the "white supremacy" speech.[41]

Nevertheless, despite the untoward revelation, at the end of two days of hearings, Carswell from outward appearances had impressed a majority of the committee. There was, to be sure, liberal apprehension when he failed to list civil rights in an exchange with Sen. Kennedy over the nation's most pressing problems, but overall the effect was minimal, so minimal in fact, that even such an ardent supporter of civil rights as Sen. Edward Brooke initially let the nomination ride.

Suddenly, with little or no warning, severe opposition to the nomination erupted. The dean of the Yale Law School, Louis H. Pollak, informed the committee that a sampling of Carswell's opinions convinced him that the candidate offered "more slender credentials than any nominee for the Supreme Court put forth in this century."[42] This estimate coincided with that of another esteemed legal authority, William Van Alstyne, of the Duke University Law School, who had applauded Haynsworth's nomination. Of

Carswell, he said, "There is nothing in the quality of the nominee's work to warrant any expectation whatever that he could serve with distinction on the Supreme Court of the United States."[43]

Yet, again, the turbulence subsided. In mid-February, the committee, with unanimous Republican backing, approved the nominee 13 to 4. Once more, confirmation appeared certain until a newly-elected Democrat from Alabama, James B. Allen, decided to filibuster against renewal of the 1965 Voting Rights Act, and in doing so, gave Carswell's opponents an additional month to maneuver. Allen had no illusions about defeating the legislation, he simply wanted to impress his constituents, but for Carswell, the delay proved fatal. The nominee's enemies inside and outside the Senate painted the Floridian as a person of no influence or individuality and when Sen. Hruska, the White House floor leader, attempted to suture the wound, he committed an unbelievable blunder. Conceding the nominee was no Brandeis, Frankfurter, or Cardozo, he publicly asked whether all judges had to be distinguished? Weren't the mediocre entitled to some representation? As *Nation* magazine commented,". . . to our knowledge this is the first time that 'the mediocre' have been identified as a specific constituency, and the first assertion that it is entitled to representation in any branch of government."[44]

On March 27, hoping to bring the Carswell issue to a head, the Senate agreed to vote on a motion to recommit the nomination to the Judiciary Committee on the first day after returning from the Easter holiday. It was the first admission that the Carswell nomination could be in serious trouble.

In hopes of retrieving the initiative, Republican leaders persuaded the President to write an open letter to Ohio's Saxbe outlining his reasons for continued support of the nominee. Had Nixon stopped at that point, the effect could have given decisive assistance, but the President went on to inform Saxbe the central issue was whether the senators could "substitute their own philosophy or their own subjective judgement" to frustrate the constitutional responsibility of the President "to appoint members of the Court."[45] Countering what he considered usurpation of the Senate's "advice and consent" authority, Brooke angrily labelled the Saxbe letter "shameful." Sen. Scott, the Republican Minority Leader, responsible for rounding up GOP votes, added privately, "One more stunt like that and Carswell will get two votes."[46]

Yet, however much the senators fumed over the impact of the Saxbe letter, when the vote on recommittal was taken, the Carswell forces came out ahead, 52 to 44, and no less an observer than the *New York Times* viewed confirmation as "probable."[47] What the writer had not realized, what, perhaps, it was impossible to foresee, was the number of senators who would vote against recommittal, but turn to block the nomination. Again, as with Haynsworth, they reached the conclusion that Carswell did not reflect the ethical standards required of members of the Supreme Court. Almost overlooked in Carswell's eventual 51 to 45 defeat were the votes of two Southern senators, both Democrats—Gore, of Tennessee, and Yarborough, of Texas—who rejected to the end the pleas of regional loyalty and paid for their independence with their political lives at the ensuing election.

To Carswell, magnanimous in defeat, the response was one of "relief" and a determination not to be "embittered by the rejection."[48] Not so, Mr. Nixon. Twice thwarted, he could not, he said, nominate successfully to the Supreme Court "any Federal appellate judge from the South" who was a strict constructionist as long as the "Senate is constituted the way it is today."[49] He continued to insist that both Haynsworth and Carswell were "distinguished jurists," demonstrating that he had learned nothing from the two rebuffs. His only concession in defeat was a promise to fill the Fortas vacancy in the "very near future" with someone "from outside the South."[50]

Notes

1. *Newsweek*, November 24, 1969.

2. *Washington Post*, May 16, 1969.

3. *Washington Post*, May 22, 1969.

4. Ibid.

5. Ibid.

6. *Washington Post*, July 20, 1969.

7. *Washington Post*, September 7, 1969.

8. *Washington Post*, August 19, 1969.

9. Ibid.

10. *New York Times*, August 19, 1969.

11. *Washington Post*, November 23, 1969.

12. *Bowman* v. *County School Board of Charles City County, Virginia*, 382 F2D 326 (1967).

13. *Green* v. *County School Board of New Kent County*, 391 U.S. 430 (1968).

14. *Coppedge* v. *Franklin County Board of Education*, 394 F2D 410 at 411 (1968).

15. *Washington Post*, August 26, 1969.

16. *New York Times*, September 17, 1969.

17. Frank Mankiewicz and Tom Braden, "Haynsworth Battle Now Centering on Nominee's Lack of Candor," *Washington Post*, November 4, 1969.

18. *Newsweek*, September 29, 1969.

19. *Washington Post*, October 3, 1969.

20. *Washington Post*, October 4, 1969.

21. *Nation*, November 3, 1969, p. 462.

22. *Newsweek*, October 20, 1969.

23. Ibid.

24. *New Republic*, November 1, 1969, p. 14.

25. *Newsweek*, November 24, 1969.
26. *Washington Post*, November 22, 1969.
27. *Washington Post*, November 15, 1969.
28. *New York Times*, November 22, 1969.
29. Ibid.
30. Ibid.
31. Ibid.
32. *New York Times*, January 21, 1970.
33. *New Yorker*, December 5, 1970, p. 61.
34. *New York Times*, January 20, 1970.
35. *New Yorker*, December 5, 1970, p. 84.
36. *New York Times*, January 21, 1970.
37. Ibid.
38. *New York Times*, January 22, 1970.
39. Ibid.
40. *New York Times*, January 20, 1970.
41. *New York Times*, January 23, 1970.
42. *New Yorker*, December 5, 1970, p. 102.
43. Ibid.
44. *Nation*, March 30, 1970.
45. *New Yorker*, December 5, 1970, p. 75.
46. Ibid., p. 78.
47. *New York Times*, April 7, 1970.
48. *New York Times*, April 9, 1970.
49. *Congressional Digest, The Month in Congress*, May, 1970, p. 129.
50. *New York Times*, April 10, 1970.

8

STENNIS IN THE SENATE— WHITTEN AND JONAS IN THE HOUSE

"I believe the debate needs to be placed on the level it deserves— the moral level—a level even higher than the Constitution itself. . . ."

Senator Jacob K. Javits, speaking on the Senate floor, February 17, 1970.[1]

Less than three weeks before President Nixon began a fruitless struggle to place two Southerners on the High Court, the House of Representatives again sought to wipe out the principles of school segregation laid down by the courts. On July 31, 1969, it passed the 1970 Labor-HEW Appropriations Bill to which the now familiar Whitten Amendments clung like a barnacle. Identical to the one adopted in 1968, the *Washington Post* described it as "an artful bit of legislative language which would, in effect, undermine a number of Supreme Court desegregation decisions and gut Title VI of the [1964] Civil Rights Act. . . ."[2] North or South, however, these proposals appeared to be gaining strength, even among liberals, because of constituents increasingly critical of busing to achieve desegregation. The Whitten Amendments were actually a legislative illusion since Congress had enacted wording in the 1964 Civil Rights Act to prevent the assignment or transportation of students or teachers "to overcome racial imbalance."[3] So the argument was a canard and the representatives knew it.

What made the Whitten Amendments so costly to school desegregation was their countenance of free-choice plans. Under them, HEW could not "force any student attending elementary or secondary school to attend a particular school against the choice of his or her parents or parent," and the Department was further enjoined from "forcing attendance of students at a particular school as a condition precedent to obtaining Federal funds otherwise available. . . ."[4] This ran directly counter to Supreme Court views about "freedom-of-choice," stated a year earlier in *Green*.[5]

For the most part, House liberals were horrified. They had tried vainly to weaken the force of the amendment by inserting language "except as required by the Constitution."[6] Then, on August 18, three Democratic veterans of the Civil Rights struggle, Donald M. Fraser, of Minnesota; John

Brademas, of Indiana; and James M. Corman, of California, wrote President Nixon, decrying his silence. Passage of the Whitten Amendments, they declared, "may have been the death warrant" of the government's effort to desegregate the nation's schools. "Your continued silence can only be construed as a deliberate effort to emasculate . . . the program."[7]

A month later, the U.S. Civil Rights Commission Chairman, Father Hesburgh, chided, "If we can get a man on the moon in nine years, I should think we can get a school desegregated in 15 years, the time that has elapsed since the Supreme Court's first declaration that desegregation is unconstitutional."[8]

In the face of Nixon's refusal to oppose the Whitten Amendments in the House, the rationale that caused him to resist them in the Senate remains obscure. Presumably, the President became apprehensive about crossing swords with the Supreme Court. In any event, HEW Secretary Finch appeared before the Senate Appropriations Committee to argue that the Whitten Amendments would cripple the government's desegregation program and perhaps lead to considerable resegregation in the South. He followed his appearance with a public telegram urging deletion of the Whitten alterations, and failing that, inclusion of the phrase the House liberals argued for: "except as required by the Constitution."[9]

On December 13, when the Senate undertook debate on the appropriations measure, the Whitten language remained, but on motion of Senator Hugh Scott, of Pennsylvania, the Republican Minority Leader the six words Finch requested were added and a bipartisan coalition adopted the amended version 52 to 37. The following day, with members of the House restive to begin their Christmas recess, the bill cleared that body with a 216 to 180 vote amid assurances the Senate amendment represented the Administration's position. However, the President vetoed the legislation, calling it too inflationary. An appropriation of $21.4 billion was considerably more than Mr. Nixon wished to authorize.

Meanwhile, Senator Stennis, of Mississippi, had begun a new campaign in mid-October to halt school desegregation. Testifying before the Senate Appropriations Committee, he reeled off "shocking" examples of Northern school segregation: Chicago, 214 schools—90 to 100 percent black, and more than 100 all black; Cleveland, 68 schools—81.3 to 100 percent black; Newark, 65 schools—81.3 to 100 percent black; East St. Louis, 24 schools— 95.2 to 100 percent black. "I don't know why it's illegal in the South and all right in the North," Stennis upbraided Finch angrily, "You haven't tried—your predecessors haven't tried" because to do so would be "politically hazardous."[10] The Mississippian insisted there was no difference between the South's de jure segregation, enforced by law, and the North's de facto segregation, which was largely the result of discriminatory housing patterns. "If it is true," he argued before his Senate colleagues on December

8, "as advocates of integration claim, that segregation deprives the Negro student of an equal education, millions of Negro students in the North are being deprived of their rights."[11]

The Senator, of course, overlooked HEW's lack of authority to bar de facto school segregation. As the *Washington Post* pointed out, "The Supreme Court has yet to go near the subject—with or without a 10 foot pole."[12] Nevertheless, Stennis plodded on, issuing additional reports on school segregation in nine Northern states and the District of Columbia. He vowed he would sponsor amendments to the House-approved $35 billion 1969 Education Act for Elementary and Secondary Education when the measure reached the Senate, to make certain the whole nation complied with the Supreme Court's *Alexander* order to desegregate "at once."[13]

When debate finally began on February 4, 1970, Stennis was ready with two amendments. Number 481 called for a freedom-of-choice "national school racial policy."[14] It bore a striking resemblance to a law enacted by the New York State Legislature and signed by Gov. Rockefeller in 1969. Stennis intended to embarrass Northern liberals who stood aghast by what a once-liberal governor had done. In the initial skirmishing, New York's Jacob Javits was asked by Senator Ernest F. Hollings (D-S.C.) whether he supported Stennis since the amendment was based on New York law. "No," replied Javits, "The New York law is very wrong. My state passes bad laws, too."[15] Stennis, a practicing politician, eventually realized that apart from the humiliation certain members felt, Amendment 481 had accomplished nothing and withdrew it.

His second amendment, Number 463, created far more controversy and stirred a variety of conflicting opinions. It stated that Federal laws dealing with school desegregation guidelines should be "applied uniformly in all regions of the United States."[16] The language expectedly raised the specter of de jure and de facto and sought to remove any statutory difference between the two.

Over the weekend of February 7, pondering the Supreme Court's schizoid interpretation of school desegregation, which allowed the North to hide behind a de facto facade, Senator Abraham A. Ribicoff, a Connecticut Democrat and former HEW Secretary in the Kennedy Administration, decided to assist Stennis. On Monday, without alerting his liberal colleagues, he rose to tell a startled Senate:

The North is guilty of monumental hypocrisy in its treatment of the black man. Without question, northern communities have been as systematic and as consistent as southern communities in denying the black man and his children the opportunities that exist for white people. The plain fact is that racism is rampant throughout the country. It knows no geographical boundaries and has known none since the great migration of rural blacks after World War II. . . .

Let us be honest with ourselves. Whether it is *de jure* or *de facto* segregation, it is segregation. I want them all treated the same way. Let us not have any illusions that then the whites in the North will start to worry about solving the problem. Our problem is that we have a racist society. . . .

I know the legal difference between *de facto* and *de jure*, but it comes down to the same thing . . . the problem of schools being segregated is due to the fact that we have a segregated society, and . . . we are not going to solve the problem . . . by busing. Who are we, whose faces are white, who send our children to white schools or private schools, to think that because a person is poor or because a person lives in the ghetto he wants his black child carted 20 miles away? . . . You are doing more harm and hurt to a child than would be done by letting him remain in a black school with decent teachers and a good curriculum.[17]

Such words cheered Southern senators who believed that Ribicoff, working alone, had scored a breakthrough for their view that the North would never submit to what Stennis called "massive, immediate integration," as required in the South.[18]

To tell the truth, however, for all Ribicoff's forthrightness, he had stated the obvious about racism without challenging the opinions of the Supreme Court. As long as these nine men refused to speak to de facto segregation, the brunt of complying with *Brown* had to fall on the South. In view of this, to accuse the North of "monumental hypocrisy" was to do absolutely nothing for the North while sabotaging the desegregation effort in the South.

In the aftermath, one Southern senator cried, "For the South, it was the Alamo. They not only went out to win, but to humble and humiliate."[19] Their task was lightened by an encouraging statement from Key Biscayne, the President's winter White House, which seemed to endorse the Stennis position without actually saying so. "The President," declared Ronald L. Ziegler, the White House press secretary, "has said every law in the United States should apply equally to all parts of the country. To the extent the uniform application amendment offered by Sen. Stennis would advance equal application of the law, the Administration would be in full support of this concept."[20] Asked whether this amounted to an outright endorsement, Ziegler refused to interpret, but the meaning could hardly be mistaken.

During the Lincoln Day recess that followed Ribicoff's speech, the Capitol remained quiet, but on Tuesday, February 17, the fireworks began again. The Senator from Connecticut, anxious to equate the meaning of de jure and de facto, proposed a modification to the Stennis Amendment, which in qualifying the term *segregation* added the words "whether de jure or de facto."[21]

In the ensuing crossfire, Sen. Stennis chided his Northern colleagues. "What is the matter with the amendment?" he shouted. "What is wrong with it? Just to get down to hard facts, what is the matter with it? Pointing to the industrial states of Illinois, Indiana, Ohio, Pennsylvania, New Jersey, and New York where HEW figures showed more segregation than before *Brown*, he said, "The people in those areas . . . do not know whether they want integration or not. . . . They have never had it applied to them. We find there is a rule that applies to the South and is ruining our public schools. I do not want to ruin the schools of the North, but I want them to find out whether or not they want this massive, immediate integration. I do not believe they do."[22] The Mississippian was especially critical of an amendment introduced by Senator Walter Mondale (D-Minn.), calling for a Senate subcommittee to study the effects of school desegregation. "If a study is needed now to determine what the facts are about segregation, or integration in the North—or the South—on what grounds did those who proposed and those who now support the Civil Rights Act of 1964 base their arguments that the civil rights law was and is needed?" To Stennis, the proposal was no more than "a smokescreen, a maneuver, which the proponents are using to avoid taking their own medicine."[23]

Ranged against him was one of the Senate's most consistent champions of civil rights legislation, New York's Republican Javits. Born on Manhattan's lower East Side, the New Yorker had held public office since 1946 when he took his seat in the House of Representatives. Reelected three times, he departed the national scene in 1954 to enter the state sweepstakes for Attorney General, becoming the only Republican to survive Averell Harriman's gubernatorial sweep. When Democrat Herbert H. Lehman retired from the Senate two years later, Javits took his place. He had engaged in the long struggle leading to the enactment of the 1964 Civil Rights Act and was now dismayed to witness only six years later an attempt to destroy what *Newsweek* magazine called "a liberal dream enshrined in law."[24]

Javits recalled that the Senate "had fought over this ground time and again." Still, he said, the crucial distinction between de facto and de jure segregation must not be forgotten. The latter resulted from state action, "whether statutorily created . . . in the South, or gerrymandered . . . in the North . . . *de jure* segregation is forbidden by law and the Constitution where it occurs—North or South—it is illegal and must be remedied." On the other hand, he went on,

De facto segregation has been caused, not established, by factors other than state action—residential patterns, for example—and it cannot be reached by any Federal law now in the books. . . . Racial imbalance is *de facto* segregation . . . action against *de facto* segregation is specifically prohibited in the Civil Rights Act of 1964, in the Elementary and Secondary Education Act of 1965, in the last two appropriation bills covering the Department of Health, Education, and Welfare, and in this very bill, where my own committee had to include the inhibition against any busing to correct racial imbalance, because without any question, that is the overwhelming sentiment in this Chamber, and no bill could be passed unless it contained that prohibition.

The pending amendment does not seek to repeal these provisions of the law; therefore, I cannot believe that it is really a serious attempt to combat *de facto* segregation. The only way we are going to combat *de facto* segregation is by redistricting or busing. It is the only recourse where there are residential patterns fixed as deeply as they are in many places.

Looking in Ribicoff's direction, he raised the argument of "monumental hypocrisy." "Naturally, this is a very serious charge to make against anyone without 'monumental proof'. What about the 'monumental hypocrisy' charge? Could it be levied," he asked, "against those who have fought enforcement of the constitutional guarantees of equal opportunity every step of the way for the last 16 years in every court and legislative body and now appear as the champions of equal educational opportunity, asking only that it be vigorously enforced everywhere?"

Throughout his extended address, Javits returned over and over to his basic theme: the question of American morality. At one point, he echoed the feelings of another New York senator of another era: "I believe the debate needs to be placed on the level it deserves—the moral level—a level even higher than the Constitution itself. . . ."[25] At another, he pointed to "the very real moral issue raised by this debate. . . . Do we slow down desegregation in the South because of residential patterns and any other factors that exist in the North, or do we proceed wherever we can with the utmost diligence to bring about justice in this country with respect to the minority groups?" We are . . . dealing with the final act of the Civil War. We are dealing with a deep and very important historic question: how to get over a deeply established social order which existed in the South for so very long. These are the most profound questions which our country faces and the most dangerous. . . ."[26]

Sadly, the press, through neglect, a shortage of space or need to report other highlights of the Stennis battle, failed to tell the American people what Javits said, as had been done so copiously with Ribicoff. Consequently, they understood neither the futility nor intellectual dishonesty of talking in favor of de facto enforcement on the one hand and passing laws on the other, which, by preventing busing to correct racial imbalance, ruled out an attack on de facto segregation that Stennis nominally wanted.

Likewise, the words of Senator Walter F. Mondale, Minnesota Democrat and close friend of Hubert Humphrey, also were largely unreported, presumably for the same reasons. Following two terms as the state's Attorney General, Mondale had taken Humphrey's Senate seat when the latter moved up to Vice-President in 1965.

Mondale, like Javits, was troubled by the South's determination to dilute Title VI of the 1964 Civil Rights Act. Racial segregation under this statute, he declared, is not per se "illegal or unconstitutional." It only becomes so "where segregated schools are the result of deliberate and official public policy . . . the trigger for school desegregation enforcement is a finding of discrimination, not simply a finding of segregation. In the case of segregated schools, the origin or cause of such segregation determines whether Title VI school desegregation program is applicable or not. I think it is terribly important not only that this distinction between *de jure* and *de facto* segregation exists, but also that the existing law is applied uniformly. Wherever *de jure* segregation is found—in the North, South, East or West—it is unconstitutional and subject to Administrative enforcement under Title VI or court action."

The mischief in the Stennis amendment, he went on, is that "it has nothing at all to do with *de facto* segregation. If it were passed, there would be nothing that could be done about *de facto* segregation. All it would do would be to put a new weapon in the hands of those who have spent their careers fighting to preserve the dual school system in this country."

Going further, Mondale said, "I do not believe that the Senate can act responsibly . . . on the basis of floor debate alone on an ambiguous amendment proposing to break ground in such a serious area."[27] Consequently, he proposed, in cooperation with Javits, the formation of a select Senate Committee on Equal Education Opportunity "to focus on the problem—and it is," he reminded his colleagues, "a national problem, found in the South as well as the North—of *de facto* segregation . . . and to see what kinds of Federal policies should be applied to deal with this problem."[28]

Because of their interest in the Stennis Amendment, the senators refused action on the Mondale-Javits measure and instead passed Ribicoff's revision 64 to 24, indicating the dramatic shift in senatorial sentiment as Northern senators vied to get aboard the Southern bandwagon in an effort to slow school desegregation.

Meanwhile, a drama was surfacing inside the White House that would have more effect on the Southern attempt to derail school desegregation than debate in the Senate. It began with a breakfast meeting in the White House on February 16, a day before argument on the Stennis Amendment resumed in the Senate. Among the Republican leaders who attended, a plethora of reactions emerged, some finding the President in favor of the Stennis Amendment, some thinking he opposed its adoption. As the conference broke up, White House lobbyist Bryce Harlow persuaded Minority Leader Hugh Scott to introduce legislation that would successfully counter the Mississippian's thrust. Scott returned to the Senate, filed the emasculating draft and informed his GOP colleagues that it had the "recommendations of the Administration."[29] As he stood talking, another breakfast par-

ticipant, John Tower, the Texas Republican, went to the telephone and
called Harlow to ask if Scott spoke for the Administration. "I spoke to Mr.
Harlow at the White House," Tower declared upon his return. "He informs
me there is not authority to give the imprimatur of the Administration on
the [substitute] amendment at the present time."[30]

Scott fumed, "My integrity has been impugned," he stormed at Harlow
over the telephone. "That's something that hasn't happened in my 12 years
in the Senate."[31] On Scott's insistence, Harlow wrote a letter on White
House stationery explaining what he had meant, but that, too, fell short. It
sounded at one point as though the President favored the Stennis Amendment as he had in his February 12 statement without actually saying so. The
bad taste remained in the Minority Leader's mouth.

Beset by these uncertainties, Republican members split and enough GOP
conservatives joined the Stennis forces to defeat the Scott Amendment 48 to
46. With the Ribicoff Amendment passed and the Scott version scuttled, the
Senate finally called the roll on the Stennis Amendment. Passage was
assured, but the margin of victory, 56 to 36, was unexpectedly high. Only
twenty-six of the senators voting "yes" were from the Southern and Border
states; the remainder came from areas formerly sympathetic to school desegregation. The amendment's author beamed, hailing the result as "a landmark . . . a new gateway, a turning point."[32] He credited Sen. Ribicoff's
speech with making the outcome possible. "Mercifully," Scott mused, "this
is mere policy and therefore not binding. It's a good thing it's policy because
a genuine attempt in good faith to enforce this language would require all
the police forces in America and a good many of our troops overseas."[33]
Moreover, he predicted demise of the Stennis Amendment in committee.
Writing of the outcome in the Senate, Tom Wicker, of the *New York Times*,
commented," [W]hat will the millions of black people believe as they see
starkly confirmed one more time—after so many precedents—the unwill-
ingness of white Americans to make good on their commitments and their
ideals?"[34]

Nor was the Southern victory yet complete. Before a final vote was taken
on the $35 billion educational authorization bill, the Senate passed still
another amendment, this one sponsored by Sam Ervin (D-N.C.), which
added a prohibition against busing "to alter racial composition."[35] Since the
bill already included a provision barring busing "to overcome racial imbalance," Ervin's amendment could only apply to de facto segregation outside the South. Opponents, principally, Sen. Javits, argued unsuccessfully
that its adoption would prevent HEW from requiring busing even in case of
de jure segregation, which was exactly what the Southern senators wanted.

The only tidbit for Northern liberals was Senate approval of the
Mondale- Javits resolution setting up a thirteen-member bipartisan committee to study school segregation in "whatever . . . form and whatever . . .

origin or cause."[36] With only five months to make its initial report, seven more to conclude, and $200,000 spending money, the committee faced a difficult task.

Over in the House on the same day, a coalition of Republicans and Southern Democrats succeeded in passing the $20.4 billion revision of the previously vetoed 1970 Labor-HEW Appropriations bill complete with Whitten Amendments against busing and one additional proposal by Rep. Charles R. Jonas (R-N.C.), which required a cutoff of Federal aid to any school district whose desegregation plan did not permit free-choice. Liberal congressmen fought again, as they had the previous summer, to qualify the provisions by inserting the language "except as required by the Constitution," but each time were rebuffed.[37] Victory for the South in both the House and the Senate now seemed assured.

As Scott had predicted, however, the gains that appeared secure suddenly eroded. First to fall, on motion of Sen. Scott, was the Jonas free-choice amendment. Then Whitten's alterations were largely nullified by two amendments introduced by Sen. Mathias (R-Md.), which added the words "except as required by the Constitution."[38] Both moves reportedly had the backing of the Administration just as their original incorporation in the House was also supported by the White House, a further indication of the President's adaptability. Four days later, the House approved the Senate's amended version, and the President signed it into law.

Virtually the same deletions occurred in conference when differences over the 1969 Education Act, occasioned by the Senate's addition of the Stennis and Ervin amendments, underwent reconciliation. On March 12, House and Senate conferees agreed to drop the Ervin Amendment. A week later, they dismembered the Stennis Amendment by establishing separate Federal policies that would be applied uniformly, but with separate interpretations, one for de jure segregation, the other, de facto, hardly what the author had in mind. On April 1, when the compromise finally reached the Senate, Sen. Ribicoff moved the bill be returned to committee for restoration of the Stennis Amendment, but this time, the Senate reversed itself, 43 to 32, and the measure was enacted as reported from committee.

So while the Southern gains in the Senate and House were wiped out within a period of five weeks, "the implications," as John Herbers, of the *New York Times*, pointed out, went "much deeper than schools and busing."[39] One of the first to sense the shift was Dr. Gallup. His poll showed Americans now believing 3 to 1 that the rate of racial integration of schools was proceeding "too fast," a feeling that Congress seemed more and more willing to accept, and the Republican party, in particular.[40] In the words of William Steif, a Washington correspondent for the *Nation's Schools*, "the GOP sensed a fundamental change in the country and was determined to ride its wave."[41]

Not only was Nixon now ridding his Administration of all liberal forces on the school issue, his backing and filling was establishing a mood of uncertainty in which opposition to desegregation took fire. It was rumored the White House strongly urged employees to read Alexander G. Bickel's February 7 article in the *New Republic*, "Desegregation—Where Do We Go From Here?" A Yale professor of law, Bickel argued that integration was creating "as many problems as it purports to solve, and no one can be sure that, even if accomplished, it would yield an educational return." It would be better, Bickel wrote, to improve black schools than to transport their students to white institutions. "Nothing," he said, "seems to be gained and much is risked or lost, by driving the process to the tipping point of resegregation."[42] This appeal for a slowdown gained added support in late February when Daniel Patrick Moynihan, the President's counselor, issued his famed memorandum for a period of "benign neglect" on racial issues.

Writing philosophically on the nation's changed attitude, Yale historian C. Vann Woodward saw a portentous parallel between the destructive struggles in Congress to weaken Title VI and the failure of Reconstruction after ratification of the Thirteenth, Fourteenth, and Fifteenth amendments. "The force of the reformist zeal expands itself," he said, "and the disenchantment sets in. The leaders of the resistance are emboldened, the Negroes feel deserted. After an era of promise, they go from disillusionment to a sense of unfulfillment, to withdrawal."[43]

Notes

1. "School Racial Policy," *Congressional Digest*, 49 (April, 1970): 113.
2. Editorial, *Washington Post*, July 29, 1969.
3. 42 U.S.C.A., 2000c-6 (1964).
4. H.R. 15931 (1970).
5. *Green v. County School Board of New Kent County*, 391 U.S. 430 (1968).
6. "School Racial Policy," p. 105.
7. *New York Times*, August 19, 1969.
8. *Washington Post*, September 13, 1969.
9. *Washington Post*, December 18, 1969.
10. *Washington Post*, October 15, 1969.
11. *New York Times*, December 9, 1969.
12. Editorial, *Washington Post*, October 18, 1969.
13. *Alexander v. Holmes*, 396 U.S. 19 (1969).
14. "School Racial Policy,", p. 105.
15. *New York Times*, February 7, 1969.
16. "School Racial Policy," p. 105.
17. Ibid., p. 118.
18. Ibid., p. 114.
19. "Requiem for a Liberal Dream, *Newsweek*, March 2, 1970, p. 19.

20. *New York Times*, February 13, 1970.

21. "School Racial Policy," p. 106.

22. Ibid., p. 114.

23. Ibid., p. 116.

24. "Requiem for a Liberal Dream," p. 18.

25. In 1850, during the Great Compromise debate, William H. Seward, New York Senator, argued that although the Constitution seemingly gave protection to slavery, there existed a "higher law" than the Constitution (March 11, 1850).

26. "School Racial Policy," pp. 113, 117, 119.

27. Ibid., pp. 123, 125.

28. Ibid., p. 127.

29. "Requiem for a Liberal Dream," p. 19.

30. Ibid.

31. Ibid.

32. *New York Times*, February 19, 1970.

33. Ibid.

34. Tom Wicker, "In the Nation: The Death of Integration," *New York Times*, February 19, 1970.

35. "School Racial Policy," p. 106.

36. *New York Times*, February 20, 1970.

37. "School Racial Policy," p. 107.

38. Ibid., p. 107.

39. John Herbers, " 'Deep and Basic' Reversal on Rights," *New York Times*, February 22, 1970.

40. *New York Times*, March 12, 1970.

41. William Steif, "Desegregation Rider Exposes Northern 'Guilt Feelings'." *Nation's Schools*, April 1970, p. 26.

42. Alexander M. Bickel, "Desegregation: Where Do We Go From Here?" *New Republic*, February 7, 1970, p. 20.

43. *Time*, March 9, 1970, p. 10.

9

A LIBERAL FLAME DIES

"Someone's poisoning the well."

Finch to Panetta.[1]

On the very day the Senate began its final debate on the Stennis Amendment, the White House maintained its quixotic record by firing Leon E. Panetta. The first inkling of what was afoot appeared in a morning headline of the *Washington Daily News:* NIXON SEEKS TO FIRE HEW'S RIGHTS CHIEF FOR LIBERAL VIEWS.[2] So precipitous was Panetta's exit that he had not had time to write a formal resignation before Ziegler announced the fait accompli. Thus ended an eleven-month effort to enforce the provisions of Title VI against school segregation.

It had taken some years for the ex-head of HEW's Office for Civil Rights to understand how discrimination and racial prejudice were tearing America apart. As a youth growing up in Monterey, California, he only knew a "happy and pleasant life, . . . typically isolated . . . that taught . . . little of the problems or concerns of other minorities." When he went on to Santa Clara University to obtain a B.A., and later a LL.B. at the law school, his experience had varied little. "There was only one black man on campus; if you came from a sheltered white environment, as I did," he wrote, "it made no impression at all. As a matter of fact, the gathering of middle to upper class white American students only tended to reinforce the isolation, and we would laugh at the racial cuts—'kike' and 'nigger'."[3]

Panetta's awakening began when he entered military service in 1964 and was assigned to the infantry school at Fort Benning, Georgia. He discovered the South contained two worlds—"blacks lived on one side of the railroad, having been confined there most of their lives, and . . . whites lived on the other side. . . . This was blatant discrimination," he concluded, "not the subtle kind that, because of property, prices and jobs, had forced blacks to settle in the outskirts of Monterey. . . . Here the law and the prejudice had been quite clear, and so were the consequences."[4]

Oddly enough, when Panetta joined HEW on December 12, 1968, no one in authority seemed to know the depth of his commitment to erasing these differences. Certainly, the South did not. In late February of the following year, a delegation of Southern Republican chairmen, headed by Clarke Reed of Mississippi, arrived in Washington to test the temper of the new Administration. Panetta got the job of giving them an inside view of HEW's operation. "We want to start communicating with school officials, bending over backward to help them meet the law," Panetta said, extending the olive branch.[5]

"The law . . . listen here," fumed Bo Calloway, of Georgia, "Nixon promised the South he would change the law, change the Supreme Court, and change the whole integration business. The time has come for Nixon to bite the bullet, with real changes and none of this communicating bullshit."[6] The contretemps grew so embarrassing that Peter Flanigan, a White House aide, felt obliged to step in. He assured the Southern Republicans that the "entire policy" of school desegregation was under study at the White House and that things would change, a harbinger of the July 3 Finch-Mitchell statement weakening the guidelines, the next coordinates on the road to liberal unwinding.[7]

When Panetta refused to change tactics, Harry Dent, White House political coordinator, remarked, "Panetta is hurting Bob Finch [HEW Secretary] and he's hurting Richard Nixon, and the President is personally quite concerned about it."[8] Likewise upset was Congressman Rogers Morton, of Maryland, chairman of the GOP National Committee and a top figure in the Republican establishment. The previous February, he announced before the same group of Southern Republican state chairmen that heard Panetta, "This is a big job and it takes all of you to help me out. As you know, I'm a Kentucky boy—a mountain boy—who believes that it's time a national party made room for the South. We've been kicked in the ass long enough. . . . I know what you fellas face. Hell, I'm from a district that had the same problems. . . . We've got a law on the books and that's a big problem. We've got to take a close look at this whole business to see where we've got some flexibility."[9] To one looking for "flexibility," Panetta's presence made no sense. He's "not going to be around very long," the Congressmen soliloquized before a HEW emissary. He "didn't understand the President's position."[10]

Incredibly though, despite the opposition, the OCR head hung on. *Human Events*, the capital's conservative guide, commented in its August 30 edition, "Unless Health Education and Welfare Chieftain Robert Finch can turn in a last-minute rescue operation, HEW's man in charge of enforcing civil rights, super-liberal Leon Panetta, will soon be out of a job."[11] In mid-September, the Secretary called him to his office to say, "Leon, we've got to do something to head off this pressure from the White House. . . . Someone's poisoning the well."[12] A month later, he declared, "Leon, I've decided to put the decision right in their laps. I've prepared a memo on your behalf. . . . But I'll need one thing to make it complete. I have to show them you're prepared to resign if necessary. All they have to do is to accept it if they don't buy my arguments."[13]

So, armed with Panetta's resignation and his own memorandum, Finch saw the President, temporarily stalling the ouster. For a time, the dike held in the aftermath of *Alexander* and Haynsworth's failure to be confirmed. In late November, however, trouble arose again following Panetta's appearance before the Senate Appropriations Committee to defend HEW's budget requests. Stennis was on hand to query him about segregation. Did Panetta believe it was equally bad in the North as in the South? Yes, indeed, as the senator contended, Federal pressure to desegregate had been greater in the South, but not because of the law but because of the way Congress had written the law. Instead of talk about letting "the North off the hook," Congress should ponder the possibility of enacting legislation to cope with Northern de facto segregation. Of course, the unsolicited advice failed to persuade the Mississippian, who merely wanted to axe enforcement in the South.

Republican conservatives reacted bitterly and for a second time *Human Events* scored Panetta. "The Administration," it said, "will really be in trouble if Panetta is allowed to mess up the Northern school systems the way he and his predecessors have messed up the Southern ones."[14] Still, the OCR chieftain toiled on, heedless to the festering opposition at 1600 Pennsylvania Avenue, which now referred contemptuously to him and other HEW liberals as "Finch's crowd."[15] The spark that finally caused the White House to explode was the spontaneous applause that greeted Ribicoff's speech in the Senate. The President, whose political finger held aloft could sense a change in the public mood, reacted vigorously. He drew a bead on anyone in HEW who still opposed him on school desegregation. Panetta had only to come within Nixon's sights for the President to fire.

The sudden explosion on February 17 caught Panetta by surprise and several times he broke down, reading his formal letter of resignation to the press. Embittered, he nevertheless noted OCR achievements during his eleven-month tenure, thanked Finch for his "courageous support," and hoped the Republican party "largely responsible for the beginning efforts to eliminate the injustices of the past, [would not be] held responsible for permitting these efforts to come to an end."[16]

To experienced reporters, accustomed to political nostrums, such talk sounded like saccharine palaver. They wanted to know whether Panetta thought Nixon had shirked his presidential responsibilities by bowing to political pressures? It was a perfect time for Panetta to answer "yes," to say what he previously had told an Associated Press correspondent, "We gave them new guidelines on Independence Day, the Stennis Amendment on

Lincoln's birthday and maybe we should shoot 10 blacks on Washington's birthday."[17]

However, he hedged and only spoke of the need for national leadership in the field of race relations. In the roll and twist of ensuing questions and answers, Panetta had a second opportunity to set the record straight on the President's lukewarm support of civil rights, but again he demurred. He said he believed that the President remained sincere in his stated determination "to bring us together."[18] Unfortunately, he went on, there were people "around the President, and others whose principal goal is not to 'bring us together', but to win the next election," and they are the "ones that are primarily responsible for the policies and developments that have occurred in this area."[19] As to Finch, who was directly affected, but had not been permitted the authority to oust his own OCR Director, Panetta remained sympathetic.

Nixon hoped the ouster would silence opposition in HEW, but the action only scotched them. One hundred and twenty-five staff members of the Civil Rights's Office, more than one-third of the employees, drew up a tough letter addressed to the President objecting to Panetta's firing. Finally, another 1,800 employees of HEW, from janitor up, signed an open petition calling on Finch to explain the Administration's civils rights policies.[20] Despite this massive shock wave—or perhaps because of it—Finch failed to appear before them. On successive occasions, he begged off giving illness as an excuse and when Under Secretary Veneman finally undertook to fill his shoes, he was booed.

With HEW now behind him, Panetta took off the gloves to blast the White House. The requirements of leadership, he assured a National Education Association civil rights conference, are "not . . . to walk away from the subject or to accept it on the busing terms in which it is now being discussed. And while leadership is not exercised through false promises, neither is it exercised through empty or confused rhetoric or, for that matter, by no rhetoric at all."[21] Busing, he termed a "phony issue and when you buy it as *THE* issue, you are buying a shabby bill of goods." The same was true for the neighborhood school, "another false issue. We need leadership to stand up and say that the issue is obedience to law, the issue is a fair break in education for kids who have lost out time and again because of rank discrimination, the issue is the future of this nation's race relations, and no amount of escape from reality will change those issues for us."[22]

Panetta had no illusions about the size of the desegregation problem or of the real enemy, white racism. He admitted he was not immune. Shortly after taking office, he confided to one writer, "I myself had some discrimination and prejudice in me. If all Americans can just get over that hump and realize what has been done in the past, then they would realize now the responsibility to do something about it. We're all guilty of discrimination."[23] The politicians' willingness to manipulate "discrimination and prejudice" to gain their ends tormented Panetta. "All of us were raised in an atmosphere of racism," he told members of the Women's National Press Club.[24] "We have to face up to that. What happens is that people like [Spiro] Agnew tend to cater to that racism like George Wallace and others. [It] divides people instead of bringing them together."[25] The result of this pandering, Panetta argued, was for the guilty to label school integration a failure. Capitulation, he said, was not only "the easy way out," but a guarantee that black children would receive an inferior education even if blacks should control the school boards. "Too much has been accomplished, too much is at stake, to let local, state or Federal leaders take the easy way out."[26]

This conviction had led Panetta, as one of his final acts before resigning, to take issue with Alexander Bickel on the subject of school desegregation. Bickel had written in the *New Republic* that it "is not going to be attained in this country very soon in good part because no one is certain it is worth the cost. Let us therefore try to proceed with education."[27] Panetta replied that "many of Bickel's assumptions of fact are so clearly wrong as to be dangerous if left unchallenged." The then OCR Director pointed to the voluminous Coleman Report which confirmed "the clear advantages to disadvantaged students learning in a desegregated environment," and the "721,261 Negro children (in 1968, possibly twice the number or more today) in former dual school systems who *are* in stable desegregated *situations* (majority white schools for the most part, to be sure). Compared with the total segregation of 1954 and the mere dozens of children desegregated in 1964, the accomplishment in terms of children in improved learning situations is comparatively staggering."[28]

Panetta agreed with Bickel that because of racial discrimination the desegregation of the school system was "enormously difficult," but the alternative suggested by the Yale professor, (to leave black schools alone and "try to proceed with education") was even worse. It would be a "conscious policy" to isolate black children and lead to their further isolation as adults.

Notes

1. Leon E. Panetta and Peter Gall, *Bring Us Together* (Philadelphia: J.B. Lippincott Company, 1971), p. 284.
2. *Washington Daily News*, February 17, 1970.
3. Panetta and Gall, *Bring Us Together*, p. 15.
4. Ibid., p. 16.
5. Ibid., p. 92.

6. Ibid.

7. Ibid.

8. Ibid., p. 235.

9. Ibid., pp. 107, 109.

10. Ibid., p. 237.

11. Ibid., p. 274.

12. Ibid., p. 283.

13. Ibid., p. 291.

14. Ibid., p. 341.

15. Ibid., p. 241.

16. Ibid., p. 363.

17. *Newsweek*, March 2, 1970, p. 20.

18. Richard M. Nixon, November 5, 1968.

19. Panetta and Gall, *Bring Us Together*, p. 364.

20. Ibid., p. 369.

21. *Washington Post*, February 21, 1970.

22. Ibid.

23. *Southern Education Report*, June, 1969, p. 29.

24. *New York Times*, February 28, 1970.

25. Ibid.

26. Ibid.

27. Alexander M. Bickel, "Desegregation: Where Do We Go From Here?" *New Republic*, February 7, 1970.

28. Leon E. Panetta, "Bickel Is Wrong," *New Republic*, February 28, 1970, p. 29.

10

NIXON DOWN—
WALLACE UP

"At least they would know that there was something to do other than chop cotton for Mr. Charlie, cook in his kitchen, mop his floors, wait on his tables and perform numerous other menial chores during his lifetime."

J. C. James, former HEW employee.[1]

Reflecting on the emerging image of the man in the White House, William Raspberry of the *Washington Post* wrote in the spring of 1970, "If Mr. Nixon knew where he wanted us to go, perhaps he could persuade us to make the necessary sacrifices, in the overriding interest of the country to go with him. But he wants us, I think, to go nowhere, neither forward nor backward which virtually guarantees that we will go backward."[2] This paralyzing attitude on the part of the President goes far to explain his reaction to the Stennis Amendment. At the same time he fabricated "full support" for the Mississippian's plea to treat de facto and de jure segregation as equally reprehensible, Nixon privately agonized over what would happen if the Supreme Court took an identical view.[3] An aroused North, angry that it had to overcome de facto segregation, would threaten his reelection in 1972.

Accordingly, to counter increasing references to his lack of leadership, the President decided to issue a policy statement about school desegregation. It would be a "personal account," one to make Nixon's position perfectly clear.[4] For a fortnight, prior to its issuance on March 24, he worked over successive drafts.

The 8,000-word message argued that the Administration's sole responsibility was to conquer de jure segregation. The President went to great lengths to spell out the differences between de jure and de facto segregation and to point out that the White House believed segregation caused by housing patterns—North and South—was outside the realm of the law and, therefore, beyond his reach. Addressing the judiciary, he said, "We should not provoke any court to push a constitutional principle beyond its ultimate limit in order to compel compliance with the court's essential, but more modest, mandate. . . ."[5]

To buttress his determination not to interfere with de facto segregation, the President said he was against busing or breaking up the neighborhood schools because such actions would threaten the peace of the community. In his view, "De facto segregation . . . is undesirable, but is not generally held to violate the Constitution."[6]

Commissioner of Education James E. Allen, Jr., who did not confer with the President about the message, tried desperately through a White House aide to reach Mr. Nixon. Allen was anxious to incorporate a statement that desegregation is essential to quality education, but he succeeded only in having the President admit that "under the appropriate conditions, racial integration in the classroom can be a significant factor in improving the quality of education for the disadvantaged."[7] Nixon refused to embrace the moral imperatives of *Brown*.

Members of Congress focused their attention on the President's last-minute promise to spend an additional $1.5 billion—half a billion in the coming fiscal year and an additional billion the following year—to assist school desegregation South and North. After fashioning a program to limit desegregation, he added $1.5 billion to achieve it. In short, the President hoped to disarm the segregationists by slowing the crackdown on dual schools and to win praise from the integrationists by promising to spend money for desegregation. This slice of pie for each neglected to focus on the real issue of whether black and white children should learn together. Prof. Coleman saw it as a dodge. "The question remains," he wrote, "not for the Federal government any more than for state and local ones: . . . are we willing to let schools be the vehicle through which the society separates into two, separate and unequal?"[8]

Nixon rejected this view. He declared that the schools and the children were already burdened with too great a share of "eliminating racial disparities throughout our society. A major part of this task falls to the schools. But they cannot do it all or even most of it by themselves."[9] The effect of such reasoning could hardly be reassuring to black America. If their President thought the process of integration too burdensome to the schools and the nation's children, black and white, he had to end up shortcutting the Fourteenth Amendment and the *Brown* decision. Indeed, the success of school integration would not stand or fall on the excess burdens that it placed on the school system and the children, but on whether the parents—the American people—were determined to make it work, and whether the man in the White House would join the struggle. Speaking to this point, sociologist Coleman wrote that even such vast problems as ghetto integration were surmountable, "but only if there is an intention to make integration work."[10] The President thought otherwise.

Two weeks after the issuance of the Nixon document, the U.S. Commission on Civil Rights pointed out that de jure segregation was not exclusively Southern. In a twenty-seven-page analysis of the March 24 statement, it said, "There is probably little legal substance to the concept of *de facto* school segregation" because so much segregation in the North bears the footprint of official acts.[11] As late as the 1940s and 1950s, the report declared, several Northern states had dual school systems. In addition, racial considerations controlled the establishment of school sites and school boundary lines. Even where so-called de facto segregation was said to be the result of housing patterns "government at all levels invariably is implicated,"[12] through such devices as zoning that requires the construction of single dwellings on one or more acres at a cost beyond the resources of most black families. "The point we are making," the six-member Federal agency wrote, "is that the current situation in which most minority group children attend school in isolation from children of the minority group is not accidental or purely *de facto*."[13]

The Commission also criticized the President's stress on the value of the neighborhood school. Actually, the report declared, "There is . . . a good deal of inconsistency and hypocrisy that all too often surrounds the lip service paid to the neighborhood school principle," because some parents only talk that way to maintain segregation.[14] As to busing, it pointed out that 40 percent of U.S. public school pupils were bused to class for nonracial reasons and some schools even bused their pupils fifty miles or more to overcome segregation.

Only Mr. Nixon's proposal to spend $1.5 billion to help desegregate the schools pleased the Commission. The President had originally intended to get the first $500 million by asking Congress to divert the money from previous budget requests, but getting funds from a budget reputedly squeezed of its last drop of fat proved too onerous. So the White House asked Congress for new funds—$150 million in an emergency appropriation, $350 million in fiscal 1971, and $1 billion in fiscal 1972. With legislation to reflect this goal, Nixon held an explanation session for newsmen and congressional leaders, but the measures he sent Congress the next day, May 23, contained a significant change. The President had added an amendment to bar the use of any funds for busing students to overcome racial imbalance. When the two intended sponsors, Sen. Javits, the ranking Republican on the Senate Education Subcommittee, and Rep. William H. Ayers, a member of the House Education and Labor Committee, heard what the White House had done, they balked. Each knew the law already contained such a prohibition and in the senator's view, the language the President had injected might even be interpreted as prohibiting the use of funds for voluntary busing. In the face of this joint refusal, Nixon backed down and agreed to eliminate the wording, the Administration gracelessly adding it would seek its ends later by urging an antibusing amendment.

The legislation that the President originally hoped would animate the Congress turned out to be an administrative nightmare. Southerners resented being asked to appropriate money to aid desegregation, while Northerners objected to Nixon's determination to spend the entire $150 million emergency funds in the South, leaving their own undernourished school districts unfed. Moreover, those representatives from Eastern and Northern urban centers, who now dominated the House Education and Labor Committee, viewed with concern any Nixon move to speed desegregation. Rep. William D. Ford, a Michigan Democrat, summed up the feelings by saying the President's "track record in this whole area" is what counts. "This has caused a number of people, for the first time since I've been on this committee, to question the motives of the people who initiated this policy, with regard to what they are actually trying to accomplish."[15] Even harsher was Rep. Augustus F. Hawkins, a Los Angeles Democrat, who belonged to that small coterie of black congressmen. Warned he, "Some of us fear that what is going to happen is that this [bill], instead of being a good tool that can be used, is going to be a dangerous tool in the hands of politically motivated individuals. It could be a sham that will end up discrediting desegregation."[16]

Apart from such misgivings, one could hardly expect Northern representatives in good conscience to aid those whose goal for sixteen years had been to thwart the dictum of the courts and Title VI of the 1964 Civil Rights Act. Only the previous February, Georgia and Louisiana had adopted laws to forbid school desegregation on any basis other than free-choice. The Georgia measure, signed by Gov. Lester G. Maddox, barred busing and other methods of desegregation ordered by the Federal courts, plus school closings, zoning, pairing, and student and teacher transfers, favored by HEW.

In such an atmosphere, it was not surprising to discover, when a delegation of five black students appeared before Sen. Mondale's newly-formed Select Committee on Educational Opportunity, that Southern "desegregated" schools were maintaining separate classrooms, separate lunch and gym periods, and separate bell systems to prevent black and white pupils from mingling in the halls. In one Louisiana parish, the school board had established separate bus schedules, collecting blacks at 5:30 A.M. and whites at a later hour. A seventeen-year-old youngster from Rocky Mount, North Carolina, described her impression of an "integrated" school as "being in a hostile jungle. If you start to question any of the rules, you are called a Communist, or you are just a black militant who is going totally insane. You can't really learn."[17] Another black from Mobile, Alabama, informed the senators that because of racial discrimination, black football players carried the ball to the one-yard line, whereupon the white coach gave a white player the honor of scoring the touchdown.

Perhaps the most melancholy development in joining Southern black and white school systems was the systematic effort of white school boards to discard the personal and cultural values of "Negro education." "This," wrote J. C. James, a former HEW employee, "was a system within a system, from elementary grades through college and university, both public and private, and to the extent *de jure* segregation was Southern, 'Negro education' was a regional phenomenon." Out of these schools—unequal and separate as they were—came the talent to administer the segregated black system. Not only did teaching provide the largest job market for the college-educated black, but it was the one profession in which prejudice did not curtail advancement. Within that isolated school system, blacks were free to vie with each other, advancing from teacher to principal to supervisor. "In the small towns and counties," as James pointed out, "they were the only educated blacks, and as a group formed the largest Negro middle class —middle class not only in terms of economics but in total outlook as well." They had become through the years the "black aristocracy," a visible cohort for young blacks to emulate. "At least they would know that there was something to do other than chop cotton for Mr. Charlie, cook in his kitchen, mop his floors, wait on his tables and perform numerous other menial chores during his lifetime."[18]

Caught in the crunch of desegregation, the number of black principals in the thirteen Southern and Border states declined more than 90 percent during the decade of the 1960s. Moreover, the shrinkage took place in a pit of hardship. In Natalbany, Louisiana, the principal of an all-black elementary school found himself assigned to teaching a fourth grade class in the morning and scrubbing the school latrines in the afternoon. In Greenwood, Mississippi, the principal of a black high school was reassigned as "hall monitor," but denied an office in the evident hope he would resign. To hurry the exit of black personnel, some boards simply assigned them to teach subjects in which they had no competence and then discharged them as soon as their unfitness could not be hidden. Evidence continued to pile up that the white boards were determined to restructure the entire school system in the white image. The first thing a Louisiana school board did, after incorporating a black school in the system, was to paint over its giant mural portraying Booker T. Washington and George Washington Carver.[19]

As a result of these developments, months passed before either the House or Senate would begin debate on the President's request. Only eight days before Christmas, as representatives were preparing to recess did the House finally agree to argue the measure. On December 21, shortly before midnight, the Administration's legislation passed 159 to 77, but not until two provisions were added at the President's insistence. One prohibited the familiar bar against the use of Federal funds to bus students in de facto segregated school districts, and the other permitted the assignment of students to classrooms on the basis of examinations testing their scholastic ability. The latter was a Southern ploy to impale desegregation. Since white students, possessing educational advantages, generally scored higher than blacks, such an arrangement allowed a striking degree of segregation to surface within the so-called desegregated school.

On the day following House action, a Senate subcommittee went into motion, announcing its opposition. " . . . a fraud upon the school children it is intended to benefit," cried Minnesota's Sen. Mondale. Anything that slowed the pace of desegregation would be a cruel hoax on black people whose commitment to integration was the "chief resource" that remained.[20] Nevertheless, despite objections from Mondale and other liberals, Senate Majority Leader Mike Mansfield was determined to call up the measure on the final day of the year. Not surprisingly, opposed as it was by Southern conservatives and Northern liberals, it lost.

Meanwhile, the White House was feeling another strain, occasioned by the Phoenix-like resurgence of Alabama's George Wallace. Two years before, after Wallace's wife, Lurleen, who succeeded him as governor, had died of cancer, a Wallace protégé, Albert Brewer, took over. This left the man who had once governed Alabama and twice campaigned for the presidency without a political power base. Consequently, Wallace decided to battle his former friend for the governorship as step one in a third presidential attempt.

In the beginning, polls showed the forty-one-year-old Brewer well in the lead. From the Tennessee Valley area in Northern Alabama, he had the support of moderates who eyed Wallace with dismay. In addition, the labor unions, the Chamber of Commerce groups, and a large portion of the state's 300,000 black voters who had not yet forgotten Wallace's unfettered pledge to maintain segregation, were in Brewer's corner.

As the campaign warmed up, however, Wallace hurt Brewer by trotting out his favorite themes: white supremacy and the South's fear of Northern interference. "They call us a redneck state," he shouted to an Albertville crowd which included one black couple among 1,500 to 2,000 whites. "I told them, if you mean by 'redneck' people, people who go out and do an honest day's work in the sun, why, we've got lots of them. . . . They want one message from Alabama. They would like you to tell them that Alabama has surrendered, that you have quit, that you're through fighting. And the vote from Alabama would be speaking for the entire South. The power's in your hands. Let's send the message out—that Alabama will not quit, that you'll fight on and on and on."[21] There was no mistaking the message. It was the historic Wallace appeal to white Alabamans to stand firm against Washington's meddling in their affairs. Indeed, he warned, "If I'm not elected, this [Nixon] Administration in Washington is going to go so far to the left, they'll be out of sight. But if you make me governor, we can keep the pressure up, the foot in the back of President and Congress. We are the balance of power."[22]

Wallace's constant reference to the "balance of power" underlined his belief that the Southern unity—under his banner—would exert more power on the President and Congress than espousal of Nixon's Southern Strategy. He was sure he had made a mistake in 1968 by spreading his candidacy too thin. If he had not radically cut his appearances in the North, he might have won their forty-five electoral votes, which coupled to the forty-six votes he did win in carrying Alabama, Arkansas, Georgia, Louisiana, and Mississippi, would have given him ninety-one. This would have prevented Nixon's victory in the Electoral College, and made the House of Representatives the final arbiter. Any winning candidate would have to get Wallace support, perhaps a quid pro quo reminiscent of Hayes's pledge to end Reconstruction by removing troops from the South.

Despite Wallace's threats and the resurgence of his fortunes, he did lose the May 5 primary, but only by 11,000 votes out of one million cast. In the run-off, scheduled for June 2, 1970, Wallace revived the race issue. In Montgomery, Wallace workers covered Brewer bumper stickers with ones that read "I'm for B and B—Brewer and the blacks." Other spurious handbills were also distributed. One warned, "White Alabama, are you going to let the niggers take over the state?" Wallace advertisements made Brewer's support among blacks a prime target, and such tactics began to pay off. Between May 5 and June 2, a total of 30,000 new voters, mostly white and mostly Wallace supporters, registered. At the end, Wallace was saying that if he lost, blacks "would control politics" for the next fifty years.[23]

The deception worked. Wallace received 51 percent of the votes cast. Brewer who said during the campaign, "I like to think that we're past the point of pitting class against class, race against race, religion against religion," called it "the dirtiest campaign I've ever observed in Alabama."[24] Although Wallace ran far behind his margin of previous years, he emerged the winner, becoming once more a political figure with national influence.

Immediately, he went on the offensive. I am, he said, "in a position to speak out, not only for Alabama, but for the people of our region, the South, about our public schools."[25] The fault with Nixon's Southern Strategy, he declared, was the President's vow during the 1968 campaign to halt busing, to return freedom of choice, and to preserve neighborhood schools, but he had not delivered on his promise.

Such inflammatory statements naturally alarmed Nixon and his White House aides, who hoped all along that Albert Brewer would somehow shove Wallace into oblivion, and thereby ensure for the President an indisputable hold on the South. Had that happened, with his Southern flank now secure, it is possible Richard Nixon would have wheeled North to woo the liberals who had been estranged by concessions to the South.

As a matter of fact, one interpretation of the Administration's decision to place greater emphasis on school integration in the spring of 1970 was the feeling that Wallace's impending defeat would give the White House a freer hand. On April 7, 1970, Secretary Finch and J. Stanley Pottinger, the young California attorney who had succeeded Leon Panetta, held a press conference. Although the HEW chieftain still refused to use the cut-off authority of Title VI—not one recommendation to terminate Federal funds had reached his desk since the previous July—he sounded ebullient over the prospects of further integration. Hopefully, he predicted the number of black children in integrated Southern schools would double from 1.2 to 2.4 million in September. He was likewise sanguine over the prospect Congress would grant his request for a staff increase in the Office for Civil Rights from 401 to 545. Concomitantly, Assistant Attorney General Jerris Leonard, chief of the Justice Department's Civil Rights Division, held a lengthy press interview. His department, he said, would make one final overture to 200 holdout Southern school districts, and if the appeal went unheeded, suits would be filed. By the time Wallace defeated Brewer, Leonard could announce that sixty-one of the recalcitrant districts had finally capitulated

However, following June 2, the mood in the White House changed significantly. Southern Strategy again became a byword, and the President moved to cleanse HEW of those who had or would antagonize the South. First to go was Robert Finch. He had underestimated the effect of a Wallace victory on his leader and told reporters while traveling through San Diego that the Administration's plans to desegregate Southern schools would remain unchanged. The next day, Nixon summoned Finch to the White House to terminate his service as HEW Secretary and to offer him the job of key counselor on domestic affairs, a role where he could be closely watched. Finch "argued strongly" against the lightening of his responsibilities. It would look as if "I was leaving the anthill," he related later, but he was "put to the wall," and had no choice.[26] A second casualty was Commissioner of Education Allen, the outspoken advocate of integration, who had further alienated himself on May 21 by decrying the Vietnam War.

With high glee, George Wallace announced on ABC's "Issues and Answers" that perhaps "my election had something to do" with Finch's departure.[27] He had done more than that. His reinstatement in the political world had made him "the balance of power."

Notes

1. J. C. James, "The Black Principal," *New Republic*, September 26, 1970, p. 18.

2. William Raspberry, "President is More Like Juggler . . . ," *Washington Post* April 17, 1970.

3. John Osborne, "The Nixon Watch," *New Republic*, April 4 and 11, 1970, p. 13.

4. Ibid.

5. *New York Times*, March 25, 1970.

6. Ibid.

7. Ibid.

8. James S. Coleman, "For Integration," letter, *New York Times*, March 10, 1970.

9. *New York Times*, March 25, 1970.

10. Coleman, "For Integration."

11. *New York Times*, April 12, 1970.

12. Ibid.

13. Ibid.

14. Ibid.

15. John Beckler, "Desegregation: Congress Wrestles with Nixon," *School Management*, August, 1970, p. 2.

16. Ibid.

17. *Time*, July 13, 1970, p. 32.

18. James, "Black Principal."

19. *Time*, July 13, 1970.

20. John Beckler, "Try, Try Again," *School Management*, March, 1971, p. 4.

21. *Washington Post*, April 20, 1970.

22. Ibid.

23. *Washington Post*, June 1, 1970.

24. *Washington Post*, June 3, 1970.

25. *Washington Post*, June 4, 1970.

26. *Washington Post*, June 7, 1970.

27. *Washington Post*, June 8, 1970.

11

SWANN v. MECKLENBURG

"Clearly one sided . . . the court is talking about the South; the North is still going free."

Jimmy Carter, Governor of Georgia, upon learning of the Supreme Court's decision in *Swann* v. *Mecklenburg*.[1]

Charlotte, North Carolina, is a bustling city of come 300,000 people, centered in the county of Mecklenburg, lying midway between the Carolinas, Atlanta, and Richmond; the Appalachian mountains; and the Atlantic seashore. In the spring of 1963, it seemed likely the city would become embroiled in the same racial protests that were enveloping other Tarheel communities. However, a voluntary desegregation of public facilities—hotels, motels, restaurants, and theatres—at the urging of the mayor and the directors of the Charlotte Chamber of Commerce helped avert violence. The spectacle of a Southern city loosening its racial shackles of its own volition drew national as well as international acclaim.

How had it happened? "[A] willingness . . . to be more progressive, to accede to reasonable requests," said the mayor, which, while understandably true, fell short of explaining the whole story.[2]

The mayor's biracial Community Relations Committee, established three years earlier during the sit-ins, played a major role. Under the tutelage of a distinguished retired president of Davidson College, the Committee had resolved many black-white differences. However, this influence, benign as it was, could not have accomplished such a profound change in city mores had not, as the president of the Chamber of Commerce put it, "the prestige leaders [taken] a stand."[3]

The Charlotte power structure had taken such a stand in part because of its supine reaction to a racial outrage six years earlier on September 4, 1957. On that day, Dorothy Counts, a fifteen-year-old black, escorted by her father, had tried to enter Harding High School. She was one of the first three blacks to be integrated into a white school under court order. While a mob followed the pair, a white woman shouted, "Spit on her, girls."[4] The jeering continued for a week until one morning someone threw a piece of tin, striking Dorothy on the head. Since neither the police department nor the school board would intervene to control the student outbursts, Dorothy withdrew. "They never came in front of me," she cried. "They always stood in back. If I turned around, there were 20 or 30 of them. . . ."[5] On the day she withdrew from Harding, Charlotte's well-known columnist, Harry Golden, and a few friends went to her father to plead with him not to remove her. According to Golden, "He showed us a pad of four pages of telephone calls of sympathy and condolences—48 names. They were the leading citizens. Anyone of them expressing what they said in public could have smashed things. But they didn't. . . ."[6] The city's prestige plummeted as news of the incident aroused worldwide censure.

By 1963, thoroughly chastened, the power structure reacted positively (if not unanimously) to the threat of racial turmoil. Nevertheless, the mood that opened Charlotte's public facilities still did not spill over into the school system. Six years after the Counts incident, a mere 2 percent of the black students—490 out of 20,000—were in integrated schools. Of this 490, more than 80 percent were in one school with seven white pupils, the remainder distributed among seven of the 103 schools in the Charlotte-Mecklenburg school system. So timid was the school board that it permitted white students to leave integrated schools if they preferred not to be with blacks. "They say we have done as little as possible," the chairman of the county school board told Pat Watters, of the Southern Regional Council, "and it may be that we haven't done all we could. But it's safer to take the conservative course than to push to the danger point. There was a great deal of fear that was without foundation about desegregation. This is what we wanted to prove—that it was without foundation. We wanted to show that it could be done, not how far we could go and how fast. If you want to build a house, you don't build the roof first. . . ."[7]

In the same year, 1964, that Watters submitted his report on Charlotte, Julius Chambers, a black civil rights attorney associated with the NAACP Legal Defense Fund, filed suit on behalf of James E. Swann against the Charlotte-Mecklenburg Board of Education, charging that the school system, forty-third largest in the nation, was continuing to operate a dual system in defiance of judgements handed down by the Supreme Court and other Federal courts. The litigation dragged on with the board deftly side-stepping the main issue. After four years nothing had happened.

In June, 1968, however, one of those unexpected events occurred that introduced a new dimension. James Bryan McMillan, the fifty-four-year-old Federal District judge for the western district of North Carolina, was appointed to hear the case. Virtually nothing in McMillan's background indicated a lively interest in the race issue. Indeed, one might assume that had there been any doubt about his belief in the sanctity of racial separa-

tion, North Carolina's Senator Ervin, one of the most inflexible segregationists in the U.S. Senate, would have blocked the nomination.

From all indications, McMillan had followed the path that other
Southern lawyers trod in reaching the Federal bench. He graduated from the
University of North Carolina and the Harvard Law School, had distinguished himself as a naval officer in World War II, and for twenty-two
years had practiced law in Charlotte. In time, he became president of the
state bar association. During an interview with Ben A. Franklin, of the *New
York Times,* he talked of growing up "on a farm at McDonalds, N.C., with
Negro tenant families who were barely a generation from slavery. They
lived together, but apart. . . . It was a system that seemed natural to him,
that he knew was changing, and whose change touched him not at all."[8]
Although prior to his appointment to the bench he had been associated with
the Chamber of Commerce that sparked Charlotte's 1963 breakthrough,
even that experience failed to evoke from McMillan any criticism of such
obvious segregation as the Charlotte school system. In short, like other
members of the city's power structure, he had found it inexpedient as a
lawyer to speak out on a subject so packed with emotion.

To the surprise of the plaintiffs, as the facts of Charlotte's racial segregation began to unfold, McMillan discovered the existence of a troubled
enclave that up to then he had barely glimpsed. Statistics revealed that by
manipulating the zoning laws, restricting the flow of public and private
capital into black housing, and using urban renewal funds to clear out
former black areas, white officialdom had bottled up 95 percent of
Charlotte's blacks in a single district west of the railroad tracks. Testimony
also showed that despite disclaimers by the school board, extensive segregation existed in the Charlotte-Mecklenburg district. Two-thirds of the 21,000
black students attending school in the city of Charlotte—approximately
14,000—attended twenty-one schools which were either totally black or
more than 99 percent black. Not until then, as the judge later admitted, had
he been aware of the extent of white discrimination in housing and public
schools, but on the basis of the plaintiffs' mountainous evidence, McMillan
ordered the county's school system desegregated. His opinion, handed
down April 23, 1969, declared that neither the neighborhood plan that the
assistant superintendent said was "working out well,"[9], nor freedom of
choice had proven effective in integrating the schools. "When racial segregation was required by law," the judge observed wryly, "nobody evoked
the neighborhood school theory to *permit* black children to attend white
schools close to where they lived. The values of the theory somehow were
not recognized before 1965."[10]

White citizens of Charlotte regarded the decision as a direct threat. How,
they asked themselves, could a white man, who had held their utmost
respect, had dined in their homes, belonged to their clubs, now condemn his

peers and order the complete desegregation of the school system? "[T]he board," McMillan declared, "is, of course, free to use all of its own resources . . . including busing. . . ."[11]

The key word "busing" was what produced the Pavlovian reaction. The image of tiny white children entering buses to be hauled miles and miles and dumped in schools alongside blacks loosened an avalanche of abuse on the judge. Sign-carrying pickets hounded McMillan whether he was at work in his office on the second floor of the Charlotte Post Office Building, or at home. Anonymous persons telephoned to threaten his life. The entire community was outraged by the fact that he had gone farther than any Federal judge to assure desegregation. He was denounced from the pulpit, censured by the school board chairman, condemned by the *Charlotte News*, and even the *Charlotte Observer*, which had once vigorously supported busing until its circulation began to decline, could offer only faint praise, saying McMillan's argument was "persuasive."[12]

However, it was the newly formed Concerned Parents Association (CPA) that gave the opposition its greatest boost. By disavowing violence, CPA gained widespread support. In the words of G. Don Roberson, CPA's co-chairman, the organization would countenance no "demonstration, marching, picketing or violence."[13] Instead, its members demonstrated their resistance to busing by flooding Charlotte with red, white, and blue "no forced busing" stickers, by collecting 21,000 signatures on an antibusing petition, by mounting public rallies throughout Mecklenburg County, and by sending delegates to Washington to describe their frustration before sympathetic members of Congress.[14] CPA's membership tent was broad enough to include groups of striking diversity. Racists worked alongside liberals whose consciences could not withstand the prick of busing, parents who resented the annoyance of busing, and those who feared their children's exposure to ghetto crime and drugs. Some were simply angered that the court should intrude in a situation that to them seemed on the point of being solved. Unfortunately, for whatever reason parents joined CPA, their activities prevented the school board from seeing eye to eye with McMillan's instructions.

In June, the court rejected the board's initial attempt to achieve integration. Although a second plan showed promise, McMillan gave orders to prepare a third in the hope of getting the kind of plan he wanted. To this admonition, the board erupted angrily, pointing out that by the judge's own admission, the Charlotte system led the region in desegregation. To their question, why more now, McMillan replied, "[C]onstitutional rights will not be denied here simply because they may not be denied elsewhere. There is no Dow-Jones average' for such rights."[15] So the board in desperation returned to the drafting tables for a third time, but again the court rejected it. By this time, convinced that neither direction nor argument would prevail against the board's stubbornness, Judge McMillan called on Dr. John Finger, an expert in education administration, who had previously testified in behalf of the black plaintiffs, asking him to help in the preparation of a viable program.

Eventually, on February 5, 1970, nearly ten months after the original decision, the court approved the Finger plan which incorporated both his and the board's ideas. To achieve a student ratio of 71 percent white and 29 percent black (the approximate breakdown taking Charlotte's total school population), McMillan directed ten all-black inner-city schools and twenty-four mostly white schools to cross-bus their pupils. The court also ratified the board's design for gerrymandering districts to achieve greater integration, and supported Dr. Finger's idea for "satellite" zoning which tied every white school district to a black one in the ghetto to make desegregation more palatable.[16] Under the plan, each school would be no more than about one-third black.

Originally, McMillan had given the school board until September, 1970, to complete integration, but as soon as the Supreme Court issued its *Alexander* opinion of October, 1969, ordering "integration now,"[17] he felt compelled to advance the deadline to April 1. Some three weeks before it was to take effect, however, Chief Justice Warren Burger declared that the High Court should help Southern communities resolve their problems of desegregation by clarifying its own position on the unanswered questions plaguing harried school boards. This comment, coming from the highest judicial authority, on top of the Charlotte School Board's appeal to the Fourth Circuit Court of Appeals to set aside McMillan's ruling, stayed the court's hand. A delay was granted until fall. It seemed a fortuitous choice, for during the April 9 hearing before the circuit appeals court, the Justice Department, taking its cue from President Nixon's March 24 speech in opposition to busing, entered the case on the school board's side. Department lawyers argued that the crucial question was whether, in ordering busing, Judge McMillan had "invoked a remedy so extreme as to constitute an abuse of discretion."[18] The circuit court accepted the argument and on May 26, 1970, by a 4 to 2 decision, laid aside McMillan's opinion for imposing an "undue burden on [the] school board."[19]

During the summer of 1970, while preparations were going forward to make a final appeal to the U.S. Supreme Court, the city of Charlotte seethed and waited. There were those who saw in the circuit court's reversal the direction the High Court would eventually take. "We have gotten one grape off the whole bunch," CPA's co-chairman jubilantly cried.[20] With school opening only days away, however, the Charlotte School Board remained in a quandary. To implement Judge McMillan's order, it insisted, would require the exorbitant expenditure of $5 million to purchase 526 new buses. Since the city had an enviable record of supporting school bond issues for capital programs, this was a stall. As McMillan said in his ruling, "The defendants have plenty of money, plenty of know-how, plenty of buses. . . . Their $5 million estimates . . . border on fantasy."[21] What was clearly annoying the board was not so much the cost of buying new buses, but the anticipated emotional outburst that would follow their use. A local stockbroker confided to a representative of *Newsweek* magazine, "You can't let the facts interfere with your understanding of the situation. I don't feel too happy about exposing my four daughters to the type of black young man I see downtown."[22] Sharing an analogous view, the mayor told the same correspondent, "If the situation explodes in September, we might have to put a policeman in every schoolroom"—not a pleasant prospect for a city that only seven years before had made national and international headlines as the city where racial breakthroughs had quietly taken place. "The nation is looking to us," he added and indeed it was, for in the last week of August, the Supreme Court refused to stay Judge McMillan's order and agreed to place the Charlotte appeal on its October calendar.[23]

Thus, its last defense gone, the school board opened the community's 104 schools on September 9 and undertook the busing of 47,000 pupils out of a total student body of 82,500. That the transition could occur without violence unquestionably reflected the majority decision to abide by the law, but it was also a result of the constant rhetoric by CPA encouraging its members to believe the Supreme Court would shortly overrule McMillan. "Though we were busing," the superintendent later admitted, "the city was not committed to the program. Many felt it would be over with as soon as the Supreme Court ruled."[24]

James T. Wooten, of the *New York Times,* visiting Charlotte a month after schools opened, found a mixed reaction. A white woman who had once wept, after learning her ten-year-old son would be bused twelve miles, now conceded, "That was sort of silly, wasn't it?"[25] For other white families, fear of busing continued to be traumatic. One woman, who was the mother of a ten-year-old-girl and whose husband was a consulting psychologist with a Purdue doctorate, told Wooten, "It's just horrible, all this. My husband and I have worked for everything we have. Why do you think we moved to this neighborhood? Because of the schools so close, that's why. It's just five minutes away from the house. Now can anyone tell me why Lisa has to go all the way 12 miles downtown to that school?" She resented the idea that anyone might think her a racist. She and her husband had lived in Little Rock during the 1957 crisis, had entertained black people in their home at the height of the tension, did not object to the idea of the racially balanced classroom, yet they foundered on the concept of busing. Since busing had turned out to be an "absurd idea . . . in the name of racial reform,"she entered her child in a private school.[26] A third parent Wooten interviewed, the mother of a lively six-year-old black youngster, was delighted to have her son sitting alongside white children. "It's simple," she said, "He can learn more." As to busing, what was all the stir about? "Shoot," she said, "black people have been riding buses miles and miles for years and years past good white schools. I was so happy to hear about the new plan I couldn't wait for Everett to get started."[27]

When hearings on *Swann* began October 12, the Supreme Court justices heard arguments about the special sanctity of the neighborhood school on the one hand and the absolute necessity on the other not to let its popular appeal prevent desegregation. Speaking for the defendants, North Carolina's Attorney General Andrew A. Vanore, Jr., said, "We contend the only realistic plan that will work for the North and the South, the only real approach is to allow a child to attend the school nearest his home."[28]

While rejecting this argument, NAACP attorney Chambers was determined not to call for "racial balance," the kind forbidden by the 1964 Civil Rights Act. "We are not arguing," he told the court, "for an absolute ratio in each school. We are asking for a plan that will disestablish all racially identifiable schools in a system." Chambers singled out schools in which the black population was more than 50 percent or the white more than 90 percent. Surprisingly, this moderate reference to Southern segregation provoked a sudden and unexpected outburst from Justice Hugo L. Black, the eighty-four-year-old Alabaman, who blamed the NAACP for attempting to "rearrange the whole country" to carry out integration. One of the two remaining jurists to take part in the original *Brown* decision, he now inexplicably excoriated the one organization that had stood Gibraltar-like in the battle for desegregation from the start. "You want to haul people miles and miles to give them equal percentages in the schools," he said, misinterpreting Chambers's argument. "I don't like this trying to condemn a whole way of living."[29]

For itself, the Justice Department carved out a position partially supporting both sides. It approved the neighborhood concept the Southerners favored, but, warned Solicitor General Edwin N. Griswold, the South could not use it as a pretext to block desegregation as charged by the NAACP. Justice would not argue that busing was unconstitutional, it only said the court should take into account the distances involved.

Affecting the outcome was the possibility the court might interpret anew the 1964 Civil Rights Act in light of Judge McMillan's decision. It had to be remembered that while the measure was under consideration in the House, Rep. William C. Cramer (R-Fla.) suggested an amendment to Title IV, later adopted by the Congress, which defined school desegregation as not meaning "the assignment of students to public schools in order to overcome racial balance."[30] Now Cramer had filed an *amicus curiae* brief to point out that Congress intended to draw a line between desegregation and racial balance. On the House floor, he argued that his amendment would "pre-

vent any semblance of congressional acceptance or approval . . . to include
in the definition of desegregation any balancing of school attendance by
moving students across district lines to level off percentages where one race
outweighs another."[31] In the Upper House, Sen. Humphrey's explanation of
the amendment followed the same reasoning. The Cramer Amendment,
said the Minnesotan, "simply seeks to preclude an inference that the Title
confers new authority to deal with racial imbalance and would serve to
soothe fears that Title IV might be read to empower the Federal government
to order the busing of children around a city in order to achieve a certain
racial balance or mix in schools."[32]

The Supreme Court's deepening dilemma, Cramer charged, stemmed
from the fact that the Fifth Circuit Court had failed to heed the meaning of
his amendment. In a series of decisions, a three-judge panel had set about to
distinguish between de jure and de facto segregation and to conclude that
the bar to racial balance applied only to de facto segregation. "From a
measure specifically designed to end segregation in the interests of education," said the Cramer brief, "it [the 1964 Act] was reframed and reformu-
lated until today it is cited as a statutory prop for balancing for balance's
sake, for destroying neighborhood integration in order to accomplish racial
integration and, in an Orwellian exercise in 'doublethink', for perpetuating
classification by race in order to remove the inequities created by racial
classification. Ironically, the present disillusionment and disenchantment
would probably never have developed had the courts and the executive kept
their respective eyes on the educational ball and on the carefully considered
measures that the people's representatives in the national Legislature framed
to assist them."[33]

While it was clear what Cramer intended to accomplish by his amendment, the phraseology lacked specific guidance. How, for instance, did one
go about defining "racial balance"? The very act of desegregation involved
the transfer of students from one institution to another and what was that
but creating a "racial balance." It was thus a matter of degree. Members of
Congress carefully avoided numerical limits, hoping naively that the courts
would somehow know the difference between desegregation and racial
balance. Now Cramer complained that the judiciary had overstepped its
responsibility and was acting improperly as the surrogate for legislative
intent.

Consequently, after three days of hearing, certain questions arose, hopefully to be answered: Would the High Court finally eliminate the judicial
interpretation separating de jure from de facto segregation? Would the justices authorize busing as a tool for school desegregation? Would they
attempt the difficult task of defining "racial balance"?

The twenty-eight-page opinion that was handed down on April 20, 1971,
attempted to answer these questions but in such equivocal language as to
encourage broad interpretations. In striving for unanimity among the jus-

tices, Chief Justice Burger presumably had had to give up lucidity for togetherness. Still, the wrinkles of discord did not extend to the joint conviction that Judge McMillan deserved to be upheld. The seeming dichotomy prompted one judge in the Fifth Circuit to remark of the total decision, "It's almost as if there were two sets of views laid side by side."[34]

At the outset, the court specifically limited its jurisdiction to de jure school desegregation. "We do not reach in this case the question," wrote Burger, "whether [de facto segregation] . . . is a constitutional violation. . . . This case does not present that question and we therefore do not decide it."[35] By taking the narrow interpretation, when overwhelming evidence showed that Charlotte's school segregation existed in large part as a result of both de jure and de facto segregation, the court passed up the chance to take the ultimate step in deciding cases of school desegregation.

The immediate outcries that arose reflected the growing bitterness among Southern whites over finding that the court still applied different rules to Northern segregation. As Jimmy Carter, then Georgia's governor, exclaimed, on hearing the decision, "Clearly one-sided . . . the Court is still talking about the South; the North is going free."[36] What fueled Southern anger was that by 1971 desegregation had proceeded much further in the South. Government figures showed that 38.7 percent of black children attended schools that were 80 to 100 percent black in the South, compared with 57.8 percent in the North and 60.6 percent in the Border states. Similarly, 39.6 percent of Southern black children were in schools with white majorities, compared with 27.8 percent in the North and 29.8 percent in the Border states.

Having proscribed de facto segregation, the Court took up the delicate question of resolving the extent to which "racial balance" or "racial quotas" could be used to correct a previously segregated system. Fearful of becoming lost in this judicial thicket, the justices refused to define desegregation in percentages of racial mix. In fact, Burger declared, if McMillan had required "any particular degree of racial balance or mixing," it would have been disapproved. "The constitutional command to desegregate schools," he went on, "does not mean that every school in every community must always reflect the racial composition of the school system as a whole." Why, then, in view of this observation, did the Court accept the McMillan decision, based as it was on a 71:29 ratio in the various schools? Burger's answer to the anomaly was that McMillan's "use made of mathematical ratios was no more than a starting point in the process of shaping a remedy, rather than an inflexible requirement."[37] If so, to establish quotas as a "starting point" would seemingly give carte blanche to almost any scheme of "racial balance" in cases involving de jure segregation.

To the Southern argument that desegregation orders should not dismantle the neighborhood school, the court replied with devastating frankness. "All things being equal, with no history of discrimination, it might well be desirable to assign pupils to schools nearest their home. But all things are not equal in a system that has been deliberately constructed and maintained to enforce racial segregation. The remedy for such segregation may be administratively awkward, inconvenient and even bizarre in some situations and may impose burdens on some; but all awkwardness and inconvenience cannot be avoided in the interim period when remedial adjustments are being made to eliminate the dual school systems."[38] Burger carefully listed the tools to be used as a "remedy" and brushed off arguments that the cure for desegregation was worse than the illness. He endorsed "pairing, 'clustering', or 'grouping' " of noncontiguous school zones even if they happened to be "on opposite ends of the city. As an interim corrective measure, this cannot be said to be beyond the broad remedial powers of a court."[39]

However, it was to the use of busing to correct state enforced racial school segregation that the Court gave its widest interpretation. Up to that time, the High Court had never defined "the scope of permissible transportation" in desegregating schools.[40] In the face of mounting pressure from the Nixon Administration against busing on the one hand and its extensive use under the McMillan order on the other, some ruling became necessary. Already, 90 percent of the nation's school districts employed busing to carry pupils to class. Indeed, by 1970, a total of 18 million—39 percent of all schoolchildren—were being transported in this way. The only argument was whether buses should be used to desegregate.

The High Court answered the question by pointing out that busing had been "an integral part of the public education system for years." Accordingly, it approved its extensive use in Charlotte, saying local school authorities could be "required to employ bus transportation as one tool of school desegregation. Desegregation plans cannot be limited to the walk-in school." To forestall criticism that the Court had gone too far, the justices agreed that busing could be limited "when the time or distance of travel" was so excessive "as to either risk the health of the children or significantly impinge on the educational process."[41]

In summary, even though *Swann* was, as *Newsweek* commented, "laid out with a number of well-clipped hedges,"[42] its conclusions impacted on the White House. Not only had the Administration's constant defense of the neighborhood school and opposition to busing been openly repudiated, but two of the justices involved were the President's own appointees. Nine days after the decision, a subdued President told newsmen that Administration officials would "continue to carry out their statutory responsibilities."[43]

A year afterwards, Frank Barrows, visiting Charlotte to find out if time had healed local wounds, wrote for the *Atlantic Monthly*, "Appearances aside, the vast majority of those parents whose automobiles sported angry stickers still think busing an outrageous injustice. But, tired and frustrated, they have wearily resigned themselves to it." In the midst of such widespread pessimism, he hearteningly reported finding islets of reconciliation. A woman who had tried to escape the McMillan order by planning private classes in the end had decided to give the new system a trial. "It hasn't upset my child like I expected," she told Barrows. "And though I'm surprised to hear myself saying this, I think in years to come, we'll see that it's something that had to be done."[44]

Barrows also spoke to Julius Chambers, NAACP's plaintiff attorney, who remained "undaunted" despite an arsonist's midnight attack in February, 1971, that left his office a charred ruin. What, asked Barrows, did Chambers think about busing? "What you are asking," he answered, "is whether the schools in the South are going to have desegregation. I'm not any kind of prophet. But if they are to be desegregated, meaningfully, there will have to be transportation. Buses." What had integration done for Charlotte youth? "There is," he stated, "a growing respect, small though it may be, between black kids and white kids, an appreciation for each other as humans. If you look beyond the lawsuits, the court decisions, the protesters' debates, all of it, that's what you find—that growing respect. To me, it's worth anything."[45]

Notes

1. *Time*, May 3, 1971, p. 14.

2. Pat Watters, "Charlotte," *Special Report* (Atlanta: Southern Regional Council, 1964), p. 11.

3. Ibid., p. 21.

4. Ibid., p. 46.

5. *New York Times*, September 6, 1957.

6. Watters, "Charlotte," p. 77.

7. Ibid., pp. 67-68.

8. Ben A. Franklin, "Judge in Charlotte Dispute," *New York Times*, April 21, 1971, p. 28.

9. Watters, "Charlotte," p. 63.

10. *Swann v. Charlotte-Mecklenburg Board of Education*, 300 F. Supp. 1358, (1969), at 1369.

11. Ibid., at 1373.

12. *Charlotte Observer*, April 25, 1969.

13. Bruce Galphin, "U.S. Judge Is Target . . . ," *Washington Post*, March 30, 1970.

14. Ibid.

15. Ibid.

16. Ibid.

17. *Alexander v. Holmes*, 396 U.S. 19 (1969).

18. *Nation's Schools*, June, 1970, p. 81.

19. *Swann* v. *Charlotte-Mecklenburg Board of Education*, 431 F.2D 138 (1970), at 139.

20. Galphin, "U.S. Judge Is Target."

21. *Newsweek*, August 24, 1970, p. 63.

22. Ibid.

23. Ibid.

24. Frank Barrows, "School Busing," *Atlantic Monthly*, November, 1972, p. 20.

25. James T. Wooten, "Parents in Charlotte . . . " *New York Times*, October 7, 1970.

26. Ibid.

27. Ibid.

28. John Beckler, "Will the Court Settle the Question of School Segregation?," *School Management*, December, 1970, p. 4.

29. Ibid.

30. Ibid., p. 5.

31. Ibid.

32. Ibid.

33. Ibid.

34. *Newsweek*, May 3, 1971, p. 27.

35. *Swann* v. *Charlotte-Mecklenburg Board of Education*, 402 U.S. 1 (1971) at 23.

36. *Time*, May 3, 1971.

37. *Swann* v. *Charlotte-Mecklenburg*, 402 U.S. 1 (1971), at 24-25.

38. Ibid., at 28.

39. Ibid., at 27.

40. Ibid., at 29.

41. Ibid., at 30-31.

42. *Newsweek*, May 3, 1971.

43. *Time*, May 3, 1971, p. 14.

44. Barrows, "School Busing," pp. 17, 18, 20.

45. Ibid., p. 22.

12

THE AUSTIN GAMBOL

"Busing, certainly, is an artificial and inadequate instrument of change. Nobody really wants it—not you, not me, not the people, nor the school boards—not even the courts. Yet the law demands, and rightly so, that we put an end to segregation in our society. We must demonstrate good faith in doing just that. . . ."

Reubin Askew, Governor of Florida.[1]

On the day following the *Swann* decision, the President met with Attorney General Mitchell and HEW Secretary Richardson, who had now replaced Finch, to discuss the court's unanimous decision and the political dent it had inflicted on Nixon's Southern Strategy. Since the White House chose not to go beyond what the law required, it was left to the President's two cabinet officers to work out a modus operandi. Despite his reputation as chief pleader for a Southern Republican renaissance, Mitchell appeared unruffled by the turn of events. Instead, the Attorney General saw in *Swann* a chance to undercut criticism of the White House by blaming the High Court for future busing woes. As he put it, "Hopefully, we can work out new plans. . . ."[2]

Soon, the first test of the government's changed stance emerged. On May 14, 1971, the Justice Department, in answer to an order by Federal District Judge Jack Roberts, of the Fifth Circuit Court, submitted a desegregation plan for Austin, capital city of Texas. It carried the unanimous approval of Mitchell, Richardson, and Edward L. Morgan, the President's assistant for civil rights, and closely followed the *Swann* dicta of extensive busing and noncontiguous zones to achieve desegregation.

Unlike most cities of the Old Confederacy, Austin was tri-cultural with white "Anglos," Mexican-Americans, and blacks. Mexican-American pupils outnumbered blacks 12,650 to 8,800. Blacks had clearly been segregated by law, but no such de jure restriction applied to Mexican-Americans (Chicanos). Hurdling this fact, HEW went boldly ahead, devising a plan that included Chicanos as well as blacks and produced the same racial and ethnic mix in each school as in the city at large (Anglo, 61 percent; Chicano, 23; and black, 16). To accomplish this, a fleet of 200 new buses would transport 85 percent of the school population.[3]

Meanwhile, the Austin School Board had developed a proposal of its own, far less demanding than HEW's plan, which it too submitted to Judge Roberts. The Austin proposal did not try to establish racial quotas in each school. It called for the transfer of black and Chicano students from junior and senior high schools where they were the greater ethnic body to high schools with Anglo majorities, and rather than destroy the neighborhood elementary school, even though segregated, it proposed to "cluster" one black and one Chicano school with four Anglo schools. Pupils from these six schools would study at least one day a week together at centers for fine arts, social science, avocation, and science, to which they would be bused. According to Austin's school superintendent, this plan would require the modest purchase of forty buses, compared with HEW's 200.

While to him this appeared "excellent," because of the reduced dependence on busing, it clearly fell short of *Swann*.[4] As May gave way to June and June to July, the Administration's reading, or misreading, of *Swann* drew mounting criticism. Had Justice and HEW gone too far? The fact that racial quotas had been allowed to stand in Charlotte's case did not imply that each desegregation plan had to be implemented in that fashion. "The constitutional command to desegregate schools does not mean that every school in every community must always reflect the racial composition of the school system as a whole," Burger had written.[5] Nor was busing, the court added, to be used indiscriminately. It could be challenged, "when the time or distance of travel is so great as to risk either the health of the children or significantly impinge on the educational process."[6] In short, the justices were looking for a flexible solution to the school desegregation problem, not an absolute one. Arithmetic ethnic ratios, they said, were not to be inflexible, indeed "no more than a starting point in the process of shaping a remedy."[7] So the question arose as to whether in fixing ratios, and resorting to extensive busing, Justice and HEW had gone beyond *Swann's* parameters. The fact that the Attorney General and the Secretary of HEW had failed to see the political consequences of their action, was, also, something to ponder. Possibly, they thought *Swann's* directional signals were apparent enough to preclude further arguments at the district level. In any event, on the basis of Mitchell's original advice to Mr. Nixon, it seems clear that developments in the summer of 1971 caught both men by surprise.

Instead of lowering the curtain on school agitation, the Administration's initial response to *Swann* placed the President in the middle of Texas politics, giving Southern segregationists a chance to revive their dying cause by focusing attention on busing. To aggravate things further, the Austin case centered on two of the state's most prominent Democrats, Will Davis and Jack Roberts. The former headed the Austin District School Board and formerly chaired the Texas Democratic executive committee, while the latter received his appointment as Federal district judge from Lyndon Johnson. Davis and Roberts were friends and according to John Osborne, writing for the *New Republic*, the White House came to suspect they "were in cahoots all along to produce a local plan and a lower court decision that the administration would be compelled to reject and appeal despite the predictable . . . adverse political effects."[8]

No one knew better than the man in the White House that Southern Strategy depended heavily on swinging Texas into the Republican camp. Of all the Southern states, Texas with twenty-five electoral votes was the largest. In 1968, Hubert Humphrey had carried the state with the razor thin percentage of 41.1 to 39.9. Now, three years later, provided the school issue did not rise to embarrass him, the President could conceivably turn the tables in 1972.

To Mr. Nixon's chagrin, *Swann's* ripples did not terminate in Austin during the summer of 1971. All across the South busing caused upheavals. In Nashville, for instance, where HEW officials had fashioned a plan to comply with *Swann*, enraged white parents filed suit on June 28 against court-ordered implementation. They charged that the proposal, which required the busing of half the city's 95,000 pupils, was excessive. In Atlanta, two U.S. district judges disapproved a plan to make racial ratios uniform throughout the city, saying it was "neither reasonable, feasible nor workable."[9] They stated that during the thirteen years Atlanta had been attempting to desegregate the city's schools, the ethnic mix had shifted from 70 percent white to 70 percent black as white families fled to the suburbs. In Richmond, Virginia, a similar metamorphosis had occurred, the black school population rising from 58 to 65 percent, after a year of court-ordered busing. Opponents singled out busing as the villain, ignoring other factors such as urban crime, overcrowding, and poverty in draining the cities of whites.

Unhappily for the White House, it was in this mood of antagonism that Southern eyes turned toward Austin to see what the court would do. On July 10, Judge Roberts rejected the HEW plan, ruling that Austin's Chicanos had never suffered school segregation and should, therefore, not be included in the proposal. Consequently, he accepted the Board's proposal.

This placed the ball in the Administration's court. Would the Justice Department appeal the decision in light of the wide disparity in the two orders? If the Administration held fast and the Fifth Circuit overruled Judge Roberts, there would in all likelihood be an uproar in Texas. Knowing this, the Lone Star's one Republican U.S. senator, John Tower, advised the President against an appeal. Although this counsel would certainly excite interest in the White House, Nixon could hardly surrender without sacrificing his reputation as a law and order President. Predictably, Nixon took the middle course, adhering neither to HEW's demanding plan, nor the more modest approach suggested by the Austin School Board. In this way, he was confident of maintaining credibility while defusing the Texas bombshell.

Had the "game plan," as the President was fond of describing his goals, emerged in a reasonable outline, little would have been forfeited. As Chief of State, he could expect credit for solving a thorny problem, with manifest political overtones, if not to the satisfaction of all concerned, still in such a way as to avoid general criticism. Instead, the combination of the Supreme Court's rejection of his stand on busing, the literal interpretation of *Swann* by his own appointees in Justice and HEW, the 351 to 36 vote in the House of Representatives the preceding day, demanding that Secretary Richardson furnish members with figures on busing to achieve racial balance, and a Gallup report showing the majority of Americans opposed busing to achieve integration—all these moves and challenges caused Nixon to over-react.

First, he announced on August 3 that Justice would appeal the Austin decision because of its alleged inconsistency with *Swann*, but "in the process of the appeal," said the President, "the Justice Department will disavow [the HEW] plan on behalf of the government."[10] This would ensure a course more rigid than the Austin Board advocated and less severe than HEW wanted. Had Mr. Nixon stopped at that point, Austin would not have become a *cause célèbre*, but unable to contain his frustration, the President challenged the High Court itself. "I am against busing as the term is commonly used in school desegregation cases," he stated. "I have consistently opposed the busing of our nation's school children to achieve a racial balance, and I am opposed to the busing of children simply for the sake of busing. Further, while the Executive Branch will continue to enforce the orders of the court, including court-ordered busing, I have instructed the Attorney General and the Secretary of Health, Education, and Welfare that they are to work with individual school districts to hold busing to the minimum required by law."[11] To make the point perfectly clear, he announced that he was sending the Congress an amendment to the $1.5 billion Emergency Assistance Act, adopted by the Senate but still under debate in the House, to prohibit spending any of the money for busing. His personal proposal "for assisting school districts in meeting special problems incident to court-ordered desegregation" was, by his own order, to have the core removed.[12]

Nixon's inconsistency produced reactions of disbelief and dismay. The absurdity of advocating desegregation on the one hand, as the President invariably did, while asking the Congress to cut off funds for busing, reminded Sen. Gambrell, of Georgia, of one who is "opposed to solitary confinement and will implement his opposition to it by cutting off bread and water from those confined."[13] In John Osborne's estimate, the Nixon statement "marked the low point of the Nixon presidency to date. It cloaked a decent and necessary action, the appeal of a Federal district judge's decision in a symbolic school case in Austin, Texas, in the misleading semantics of busing 'to achieve a racial balance' with which Mr. Nixon has been deceiving his white Southern constituency and the entire country since

1968. It taught me never to assume . . . that the President is capable of acting or letting his subordinates act in good faith on desegregation. The politics of the issue is simply too much for Mr. Nixon and for whatever sense of
public integrity he may retain."[14] Other voices, too, were incensed by his
slashing attack on busing that offered no alternatives. Gov. Askew, of
Florida, for one, told graduates at the University of Florida, "Busing, certainly, is an artificial and inadequate instrument of change. Nobody really
wants it—not you, not me, not the people, nor the school boards—not even
the courts. Yet the law demands, and rightly so, that we put an end to segregation in our society. We must demonstrate good faith in doing just
that. . . ."[15]

Unhappily, White House opposition to busing encouraged the American
people not to accept desegregation if it involved busing. The President
knew, as Askew noted, "nobody really wants it," and measuring that reluctance, the White House now pandered to the racist appeal in order to boost
Nixon's political standing. In the process, the President made the Supreme
Court the whipping boy on which angry citizens could vent their rage.
Nixon had come to insist on the barest law and order the courts would
allow.

The stratagem worked. In Jackson, Mississippi, where civil rights leader
Medgar Evers had been gunned down in June, 1963, the city had finally
wriggled out of its segregation coil. After eight years of losing court battles,
the Board of Education finally capitulated and voted to bus 9,000 black and
white children in the spirit of *Swann*. Goaded by an energetic business
community that wanted no more battles over school desegregation, the
Board approved a singularly imaginative plan for the development of interracial educational parks at opposite ends of the city. All along, they had
assumed that the Federal government would underwrite the $6 million cost
of the program. "Now," charged an angry Jacksonian, "the white community will want to know why the school board acquiesced to a busing plan
when the President is telling them to continue fighting."[16]

What little possibility there might have been of changing the President's
mood evaporated when George Wallace announced on August 5 he would
again campaign for the presidency in 1972. Busing would be a key campaign
issue, he told the press, one on which he could rightly charge that President
Nixon had stood "forthrightly on both sides of most questions."[17] Wallace
argued that the President's action in disavowing the Austin plan was not a
"reflection" of a change in heart at the White House. "He just keeps on saying he's against busing and our children just keep getting bused."[18] This
needling was followed by an embarrassing telegram to Nixon urging him to
seek a court ruling that busing for the purpose of desegregation was unconstitutional.

A jittery President lost no time reacting to the renewed Wallace threat.
Through press secretary Ron Ziegler, Nixon warned government officials to
obey his order not to use any more busing than the minimum required

by law. Those who failed to heed the caveat would "find themselves involved in other assignments or quite possibly in assignments other than the
Federal government."[19]

This was countered the following day by a blast from the United States
Civil Rights Commission whose members rose to the top of their moral toes
to excoriate the Administration. In a statement, signed by all six members,
the Commission accused the President of undermining school desegregation
by adhering to a policy of minimum busing. "Transportation of students,"
it read, "is essential to eliminating segregation; [it] has been a common fea-
ture of American education." Instead of the White House giving way to the
threat of political reprisal, "what the nation needed was a call to duty and
responsibility, for the immediate elimination of the dual school system, and
for support of all those officials who are forthrightly carrying out their legal
obligations. . . . Had [the President] presented an effective alternative, the
statement would have found acceptance among those who have waited 17
years after the Supreme Court decision to see the law of the land implemented." In one final castigation, the Commission deplored Mr. Nixon's
proposal to prohibit the use of Federal funds to finance the purchase of
buses, warning that "to eliminate a major source of financial support for
busing—an important and potentially expensive remedy for school desegregation—would almost certainly cripple the bill and render it far less
effective."[20]

Oddly enough, on the day the President ordered Justice and HEW to curtail busing in future desegregation plans, an article by J. Stanley Pottinger,
titled "HEW Enforcement of *Swann*" appeared in *Inequality in Education,* a
publication of the Harvard Center for Law and Education. Pottinger, the
new director of HEW's Office for Civil Rights, described what steps the
Department was taking to comply with *Swann.* All districts in the seventeen
Southern and Border states were being reviewed to see which had racially
identifiable schools requiring desegregation. "Of the districts surveyed,"
Pottinger reported, "about 650 were found to have had one or more schools
of this kind. . . . Of these 650 districts, about 350 were found already to be
under court order or in litigation, leaving about 300," of which seventy-five
were eliminated because the districts lacked disproportionate majorities.[21]

In view of Pottinger's role in the Austin case, which went beyond the
minimum required by *Swann,* there is no reason to suspect he originally
expected to undercut the High Court's directive. However, following the
White House ultimatum of August 3, together with the presidential threat to
fire recalcitrants, he backed off. Administratively, HEW simply put aside
134 of the districts from further consideration and mailed the remaining
ninety-one the so-called *Swann* letters in which HEW declared each district
would be contacted "directly to determine together what steps may be
necessary" to comply with the court's edict. Prior to that, on July 15,
Pottinger had said HEW would either get the offending districts to acquiesce

by fall, or failing that, send their cases to Justice for prosecution or commence hearings under Title VI to cut off whatever Federal funds they were receiving. Now, of the ninety-one districts contacted, only thirty-seven submitted desegregation plans, three went to Title VI proceedings, and nine were found not to come under *Swann*. The remaining forty-two districts were placed in a category labelled "in review."[22]

In December, 1971, three months after the Pottinger "deadline," when questioned about the delay, he frankly admitted that he was still negotiating and hoping for a successful conclusion in the "coming months."[23] In short, by direction of the White House, the directives of the Supreme Court were being ignored. Moreover, of the 134 districts that had not received *Swann* letters, eighty-five had one or more schools whose racial mix was 20 percent or more disproportionate. Knowing this, HEW still did nothing, although *Swann* declared it was the district's obligation to satisfy the Department that its racial composition was "not the result of [the district's] present or past discriminatory action."[24]

In the midst of these transgressions, a third event bubbled up to slow school desegregation. On August 31, Chief Justice Burger surprised the judiciary by admonishing those district court judges who ordered extensive busing on the unjustified belief that *Swann* required racial balance in each school. Although he refused to stay an elaborate racial balance plan for Winston-Salem, North Carolina, Burger used the occasion to clarify the interpretation of his own *Swann* opinion. In an unusual ten-page statement, he stated that if lower court judges "read this court's opinion as requiring a fixed racial balance or quota, they would appear to have overlooked specific language in the *Swann* case . . . ," going on to remind them of his words "the constitutional command to desegregate schools does not mean that every school in every community must always reflect the racial composition of the school system as a whole."[25] However, Burger had written into the same opinion the directive that the "district judge or school authorities should make every effort to achieve the greatest possible degree of actual desegregation . . . ,"[26], and in Charlotte's case, the court had approved a plan for massive busing.

Burger evidently wanted to hedge, and by hedging, his "clarification" made matters worse. In his own mind, Burger already seemed to be having grave doubts about the judiciary fashioning a new social order. Legislative bodies were created for this purpose. He saw a potential danger in nine men deciding issues that properly were not theirs to evaluate. As a conservative, Burger approved the court's prime function (protection of constitutional rights), and feared the consequences of going too far afield. Like Finley Peter Dunne's turn-of-the-century "Mr. Dooley," Burger was convinced that, "No matter whether th' constitution follows th' flag or not, th' Supreme Court follows th' ilection returns [*sic*]."[27] He sensed all too well that public sentiment had shifted on school desegregation and busing and now he foresaw the judiciary losing its parity in the tripartite system of checks and balances by continuing to hand down decisions that angered the majority. Moreover, Burger was by nature too jealous of his prerogatives to permit impairment of the High Court's prestige. Yet, in telling the courts to slow down, Burger had avoided the key issue: was there in his admonishment, the intimation of Executive supremacy? Clearly, the people needed a moral touchstone to keep them from losing their way, a role the President disavowed for himself. The fact that Burger now rapped the knuckles of the lower court justices for going too far indicated that they were in danger of losing the full support of the one institution that had stood so tall since 1954.

If the Chief Justice had any idea the national legislature—as the third branch of U.S. government—would lift the question of school desegregation from the back of the judiciary, this theme was put to rest early in November. After weeks of delay, the House began debate on the President's $1.5 billion measure to desegregate the schools. Without an amendment to prohibit the use of funds for busing, it lost 222 to 135. For several days nothing happened, but late on the evening of November 4, the antibusing spokesmen asked the chair for permission to add an amendment to the Higher Education Act which was then under discussion. Since the appeal included provisions affecting both elementary and secondary schools, the chair ruled the request in order and as John Beckler, of the Associated Press, wrote, "the dam burst." For four frenzied hours, ending at 3 A.M., in one emotional outburst after another, the House adopted three of the most restrictive antibusing amendments ever passed. One would prohibit the use of Federal money for busing. A second would prohibit the Federal government from requiring or even encouraging a state or local community to spend its funds on busing. The third, whose impact was hard to gauge, would halt implementation of Federal court busing orders until all appeals had been exhausted or until the time for appeals had expired.

The ferocity of the debate took on a harshness rarely heard in the House. Black representatives were especially bitter. Their chief spokesman, John Conyers, Jr. (D-Mich.), who led the opposition, lamented: "The opponents of busing are hiding behind their children to protect themselves from the truth. Busing is not the issue and children are not the issue. The real issue is whether or not the country will become what it says it wants to be—that place in the world where freedom and equality exist for all."[28] He was joined by Shirley Chisholm, the Brooklyn Democrat, the first black woman to enter Congress. "Let me bring it down front to you," she shouted, turning pointedly to the whites. "Your only concern is that whites are affected. Come out from behind your masks and tell it like it really is. Where were you when black children were bused right past the white schools?"[29] Rep. Parren J. Mitchell (D-Md.), brother of NAACP's chief Washington delegate, Clarence Mitchell, stood up to deplore that "more and more black Americans in increasingly large percentages are demonstrating an absolute lack of credibility in the white-dominated institutions of this country. . . . How, in the name of God," he asked, "can I or others restore credibility when we see this body act as it did . . . and when we see our liberal friends turn away from us in terms of this important legislation."[30]

To be sure, some white voices opposed precipitous action. Hale Boggs, of Louisiana, the House Democratic leader, pointed out that busing was now being ordered by the courts, and nothing we do will change it. "You are simply requiring that local people pay the cost and bear the burden."[31]

In the rush to judgement, the majority had no stomach for such talk. They preferred the old-fashioned appeal of Rep. Edith Green, the Oregon Democrat, mother of two grown sons, who as well as being the chief House authority on school problems, was a devoted friend of the neighborhood school. "The evidence is very strong that busing is not the answer to our school problem" she informed a House suddenly stilled. "I never bought a home without looking first to find out about the schools my boys would attend. Now, the Federal Government is reaching its long arm in and telling me I can't send them to that school. And that's going too far."[32]

In the end, scores of representatives disgorged their previous convictions. Dozens of erstwhile liberals tramped down the aisle to register their votes for the antibusing amendments amid cheers and jeers from Southern legislators who for years had endured their barbs over Southern school segregation. Now that the waters were rising in their own constituencies, they streaked off to escape the flood.

An ecstatic President, vacationing in Key Biscayne, Florida, telephoned Rep. Gerald Ford the day following the House vote to thank the Minority Leader for what he had done, especially his role in passing the amendment to prohibit the use of Federal funds for busing. It was Mr. Nixon's view, said Press Secretary Ziegler, that the $1.5 billion should be used "to assist the school districts with special services and other costs in the desegregation process— and not for busing."[33]

For the rest of 1971, no attempt was made to settle the many differences between the higher education and emergency school aid bills adopted by the Senate and House. Before the measures could go to a House-Senate conference to reconcile the two versions, the Senate had to repass them as one piece of legislation, to conform with the previous House action. This the Senate leadership refused to do, citing the lateness of the session. Also, a group of Southern senators, led by Sam J. Ervin, Jr., of North Carolina, determined to add the House's antibusing amendments to the Senate legislation, a move that would automatically involve the Senate in long debate.

By the time the Senate reconvened in January, 1972, a distinct drift was observable in that body from sentiment *for* to sentiment *against* busing.

New York Times correspondent, David E. Rosenbaum, reported that "The civil rights coalition in the Senate—that group of Northern Democrats and moderate Republicans that, for a decade, has formed a majority on nearly every major piece of civil rights legislation—is in danger of collapse."[34] Members of the coalition, it seemed, had been badly frightened by what their constituents told them over the Christmas holidays, one Eastern Republican even saying the antibusing attitudes he heard "would fill an auditorium five times over." Those facing reelection in November were under particular pressure to change their stance.[35]

Just as the busing dike appeared to be springing irreparable leaks, the two Senate leaders inserted their fingers in the openings. Democrat Mike Mansfield and Republican Hugh Scott proposed a compromise that would presumably gain the support of the majority as well as reduce the mounting pressure for some legislative or constitutional action to halt busing. Amendment One provided that Federal money could not be used for busing unless voluntarily requested by local school authorities and then only on condition that the busing was not so time-consuming or lengthy as, borrowing *Swann* language, "to risk the health of the children or significantly impinge on the educational process."[36] A second provision of the Mansfield-Scott compromise could have barred Federal officials, but not the courts, from ordering any school board to bus if the busing was not "constitutionally required," or if the education a student might receive was inferior to that in his home district.[37] Finally, the proposal would delay the execution of court orders requiring the busing of students across district lines until all appeals had been exhausted, or until July 1, 1973.

Taken together, the three provisions produced an antibusing imprimatur that satisfied opponents, but gave little ground. True, Federal funds were not available for busing unless requested locally, but surely school districts would seek them, if ordered to bus, rather than spend their own revenues. Moreover, the White House had already instructed HEW and Justice to curtail busing to the minimum required by law and the law was the interpretation given it by the courts. The other provisions were, in reality, largely redundant for they referred for the most part to nonexistent situations. In view of what the President had said, no Federal official would order busing that was either not "constitutionally required," or the means of sending a white student to a black central city school; and with one exception, up to then, no Federal judge had ordered the "busing of students across district lines."

The Senate passed all three measures on February, 24, 1972, amid varying predictions of their ultimate effect. Abraham Ribicoff, speaking mournfully, claimed the amendments were "public notice that we have given up the struggle to end discrimination."[38] The man in the middle of the drafting process, Jacob Javits, of New York, declared it was a case of "giving up something" to forestall something worse.[39]

Nevertheless, the Senate mood continued to be volatile. Despite approval of the Mansfield-Scott amendments, within twenty-four hours a far stronger antibusing measure, introduced by Republican Whip Senator Robert P. Griffin, of Michigan, passed 43 to 40. It would have stripped Federal courts of their authority to bus children "on the basis of their race, color, religion, or national origin."[40] This bald attempt to circumvent *Swann* posed a constitutional crisis by taking from the courts the freedom to exercise jurisdiction in the desegregation of schools. Surprisingly, its author had once strenuously championed civil rights, but now to accommodate growing antibusing sentiment in Michigan, had turned a somersault.

Although nettled by the unexpected outcome, Mansfield and Scott promised a second vote for the following week. They looked forward to the return of a number of Democratic presidential hopefuls who were off on the stump and expectedly would support the Mansfield-Scott compromise. As Sen. Scott bluntly informed a newspaperman, they are "being paid $42,500 a year plus travel expenses and stationery allowance to be here. This is where they are needed."[41] Not only did Senators Muskie, Humphrey, and McGovern leave the campaign trail to take part in the voting, a total of fourteen senators who had been absent or paired, in the first go-around, took part in the second tension-filled debate and roll call. The final tally showed Griffin had lost 50 to 47. This done, the senators supported for a second time the Mansfield-Scott compromise 63 to 43. Next day, March 1, they adopted 88 to 6 a compromise Higher Education Bill to which Nixon's $1.5 billion desegregation proposal and the Mansfield-Scott Amendment had been added. A major retreat on school desegregation was thus narrowly avoided.

Any hope the House would now follow the Senate's lead disappeared with the former's 2 to 1 decision on March 8 to stand firm against any conference compromise that would weaken its three antibusing amendments. It reaffirmed this stand a second time on May 11, after the Senate-House conferees had been meeting for two months without yet tackling the issue of busing. A week later, however, after an all-night session, the conference struck a compromise that was much weaker than the House version. For the most part, it followed Senate language. Instead of permitting court-ordered busing appeals to run their course, as the House had insisted, the conferees placed a time limit on such delays, but in deference to House sentiment, the cut-off was extended six months from July 1, 1973, to January 1, 1974. Instead of prohibiting the use of Federal money for busing, as the House demanded, the conferees accepted the Senate idea of allowing its use if sought by local officials, so long as it did not endanger the health of students or require them to be placed in inferior schools.

The Senate approved the compromise 63 to 15, as did the House two weeks later by the narrower margin of 218 to 180. Finally, on June

23—more than twenty-six months after his initial message to Congress—
President Nixon added his signature, but not without branding it a "clever
political evasion."[42] The man who had done more than any other American
to halt school integration through his imprecations against busing now
fumed that, "Congress has not given us the answer we requested. It has
given us rhetoric. . . . Not in the course of this Administration has there
been a more manifest Congressional retreat from an urgent call for responsibility."[43]

Against all the hopes and aspirations for a unitary school system, which
Brown had envisioned in 1954, the President was determined to destroy the
one tool necessary to its fulfillment. He threatened "to go to the people" in
the coming presidential campaign to rally support for a constitutional
amendment to prohibit the use of busing to achieve school integration.[44]

Notes

1. Cynthia Brown, "Busing: Leaving the Driving to U.S. . . . ," *Inequality in
Education*, December, 1971, p. 6.
2. Charles Rabb, "Education Report," *National Journal*, June 17, 1971, p. 1305.
3. *New York Times*, August 8, 1971.
4. Ibid.
5. *Swann v. Charlotte-Mecklenburg Board of Education* 402 U.S. 1 (1971), at 24.
6. Ibid., at 30-31.
7. Ibid., at 25.
8. John Osborne, "Austin Story," *New Republic*, August 21, 1971, p. 15.
9. *U.S. News*, August 16, 1971, p. 38.
10. Richard M. Nixon, "Statement on Busing," *New York Times*, August 3, 1971.
11. Ibid.
12. Richard M. Nixon, *New York Times*, March 25, 1970.
13. Brown, "Busing."
14. Osborne, "Austin Story," p. 13.
15. Brown, "Busing," p. 6.
16. *Newsweek*, August 16, 1971, p. 47.
17. *New York Times*, August 6, 1971.
18. Ibid.
19. *New York Times*, August 12, 1971.
20. *New York Times*, August 13, 1971.
21. J. Stanley Pottinger, "HEW Enforcement of Swann," *Inequality in Education*,
August 3, 1971, p. 8.
22. *Adams v. Richardson*, D.D.C. Civ No. 3095-70, Plaintiffs' Points and Authorities in Support of Motion for Summary Judgment (December 17, 1971), pp. 43-46.
23. Ibid., p. 44.
24. *Swann v. Charlotte-Mecklenburg*, at 26.
25. *New York Times*, September 1, 1971.

26. *Swann* v. *Charlotte-Mecklenburg*, at 26.

27. Finley Peter Dunne, *Familiar Quotations by John Bartlett* (Boston: Little Brown and Company, 1940), p. 796.

28. *Nation*, November 22, 1971, p. 516.

29. *New York Times*, November 5, 1971.

30. *Nation*, November 22, 1971.

31. Ibid.

32. *New York Times*, November 5, 1971.

33. *New York Times*, November 7, 1971.

34. *New York Times*, January 23, 1972.

35. Ibid.

36. *Swann* v. *Charlotte-Mecklenburg*, at 30-31.

37. *New York Times*, February 25, 1972.

38. Ibid.

39. Ibid.

40. *New York Times*, February 26, 1972.

41. Ibid.

42. *New York Times*, June 24, 1972.

43. Ibid.

44. Ibid.

13

ADAMS v. RICHARDSON

"You're happier if you lead an integrated life."

Joseph L. Rauh, Jr. [1]

The 1964 Civil Rights Act has aptly been called "the most far-reaching and comprehensive law in support of social equality ever enacted by Congress."[2] It was only enacted after 500 amendments and 534 hours of debate. At the behest of a powerful civil rights coalition, Congress voted to protect racial minorities and disadvantaged groups by ordering a cut-off of Federal funds to any entity found guilty of discrimination. It was a carrot-and-stick approach, based on the theory that communities would rather outlaw discriminatory practices than give up their share of national revenue, particularly in the field of public education which was already becoming prohibitively expensive. The chief white lobbyist for this monumental achievement was a Washington-based lawyer, fifty-three-year-old Joseph L. Rauh, Jr., called by Senator Philip A. Hart, of Michigan, "the *real* conscience of the Senate."[3]

Rauh was born in Cincinnati and received degrees from Harvard College and Harvard Law School, graduating from both magna cum laude. Thereafter, he was law secretary to two of the most renowned justices in Supreme Court history—Benjamin N. Cardozo and Felix Frankfurter—counsel to the SEC, the Department of Labor, the FCC and just prior to World War II, the Lend-Lease Administration. In 1946, after serving on General Mac-Arthur's staff in the Southwest Pacific area, he became a private practitioner in Washington.

Unlike many lawyers who grew up in Washington during the New Deal and went on to profit handsomely from their governmental contacts, Rauh early on demonstrated a deep concern for the people's rights. "Anybody who has had the advantage of working for Benjamin Cardozo, Ben Cohen or Felix Frankfurter will have the public interest drummed into him in a way that he can never forget it," he says, reminiscing about the past.[4] Nature

endowed Rauh with a love for people, all people. In much the same vein
Hubert Humphrey used to describe the joy of politics, Rauh exudes his own
aphorism, "You're happier if you lead an integrated life."[5]

Rauh's support of liberal causes made him a founder of the Americans for
Democratic Action, and when a combination of civil rights organizations
established the Leadership Conference on Civil Rights, he was their natural
selection for general counsel. Not only was he an able litigant, he possessed
the physical presence to command attention. The combination of a massive
head atop a huge frame coupled to an aggressive personality generated the
power with which to dominate others.

Predictably, Rauh was angered when he learned on July 3, 1969, that
Attorney General Mitchell and HEW Secretary Finch were planning to
abandon the strict enforcement of Title VI of the 1964 Act. As noted in
Chapter Four, the Administration's subterfuge was couched in phrases of
undying fealty to school integration, but subsequent facts told what the
White House was planning. In the year before the statement, HEW terminated Federal assistance to forty-four school districts; in the twelve months
following Finch-Mitchell, it took away aid in only two districts.

In the face of this attack on Title VI, Rauh, his partners John Silard and
Elliott Lichtman, and the NAACP Legal Defense Fund decided to bring suit
against HEW and charge it with defaulting on its statutory obligation to
enforce the 1964 legislation.

Over a period of fifteen months, they had constructed their case around
six children of the Adams family, aged eight to sixteen, residents of Rankin
County, Mississippi, and other schoolchildren and their parents. Although
each was admittedly a victim of school segregation, HEW had not used the
authority of Title VI to suspend or terminate Federal aid to the district.

Meanwhile, on June 7, 1970, Under Secretary of State Elliot L.
Richardson replaced Finch as Secretary of HEW. A Massachusetts native,
the son, grandson, and brother of eminent physicians, Richardson excelled
as both an elective and appointive official. Now forty-nine, he had clerked
for Supreme Court Justice Felix Frankfurter and served a term as the Commonwealth's Lieutenant-Governor before joining the Nixon Administration. At the State Department, after eighteen months, he "dazzled older
hands with his ability to master . . . the . . . Department's internal
management."[6] To some, he was "probably the most effective administrator
at Foggy Bottom in the last decade."[7] Upon learning HEW was to come
under fire, he reacted indignantly. Chancing to meet Rauh at the Washington Star International Tennis Tournament, he said. "I understand you are
going to sue me."

"Yes, you are not enforcing Title VI, Elliot," Rauh replied.[8]

The new Secretary argued that HEW could not lose, and therefore, the
suit was only being engineered to embarrass him and the Administration.

Why the worry, countered Rauh, if there is no chance of success, and the two parted to face each other in court.

When the U.S. District Court for the District of Columbia finally received the plaintiff's complaint on October 19, 1970, the case against HEW had grown to six different counts, all designed to test HEW's alleged failure to enforce Title VI.[9]

Despite overwhelming evidence, Richardson and Pottinger countered on December 9, 1970, with a motion to dismiss, contending that the enforcement responsibilities of executive officials under Title VI were "completely discretionary in nature."[10]

Eight days later, Adams and his colleagues replied by denying unlimited discretion. "Section 602," they pointed out, "gives HEW discretion as to the *means* which it chooses to enforce the right specified in Section 601; it has no discretion simply to countenance a continuing violation of plaintiffs' Section 601 rights which are absolute and unqualified."[11] If HEW's "discretionary" view were tenable, they went on, "Title VI would permit and sanction what the Constitution forbids. . . . The ultimate incongruity of HEW's statutory interpretation is that Title VI actually becomes more helpful to segregation and discrimination than to the specific class of persons given rights by Section 601. . . ."[12] Sixteen years after *Brown*, [13] and six years after the passage of Title VI, it is outrageous for HEW under the mantle of 'discretion' to attempt to justify its continuing injury to plaintiffs' statutory and constitutional rights."[14]

About six months passed before John H. Pratt, United States District Judge for the District of Columbia, denied Richardson and Pottinger's motion, passing the case along to further litigation. To buttress their case, plaintiffs filed on December 17, 1971, a detailed amplification to their original complaint.

The first charge was that HEW had failed to terminate Federal aid to colleges and universities that openly discriminated against minorities. Rauh's firm and the Legal Defense Fund could point to a long history of inaction and neglect. As far back as the fall of 1967, the Department recognized the existence of discrimination. A survey revealed that Southern institutions continued to receive millions of dollars annually despite pervasive segregation. "Sister" schools, one white, the other black, existed side by side, virtually duplicating courses and services. At the three branches of Southern University in Baton Rouge, New Orleans, and Shreveport, Louisiana, not a single white student was enrolled, while in the same cities at Louisiana State University, only 4 percent of the student body was black. Between January, 1969, and February, 1970—the Panetta months—the Nixon Administration had used the data to dispatch letters to ten states, requesting the submission of desegregation plans within 60 to 120 days. Five states, Louisiana, Mississippi, North Carolina, Oklahoma, and Florida, ignored the ultimatum and the others merely offered unacceptable plans.

Yet, the plaintiffs pointed out, HEW steadfastly refused "to commence any administrative or judicial proceedings against *any* of these states."[15]

Louisiana's record was especially instructive, as recalled by Leon Panetta, head of OCR during the first year of the Nixon Administration. The original letter, mailed January 13, 1969, drew no response. On July 8, a second letter went out requesting an outline plan. No response. A third one followed on October 21. Still no response, although this time HEW threatened administrative proceedings if the state failed to produce an outline by mid-December.

At the mention of punitive action, Louisiana's Governor, John McKeithen, exploded: "We are tired of being treated as guinea pigs and second-class citizens in this state."[16] In this impasse, only the use of U.S. marshals could compel Louisiana to integrate, and McKeithen, fearing for his political life, did not hesitate to warn Panetta, "You know, this race thing could blow up my whole state. . . . you'll make all of Louisiana like Washington, D.C.; the whites will just move out and we don't want that."[17]

As soon as Pottinger replaced Panetta, the fever subsided, and officials in Louisiana and other Southern states concluded the Department had softened its stance and declined to act. Pottinger's defense for this "abysmal" performance,[18] as stated in an affidavit to the plaintiffs, was that he needed time to negotiate, to which the Rauh group replied the enforcement of Title VI was not negotiable. The law granted HEW the right initially to use voluntary means to assure compliance, but did not empower the Department to sanction perpetual evasion. Seven years had now passed since Title VI became law and still Pottinger insisted on "complete discretion" to continue endless negotiations.[19]

A second excuse Pottinger gave for not desegregating the statewide institutions of higher learning was their alleged complexity. To his statement that it might "take a decade," plaintiffs replied he could take many intermediate steps to quicken the process.[20] Panetta had mentioned several of these in testimony before the court. They included such devices as putting black and white "sister" colleges and universities together in an "exchange of courses, faculty, students, and resources between each 'pair' of schools."[21]

Further, Elias Blake, an expert on education, described how HEW could break down the segregation that separated these "sister" institutions. Why not, he asked rhetorically, have a system of "single registration" so that "when the course in educational psychology is filled at one institution . . . the additional enrollment could enroll in that course at the other institution?"[22] Beyond that, HEW could have ordered the reconstruction of state governing boards of higher education. What could one expect from boards that were either all white or contained only a token black or two? Since most members were political appointees, HEW had the power, reasoned Blake, to require their immediate desegregation, a step that

Pottinger frankly admitted he had never "required," or even "requested" and perhaps never thought of.[23] Additionally, Blake went on, since higher education staffs are "generally hired by the people on these boards," the desegregation of the board would have reverberations down the line.[24] As to graduate and professional schools, they could be desegregated at once, faculty and students exchanged, and "other race" scholarships established in order to attract blacks to "white" campuses.[25] In short, as the plaintiffs indicated, "even if comprehensive desegregation on a state-wide system [were] complex, there [were] numerous significant movements toward desegregation which HEW [could] immediately require."[26]

Pottinger's apologia concluded with the view that *Alexander's* mandate to desegregate "at once" did not apply to higher education.[27] This, the plaintiffs retorted, was "out of the whole cloth."[28] There was nothing in the High Court's opinions, beginning with *Brown*, that suggested that rulings did not apply to higher education. Pottinger had conjured up the theory in order to justify the Department's "unlawful and unconstitutional expenditure of tens of millions of dollars to segregated systems of higher education."[29]

The plaintiffs' count two against HEW focused on elementary and secondary education. They reminded the court that HEW's original enforcement proceedings under Title VI had succeeded. Administrative efforts against 600 Southern districts between 1964 and 1970 ended aid to 200 of them. In all but four instances, after districts submitted satisfactory desegregation plans or promised HEW to comply with court orders, Federal assistance had been restored. It was a chapter and verse proof demonstrating the efficacy of properly administering the provisions of Title VI. However, because the Nixon Administration insisted on changing the rules, HEW faced the galling problem of pressuring again those districts that were once in compliance, but now through rejection or noncompliance, were violating Title VI.

During the school years 1968-69 and 1969-70, the Department's regional offices referred the names of ninety-nine such recalcitrant districts to Washington, but the record showed few efforts to force compliance. HEW did refer seventeen of the ninety-nine cases to the Justice Department, and in September, 1969, Justice obtained ten temporary restraining orders. No action, however, was ever initiated against twenty-four of the delinquents. As with higher education, in the face of deteriorating enforcement proceedings, HEW came to rely more and more on protracted negotiation and persuasion, hoping thereby to still or at least temper Mr. Nixon's imprecations against Title VI.

Plaintiffs' third complaint was HEW's refusal to speed up desegregation as the Supreme Court had demanded. Prior to *Alexander*, HEW had permitted eighty-seven school districts to delay desegregation "at once"; the Department still dawdled.[30] In the case of the Osceola Arkansas School District, HEW not only failed to require immediate desegregation, but six months later, agreed to a fifteen-month postponement. In October, 1970, after litigation began in *Adams* v. *Richardson*,[31] HEW granted a further extension, this time admittedly "in error."[32] Eventually, Pottinger gave up negotiating and turned the case over to Justice where it was finally resolved in February, 1973—forty months after *Alexander*.

A fourth objection, raised by Adams et al., centered on HEW's failure to monitor segregated schools for deaf, blind, and mentally handicapped children in seventeen Southern and Border states which operated in violation of Title VI. To cover this illegality, HEW accepted "statements of compliance," mere scraps of paper, on which the state "assured" the Department of compliance and then reneged.[33] Dishearteningly, HEW continued to pour millions into the support of these segregated schools.

For its fifth point, the plaintiffs charged HEW with refusing to monitor 640 districts in the seventeen Southern and Border states under court order to desegregate. Although they constituted nearly 15 percent of the 4,380 cited districts, HEW steadfastly excused its inaction by referring to Public Law 90-247, enacted in 1968, which defined compliance with Title VI as "compliance by such agency with a final order or judgment of a Federal court."[34] Under HEW's interpretation, if a Federal district judge handed down a final order that did not strictly accord with Title VI, the Department had no right to step in. In this way, the 640 districts mentioned above escaped. Presumably, it was the duty of Justice to monitor compliance, but Pottinger was ignorant of what had been done. He even conceded to the plaintiffs that "it is possible that gross violations of court orders may be occurring in court ordered districts, some of which are the largest in the South, and HEW doesn't know. . . ."[35] His words indicated HEW's new direction. Before *Adams*, former Secretary Finch had announced on April 7, 1970, that "school districts now under desegregation court decrees, as well as those which may come under court decrees as a result of action by the Department of Justice" would be monitored.[36] When that did not happen, it constituted one more proof of the White House's determination to undercut school desegregation.

Pottinger sought to circumvent the criticism by saying he had done so to avoid "possible interference" with the courts.[37] He cited *Lee* v. *Macon County Board of Education*[38] in which a three-judge panel allegedly "found a conflict in jurisdiction and booted HEW out of the court order districts.[39] When asked where in that case did the court preclude monitoring, Pottinger hedged. What *Lee* expressly recognized was "HEW's 'duty' to monitor such court order districts."[40] Checkmated, Pottinger reversed himself, claiming his failure to monitor must be blamed on the Department's lack of personnel. Although HEW was admittedly understaffed, Pottinger could hardly argue both that the Department had no duty to monitor, and that it lacked the resources to do the job. Pouncing on this inconsistency, the plaintiffs said "[T]here is absolutely no integrity to the 'defenses' proffered by HEW and Mr. Pottinger. One excuse impugns the second. When a rationalization becomes tenuous, it is promptly disavowed in favor of another."[41]

Finally, the plaintiffs scored HEW's reluctance to suspend and/or recapture Federal aid from schools that violated Title VI. Interestingly, Sidney P. Marland, Jr., Commissioner of Education, had only recently told a nationwide television audience that HEW was recovering "roughly an average of a million dollars a state" from six states that had improperly spent funds under Title I of the Elementary and Secondary Education Act of 1965.[42]

At the same time its failure to prosecute school districts in violation of Title VI produced predictable results. They deliberately delayed administrative procedures, knowing that the litigation could take several years during which government funds would continue to flow from Washington. Argued the plaintiffs, "Only this court's intervention can restore the spirit and letter of Title VI in the area of public education."[43]

Some eleven months later, on November 16, 1972, Pratt found in favor of the plaintiffs.[44] In another three months, on February 16, 1973, he ordered HEW to begin action within 120 days against the states listed in the complaint.[45] In addition, the Department was "required and enjoined" to afford the plaintiffs such information as would tell whether the Department was conforming to Title VI. Within 150 days, HEW would have to report what had been accomplished, and thereafter every six months "for a period of three years, so as to permit evaluation of the reasons for any delays. . . ."[46] Similarly prickly injunctions were applied to almost all the other counts.

The decision represented an extraordinary victory for the plaintiffs. Not only had they succeeded in routing HEW's contention that Title VI permitted the Department "discretionary" powers to delay, but as a matter of law, they had established the principle of judicial review of administrative nonfeasance. The fact that members of the executive branch, appointed by the President, were now accountable for their interpretation as well as their enforcement of the law by a member of the judiciary was writing a new chapter—a vital one—in the history of American jurisprudence.

The incisiveness of the Pratt decision brought a sharp response from HEW, but on appeal, the plaintiffs were affirmed. The U.S. Court of Appeals unanimously upheld the Pratt ruling on April 9, 1973, after forty-five months of litigation.

Notes

1. Stephen Gillers, "Joe Rauh An Integrated Life," *Juris Doctor*, February, 1975, p. 37.

2. John Hope Franklin, *From Slavery to Freedom, a History of Negro Americans* (New York: Vintage Books, 1969), p. 635.

3. Philip A. Hart, autographed photograph of Hart, presented to Joseph Rauh, Jr., a year before Hart's death on December 26, 1976.

4. Gillers, "Joe Rauh An Integrated Life," p. 40.

5. Ibid.

6. *New York Times*, June 8, 1970, p. 44.

7. Ibid.

8. Author's conversation with Rauh, August 2, 1977.

9. Pub. L. 88-352, Title VI, Section 601, July 2, 1964, 78 Stat. 252.

10. *Adams* v. *Richardson*, D.D.C. Civ. No. 3095-70, Defendants' Motion to Dismiss or In the Alternative for Summary Judgment, December 9, 1970, p. 13.

11. *Adams* v. *Richardson*, D.D.C. Civ. No. 3095-70, Reply Memorandum for Plaintiffs, December 17, 1970, p. 13.

12. Ibid., p. 8.

13. *Brown* v. *Board of Education*, 347 U.S. 483 (1954).

14. *Adams* v. *Richardson*, Reply Memorandum, p. 14.

15. *Adams* v. *Richardson*, D.D.C. Civ. No. 3095-70, Plaintiffs' Points and Authorities in Support of Motion For Summary Judgment, December 17, 1971, p. 10.

16. Leon E. Panetta and Peter Gall, *Bring Us Together* (Philadelphia: J.B. Lippincott Company, 1971), p. 323.

17. Ibid., pp. 329-30.

18. *Adams* v. *Richardson*, Plaintiffs' Points, p. 17.

19. Ibid., p. 21.

20. Ibid., p. 23.

21. Ibid., p. 24.

22. Ibid.

23. Ibid., p. 25.

24. Ibid.

25. Ibid., p. 26.

26. Ibid.

27. *Alexander* v. *Holmes*, 396 U.S. 19 (1969).

28. *Adams* v. *Richardson*, Plaintiffs' Points, p. 27.

29. Ibid.

30. *Alexander* v. *Holmes*, 396 U.S. 19 (1969), at 20.

31. *Adams* v. *Richardson*, 351 F. Supp. 636 (1972).

32. *Adams* v. *Richardson*, Plaintiffs' Points, p. 40.

33. Ibid., p. 48.

34. 42 U.S.C.A. Sec. 2000d-5.

35. *Adams* v. *Richardson*, Plaintiffs' Points, p. 52.

36. Ibid., p. 54.

37. Ibid., p. 55.

38. *Lee* v. *Macon County Board of Education*, 270 F. Supp. 859 (M.D. Ala., 1967).

39. Deposition of defendant Pottinger, Plaintiffs' Exhibits, (Tr. 21), (December, 1970).

40. *Lee* v. *Macon County*, at 866.

41. *Adams* v. *Richardson*, Plaintiffs' Points, p. 57.

42. Ibid., p. 68.

43. Ibid., p. 80.

44. *Adams* v. *Richardson*, 351 F. Supp. 636 (1972).

45. *Adams* v. *Richardson*, 356 F. Supp. 92 (1973).

46. Ibid., at 95-96.

14

BUSING MOVES NORTH

"Suppose I send my daughter to school and she gets thrown through the window and breaks her neck, or she gets molested or stabbed."

Pontiac mother opposing school integration.[1]

In the autumn of 1971, while Congress was still battling to curtail the use of Federal funds for busing, HEW began collecting figures on school desegregation. The data revealed a frightening disparity in racial isolation between North and South. Principally as a result of white migration to the suburbs, the public schools of New York, Chicago, Philadelphia, Baltimore, Washington, Cleveland, Detroit, and Los Angeles no longer had white majorities. As a measure of the "apartheid" that existed above and below the Mason-Dixon line in twelve major cities of the North and West, there were approximately 380,000 blacks in all-black schools.[2] In twelve comparable Southern cities, about 8,800 blacks attended all-black schools.[3] In the days preceding the HEW survey, school "blackness" had increased by 2 percent in the above-mentioned Northern and Western cities, while falling 25 percent in the corresponding Southern communities. In short, because of the North's failure to desegregate its schools, more—not less—racial segregation existed in America's public schools seventeen years after *Brown*.

Tragically, for America's children, the High Court had refrained from outlawing both de facto and de jure segregation. In formulating *Brown*, the justices used two guidelines: one that a dual educational system was "inherently unequal"[4] because it violated the "equal protection" clause guaranteed by the Fourteenth Amendment, and the other, psychologically rooted, yet equally unconstitutional, that minority children could not be isolated without generating "a feeling of inferiority . . . unlikely ever to be undone."[5] The first spoke to desegregation, the second to integration, and therein lay the rub, for if separate schools were "inherently unequal," as the court ruled in *Brown*, then the distinction between Southern de jure and Northern de facto had no constitutional relevance.

Nevertheless, the Supreme Court refused every opportunity to be drawn into the argument, stating only that de jure segregation was illegal. Consequently, the North escaped the judgments handed down to the South. Moreover, the court's decision to limit its jurisdiction gave Northern liberals in Congress a grace period of several years, long enough to hide behind the iron curtain of de facto segregation while writing civil rights legislation that applied only to Southern schools.

By 1971, however, the atmosphere was changing, as Northern Federal judges began to rule that cases, formerly considered de facto, were in reality de jure. As with Charlotte, it was seen that municipal authorities used their office to create school segregation.

Among the first cities to feel the judicial whip was San Francisco. Shortly after *Swann*, a Federal district judge found historical evidence of de jure segregation in the record of the school board. It had, the court declared, been guilty of constructing and remodeling schools, establishing attendance zones, and assigning inexperienced teachers in a manner to preserve the dual system. Moreover, it had failed to establish racial balances as prescribed by the state board of education. Accordingly, the court ordered the city to integrate its 46,000 children in ninety-seven elementary schools, a task that involved the busing of 25,000 at an annual cost of $2.5 million.

By the time school was to open in the fall of 1971, the city had become a powder keg. As many as 1,000 angry parents marched to school board meetings to protest the plan and even the presence of three dozen policemen could not prevent rampaging, heckling, and fist fights. Leading the opposition was Mayor Joseph Alioto, who up to the time he sniffed public hostility, had been renowned for his strong advocacy of civil rights.

On opening day, an estimated 20,000 students stayed home, and a number of well-to-do white parents enrolled their children in private or parochial schools rather than allow them to be bused into black neighborhoods. Especially bitter was the Chinese community whose spokesmen feared their youngsters would lose their ethnicity in a cultural amalgam. Yet, despite the many obstacles, by the second week, almost 70 percent were in class, and San Francisco's school superintendent was comparing the situation to a football team that had driven to the ten-yard line. "Those last 10 yards come very hard," he sighed.[6]

With all the confusion, however, it was not San Francisco, but Pontiac, Michigan, a tough factory town twenty-five miles northwest of Detroit, that produced the major headlines that fall. Decades of migration had made the city ripe for racial strife, as poor white families from Appalachia poured in seeking jobs in the giant General Motors plants which employed 40 percent of the city's population. They competed with Southern blacks, who by 1971, comprised a fifth of the city's population. In the previous decade, their numbers had jumped 60 percent, while the white population was dropping almost 10 percent. "Racial clashes are endemic here," wrote Daniel Zwerdling in the *New Republic*. "White and black communities battled . . . over the location of a new $15 million high school, turning one school board meeting into a chair-throwing melee. . . ."[7]

In 1969, with feelings running high, the Pontiac branch of the NAACP started a class action suit, charging the school board with having violated *Brown I*. Since a favorable decision would require an affirmative showing of de jure segregation, the national organization refused to take the litigation seriously. However, after listening to the NAACP's complaint, U.S. District Judge Damon J. Keith, a black jurist from Detroit, a Lyndon Johnson appointee, ruled that while the board had given lip service to the idea of desegregation, it actually had kept the system segregated by planned site selection and teacher placements. "Sins of omission can be as serious as sins of commission," he wrote.[8]

Under the Keith decision, about 9,000 children, or 37 percent of the student population, would be bused to thirty-six preponderantly white schools, assuring a black mix of between 20 and 36 percent.

It was not a particularly ambitious program, but rather than comply, the board decided to appeal the decision to the Sixth Circuit, which in turn refused to act until the High Court reached a decision on the legality of busing to achieve desegregation. Finally, relying on the *Swann* opinion of April, 1971, the Circuit Court upheld Keith's order.

Overnight, a group of Pontiac white mothers—all militant segregationists —organized an Antibusing National Action Group (NAG) to prevent compliance with the court order. Led by Irene McCabe, a thirty-six-year-old housewife, who swore NAG's opposition to busing was not racial, the organization's first public act was to sponsor a rally in Wisner Stadium where a crowd of 5,000 listened intently while George Wallace praised their stand. On August 30, one week before school opening, citizens awoke to an explosion that blew ten of the city's school buses to bits at a loss of about $50,000. Criminals had cut a passage through the chain-link fence securing the vehicles and planted dynamite. The FBI suspected the Ku Klux Klan and two weeks later picked up six alleged members, charging them with conspiracy.

Although NAG leaders condemned the bombing, they began a campaign of picketing and boycotting that also led to violence. On the same day school began, five women chained themselves to the bus yard gates to keep the buses from operating. They were arrested along with four other women who staged a sit-down in front of the gate. When black children arrived to enter previously all-white schools, NAG pickets joined in shouting "nigger, nigger" as they passed. Rocks flew. For three days massive demonstrations continued. Demonstrators carried placards trumpeting, "We're fighting for OUR civil rights now," and "Do you smell communism when one man overrules 99 percent of the people?"[9]

Although white attendance on opening day dropped to 66 percent, by week's end, the figure had swollen to almost 80 percent, and the conflagration seemed to be dying out. Then, on Wednesday of the following week, NAG protesters gave the embers a kick by massing pickets in front of the

General Motors' Fisher Body plant and forcing a work stoppage of the 4,200 workers. Fear took hold. In the words of one NAG mother, "We want to keep our children in our neighborhood where we know they're safe. Suppose I send my daughter to school and she gets thrown through a window and breaks her neck, or she gets molested or stabbed."[10]

Security forces had no heart for keeping NAG under control. In fact, the Pontiac Police Officers Association had already contributed $300 to the NAG cause, and according to observers on the scene, "Most policemen covering the demonstrations idled on the sidewalks."[11] Organized labor also displayed negativism. Pontiac school superintendent Dana Whitmer told a staff writer for the *Detroit Free Press*, "The UAW hasn't done anything."[12] The lone exception was UAW's head, Leonard Woodcock, who insisted that its Pontiac local not contribute to the NAG effort. The union's leadership, however, had no stomach for opposing its membership. Nor did the city's foremost employer, General Motors. Company policy called for noninterference in controversial subjects. Thus, Pontiac became another example of a community cut adrift by the very people who could have controlled the situation. Through creating a vacuum, the leadership elite permitted the raucous elements to take over.

As one might expect, each party had a different excuse for defaulting. The police chief thought his men had shown remarkable restraint. "If we wanted to get technical," he observed quite fecklessly, "we could have arrested hundreds."[13] He either could not—or would not—admit that his force acted in one fashion toward blacks demonstrating at school board meetings, and another toward white NAGs demonstrating around school properties. He had to arrest blacks, he argued, because he "heard them shouting obscenities at male and female members of the school board," yet would not move against whites, preferring the use of "gentle persuasion and logic."[14]

Union reaction to the Keith order made just as reprehensible reading. The UAW enjoyed a national reputation for liberality. Under the leadership of the late Walter Reuther, it had opened positions in its top ranks to blacks in increasing numbers. No union in America had been so forthright in the support of civil rights, guaranteed wages, adequate housing, improved health, and quality education, but confrontation with white ethnics over the question of school integration caused a panic. On the other hand, had it made the effort to explain the rationale for the Keith plan, undoubtedly Pontiac passions would have cooled.

No less peccant was General Motors. By refusing to enter a controversial community issue, the company jettisoned all claim to community leadership.

With so many negative forces in play, the wonder is that eventually a positive force in the form of the Parent-Teacher Association did arise to support the plan and assure its success. Additionally, as time went on, many students worked hard to maintain racial peace. When school opened in the fall of 1972, the district's racial troubleshooter could boast, "We had the quietest school opening since '63; it's even hard for us to understand."[15] Moreover, relief from racial tension among the students permitted school authorities to take a fresh look at curriculum. Busing, he said, "is making us look at ourselves as we've never done before. We've had kids graduated from high school that couldn't read the words on their diplomas."[16]

Despite this encouraging report from the school system, the positive effect of desegregation had had little effect on the city's white ethnics. Although busing was not new, they bristled at the thought of its use for racial balancing, and believed it would destroy their neighborhood identity. As long as ancient enclaves survived, Poles could preserve their neighborhood schools, Russians theirs, and so on.

White ethnicity in conflict with blacks was not unlike the canyon separating blacks from WASPs. The latter could not disengage themselves from the assumption that blacks were somehow inferior, a view that slavery had long ago embedded in their psyche. Accordingly, discrimination and prejudice, as much as they liked to deny its existence, permeated their thinking and their actions regardless of religious appeals and the pressure of antibias laws.

Of more recent incorporation in the American scene, white ethnics feuded with blacks on other grounds. Their hostility sprang from three roots: first, they had to compete with blacks for jobs that initially belonged to the ethnics, particularly in the building trades. In their struggle they came to view antibias laws, enacted to help minorities, as a weapon that actually denied them equality.

Second, the upheaval that occurred in every Northern city after World War II with the sudden rise in the number of blacks was about equally balanced by the number of whites departing for suburbia. In such a vast demographic cataclysm, new residents inevitably got the blame for much of the city's woes. Minority envelopment of the schools, higher welfare costs, deteriorating housing, increased crime, and narcotics addiction—all were charged up to black intrusion.

A third obstacle, linked to the second, evolved from the growing threat blacks posed to the retention of white ethnicity. A challenge at work, away from their families and neighborhoods, was unsettling enough, but with the rising emphasis on U.S. pluralism, as illustrated by the battle for school integration, white ethnics saw themselves hemmed in by forces that could terminate their continuing entity on which they placed a high price.

Notes

1. Daniel Zwerdling, "Block Those Buses," *New Republic*, October 23, 1971, p. 15.

2. Chicago, Baltimore, Cleveland, Columbus, Detroit, Indianapolis, Kansas City, Los Angeles, Milwaukee, Newark, St. Louis, and Washington.

3. Atlanta, Austin, Miami, Dallas, Jacksonville, Tampa, Houston, Birmingham, Nashville, Norfolk, New Orleans, and San Antonio.

4. *Brown* v. *Board of Education,* 347 U.S. 483 (1954).

5. Ibid.

6. "Boycotting the Buses," *Newsweek,* September 27, 1971, p. 43.

7. Zwerdling, "Block Those Buses," p. 14.

8. *New York Times,* February 18, 1970.

9. Zwerdling, "Block Those Buses."

10. Ibid.

11. Ibid.

12. William Serrin, "They Don't Burn Buses Anymore in Pontiac," *Saturday Review,* June 24, 1972, p. 8.

13. Zwerdling, "Block Those Buses," p. 15.

14. Ibid.

15. *New York Times,* November 26, 1972.

16. Ibid.

15

NIXON'S SECOND MANDATE

"I hate to see a cannon used to shoot a gnat."

Senator Howard H. Baker, Jr., Tennessee.[1]

During the early summer of 1971, it appeared for a time that the clamor over busing and school desegregation had finally run its course. In *Swann*, the Supreme Court approved busing to desegregate dual school systems, and Nixon thereafter promised to cooperate.

Then, suddenly, the structure of collective action crumbled. The political questions raised by HEW's ambitious Austin proposal caused the President to reverse himself. Sensing that school desegregation was once more filling the campaign trough, George Wallace also decided to add his bit. On the day following Nixon's disavowal, the Alabaman directed the Jefferson County School Board to assign a fifteen-year-old suburban Birmingham white student to a predominantly white high school, four miles away, instead of busing her twenty-two miles to help integrate a high school, 95 percent black. Although it turned out the school board's action stemmed from a clerical error, the Governor's action clearly defied a Federal District Court order. "My order," barked Wallace, "transcends the order of the court,"[2] and knowing how rankled the President would be, he twitted, "This is going to give him a chance to carry out his wishes. You might say Governor Wallace is working closely with the President to help carry out his desire not to have massive busing."[3]

Within a month, the Wallace ruse produced results. *New York Times* reporter James Wooten, writing from Atlanta, reported heightened resistance to desegregation spreading throughout the South. Opposition in Tennessee was especially virulent as the result of an unpopular court order imposed upon Nashville. When front-running Democratic presidential hopeful Senator Edmund S. Muskie, of Maine, visited Chattanooga in September, he was queried about busing. "Inequality of educational opportunity," he replied with commendable frankness and shaky syntax, was "a wrong that must be righted. . . . The courts have told us that busing is a way, . . . and in many cases the only way to get at that wrong. So I don't think we ought to exclude it as a tool for doing just that."[4] The state's Democratic hierarchy thought otherwise and cancelled Muskie's invitation to address a fund-raising dinner in Nashville.

For Muskie, as well as for other aspirants for the Democratic nomination, the approaching campaign looked increasingly more like the winter of their discontent. All but Wallace had ardently advocated civil rights, and during the 1960s, had voted to desegregate Southern schools. Now that the shoe was passing to the Northern foot and Federal judges were citing Northern school systems for de jure segregation, the "chickens" were coming home to roost, as Sen. Stennis had long predicted.

For Sen. McGovern, "school busing and redistricting as ordered by the federal courts are among the prices we are paying for a century of segregation in our housing patterns."[5] As with Muskie, he knew that a "wrong" had to be "righted," and while sympathizing with parents who opposed busing, McGovern would not discard busing as a necessary tool in the integration of the school systems. "For 50 years," he continued, "we have been busing white and black children out of their neighborhoods to attend other schools in order to preserve the principle of segregation. Now the court has said we're going to use busing for a different purpose. . . . I think that is a concept worthy of our support."[6]

For Washington's Senator Henry Jackson, the answer to busing had all the complexity of Churchill's "riddle wrapped in a mystery inside an enigma."[7] The only Democratic candidate professing a belief in civil rights to send his child to an integrated public school, Jackson nevertheless proclaimed his opposition to "massive busing for purposes of racial integration."[8] He rationalized his stand by arguing that blacks in his daughter's school had been "bused from a bad school to a good school." This he found acceptable, but not had it been the reverse, "from a good school to a bad school."[9] That all children could not be bused from "bad to good" did not apparently trouble the Senator. Instead of admitting that all children deserved not better, not worse, but equal treatment, he had concocted a constitutional amendment that would deny the Supreme Court school decisions beginning with *Brown*. It would have, in Jackson's words, prohibited "mandatory busing of children by declaring that every parent has the freedom of choice and the right to have his or her children attend their local neighborhood school."[10]

During the early weeks of 1972, the Jackson proposal represented but one of several antibusing suggestions then circulating in Washington. The idea with the widest support was an amendment proposed by Representative Norman F. Lent, a New York Republican from suburban Nassau County.

It read, "No public school student shall, because of his race, creed or color, be assigned to or required to attend a particular school."[11] Members of both houses of Congress found its simplicity appealing. Lent was no stranger to antibusing legislation. While still a state senator, he had won acclaim for authoring an antibusing measure (later declared unconstitutional) that helped him to defeat the liberal Democrat, the late Allard Lowenstein, in a 1970 race for the House. For all his experience, however, Lent had a blind spot about civil rights that prevented his understanding the implications of *Brown*. He was, in fact, an apostle of the "color-blind" school, which held that *Brown* was the harbinger of racial nondiscrimination, not racial equality. As Lent saw it, blacks and whites should enjoy free-choice, freedom to resegregate their children in neighborhood schools, as the Southerners had done. Naturally, their congressional spokesmen signed a discharge petition to get Lent's amendment out of the House Judiciary Committee. Of the 218 signatures needed to outflank Chairman Emanuel Celler, of Brooklyn, Lent had 134 in his pocket by mid-January and on January 25, 1972, House GOP leader Gerald Ford added his name, saying he did not usually sign discharge petitions "as a matter of principle," but this time he had "because of the extreme urgency of the question involved."[12]

Conceivably, Celler could still have stood his ground, but when Rules Committee Chairman William Colmer, the veteran Mississippi Democrat, threatened to use his parliamentary powers to bypass Judiciary, Celler promised to begin hearings on Lent's Amendment and other suggested plans commencing February 28.

About the same time, with his penchant for detecting the latest shift in antibusing winds, the President jumped into the fray. On February 12, he too announced interest in a constitutional amendment that would restrain the courts. Ostensibly seeking advice, Nixon called in seven senators and representatives, as well as Attorney General Mitchell, HEW Secretary Richardson, Budget Director George Shultz, and chief domestic adviser, John Ehrlichman. Mincing no words, the President declared, "We don't need to spend a lot of time selling each other the case against busing. I am against busing for the purpose of achieving racial balance, and I know you are. The question is: What do you do about it?"[13] Senator Howard Baker responded with three alternative suggestions: let the Justice Department intervene against busing; let the White House support legislation to counter extensive busing; let the Administration take the lead in adopting a constitutional amendment to prohibit racial-balance busing. "I hate to see a cannon used to shoot a gnat," Baker added, referring to the final proposal, "but it may be necessary if all else fails."[14] During the verbal interplay, Nixon took notes on the back of an envelope, then pounding the Cabinet Room conference table with his fist, he vowed action. "I'm not going to leave the situation as it is," without revealing what he intended to do.

About to leave on his initial trip to China, he asked that "option papers" be prepared for review upon his return.[15]

From the start, the possibility of adding an antibusing amendment to the Constitution did not appear bright. Although his advisers put together something to curb the courts and prevent "rolling back 17 years of desegregation already achieved,"[16] the result was said to be unbelievably massive, "almost as long as the Constitution itself."[17] "There is no way," observed Yale Law Professor Alexander Bickel, viewing the effort, "to fine tune a constitutional amendment to deal solely with busing. It is beyond the wit of the most articulate draftsman and it trivializes the Constitution."[18] Top figures in the Administration agreed. Vice-President Agnew opposed an amendment because "it fuzzes and obfuscates the entire issue."[19] Secretary Richardson, while acknowledging that "excessive" busing existed in some areas,[20] still felt a corrective amendment would undermine the progress in desegregation that had taken place. In that he was joined by Attorney General Mitchell who let it be known that he, too, was opposed to an antibusing amendment. Not only was it a matter of finding appropriate language, but the amendment process (two-thirds affirmative votes in the House and Senate and the approval of three-fourths of the state legislatures) seemed insurmountable. In the Senate, Walter Mondale, the Minnesota Democrat, was certain to mount a lengthy filibuster, and Republican Charles Percy, of Illinois, had promised to join in "as long as there's breath left in my body," and as Edward A. Behr, of the *Wall Street Journal*, commented, "Senator Percy's wind is excellent."[21]

Opposition to busing in the House, however, was so strong, an amendment might muster the necessary support. When the Judiciary hearings opened, both Celler and William M. McCulloch, of Ohio, the ranking Republican, sought to calm angry demands for immediate action. McCulloch said disarmingly:

Never before to my knowledge have we amended the Constitution to change a practice which is itself only temporary. A social issue of such great controversy as this cannot be illuminated by statements of opposition to "unnecessary" busing or busing to "overcome racial imbalance." Such statements create the impression that Federal judges are arbitrarily ordering massive, crosstown busing without any justification other than [that] the racial composition of a particular public school does not reflect the racial composition of the entire school system.

But the truth is that every court order operating today is predicated on a finding that the Constitution has been violated by agents of the state, discriminating on the basis of race. In view of the facts, such statements are highly inflammatory and most irresponsible.[22]

Had the occasion been less explosive, McCulloch's words might have quieted the uproar, but bent on cuffing an unpopular idea as the opponents were, nothing could stop them. "More than 11,000 children are bused solely to achieve court-ordered racial balance in my hometown of Winston-Salem," angrily charged Republican Wilmer D. Mizell, of North Carolina.[23] Lent argued the proposition that court orders that required extensive busing were making a "shambles of the nation's public school system,"[24] a charge that so infuriated Father Hesburgh, U.S. Civil Rights Commission head, he accused the New Yorker of supporting a "fundamentally antiblack" amendment.[25] The real question, he told the Judiciary Committee, was ". . . whether we are going to give minority citizens an opportunity to learn, to earn and to live at the same level as the rest of society, or whether we are going to forget about the future of generations of minority children."[26]

In the midst of the Celler hearings, the antibusing motif suddenly shifted to the South. In Augusta, Georgia, hundreds of white parents organized a boycott to protest a court order integrating the county's sixty public schools. As busing began, more than 19,000 of 36,000 pupils stayed away. "The white people don't want to send their children into any Negro neighborhood," stated the sixty-four-year-old superintendent. The court order "stinks. It is a filthy shame, hauling children back and forth just to force them to sit together."[27] His animosity was shared by Jimmy Carter, then the Peach State's Governor. Despite his vaunted reputation as a member of the avant-garde of Southern liberalism (on being inaugurated, he declared, "I say to you that the time of segregation is over"[28]), he announced he would show his sympathy for the people of Augusta by supporting a one-day statewide school boycott unless Georgia legislators enacted a resolution calling for an antibusing constitutional amendment.

In contrast, Florida's Reubin Askew remained remarkably courageous in the face of similar antiblack outbursts. The Governor fought openly to turn back such a constitutional bar to busing. He promised friends to act "as forcefully as I know how," because "many Southerners and many Northerners, too, had been deluded into thinking a retreat from desegregation was possible or that the goals of a just and equal society could be abandoned once the transition got rough."[29]

Askew was the youngest of six children, reared in poverty by a mother who eked out a living as housekeeper in a Pensacola hotel. In his first year at the state house, the forty-three-year-old Democrat had fought the special interests that up to then had controlled the state. He said he would increase the tax on their corporate profits and as soon as the Askew-supported measure became law, General Motors found itself charged $2.4 million instead of the paltry $1,500 it previously paid annually.

No high official in Florida's history had appointed so many blacks to influential posts in state government. "We've got to break the cycle of black poverty," he declared emphatically. "We can't afford to isolate and not utilize 12 percent of our people. No large corporation would do it."[30] Accordingly, he placed blacks for the first time on professional examining and licensing boards. One of his appointees was the first black to sit on a court of superior jurisdiction. In addition, he appointed blacks to head the socially sensitive Department of Community Affairs and the State Division of the Office of Economic Opportunity.

Largely because of Askew's activity and Nixon's Southern Strategy, Florida became the natural platform to air the busing controversy in the spring of the 1972 presidential race. Five weeks prior to the March 14th election, Republican members of the state legislature pushed through a measure to query voters on the question: "Do you favor an amendment to the U.S. Constitution that would prohibit forced busing and guarantee the right of each student to attend the appropriate public school nearest his home?"[31] Since the Governor had always stood for the public's right to vote on any issue, including a straw ballot, he could not refuse to go along. Before signing the measure, however, Askew did force his legislative adversaries to ask a second question: "Do you favor providing an equal opportunity for quality education for all children regardless of race, creed, color or place of residence and oppose a return to a dual system of public schools?"[32] This, he hoped, would show that although Floridians opposed busing for racial purposes, they opposed a return to the dual school system, too.

In so doing, not only did Askew leap into the middle of the primary, he became, after Wallace, the chief figure in the campaign, and in reality the Alabaman's chief opponent. Additionally, as a Southerner, he was the only one who could lecture white Floridians on the iniquity of their ways. "We cannot achieve," he said with Lincolnesque directness, "equal opportunity in education by passing laws or constitutional amendments against bus-ing—they could deny us what I believe is the highest destiny of the American people. That destiny, of course, is to achieve a society in which all races, all creeds and all religions have learned not only to live with their differences—but to thrive upon them. No other civilization has learned to do that. But we can. And we must"[33]

To persuade the voters, the Governor raised $25,000 to pay for a series of television programs, designed especially to rally support among Florida's 1.1 million blacks. Unfortunately for Askew, although most blacks considered busing "absolutely essential" to desegregation of the schools,[34] they demonstrated, according to Marvin Davies, NAACP's top state official, little interest in the outcome of the primary. Nevertheless, the Governor struggled on, admitting all the while that the "yes" vote on the antibusing straw poll would exceed 90 percent. Against the prediction of one Northern Democratic governor that the campaign would kill Askew politically, he professed indifference.

In the end, nothing could hold back the avalanche of antibusing. For twenty-nine days, before crowds numbering 1,000 to 10,000, George Wallace hammered away at busing, telling Floridians "they were being screwed by pointy-heads in Washington and New York."[35] Quickly, it became a question of not who would win, but by how much. In a Jacksonville shipyard, political reporter Richard Reeves overheard two pipe fitters discussing Wallace's chances. "He's got 90 percent of the vote in this yard," said one. "That's crap," said the other, "he ain't got more than 75 percent."[36]

Seemingly unconcerned by the signs, Mayor John Lindsay of New York City, spent a half million dollars to spread the liberal creed. According to editors of the *Miami Herald*, he told voters "things that no serious candidate for public life had told them in a hundred years. He endorses 'the progressive income tax' so easily that it almost seems he is unaware of the hysteria Florida politicians engage in whenever the subject comes up."[37]

Wanting to avoid the busing entanglement, Hubert Humphrey sought the high road and came down heavily on conservation. "You cannot take from the land, the water and the air," he proclaimed, "unless you return that land, that water and that air to its original source, unpolluted, uncontaminated and unscarred."[38] Shortly after the Senator delivered this homily to about one hundred people gathered at a seafood festival and his caravan had disappeared around a corner, the ever-watchful Reeves saw Humphrey's Brevard County coordinator throw her seafood platter out the car window. "The paper plate, napkins, plastic fork and spoon and ketchup at the foot of a palm tree," he wrote, "could have been the official symbol of the 1972 Florida primary."[39] Except for the lonely pleading of Governor Askew, the judgement was valid. Askew's voice, like the biblical prophets of old, rang clear and true, but like theirs, fell on deaf ears.

When the votes were tallied, Wallace had won a smashing victory, capturing seventy-five of the state's eighty-one Democratic delegates. Although the other ten contestants spent $3 million to defeat him, the Alabaman had twice as many votes as Humphrey, who won the remaining six convention delegates; he had three times Jackson's total, four times Muskie's, five times Lindsay's, and six times McGovern's.

No one could mistake the public's mood. Although the school busing ban carried 3 to 1, Floridians had done as Askew predicted. They had voted in even greater strength for quality education regardless of race. To Askew this meant that "Florida is not a racist state:" in fact, he wondered whether the result might even be the "high point" of the antibusing fervor if only President Nixon would now lead the nation "into an arena where the problem can be solved."[40]

Askew overestimated the man in the White House. The President was too dichotomous to land on the unpopular side of a vote-laden issue. He had spent a long weekend at Camp David just prior to the Florida primary working over a new position paper on school busing, which he promised to reveal in a nationwide radio and television broadcast. His options varied little from those two years before when he issued an 8,000-word statement on school desegregation. Then, as now, Nixon asked top Administration figures whether they favored congressional action or a constitutional amendment to interdict busing. In 1970, William Rehnquist, then a powerful force at Justice, advocated the amendment route. More stridently, the President's speech writer, Patrick J. Buchanan, argued that Nixon should veto "compulsory integration anywhere in the country. . . . there will be blood in the streets," he warned, if Northern suburban kids are bused into central city schools. "The second era of Reconstruction is over; the ship of Integration is going down; it is not our ship, it belongs to national liberalism—and we cannot salvage it; and we ought not to be aboard."[41]

An instinct for the middle road kept Nixon from adopting either Rehnquist's or Buchanan's advice. Instead, he decided to elaborate on his February statement to the press of opposition to "busing for the purpose of racial balance."[42]

On the evening of March 16, he equated busing with racial balance no less than four times during a twelve-minute address, using such expressions as "busing for the purpose of achieving racial balance in our schools" and "massive busing to achieve racial balance." To turn back the clock, he proposed a congressional "moratorium" on the Federal courts in order to halt further attempts to achieve "racial balance."[43]

This call to restrain the judiciary flew in the face of the President's progress in reshaping its philosophy. He had already appointed four Supreme Court justices, plus 161 judges to the lower Federal courts, all presumably carrying his stamp of approval.[44] To excoriate the judiciary, as Nixon now appeared intent on doing, could only undermine the system. As the *New Yorker* magazine commented, "Now that the courts have carried out the responsibility that President Nixon thrust upon them, he has attacked them for doing their duty, and has thereby intimated to the people that an unpopular law—in this instance a law that he, more than anyone else, made unpopular—can be got around. That kind of suggestion, whatever the political profit to be derived from it, can only damage the country. If legislation is enacted to stop busing and then judicially overturned, the public wrath against the courts, which is threatening as it is, may get out of hand. And if that should happen, the federal judicial system could be altered practically overnight."[45]

Despite this, the President wanted court jurisdiction narrowed. "There are many," he said in his televised message, "who believe that a constitutional amendment is the only way to deal with this problem." As an answer to the immediate problem of stopping more busing now, "the constitutional amendment approach has a fatal flaw—it takes too long." Consequently, he announced he would ask the Congress both to place a "moratorium" on the courts and appropriate $2.5 billion for an Equal Opportunities measure to aid disadvantaged children in the inner city.[46]

The specifics emerged the next day when the two measures were delivered to Capitol Hill. As part of their future school rulings, courts would be required to follow a list of priorities in handing down opinions on school desegregation. If the first priority failed, the second would trigger and so on down the list, much like the soldier retreating from one previously prepared position to another, defensible but offering less cover. The most favored solution was the neighborhood school, then came pairing of blacks and whites, next school clusters, new construction, and educational parks. Only as a last resort could busing be ordered and then only for grades nine to twelve. Seen in its entirety, it was, as *New York Times* reporter Robert R. Semple, Jr., described it, "yet another Presidential commitment to the 'principle' of desegregation and yet another Presidential rejection of the available means—in this case, busing—to reach the objective."[47]

As in 1970, Nixon attempted to stifle opposition by offering to spend $2.5 billion for "compensatory education" regardless of mounting evidence that challenged the efficacy of such largesse. Even the President's own Commission for School Finance had written the previous December that "virtually without exception, all of the large surveys of the large national compensatory education programs have shown no beneficial results on average."[48]

The Nixon message, nevertheless, had a shattering effect on the Democratic presidential candidates, Wallace excepted. They were hoping, with Florida behind them, that the issue would die. Yet, here was the President demanding action and dumping the problem back in their laps. Humphrey became so piqued, he blurted out, "Thank goodness that at long last the President has been able to get his finger up in the air and sense what's going on and has decided that he would say amen to some of the things that some of the rest of us have been trying to do."[49] Coming from the Minnesotan, the retort seemed so out of character that after several days, friends persuaded him to retract the statement.

On Capitol Hill, questions immediately arose over the constitutionality of the Nixon program. Did Congress have the authority to prescribe rules and regulations for the judiciary? Acting Attorney General Richard G. Kleindienst declared there was "no legitimate doubt whatsoever," that Article III, Section 2 of the Constitution gave Congress power to regulate the Supreme Court's appellate jurisdiction, and Section V of the Fourteenth Amendment gave Congress authority to interpret its provisions with appropriate legislation.[50] However, such assurances failed to calm the opposition, among them NAACP's Clarence Mitchell, who threatened to challenge its enactment in the courts "before the ink is dry."[51]

When HEW Secretary Richardson attempted to defend the President's views before the Senate Education and Labor Committee, he encountered strenuous opposition. New York's Javits attacked the need for a moratorium, drawing from the Secretary an admission that from 1969 to 1971, when school desegregation rose impressively, the percentage of public school children who were bused increased only 42 to 44 percent, a jump of 500,000[52]—and not all that was due to school desegregation. As the hearings dragged on, testimony became embarrassingly one-sided and apart from Richardson, only Roy Ennis, of CORE, spoke favorably, and then only from a desire to get Federal funds to equip all-black schools controlled by blacks.

While unrest over busing continued, tragedy unexpectedly befell George Wallace. While campaigning in Laurel, Maryland, he was critically wounded on May 15, shot by a demented twenty-one-year-old Milwaukee resident, Arthur Bremer. The attempted assassination occurred at a time when Wallace was gaining steadily. On the day following the shooting, he captured his first Northern state, soundly trouncing McGovern and Humphrey in Michigan, the former two-to-one and the latter three-to-one. Although the Governor insisted on remaining in the race, despite paralysis in both legs, the public knew he was no longer a viable candidate, as did the man in the White House. Temporarily, busing lost its sting.

By the time the Democratic convention opened in Miami Beach in mid-July, the platform committee refused to follow Wallace's plea for a strong plank against busing. Instead, it stated the controversial fact that busing was "one of several tools for desegregation" which "must continue to be available according to Supreme Court decisions. . . ."[53]

Not wishing to be tarred with this moderate statement, the House leadership fired its own antibusing sentiment in mid-August by voting 282 to 102 to bar the judiciary from ordering long-distance busing to balance racial differences, in keeping with the President's March proposals.

Two weeks later, on September 6, Sen. Allen, an Alabama Democrat, succeeded in placing the House's antibusing measure on the calendar and within a month it reached the floor. There a combination of liberal senators joined in filibustering. Three times it came to a vote on cloture, on October 10, 11, and 12, and each time Allen was turned back. With the final tally, Nixon's 1972 effort to hobble the courts ended.

Meanwhile, sensing there might be a political advantage in adopting a sterner antibusing stance than the Democratic delegates had, Republicans gathering in Miami Beach approved a plank that was even stronger than the White House advocated. It proclaimed that in the event Congress failed to pass appropriate legislation, the people should press for a constitutional amendment to outlaw busing as a method of achieving school desegregation.

In November, Nixon swamped George McGovern, the liberal Democratic nominee, and in a post-election interview, promised his continued opposition to busing when used to overcome racial imbalances.

Notes

1. *Newsweek*, February 28, 1972, p. 15.
2. *Time*, August 23, 1971, pp. 10-11.

3. *Newsweek*, August 23, 1971, p. 21.

4. John Herbers, "School Busing . . . ," *New York Times*, October 3, 1971.

5. "How the Candidates Stand on Busing," *Life*, March 3, 1972.

6. *U.S. News and World Report*, February 28, 1972, p. 27.

7. Winston Spencer Churchill, broadcast, October 1, 1939.

8. Stewart Alsop, "I'm Gonna Shake Their Eyeteeth Out," *Newsweek*, February 7, 1972, p. 80.

9. Ibid.

10. *New York Times*, February 15, 1972.

11. *New York Times*, January 26, 1972.

12. Ibid.

13. *Newsweek*, February 28, 1972.

14. Ibid.

15. Ibid.

16. Robert B. Semple, Jr., "President Leaves . . . ," *New York Times*, February 21, 1972.

17. Ibid.

18. "The Busing Issue Boils Over," *Time*, February 28, 1972.

19. *New York Times*, February 15, 1972.

20. *New York Times*, February 17, 1972.

21. Edward A. Behr, "Politics and Race," *Wall Street Journal*, February 23, 1972.

22. John Herbers, "Rift on Busing . . . ," *New York Times*, February 29, 1972.

23. Ibid.

24. John Herbers, "Hesburgh Warns . . . ," *New York Times*, March 2, 1972.

25. Ibid.

26. Ibid.

27. Jon Nordheimer, "Gov. Carter . . . ," *New York Times*, February 17, 1972.

28. Jon Nordheimer, "A Man to Watch," *New York Times*, March 5, 1972.

29. Ibid.

30. Ibid.

31. Tom Wicker, "To Bus or Not To Bus," *New York Times*, February 17, 1972.

32. Jon Nordheimer, "Busing on Florida Ballot . . . ," *New York Times*, February 17, 1977.

33. Nordheimer, "A Man to Watch."

34. Martin Waldron, "Busing Held Key Issue . . . ," *New York Times*, March 3, 1972.

35. Richard Reeves, "Eleven Alligators in Florida's Political Swamp," *New York Times*, March 12, 1972, p. 106.

36. Ibid.

37. Ibid.

38. Ibid.

39. Ibid.

40. Douglas Robinson, "Busing Ban Wins . . . ," *New York Times*, March 15, 1972.

41. Patrick J. Buchanan, "Memorandum to the President," *Harper's*, June, 1972.

42. John Herbers, "President Orders a Study . . . ," *New York Times*, February 11, 1972.

43. "Transcript of Nixon's Statement on School Busing," *New York Times*, March 17, 1972, p. 22.

44. John Herbers, "Nixon Busing Curb . . . ," *New York Times*, March 25, 1972.

45. "The Talk of the Town," *New Yorker*, March 11, 1972.

46. "Transcript of Nixon's Statement."

47. Robert B. Semple, Jr., "Busing—A Plan by Nixon . . . ," *New York Times*, March 19, 1972.

48. John Herbers, "Basis of Nixon Pupil Aid Shift Doubted," *New York Times*, March 24, 1972.

49. Marjorie Hunter, "Nixon's Plans Splits Rivals . . . ," *New York Times*, March 18, 1972.

50. John Herbers, "President Seeks Permanent Curb . . . ," *New York Times*, March 18, 1972.

51. *New York Times*, March 29, 1972.

52. Herbers, "Nixon Busing Curb."

53. *New York Times*, July 13, 1972.

16

UNBELIEVABLE FERNDALE

"The people here just can't believe the area in which they've lived most of their lives can be described as racially discriminatory."

John J. Houghton, Ferndale School Superintendent.[1]

In the long and devious history of school desegregation, Ferndale, Michigan, stands out as *the* example of a Northern community evading the provisions of Title VI of the 1964 Civil Rights Act. Situated eight miles northwest of Detroit, Ferndale is a predominantly white suburban community of 25,000 persons. Employees of the Ford Motor Company's Highland Park plant founded it in the early years of the twentieth century, and built for themselves modest homes of wood and brick. From its incorporation in 1918 as a village, Ferndale evidenced more than once remarkable civic pride. Strict zoning ordinances confined industry to one area, retail stores to another. Seven major parks provided recreational space. In 1954, a bond issue of $300,000 built a library and three years later, Ferndale constructed a new high school costing $6.5 million.

The idyll, such as it was, ended in 1968. That fall white residents were infuriated to learn that Federal investigators from HEW, after examining school records, had charged the Ferndale system with racial discrimination. "The people here just can't believe the area in which they've lived most of their lives can be described as racially discriminatory," agonized John J. Houghton, a fifty-year resident, who had been successively teacher, principal, and superintendent.[2] The source of the charge was the all-black Ulysses S. Grant Elementary School, situated in the all-black Royal Oak Township, a tiny three-quarter square mile enclave within the Ferndale School District.

The township had been settled in 1921 by Southern blacks coming North in search of work who then bought property in Royal Oak from the wealthy board chairman of the Detroit Urban League. A second wave that rolled in during World War II lived in hastily erected barracks, courtesy of Uncle

Sam, and while hostilities lasted, gave the area an air of prosperity. Once that tap closed, "Little Egypt," as it was known, became nothing more than a "dreary row of boarded windows, shut theatres, broken down bars and burned-out buildings."[3] By 1959, a survey of Oakland County's sixty-one municipalities listed Royal Oak Township as the most overcrowded with the worst economic conditions. In advocating immediate Federal and state aid, the report labelled such assistance as necessary to end the "deprivation, frustration, discontent and low self-esteem."[4] These two communities— Ferndale and the Royal Oak Township—one white, one black, one prosperous, one depressed, existed cheek by jowl, yet remained wholly separate culturally and economically. Presumably, an isolated black community posed no threat to white dominance, and the blacks were, as Ralph Ellison's hero found out, largely "invisible."[5] After more than four decades of eremitic living, residents of Ferndale had no desire to change their ways, especially when the secondary school grades were integrated. What did it matter that one elementary school should be all-black?

Indeed, Ferndale residents, for the most part, had forgotten the history of the Grant Elementary School. Back in the summer of 1925, after Dr. Ossian Sweet, of Detroit, a black physician, moved into a white neighborhood, racial warfare erupted. A mob of more than 400 stone-throwing whites menaced a dozen blacks holed up in the Sweet home. In the melee, one white was shot to death, unloosing a torrent of racism, topped off with cross burnings by the Ku Klux Klan. One month after the Sweet incident, the Ferndale school district decided to build a new elementary school in Royal Oak, although a mere four blocks away stood Jefferson Elementary, erected the previous year and still unfilled. Following the construction of Grant, black pupils from Jefferson were transferred, making Jefferson all white and Grant all black. Despite the record, Ferndale school authorities maintained that residents of Royal Oak "begged" the board to build a school in the neighborhood. "We didn't give a damn about race," declared octogenarian William Norton, president at the time the decision had been made. "Color was never a question, but getting schools built for children was."[6]

To back up his assertion of gratuitous meddling by HEW, Houghton claimed to be making extraordinary efforts to improve the quality of education for black youngsters. "Grant now has a 17.2-1 pupil teacher ratio," he said, "while the other nine elementary schools have a 27-1 ratio."[7] Nevertheless, the Department stuck by its charge of segregation. Grant had 315 students, *all* of them black. Of the remaining elementary schools, three were all-white; two contained one black each; two, three blacks each; one had five; and one, ten. Moreover, HEW attorneys cited "circumstantial evidence" of the school board's bias. Back in the 1930s, construction of a swimming pool at the former Lincoln High School had been halted because of community objections to black and white students swimming together. Furthermore, up to 1964, Grant had black teachers only. "We raise these issues," one HEW attorney explained to Burton R. Shifman, attorney for the Ferndale Board, in the course of an informal hearing in Washington, "because you give the impression that Ferndale is the greatest integrated district in the world."[8] After Shifman objected by saying that he had "gone through the recollections of hundreds of people" and had heard no one state that Grant "was built for purposes of segregating black students," the former went on, "I don't disagree with you that every action in this case can be interpreted one way or the other," but taken together, they "point to one conclusion—that discrimination was intended."[9]

Despite the weight of the evidence, twenty-two months passed before HEW finally on September 28, 1970, found Ferndale guilty of violating Title VI. It was the first Northern school system to be so cited. In a fifty-seven-page opinion, HEW recommended the elimination of Federal funds amounting to $265,000. The government claimed that Grant had been built to segregate black students and was simply the "Negro annex" of nearby Jefferson school.[10] Had Ferndale simply submitted an acceptable plan to desegregate the school, no doubt HEW would have vacated its citation, but the school board, feeling itself unfairly treated, grew stubborn. "We have no plan," admitted Houghton, "because we think we can win this, and we'll do everything in our power to do so."[11]

Likewise, this decision reflected the prevalent white mood. In the spring of 1968, just months before HEW acted, Ferndale tried vainly to form a committee to study the district's racial isolation. No one volunteered to head the survey. A year later trouble began at Ferndale High School when 138 black students demonstrated to make the curriculum more black-oriented and the faculty more representative of blacks. They demanded a course in black history and black literature and pointed to the fact that the school had no black student counselors, that all eight coaches were white, and that only three of the school's 115 teachers were black. For their efforts, all 138 were suspended.

Three months after the HEW citation, in December, 1970, black students again revolted. This time the controversy involved a black social studies teacher whom the board denied tenure. When the National Youth Alliance, a right-wing organization, used the occasion to circulate hate literature in the high school, urging "white students to unite against the blacks," violence erupted.[12] Two teachers and eleven students suffered minor injuries in the outbreak. Of the 200 students involved, seventeen black and nine white students were suspended.

With feelings running high, black parents sought an open forum to air their grievances. Through Holbert Maxey, Executive Director of the Royal Oak Township Community Relations Council, they informed a tense crowd of more than 600 black and white parents, jammed into the junior high gymnasium, that culpability for the riot should be thoroughly investigated, that suspended students should be immediately reinstated, and that greater police protection should be provided at the school in the future. For once, the board, responding to this goad, acted impressively: within a month the high school principal and three assistant principals had been fired.

However, punitive actions would no longer stifle the discord. Ferndale High had hardly opened its doors the following September when racial violence again broke out. After twelve hours of rioting, classes were closed and a curfew imposed. Fifty police from five neighboring communities had to be called in to disperse an unruly crowd of black and white students. As before, fear permeated the community, one nearby resident even standing guard on his lawn with raised shotgun. At first, the board ordered the school closed indefinitely, then four days later, the members reversed themselves.

Unfortunately, the ease with which the board changed course did not extend to its dealings with HEW. Nothing could make its members order the desegregation of Grant, not even the threat of Federal retaliation. Finally, on April 19, 1972—twenty-nine months after HEW's initial investigation—the government acted. Secretary Richardson announced that within thirty days the district would lose its Federal assistance. However, the Secretary seemed almost apologetic. "Every effort has been made to obtain compliance by voluntary means," he said in dulcet words, "but there was no alternative."[13] Even that soft answer could not contain the board's wrath, and with the majority vowing to remain firm, Superintendent Houghton declared with apparent pride, "Ours is not a radically discriminatory district."[14]

For the first time, however, in light of HEW's action, some board members dissented, saying Grant should be integrated. Their apprehensions were confirmed when William Waterman, NAACP counsel, threatened to bring suit against Ferndale, citing the board and HEW which, taking its cue from the President, was now saying it would not cut off funds if desegregation involved busing. Since the board doubted whether Grant could be integrated without busing, it hoped to have time to vindicate its position.

What gave Waterman's threat special sustenance was his allegation that a cut-off "primarily hurts black kids."[15] Severance of the remedial reading project, for instance, would apply to 617 students, 30 percent black, and withdrawal of the headstart plan would affect sixty students, 68 percent black, in a total school population, 10 percent black.

In its quest for relief, the board decided to ask its congressional representative, William Broomfield, a Royal Oak Republican, to intercede with Secretary Richardson. While the latter preferred the velvet glove, the law being the law, he rejected the appeal.

Thus rebuffed, the board now appealed HEW's order to the Sixth Circuit Court of Appeals in Cincinnati, forcing Justice to file a brief in the government's behalf. "There was ample evidence showing," wrote Justice, "that the [school] board in designing the size, location, and attendance area for Grant was aware of the segregatory effect its decision would have. Even when Grant became seriously overcrowded, the school district would not transfer students to the near-by, all-white Jefferson school, which had ample room. Today, the school district still refused to take steps to desegregate Grant even though such action would not require busing of students." The government by carefully avoiding the de jure-de facto argument, contended that Grant furnished an example of the former and was, therefore, illegal. It did not, the brief maintained, "seek relief from racial imbalance caused by other forces," notably neighborhood housing patterns.[16] Arguments took place on February 14, 1973, and three weeks later, the court upheld HEW.

Still, the Ferndale board refused to bow. By a 4 to 2 margin, it voted to appeal the decision to the U.S. Supreme Court. One dissenter, the board's only black member, vainly called on the board to do its duty "to uphold the law of the land."[17] The majority reasoned that to suggest a plan for desegregation would be an admission of guilt, an inadmissible concession. Besides, loyalty to a majority of their constituents seemed to outweigh allegiance to a government of laws. "I am concerned about what will happen when we tell people to take their children out of one school and put them in another," said one worried member. "You could still have a riot here. I'd hate to think I did anything to bring that about."[18] A second argued, "I don't agree with what the Sixth Circuit Court decided. This is the only way to protect the wishes of the majority of the people. HEW is only worried about socio-economics. As far as I'm concerned they can take their money and bag it. HEW doesn't give a damn about our education. I am tired of liberals telling me that they are talking for the whole community. They are only a small part of the community."[19]

So an appeal went forward, and five months later—nearly five years after the original citation—the Supreme Court denied Ferndale's petition and in a way that must have galled the recalcitrants, offered no explanation. The board by then had spent more than $60,000 in legal fees in a fruitless effort to avoid the law. As though this meant nothing, the board proceeded to vote 4 to 3 to petition the Supreme Court a second time, and again was turned down.

Three months following the rejection, the board grudgingly offered parents a choice of sending their children to segregated Grant or to any one of the nine other elementary white schools. At that, the author of the change, the Reverend Joseph E. Biscoe, was severely criticized by one resident in the audience blurting out, "You invade our community as a minister and come to our churches to speak and invite blacks to sing in your church, but you are a hypocritical racist."[20] Whatever emollient Biscoe hoped to add, it was naive to think Ferndale white parents would volunteer to put their children in an all-black school. After six years of argument and controversy, the situation at Grant was shifting rapidly. Because it operated at 45 percent of capacity, Grant was now the most expensive school in the district, and in one board member's words "was being set up to be closed."[21] A survey of 3,400 homes, authorized by the board, revealed that no white students had volunteered to attend Grant and only two black students wished to enter a white elementary school.[22]

In January, 1975, seventy-four months after HEW initially cited Ferndale, a new wrinkle creased the impasse. The Office of Revenue Sharing in Washington threatened to cut off Michigan's share of Federal largesse, estimated at $90 million, unless Ferndale stopped operating a segregated school system. The government noted that the state placed a portion of its Federal allotment in a pension fund for retired teachers. Since Ferndale benefited, the state had directly violated the Revenue Sharing Act of 1972 which prohibited payment to any unit that discriminated. In announcing the ultimatum, ORS Director Graham W. Watt declared, "I see no alternative to the state taking action to terminate the discrimination by the school district."[23]

At that point, hobbled by pressures from the state as well as confrontations with HEW and Justice, the board sought a meeting with the latter to discuss Grant's problems, taking even this tentative step with serious misgivings. One board member decided to resign and accused the others of "selling out the children of the district." Another member hoped the entire board "would resign" if the government forced Ferndale to bus students to achieve integration.[24] Nonetheless, the board did finally submit four proposals to the Justice Department, all of them voluntary free-choice plans which the Supreme Court had outlawed seven years before in *Green*.[25] We "reject the concept of involuntarily moving bodies by race where it would not contribute to the improved education of the children," they said in way of explanation.[26] It took only two weeks for Justice to say "no," that in its experience, proposals like Ferndale's did not "work,"[27] and forthwith announced its intent to file suit against Ferndale.

The board responded to the latest governmental move by asking Representative James Blanchard, a Democrat, who now represented Ferndale in the House, to seek an intercession from President Ford, who had replaced Nixon upon the latter's resignation. Although Operation White House failed, Blanchard did succeed in closeting himself for seventy-five minutes with Edward H. Levi, the newly appointed Attorney General. Levi made no promises except to say no suit would be filed without his prior approval, and even this seeming delay vanished when Justice filed suit against Ferndale and the state of Michigan on May 22, 1975. When the case came before Federal District Judge Cornelia Kennedy, of Detroit, she dismissed the charge on the ground that the 1974 Equal Educational Opportunity Act required the plaintiff in such cases to be an aggrieved individual and Justice had merely written in the "United States of America."[28]

Without an adverse ruling, the board could undertake its own desegregation plan which consisted of busing 169 white and 32 black children to special classes at Grant. Unaccountably and contrary to its previous adamancy, the board had now purchased two buses to implement the plan at a cost of approximately $30,000.

Again, Justice appealed, this time to the U.S. Circuit Court of Appeals, asking an expedited hearing. Two months passed and the court agreed to review the Kennedy decision. This time, to obviate any misunderstanding, Levi certified that he had received "a complaint in writing signed by parents of minor children alleging [they] are being deprived of equal protection of the law."[29] School officials wanted to learn the names of the accusers so that, as the superintendent said, "we can try to rectify their particular problem,"[30] but Federal officials held back the names under the guarantees of a statute passed in the late 1960s which protected the identity of black parents in the South.

Not until May 17, 1978—now nine and one-half years after the case was opened—did the Sixth Circuit finally order Judge Kennedy to reopen the case and conduct a trial within sixty days. The higher court ruled that she had wrongfully dismissed the government's allegations. "Every effort should be made to resolve the issues in this case prior to the commencement of the 1979-80 school year," the appeal judges declared.[31]

On September 13, Judge Kennedy demonstrated her disregard for the appeals court opinion by finding the Ferndale school board not guilty of intentional segregation of black pupils in the Grant School. Stated the jurist: "Segregated housing patterns . . . were responsible."[32] Jubilantly, board attorney Shifman termed the decision a "vindication," adding, "The U.S. Justice Department was just looking for a Northern guinea pig. This was a classic case of government overkill."[33]

Again, the Sixth Circuit disagreed. Sixteen months later, a three-member panel ordered Ferndale to submit a plan "to accomplish wiping out the vestiges of segregation . . . —root and branch," thereby reversing Judge Kennedy who was by now a member of the appeals court and took no part in the decision.[34]

Still, the board was adamant. It voted to petition for a rehearing, and to apply once more to the U.S. Supreme Court if turned down by the Sixth Circuit. Only Shifman's estimate of $120,000 in legal fees and trial expenses plus the realization that Ferndale had now lost $3 million in Federal funds convinced the board to reverse itself.

In May, 1980, the board voted to submit another plan to Justice, but after eleven and one-half years of litigation, it again refused to endorse a mandatory scheme, preferring a voluntary solution and hoping it would get the court's approval.

Again, the court intervened. Federal District Judge Horace W. Gilmore, of Detroit, rejected the board's action. Busing black students from Grant, as contemplated, would result in "one-way busing," Gilmore declared, placing "all the burden for integration on the blacks . . . and none on the district's white students."[35]

The court ordered the school to submit a new integration plan by August 4. Thus goaded, school officials offered to bus 204 white students to Grant and transfer 180 blacks to other Ferndale elementary schools. While this proposal marked a departure from the board's previous intransigence, it failed to get the approval of either Iris Green, a Justice Department attorney assigned to the case, or William Waterman, the NAACP's Pontiac lawyer. Both believed the district's plan still placed a greater burden on black than white students.

Judge Gilmore agreed. On October 8, he ordered the Ferndale School District to follow a plan drawn up by D. William Gordon, a Miami University professor of education, who had helped with the preparation of eighty different school desegregation plans. Under Gordon's proposal (1) pupils in grades one through three from Grant (black), and Jefferson (white), and Taft (white) would attend Grant, and (2) Grant children in grades four to six would move either to Jefferson or Taft, and Jefferson and Taft students, grades four to six, would remain in place. An additional 300 youngsters would be bused in the exchange.

"We are relieved to get a final decision," glowed William G. Coyne, Ferndale's new superintendent. "[T]he community is going to make it work." And work it did as the community finally gave its assent. School officials enlisted the aid of the federally financed Program for Educational Opportunity, held workshops, appointed committees, and enlisted parental assistance. On January 5, 1981, "everything went super." Superintendent Coyne did not hear "a single protest" from a parent.[36] Parents had already offered their support, volunteering as "luggers or huggers," the former carrying material from building to building, the latter standing at the entrances to give "a familiar child a welcoming embrace."[37]

Thus ended more than twelve years of litigation at a cost to the Ferndale District of some $3 million in Federal aid.

Notes

1. *Detroit News*, April 20, 1969, p. 24-A.
2. Ibid.

3. Ibid.

4. Ibid.

5. Ralph Ellison, *Invisible Man*, (New York: The Modern Library, 1947).

6. *Detroit News*, May 24, 1972, p. 10-B.

7. *Detroit News*, April 20, 1969.

8. *Detroit News*, April 21, 1969, p. 4-A.

9. Ibid.

10. *Detroit News*, September 29, 1970.

11. Ibid.

12. *Detroit News*, February 23, 1971.

13. *Detroit News*, April 20, 1972, p. 3-A.

14. Ibid.

15. *Detroit Press*, April 23, 1972, p. 3-A.

16. *Detroit News*, December 9, 1972.

17. *Detroit News*, April 2, 1973, p. 3-B.

18. Ibid.

19. Ibid.

20. *Detroit News*, May 8, 1974, Section B.

21. Ibid.

22. *Detroit News*, June 5, 1974, Section B.

23. *Detroit News*, January 25, 1975.

24. *Detroit News*, February 4, 1975.

25. *Green* v. *Board of Education of New Kent County*, 391 U.S. 430 (1968).

26. *Detroit News*, February 11, 1975, p. 3-A.

27. *Detroit News*, February 25, 1975, p. 10-A.

28. *Detroit News*, July 4, 1975.

29. *Detroit News*, April 29, 1976.

30. *Detroit News*, May 5, 1976.

31. *Detroit News*, May 18, 1978.

32. *Detroit News*, September 14, 1978.

33. Ibid.

34. *Detroit News*, January 31, 1980.

35. *Detroit News*, July 18, 1980.

36. *Detroit News*, January 5, 1981.

37. *Detroit News*, December 7, 1980.

17

BRADLEY v. MILLIKEN

Roth "should be crated up and shipped back" to Hungary.

Orville L. Hubbard, Mayor of Dearborn.[1]

Since the early twentieth century, the capital of America's automobile industry has been Detroit and its environs. Like a gigantic magnet, the community attracted thousands of job-seeking workers and their families from all parts of the U.S. and from abroad. During World Wars I and II, Southern blacks and whites from Appalachia, eager to earn the inflated wages, joined the march. Predictably, the resulting racial mix was extremely volatile and in 1943 exploded. Thirty-four persons died in a riot described as the "bloodiest in the United States in a span of two decades."[2] It was, recalled George Edwards, Judge of the United States Court of Appeals for the Sixth Circuit, and Commissioner of the Detroit Police Department from 1961 to 1963, "open warfare between the Detroit Negroes and the Detroit Police Department."[3]

Describing this hostility in which white policemen acted as white surrogates, Edwards added that "although local police forces generally regard themselves as public servants with the responsibility of maintaining law and order, they tend to minimize this attitude when they are patrolling areas that are heavily populated with Negro citizens. There, they tend to view each person on the streets as a potential criminal or enemy and all too often that attitude is reciprocated."[4] His 1961 prediction that "Detroit was the leading candidate in the United States for a race riot,"[5] came true on July 22, 1967, when forty-three persons—thirty-three black and ten white—died in a confrontation that cost Detroiters $50 million in property damage.

As an antidote to these racial antagonisms, sporadic attempts were made to relieve tension. In the summer of 1962, a thirty-five-member Citizens Committee on Equal Education Opportunities, appointed by the Detroit Board of Education, asked that at least one black teacher be assigned to every school in the city. As black committee members and future Federal District Judge Damon J. Keith observed, it was time white children saw blacks as "something more than chauffeurs or domestics."[6] Although the committee failed to obtain pledges, the community did respond by electing a liberal majority to the school board in 1964. The board then hired an egalitarian superintendent, aggressively recruited black teachers, and promoted black administrators. By the spring of 1970, no large city in the North could equal Detroit's record for advancing blacks within the school system.

Having come that far, the board decided to take on the next racial redoubt, the white school enclave. By a 4 to 2 vote, it adopted on April 7, 1970, a plan that would change the boundary lines for eleven of the city's twenty-two high schools, affecting 33,000 students. To its surprise, as many as 1,000 angry Detroiters tried to jam the hall at the plan's unveiling, chanting, "Hell no, we won't go."[7]

"All the trouble," explained a humiliated board president, A. L. Zwerdling, labor lawyer and ex-administrative assistant to the late Walter Reuther, "was because for the first time we devised a plan that not only moved black students into white schools, but also required white students to go to black schools."[8] Other members of the board's liberal bloc were equally upset. Not one had accurately read the emotional response to their action.

One exception, however, was Patrick A. McDonald, a white, who cast a negative vote. He arrived at the following meeting with three bundles containing 1,100 telegrams, 250 letters, and petitions bearing 5,000 signatures. "Only six favor the boundary change," he revealed. "All . . . are Detroit residents."[9]

In no time, a group calling itself the Citizens Committee for Better Education (CCBE) asked for the recall of the board's majority, accusing them of "forcing integration to drive the white people out of town."[10] Soon it had collected 114,000 signatures to qualify for a special election.

Meanwhile, the state legislature decided to initiate its own program to strike down the April 7 plan, and Gov. William M. Milliken promptly cooperated by signing the measure. In fear-ridden Detroit, the mayor washed his hands of the controversy.

Only the United Auto Workers disputed the popular trend. It managed to run a newspaper advertisement bemoaning the recall, but then only because in the words of one officer, "We couldn't raise a dime anywhere else."[11] In vain did Andrew Perdue, a black attorney, elected to the board two years before, ask, "Where is everybody? Where are the people who helped get us elected—the UAW, the NAACP and the others? Don't they care anymore?"[12]

Recall carried three to two, almost exactly the margin of whites over blacks in the city voter registration. "My daughter was being sent to a black school," explained a white policeman, an early supporter of CCBE. "We knew we were going to win, because we were fighting for our children. They were only fighting for an idea."[13]

"They" in this instance referred to Detroit's chapter of the NAACP which for years had advocated integration of the city's public schools. "I know of no other way to prevent the Negro child from being short-changed in education in the years ahead," said Executive Director Arthur L. Johnson.[14] With integration now at an end, the NAACP decided to challenge the constitutionality of the state's recently enacted statute, outlawing the April 7 plan.

On August 18, 1970, suit was filed in Detroit's Federal District Court on behalf of a number of black students. Since Ronald Bradley, a six-year-old, topped the plaintiffs' list and Gov. Milliken was the principal defendant, the case went on the calendar as *Bradley* v. *Milliken*.[15] The suit accused Milliken, State Attorney General Frank J. Kelley, the State Board of Education, and the Detroit Board of Education of actions and inactions that had produced de jure segregation of Detroit's public schools.

Assigned to hear the case was sixty-two-year-old Stephen J. Roth. A Hungarian by birth, he was the son of a nobleman's custodian who emigrated with his wife to America in 1911, leaving Stephen and an older sister temporarily behind with relatives in Sajo Szoged.

After settling in Pennsylvania for a time, the Roths moved on to Flint where Charles Roth found a position in the Buick plant. Two years later, Johanna Roth returned to Hungary, picked up Stephen and his sister, and booked passage back in steerage. Thereafter, living in a working-class neighborhood on Flint's north side gave young Roth a taste of rough and ready living. Such words as *hunky*, *kraut*, *wop*, and *nigger* were in common use. "We were all in the melting pot," Roth later recalled, "but only the blacks had the handicap of color."[16]

Roth was a bright youngster, completing four years of high school in two and one-half years, and graduating at age 16. For three years, he worked in Flint on the assembly line, as bank messenger and cashier, short order cook, and spot welder. Finally, deciding to study law, he entered the University of Notre Dame, graduated in 1931 and from the Michigan University Law School four years later. Back in Flint, Roth gravitated to politics, but failed his initial test when he fell three votes short of gaining a seat on the Flint City Commission. Unperturbed, he continued to work—and to wait. When World War II came, despite his thirty-four years, he joined the army and served twenty months overseas in North Africa and Italy as a criminal investigator, rising from private to second lieutenant.

By 1948, Roth's widening friendships and growing political influence enabled him to win the Democratic nomination for state attorney general. On a ticket headed by G. Mennen "Soapy" Williams, Michigan's youthful vote getter, Roth won but by only 1,163 votes and two years later was defeated for reelection. His star, however, continued to rise. A Democratic poll the following year put him at the top of the list among those to succeed U.S. Senator Arthur Vandenburg when the famed head of the Foreign Relations Committee died. However, Gov. Williams passed him over and, partly to assuage the rebuff, named Roth to the Genesee Circuit Court, a post he held until John F. Kennedy appointed him to the U.S. District Court for eastern Michigan in May, 1962.

Roth's assignment to hear *Bradley* v. *Milliken* did not particularly elate the NAACP. Although the judge was once poor, he now lived in the exclusive and expensive Warwick Farms subdivision, south of Flint. As with self-made men, he rejoiced in the ways of his youth. He liked to say he had never bought on credit or owned a credit card. He had a distaste for liberals who were forever trying to unravel his society. As late as December, 1970, Roth had announced his opposition to court-ordered integration plans, if they involved forced busing.

Once the trial began, however, and fact piled on fact, he saw something different that changed his mind. NAACP attorney Louis R. Lucas, of Memphis, provided chapter and verse showing black students victimized by de jure segregation. Alexander Ritchie, representing CCBE, explained the impossibility of desegregating the Detroit school system, already preponderantly black, unless the city were joined to the largely white districts in surrounding Oakland, Wayne, and Macomb counties. "If all the 85 school districts were included with Detroit," he informed Roth, "the total of 942,500 students would be only 20 percent black."[17] Integration on this 80/20 basis would involve busing 130,200 black students out of Detroit daily and busing in 130,000 white students from the suburbs. Without such action, warned Ritchie, Detroit would be 85 percent black by 1980 and the legal promise of desegregation would be meaningless.

Eventually, after sifting through 6,000 pages of testimony, on September 27, 1971, Roth found the state of Michigan and the Detroit Board of Education guilty of fostering racial segregation. He did compliment the city for having a "higher proportion of black administrators than any other city in the country,"[18] and a greater percentage of black teachers compared with the city's black mix, but this would hardly compensate for what "pervasive and long standing" residential segregation had done to the school system. Nor was it the de facto kind on which the Supreme Court had failed to reach a conclusion. "Government actions and inactions at all levels, federal, state and local," he wrote, "have combined, with those of private organizations . . . and brokerage firms, to establish and to maintain the pattern of residential segregation throughout the Detroit metropolitan area."[19]

Black realtors had informed the court that white-owned homes in Detroit and the suburbs were unavailable to them despite Federal and state open housing laws. Black families could not get mortgages in areas that had been "red-lined" by Detroit's banks and lending institutions. They singled out the

Burton Abstract and Title Company, a large Detroit title insurance establishment, charging attachment of racially restrictive covenants to its real
estate contracts as late as 1969, despite the fact that the U.S. Supreme Court
had outlawed such contracts twenty-one years before. Further testimony
revealed that the Detroit Housing Commission had built large projects in
the city's black areas to contain the minorities rather than construct moder-
ately sized developments throughout the city that would have integrated the
population.

On this basis, Roth reasoned, "the natural and actual effect of these acts
and failures to act has been the creation and perpetuation of school segregation. There has never been a feeder pattern or zoning change which placed a
predominantly white residential area into a predominantly black school
zone or feeder pattern. Every school which was 90 percent or more black in
1960, and which is still in use today, remains 90 percent or more
black. . . . The public schools operated by defendant board are thus segregated on a racial basis."[20]

Roth indicated that the board's site selection policy had compounded segregation. Of fourteen new schools opened in 1970-71, eleven had a black
student population of more than 90 percent and one had a white population
of more than 90 percent. "Since 1959," Roth added, "the Board has constructed at least 13 small primary schools with capacities of from 300 to 400
pupils. This practice negates opportunities to integrate, 'contains' the black
population and perpetuates and compounds school segregation."[21] Roth
wanted the state to share the blame. The legislature had refused, until the
previous session, to provide funds to bus pupils "with Detroit, regardless of
their poverty or distance from the school to which they were assigned,
while providing in many neighboring, mostly white, suburban districts the
full range of state supported transportation."[22] Moreover, what funds the
board raised locally to bus students were used to transport "black pupils
past or away from closer white schools with available space to black schools
. . . . With one exception (necessitated by the burning of a white school),
defendant board has never bused white children to predominantly black
schools . . . despite the enormous amount of space available in inner city
schools. There were 22,961 vacant seats in schools 90% or more black."[23]

The weight of the evidence had now made a profound impression on
Roth. He found it "unfortunate that we cannot deal with public school segregation on a no-fault basis, for if racial segregation in our public schools is
an evil, then it should make no difference whether we classify it *de jure* or
de facto. Our objective, logically, . . . should be to remedy a condition
which we believe needs correction,"[24] stating at another point that "a school
board [and inferentially the court], may not, consistent with the Fourteenth
amendment, maintain . . . or permit educational choices to be influenced
by community sentiment or the wishes of a majority of voters."[25]

Hinting at what he had in mind, Roth went on to say that "judicial remedial steps" could not be taken without adding as defendants "a great number
of Michigan school districts located out-county in Wayne County, and in
Macomb and Oakland counties."[26] In directing Michigan officials to draw
up such a plan, he told the press, "During the course of this trial, I have
developed certain reservations about the possibility of desegregating the
schools within the city. It appears to us only a plan that encompasses all or
part of the metropolitan district can guarantee the constitutional rights of
all the people in that district."[27] Yet the judge was in no hurry to reach a
final decision. "[N]ine wiser men than myself took a year to decide the first
school integration case in 1954," he said.[28]

In the suburbs such comments struck a raw nerve. As soon as white families sensed the court's direction, pandemonium erupted. Within a week,
10,000 residents of Warren, in Macomb County, had organized an antibusing group—Save Our Children (SOC)—and called a school boycott. About
20,000 students, almost a third of the school population, cut classes. In
nearby Bloomfield Hills, in Oakland County, a mother told the *Detroit
News*, "I would never know if my children were safe. We pay high taxes for
good schools and now they want to bus my children to an inner city school.
No way. I'll fight first."[29] In the face of this hostility, Roth refused to budge.
"If there is segregation," he said, "it is the responsibility of all of society.
The schools, as the agent of social change, should take the lead in bringing
about integration."[30]

Within a week of the ruling, the Mayor of Warren, Ted Bates, was
closeted in Washington with his congressman, Representative James G.
O'Hara. Bates had come with petitions signed by 50,000 residents calling for
an antibusing constitutional amendment. Up to then, O'Hara had been one
of the most outspoken liberal Democrats in the House. He had once chaired
the 125-member House Democratic Study Group, formed in 1959 to promote progressive legislation. Four times he had voted against the Whitten
Amendments to restrict busing—once in 1968, again in 1969, and twice the
following year. Then the clamor from Michigan whites against integration
became frightening. Panic surfaced most noticeably in the overwhelmingly
white suburbs that O'Hara represented. Out of 179,000 people in Warren,
only 132 were black. On April 7, 1971, the anniversary of the Detroit
school board's effort to erase segregated school boundaries, the House
voted a fifth time to restrict busing. O'Hara could not yet bring himself to
approve the Whitten Amendments so he simply neglected to vote.

All the same the handwriting was there. If O'Hara wanted to retain his
seat, he had to forswear his integrity. On the day following his conversation
with Bates, he joined two other members of the House Education and Labor
Committee in vetoing the use of any part of President Nixon's request for
$1.5 billion in desegregation funds to bus children.

O'Hara had company in retreat. Faced with the same choice, the remaining five congressmen with constituencies in the city's white suburbs cut and ran. Lucien N. Nedzi and William D. Ford, both Democrats, had voted five times against Whitten; John D. Dingell, another Democrat, four times; and the two Republicans, Jack H. McDonald and William S. Broomfield, twice each. Following the Roth ruling, no recanting was too harsh to convince their constituents that it had all been a gross political mistake.

Indeed, on October 28, 1971, Rep. Broomfield introduced legislation to postpone the effective date of any Federal court order requiring busing until all appeals had been settled or the time for them had expired, a procedure that would delay the judicial process indefinitely. He was joined by O'Hara, Ford, Nedzi, and McDonald as co-sponsors. One week later, during four hours of frenzied post-midnight debate, in which frightened legislators hastened to go on record against busing, the House overwhelmingly adopted the Broomfield measure 235 to 125. "More than half of those votes," reported the *Congressional Quarterly*, "were cast by Representatives from states outside the South. Fifty-six Democrats from Northern and Western states—considered the most liberal voting group in the House— voted for the [Broomfield] amendment."[31] Events back home had so unnerved the entire Michigan delegation that *every* white Representative voted in the affirmative. Twenty months before, on March 3, 1970, the same members had voted 16 to 1 against the Whitten Amendment to restrict busing. After witnessing the vote from the House gallery, Clarence Mitchell, the NAACP's capital spokesman, lamented, "The people of each congressional district should study the roll calls on busing. This is a reliable list of the true racists and promoters of discord in the United States. They may wear the business suits of congressmen, but in their hearts they wear the robes of the Ku Klux Klan and this night they put the torch to the Constitution of the United States."[32]

Back in Lansing, on the evening before the Broomfield Amendment passed, Gov. Milliken went on both radio and television to announce he was appealing Roth's decision. He was convinced the judge had gone too far. As with Michigan's congressmen, he tried to take the glare off busing by emphasizing the need for "quality education" instead of integration. "Simply put," said the Governor, without blinking, "children—white or black— don't learn by riding buses,"[33] neglecting to mention, of course, that Michigan was spending millions of dollars annually busing white pupils in suburbia to predominantly white schools.

Taking its cue from Milliken, Detroit's Board of Education likewise decided to appeal, but its obdurateness, instead of softening Roth's attitude, seemed to harden it. After studying the two desegregation plans that the Board finally submitted, Roth told its members, "These seem to be a form of bargaining, and this court is not about to bargain. I made it plain the first job was desegregating the Detroit schools, and this was a primary responsibility of the Detroit board."[34] Accordingly, this time he asked the NAACP to assist in designing a plan and informed attorney Lucas to tell the court if the Board failed to cooperate. Three months of study and analysis produced three Detroit-only plans, but after five days of hearings before Roth, witnesses generally agreed on the educational and social preferability of a metropolitan plan.

Consequently, Roth scrapped the Detroit-only concept. His pronouncement on March 28, 1972, that the court "must look beyond the limits of the Detroit school district for a solution to the problems of the Detroit Public Schools,"[35] brought an immediate rejection from Detroit's Scripps-Howard publication. "Despite all the hazards of cross-district busing," the *News* editor wrote sardonically, "Judge Roth seems to feel compelled toward a cross-district order by a constitutional mandate, specifically the Supreme Court's finding against the concept of 'separate but equal' schools. . . . Roth, like some other federal judges, is pursuing the chimera of perfect racial ratios in the public schools. That is not to be—unless, of course, the entire United States becomes one single school district and the government starts jetting students to school from, say, Detroit's inner city to Great Falls, Mont."[36]

On May 16, the 1972 presidential primary election gave voters in twenty-seven metropolitan Detroit communities an additional opportunity to tell Roth how they objected to cross-district busing. In Dearborn, with a segregated population of thirteen blacks out of 104,000 residents, approximately 85 percent of those voting favored an antibusing constitutional amendment that would "guarantee the right of each student to attend his neighborhood school."[37] In Macomb County, which included Warren, more than 94 percent said "no" to busing and according to Stephen W. Dane, chairman of the County Board of Commissioners, "this was not just a Warren issue. The 15-1 margin was prevalent throughout Macomb County."[38]

However, if the voters thereby hoped to send a message to the imperturbable Roth, his line was dead. Within the month, the judge issued an eleven-page order, the most extensive busing order in the nation's history, calling for the integration of 290,000 children in Detroit's schools, where black pupils outnumbered whites 2 to 1, with 490,000 children from fifty-three peripheral suburban school districts, where white students outnumbered blacks 48 to 1. A total of 310,000 children would be bused from city to suburbs and suburbs to city with both black and white pupils assuming equal responsibility. "The order," wrote Jerry M. Flint, of the *New York Times*, "would combine Detroit's students with children from the rich Grosse Pointes; integrate working class suburbs such as Warren, where anti-black feeling has been fierce in the past; integrate Birmingham and Bloomfield Hills, the home of the auto rich; include Oak Park and Southfield, suburbs where the bulk of the area's Jews live; and include Dearborn, another community noted for anti-black sentiments."[39] Under Roth's ruling no school would have "less than 10 percent black faculty and staff."[40] Although Detroit's teaching staff of 1,000 was more than 40 percent black, in the suburbs, white naturally predominated.

On the subject of busing, Roth pointed out that its use was widely accepted. The only difference, in this case, is "the direction of the buses."[41] Four out of ten schoolchildren in the metropolitan district would travel up to twenty miles each day to achieve a classroom mix approximately 25 percent black. To forestall or at least reduce the trauma associated with busing young children, the judge limited the transportation of kindergarten pupils to forty-five minutes one way, which he said "does not appear unreasonable, harmful or unsafe."[42] A nine-member panel would flesh out the plan and final desegregation commence with the 1973 fall term.

Local scorn for Roth and his order was ubiquitous. Dearborn Mayor Orville L. Hubbard predicted "massive resistance," and said Roth, "should be crated up and shipped back" to Hungary. He was not "surprised," he added, that such a wild decision "would come from a man who has been a U.S. citizen only 39 years."[43] In Warren, the school board gave permission to an irate parents group to form a private school that would use the public school buildings at night. Even the teachers, who might have understood what Roth was trying to accomplish, were aghast. "It boggles the mind," announced Mary Ellen Riordan, president of the 11,000 member Detroit Federation of Teachers. "All I see ahead is chaos, utter chaos. I just don't see how it can possibly work."[44] She calculated that Roth's order would require moving 4,000 black teachers from Detroit to the suburbs to achieve the 10 percent minority representation in each school. "I've talked to a great many of them," she said, "and they are extremely reluctant, first to have to go to an area where they could not get hired if they had wanted to, and second, because it would mean a major loss of income for many."[45] Detroit's starting scale of $9,000 was the highest in the state.

Amid the threats, groans, and anger, the only positive note came from the city's religious groups. Detroit's top Catholic, Protestant, and Jewish spokesmen issued a joint statement calling upon "all persons in this metropolitan area to respect the order of the court and to work toward the goals which this decision seeks to achieve. . . . We must remember that the court's decision has one basic purpose—namely to forward the American goal of good public education in an integrated setting for all children in this society. . . . We ask that you look beyond the court's decision and see what it is trying to achieve. In that light it can be seen, not as a crushing burden, but as a new opportunity to achieve goals that we have often sought in vain."[46]

Notwithstanding this appeal for understanding, the chance to fish in troubled waters proved irresistible to the President of the United States. Mr. Nixon informed the Washington press corps that Roth's decision was a "flagrant" violation of the neighborhood school concept and followed this with a letter to Rep. Broomfield, replying to the latter's request for White House intervention, in which he promised to do whatever the government could do to prevent busing in the Detroit area. "Under the circumstances," he informed Broomfield, "we must leave no stone unturned. . . ."[47]

The possibility of overturning Roth's order by a higher court was not lost on the Milliken administration which ordered its Solicitor General Robert A. Derengowski to ask the Court of Appeals for a stay, arguing the court's decision would cause "irreparable harm."[48] In this way, execution of the Roth order was halted pending a three-judge panel review. On August 24, 1972, Derengowski told the court that Roth would probably be reversed by a higher court since segregation in one school district could not be judicially eliminated by integration with another district or districts—in this case the suburbs—where segregation had not been proven to exist. Without a precedent, Roth, claimed Derengowski, could not order state officials to perform actions not permissible under state law.

Concluding that Derengowski erred, the panel upheld Roth for ordering cross-district busing, but said he was wrong in not making the suburban school districts a party to the suit. Unanimously, the court agreed that a Detroit-only plan would not integrate the city's schools. Therefore, it was both "legal and proper" to include the suburbs.[49] The fact that eighteen of the fifty-two suburban school districts involved in the plan had not been included in the suit convinced the judges to order a new desegregation plan. To Roth, who now lay stricken in Ford Hospital with a serious heart attack, the affirmation of his order had to be profoundly gratifying. The panel had written, "It will not be necessary for the District Court to find discriminatory conduct, either *de jure* or *de facto*, as a prerequisite to including such district in a desegregation area."[50] In the eyes of Louis Lucas, NAACP attorney, the result was "absolutely beautiful. The language is that school district boundaries are not sacrosanct and that it's not necessary for the court to find segregation in the suburbs. The court is saying the suburban districts should be heard from on the question of remedy, but not on the question of fault."[51]

Astonishingly, some months prior to the ruling, by now convinced that cross-district busing would become a reality, thirty-five area groups had formed the Metropolitan Coalition for Peaceful Integration. Such major organizations as the Detroit Archdiocese, the UAW, the AFL-CIO, the American Jewish Congress, the Metropolitan Detroit Council of Churches, the League of Women Voters, Urban League, and Michigan Federation of Teachers formed the hard core. Its leader, Elwood Hain, a Wayne State University constitutional lawyer, described the coalition as neither for nor against busing, but a group that would help "to identify the problems which are worrying people."[52]

"Suburban parents," Hain continued, "worry about the physical safety of their children in city schools where there have been a number of instances of violence. Black parents . . . worry about the psychic damage to their children when they move from a predominantly black school to one where they are in the minority. . . . We have also discovered there is virtually no interaction between suburban schools and the police. In the city, the police and schools do have a working relationship, but any school matters in the suburbs are largely ignored by the police."[53] Hain was surprised by the public's "level-headedness." He found some to be "rabidly anti-busing," but still aware of the need to prepare for what seemed a "certainty." The businessmen provided special help. As "pillars of their own communities," they were eager to have a "peaceful transition" and offered to cooperate regardless of personal misgivings.[54]

In view of this concerted preparation, and the unanimous ruling of the Appeals Court panel, Detroit residents were bewildered to learn on January 16, 1973, that a majority of the nine appellate judges had voted to reopen *Bradley* v. *Milliken,* setting February 8 as the date for hearing arguments. This decision returned the case to the previous August when debate began on Roth's order.

Not until June 12, 1973, did the en banc court announce its 6 to 3 agreement with the Roth decision. The majority opinion, again written by Chief Judge Phillips, declared that the state of Michigan and the Detroit School Board were guilty of discrimination. "Even if the segregation practices were a bit more subtle than the compulsory segregation statutes of Southern states," he wrote, "they were nonetheless effective. . . . That the court must look beyond the limits of the Detroit school district for a solution to the problem of segregation in the Detroit public schools is obvious. . . ."[55]

Not so, said dissenting Justice Paul C. Weick, of Akron, Ohio. He termed Roth's decision a "legal monstrosity."[56] It was "incredible," he said, that Roth would say in a pre-trial conference that "our courts are called upon, in these school cases, to attain a social goal by using law as a lever . . . courts are not called upon to integrate the school system. . . . Nor should judges assume to act as legislators, for which they are neither fitted nor qualified."[57] Weick refused to admit any duplicity on the part of the state or Detroit's Board of Education in prolonging school desegregation in the metropolitan area. There was "not an iota of evidence, . . . that the boundaries of the Detroit school district . . . were established for the purpose of [segregating] the races. . . . the School Board . . . ought not to be blamed for the heavy concentration of blacks in the inner city. . . ."[58] According to Weick, Roth's decision would cost "untold millions," and bus hundreds of thousands of children, none of whom had "committed any offense for which they should be so punished."[59]

Although the circuit court had overwhelmingly supported Roth, the state and suburbs would not give way. Soon after the ruling, they prepared briefs for an appeal to the U.S. Supreme Court, and on November 19, the land's highest tribunal granted the request, setting the stage for the final act in the Detroit drama.

Notes

1. *Detroit News*, June 15, 1972, p. 8-B.

2. *Report of the National Advisory Commission of Civil Disorders* (New York: Bantam Books, 1968), p. 85.

3. Ibid.

4. Ibid.

5. Ibid.

6. *Detroit News*, August 22, 1962.

7. William Grant, "Integration's Last Hurrah, 'Where Did Everyone Go To?'," *New Republic*, September 12, 1970, p. 20.

8. Ibid.

9. *Detroit News*, April 29, 1970.

10. Grant, "Integration's Last Hurrah."

11. Ibid.

12. Ibid.

13. Ibid.

14. *Detroit News*, May 21, 1963.

15. *Bradley* v. *Milliken*, 338 F. Supp. 582 (1971).

16. *Detroit News*, October 10, 1971, p. 3-A.

17. *Detroit News*, August 1, 1971.

18. *Bradley* v. *Milliken*, at 590.

19. Ibid., at 587.

20. Ibid., at 588.

21. Ibid., at 589.

22. Ibid.

23. Ibid., at 588.

24. Ibid., at 592.

25. Ibid., at 593.

26. Ibid., at 595.

27. *Detroit News*, October 4, 1971.

28. Ibid.

29. *Detroit News*, October 5, 1971.

30. Ibid., p. 16-A.

31. "Busing Opponents: New Friends in the House," *Congressional Quarterly*, 29 (December 11, 1971): 2559.

32. *Detroit News*, November 5, 1971.

33. *Detroit News*, November 4, 1971.

34. *Detroit News*, December 20, 1971.

35. *Detroit News*, March 29, 1972.

36. Editorial, *Detroit News*, March 30, 1972.

37. *Detroit News*, May 17, 1972.

38. Ibid.

39. *New York Times*, June 15, 1972.

40. Ibid.

41. *Detroit News*, June 15, 1972, p. 3-A.

42. Ibid.

43. Ibid., p. 8-B.

44. Ibid., p. 13-B.
45. Ibid.
46. *Detroit News*, June 17, 1972.
47. *Detroit News*, June 29, 1972.
48. *Detroit News*, July 20, 1972.
49. *Detroit News*, December 8, 1972.
50. *Detroit News*, December 12, 1972.
51. *Detroit News*, December 9, 1972.
52. *Detroit News*, December 19, 1972, p. 3-A.
53. Ibid.
54. Ibid.
55. *Bradley* v. *Milliken*, 484 F. 2d 215 (1973), p. 244.
56. Ibid., at 260.
57. Ibid., at 261.
58. Ibid., at 260.
59. Ibid., at 259-60.

18

THE PATH LEADS DOWN

"Our nation, I fear, will be ill-served by the Court's refusal to remedy separate and unequal education, for unless our children begin to learn together, there is little hope that our people will ever learn to live together."

Thurgood Marshall, Justice U.S. Supreme Court.[1]

By now, the High Court had donned a new face. Of the six pillars in the Warren Court—Black, Brennan, Douglas, Fortas, Marshall, and the Chief Justice—only three remained. Warren had retired in June, 1969. Fortas resigned in the spring of 1969, driven out by public outrage over revelations of financial improprieties. Black had departed in the fall of 1971, only weeks before his death. Of the three others—Harlan, Stewart, and White—only the latter two were left. Harlan, sick with terminal cancer, made his exit, like Black's, in the fall of 1971. Thus, to Richard Nixon came the unique political windfall of naming four justices in his first term—only George Washington, who had to nominate the entire court, and William Howard Taft, who nominated six, matched the Nixon opportunity.

It should have been a labor of love, filling the seats of three known liberals, Warren, Fortas, and Black and one conservative, Harlan, presumably with men who would be strict constructionists. Instead, after Burger was named Chief Justice, the nominating process had deteriorated into two abrasive and bruising battles with both Haynsworth and Carswell rejected.

Thereafter, a piqued Chief Executive, vowing the Senate would not confirm a Southerner because of regional bias, looked elsewhere for a nominee. The search, lasting barely a week, concluded on April 14, 1970, with the naming of Harry Andrew Blackmun, sixty-one, of Rochester, Minnesota, who was then a member of the United States Court of Appeals of the Eighth Circuit. The nominee had met privately with the President prior to the announcement, and according to Press Secretary Ziegler, Mr. Nixon was "highly impressed by Judge Blackmun's personal qualities."[2] Having left the choice of Haynsworth and Carswell entirely to Attorney General Mitchell, this time the President took a direct hand. He requested John Ehrlichman, his domestic aide, to sound out Clarence Mitchell of the NAACP's Washington office and other black leaders to get their opinions in advance. Chief Justice Burger also played a significant role in the selection. Burger had known Blackmun since the two attended kindergarten and grade school together in St. Paul, Minnesota. Life-long intimates, Blackmun had been best man at Burger's wedding in 1933, and the Chief Justice evidently had no qualms about urging Blackmun's appointment.

Nixon's latest nominee was born on November 12, 1908, in Nashville, Illinois, but spent most of his adult years in Minneapolis and St. Paul. A bright youngster, he entered Harvard on a scholarship, majored in mathematics, and won a Phi Beta Kappa key. Working to pay his tuition, he graduated from Harvard Law School in 1932, then returned to Minneapolis to spend two years as law clerk and law teacher at the city's William Mitchell College of Law. Following this, he joined the prestigious firm of Dorsey, Colman, Barker, Scott and Barber which provided legal services for the famed Mayo Clinic. Since this litigation required a full-time counselor, he moved to Rochester, Minnesota, the Clinic's headquarters, in 1950 to take the job of General Counsel. Nine years later, Dwight Eisenhower named him to the Eighth Circuit, covering the states of Minnesota, Iowa, Missouri, Arkansas, Nebraska, and the two Dakotas.

Quietly intellectual, naturally reserved, Blackmun made a specialty of tax law and did not seem destined for controversy. His record on the Eighth Circuit stamped him as a moderate on civil rights. For example, he reversed a lower court's ruling that sanctioned "racially indentifiable and completely black" elementary schools.[3] On another occasion, he ordered an Arkansas school district to rehire black teachers who were fired as unqualified upon an all-black school's closing.

Yet, when the opportunity arose to turn new ground on civil rights, Blackmun demurred. He refused to authorize the purchase of a residence in an all-white East St. Louis housing development by an interracial couple whose defense was the almost forgotten 1866 antibias housing law, enacted over President Andrew Johnson's veto. Blackmun hesitated, he said, out of respect for judicial restraint. The High Court later approved the constitutionality of the law, thus overturning Blackmun's opinion.

What caught President Nixon's eye was the nominee's philosophy on law and order which closely resembled Chief Justice Burger's. Blackmun believed the Warren Court had gone too far in protecting the rights of criminal defendants, a conviction the White House shared, where Blackmun was already seen as fitting nicely into the Nixon Supreme Court mold.

Confirmation hearings proceeded without fanfare. Unlike Haynsworth, who had equities in excess of a million dollars, Blackmun showed a net worth of $125,000 and unlike Carswell whose opinions were said to read like a plumber's manual, Blackmun's prose breathed scholarship from every pore. Prior to hearings before the Senate Judiciary Committee, he received the top endorsement of the American Bar Association's Committee on the Federal Judiciary. No groups—civil rights, labor, or any other—asked to speak against him. The Senate confirmed his nomination 94 to 0, and on May 14, 1970, exactly one year after Fortas had resigned, Blackmun took his seat. Although issues were to arise on which Burger and Blackmun disagreed, there is little doubt that in Blackmun the Chief Justice found a colleague who at first most nearly reflected his ideology. If Burger should succeed in negating the very liberal legacy of the Warren Court, Blackmun would be his trusted lieutenant, much as Joseph Story seconded the nationalism of John Marshall.

For sixteen months, the make-up of the Court remained unchanged. When Justices Black and Harlan retired, Nixon turned first to Richard Poff, a conservative Republican congressman from Virginia. However, Poff had signed the 1956 Southern Manifesto, which contemplated a reversal of *Brown I*,[4] and consistently opposed civil rights legislation. Bitterness erupted as with Haynsworth and Carswell. AFL-CIO President George Meany, one of many critics, stigmatized Poff as a racist. By the first week of October, 1971, he had had enough and asked the President to withdraw his name from consideration.

In view of the President's oft-stated view that a Chief Executive's place in history is largely dependent upon his appointments to the Supreme Court, it is difficult to reconcile what happened next. There is some reason to believe Nixon wanted a woman on the Court, but could not find one to his liking. While the search continued, Attorney General Mitchell, by chance, met Mildred Lillie, of the California Court of Appeals. Impressed by her law-and-order record, he invited Lillie to Washington for further consultations and submitted her name to the American Bar Association (ABA) for scrutiny. At the same time, he became interested in Herschel Friday, a prominent Little Rock lawyer, of whose conservative record, *Time* magazine wrote, "for 14 years [he] had compiled a record of unsuccessful efforts to defend Arkansas school boards against desegregation. His firm's fees for such cases amounted to some $220,000."[5]

Although the Majority Leader of the Senate, West Virginia's Robert Byrd, was also said to be under consideration, his candidacy lacked the necessary credentials. He was revealed as a former agent of the Ku Klux Klan and a lawyer without portfolio. After earning a night school degree, Byrd had declined to take the bar examination that would have qualified him to practice. Nevertheless, his name was one of six candidates that went to ABA. In order to disguise Administration interest in Lillie and Friday, Mitchell added the names of two justices from the Fifth Circuit Court of Appeals, one from Mississippi, the other from Florida, as well as a second woman, Sylvia Bacon, of the District of Columbia Superior Court.

It took the media only one day to find out who was on the list, and the uproar that followed shocked the White House. "Utter contempt for the court," snapped Edward Kennedy.[6] Thirty-four Harvard Law School faculty members signed a petition objecting to the nominees. When ABA judiciary chairman Lawrence Walsh protested that one week (the time Mitchell had allotted to investigate all six) did not provide for sufficient probing, the Attorney General ordered him to concentrate on Lillie and Friday and forget the others, clear evidence of the White House's intentions.

It seemed only an adverse ABA vote, bringing with it the prospect of yet another struggle in the Senate, could derail the President's determination. Walsh's committee of twelve lawyers met and debated the potential nominees' qualifications. On Friday, they split 6 to 6; on Lillie the vote was a negative 11 to 1. According to ABA rules, lacking a two-thirds affirmation, both failed to qualify. Only two days now remained before the expiration of Nixon's promise to announce his choices within a week of his submission of the names to Walsh. What would the President do? Already, the same group of Senate liberals who had united behind Birch Bayh and Edward Kennedy to block the confirmation of Haynsworth and Carswell were preparing to stage a fight against Friday and Lillie.

In the crisis, Nixon acted very much alone. He telephoned Lewis F. Powell, Jr., a Richmond lawyer, and offered him the nomination. Here age posed a barrier. Powell, sixty-four, had previously asked that his name be withdrawn from consideration. Now, under the President's personal appeal, he agreed to weigh the new offer. Late the next day, Powell accepted, and during the following twenty-four hours, the White House quietly decided to add the name of William H. Rehnquist, Assistant Attorney General.

A startled nation then learned through television what had happened, that Powell and Rehnquist had taken the places of Friday and Lillie. Not until an hour before the President was to go on the air were the latter two told of the change in signals. Blithely, Mr. Nixon told the public, "[Ten years of Powell] is worth 30 years of most."[7] He went on to pontificate that a Supreme Court Justice should not "twist or bend the Constitution in order to perpetuate his personal political and social views," adding his belief that some Court decisions had gone too far "in weakening the peace forces as against the criminal forces in our society."[8]

The President, however, failed to sort out the ambivalence of the two views. For how could he pay homage to the one without denying the other? To encourage a conservative trend, as Nixon advocated, but only in a judicial, not a political sense, was pure nonsense. As Alan Dershowitz, of the Harvard Law School, said in commenting on Nixon's appointees, a judicial philosophy "if it is truly judicial rather than 'political' or 'social' does not speak in terms of giving the peace forces 'tools' to 'protect the inno-

cent from criminal elements' . . . Most important, a judge with conservative judicial philosophy abjures employing the courts to effectuate his own
political or social program—he is a decider of cases rather than advocate of
causes" which support his contention.[9]

Since, in Powell and Rehnquist, the President had named two men with
conservative instincts, the only important issue to settle was whether they,
like Burger and Blackmun, could be expected to rely on their "individual
political [or economic or social] views" to decide questions of law. Since
neither had served in a judicial capacity, there were no precedents to go by.
One, therefore, must look to their backgrounds and writings for possible
insights.

Lewis Powell, born in Suffolk, Virginia, could trace his American for-
bears back to 1607 when the first Powell stepped ashore to help build the
Jamestown colony. He had been Phi Beta Kappa at Washington and Lee
University where he also earned a law degree before going on for a master's
degree at Harvard Law School. For thirty-four years (with time out for OSS
service in World War II) Powell had been a partner in Richmond's widely
known firm, Hunton, Williams, Gay, Powell, and Gibson. His standing in
the profession was confirmed by the honors heaped on him: president of the
American Bar Association (1964-65), president of the American College of
Trial Lawyers (1969-70), and president of the American Bar Foundation
(1969-71). Politically, Powell supported Virginia's famed Byrd organization. In the civic world, his chief interest lay in education. As chairman of
the Richmond public school board between 1952 and 1961, he was instru-
mental in persuading the board not to endorse the irresponsible wave of
"interposition" that was sweeping the South. The doctrine of state opposition to Federal integration of the school systems he termed a "lot of rot."[10]
According to Booker T. Bradshaw, the first black member of Richmond's
school board since Reconstruction, Powell "was opposed to the state's massive resistance laws on constitutional and moral grounds. He was a great
moving force. . . ."[11] In gratitude, his nomination to the High Court was
immediately endorsed by Virginia's NAACP leadership.

An examination of Powell's writings and observations, prior to his selection by Nixon, point to one ineluctable conclusion: articulate, fair, and
impartial. "I don't categorize myself," he once remarked, "I think of myself
basically as a lawyer with a wide spectrum of experience. My views may be
liberal on one issue and conservative on another. I regard myself as an independent Democrat."[12]

What impressed the President were his statements on law and order.
Powell, like most conservatives, believed the Warren Court had gone too
far in protecting the rights of the defendant. "The key problem," in his
words, "is one of balance. While the safeguards of a fair trial must surely be
preserved, the right of society in general, and of each individual in particu-

lar, to be protected from crime must never be subordinated to other rights."[13] On balance, however, he would point out that because "wealth, social position and race . . . may affect the standards of justice available, it is small wonder that the public at large should be less enthusiastic about the administration of justice."[14] In his view, it was entirely possible for law enforcement officials bent upon uprooting crime to endanger the rights of defendants. Again, the true criterion was restraint. To demonstrate his concern for impoverished litigants, whose faith in the justice system had been undermined, he supported Lyndon Johnson's call for legal aid to the poor.

Only on the subject of wiretapping did Powell's views arouse certain misgivings. "The outcry against wiretapping," he wrote for the August 1, 1971, edition of the Richmond *Times-Dispatch*, is "a tempest in a teapot. There are 210 million Americans. There are only a few hundred wiretaps annually," forgetting the number had nothing to do with the principle of one's right to privacy. "There may have been a time," he added, "when a valid distinction existed between external and internal threats. But such a distinction is now largely meaningless."[15] That Powell spent his war years in espionage may well account for what followed: ". . . the 'radical left' strongly led and with a growing base of support, is plotting violence and revolution. Its leaders visit and collaborate with foreign Communist enemies. Freedom can be lost as irrevocable from revolution as from foreign attack."[16]

In view of these statements, nothing can better indicate the difficulty of categorizing Powell's thinking than the fact that he wrote the Supreme Court's unanimous decision, ten months later, outlawing the unlimited practice of placing surreptitious telephone taps on domestic radicals considered dangerous to the national security. "Fourth Amendment freedoms against 'unreasonable searches and seizures' cannot be properly guaranteed if domestic surveillances may be conducted solely within the discretion of the executive branch," warned Powell.[17]

This even-handedness, this facility for change, was not to be found in Nixon's second choice, William Rehnquist. He was, like Powell, a judicial conservative, but unlike Powell, a judicial activist as well. One of the youngest men to be named to the Supreme Court, Rehnquist was barely forty-seven when Nixon tapped him. Born in Milwaukee, he, too, was a Phi Beta Kappa key holder, earning bachelor and law degrees from Stanford University. He then worked two years as a law clerk for Supreme Court Justice Robert H. Jackson. Becoming disenchanted with the operation of the Warren Court (samples: Chief Justice Warren and Associate Justices Douglas and Black were "making the Constitution say what they wanted it to say," and Warren was a "fine California politician, but not much of a lawyer. He was a vote-getter who held one political job after another, but was 58th out of 65 in his law school class."[18]), Rehnquist moved to Phoenix to take up what he called a "cats and dogs" practice of law involving every form of litigation.[19] Soon he was hobnobbing with far-right Republican personalities. "Unlike a lot of Arizona politicans who tried to follow the public thought," a fellow lawyer commented, "Rehnquist is a deep philosophic conservative. He apparently just sat down and decided intellectually that he is against anything liberal."[20]

In striking a balance between the rights of the individual, espoused by liberals, and the rights of society, advocated by conservatives, he tipped toward the latter. The 1960s crusade for civil rights, often erupting into civil disobedience, was an anathema to Rehnquist. "There is a certain amount of arrogance," he wrote, "in insisting that one's own personal predilections will not permit him to obey a law which has been duly passed. . . . The claim for conscientious disobedience is at war with the basic premise of majority rule."[21] The man simply could not admit that more was needed than majority rule to guarantee individual minority citizens their constitutional rights. Not surprisingly, when the Arizona state legislature debated a civil rights law in 1968, Rehnquist was among the few opposing its passage —"the only major person of stature in the state," said a leader of Arizona's NAACP.[22]

During the period of his active association with the Arizona GOP, Rehnquist formed close friendships with Senator Barry Goldwater and Richard Kleindienst, a Phoenix lawyer. In the presidential campaign of 1964, Kleindienst asked Rehnquist to write speeches for Goldwater. When Kleindienst was asked to join John Mitchell's Justice Department in 1969, as number two man, he invited Rehnquist to head the Department's Office of Legal Counsel, a post the President referred to as the "President's Lawyer's lawyer."[23]

In his thirty-three months as a Justice counsel, Rehnquist had stoutly upheld White House policy, adding his commentary to current happenings. When the President wanted a constitutional amendment outlawing forced busing, it fell to Rehnquist to author it. When Mr. Nixon wanted to place a straitjacket on criticism of his Austin policies in the fall of 1970, it was Rehnquist who upheld the White House's right to fire those who disobeyed. When the Administration was forced to contend with student demonstrators protesting the Vietnam War, Rehnquist scornfully accused them of being the "new barbarians." When they tried to "shut down" Washington on May Day, 1970, he sanctioned the mass police arrests as "qualified martial law."[24]

Beyond this loyalty to the White House, it was Rehnquist's total dedication to law and order that captured the President. For example, Rehnquist had told the Senate Subcommittee on Constitutional Rights that he would "vigorously oppose any legislation" restricting the government's right to wiretap American citizens, going so far as to inform the chairman, North

Carolina's Sam J. Ervin, Jr., that while it would be "inappropriate" and a "waste of taxpayer's money" to place him under surveillance, it would not be unconstitutional.[25] At another point, he said, "Self-discipline, on the part of the executive branch will provide an answer to virtually all of the legitimate complaints against excesses of information gathering. . . ."[26]

Confirmation of Nixon's two appointees produced few fireworks. Within four days, Powell had moved to counteract criticism of his owning stocks valued at $1 million, and promised to do whatever was "necessary and proper" to avoid any possible conflict of interest.[27] He was a director of eleven corporations and vowed he would resign from all boards that had "commercial implications."[28] His assertions, in addition to his record, got him the ABA's highest rating by a unanimous vote. On December 6, 1971, he was overwhelmingly approved by the Senate 89 to 1, the first Southerner to be so honored since the appointment of James F. Byrnes, thirty years before. Commenting on the result, Washington's Senator Henry Jackson huffed, "A rebuff to those who suggested that the Senate would not confirm a Southerner to serve on the Supreme Court. One wonders why it has taken so long to propose a man of Mr. Powell's stature."[29]

In marked contrast was Rehnquist's reception both in and out of the Senate. A 1964 incident came to light revealing that the nominee had written the *Phoenix Republic* to condemn a proposed city public accommodations ordinance as a "mistake" that would produce a confrontation between the "unwanted customer and the disliked proprietor glowering at one another across the lunch counter."[30] Again in 1967, he had similarly opposed an effort to integrate the city's high schools. "The school's job," he wrote, "is to educate children. They should not be saddled with a task of fostering social change which may lessen their ability to perform their primary job," adding "we are no more dedicated to an 'integrated society' than we are to a 'segregated' society; that we are instead dedicated to a free society in which each man is equal before the law, but in which each man is accorded a maximum amount of freedom of choice in his individual activities."[31]

Now before the Senate Judiciary Committee, Rehnquist backpedaled. He admitted that he was wrong to oppose the right of minorities to patronize public places. The ordinance had proven its value, and "I would not have the same feeling now," he promised. As to busing schoolchildren to achieve racial integration, he was still against "transporting people long distances," but now pointing to the fact his children attended integrated schools in Virginia, he admitted they were "better off" for that experience.[32]

These postulations, however, did not appease civil rights leaders. Clarence Mitchell, the NAACP's lobbyist, cried out, "The Rehnquist nomination raises grim warnings. Through that nomination the foot of racism is placed in the door of the temple of justice. The Rehnquist record tells us that the hand of the oppressor will be given a chance to write opinions that will seek to turn back the clock of progress."[33] More violent was Joseph Rauh, of the Americans for Democratic Action, who accused Rehnquist of being "a laundered McCarthyite."[34] Despite the nominee's affidavit to the contrary, Rauh went on to accuse him of "connections" with far-right groups similar to the John Birch Society.[35] At this, even Sen. Kennedy, himself a liberal, stepped in to chide Rauh.

As with Haynsworth and Carswell, a group of Senate liberals, led by Indiana's Birch Bayh, tried to block the nomination, but were handicapped by a general feeling that Rehnquist, whatever his previous views, would sublimate them to the mandates of the Constitution. Moreover, the ABA had endorsed his nomination 9 to 3, attesting to his standing with the bar. The final affirmative vote of 68 to 26 was, therefore, not unexpected.[36]

Yet, even in victory, there was about the man a cloud of uncertainty about his judicial flexibility. William V. Shannon, of the *New York Times*, expressed it nicely by previously calling Rehnquist "an ideological zealot given to writing letters to the editor and making public speeches in which he has vigorously advanced a narrow set of strongly right-wing views. This," he said, contrasts strongly with Powell who "comes across as a true conservative, as a potential judge who would be reluctant to venture into new thickets of controversy, but would also be slow to reverse Court decisions, regardless of what he thought of them, and who would be wary of using the Court's great power to overrule Congress and the state legislatures."[37]

On January 10, 1972, both men joined the High Court, giving the tribunal a strong conservative nudge for the first time since Warren's ascension two decades before. Within a day of the swearing-in ceremony, a Federal District Judge for the first time ordered the formation of a metropolitan school district to solve an urban segregation problem. Robert R. Merhige ordered Virginia's state officials to consolidate Richmond's school system (70 percent black) with two peripheral counties, Chesterfield and Henrico (91 percent white). To cope with white flight to the suburbs, the Judge had accepted this innovative move, knowing that from 1954 to 1971, the percentage of whites in Richmond schools had dropped from 57 to 31 percent, while the percentage in Chesterfield and Henrico had exploded by some 250 percent. The "invidious intention . . . on the part of certain officials," the court ruled, had strongly influenced the result.[38] By deliberately constructing a network of superior suburban schools, they had stimulated a white exodus. Their actions violated the Equal Protection Clause of the Fourteenth Amendment, and were, therefore, unconstitutional. Moreover, Merhige contended, school boundary lines were not inviolate, only "political demarcations."[39] Since they were a creation of the state, not unlike a water or sewer district, they could be obliterated to form others. The new districts would contain 104,000 pupils, more than twice Richmond's school

population, but increase the 68,000 already bused by only 10,000. No
school would be more than 40 percent black.

As usual, anguish flowed in the wake of this 325-page ruling. Richmond's
foremost publication, the *Times-Dispatch*, ridiculed it as "a nauseating mixture of vacuous sociological theories."[40] The state's House of Delegates and
the State Senate dutifully demanded a constitutional amendment barring
busing to achieve racial balance. Abuse of Merhige became so intemperate
that United States marshals were called to guard his home. Only the
NAACP Legal Defense lawyers, who argued the case, saw a future in which
no "metropolitan area in the country" could escape the "implications" of the
decision, assuming, of course, Merhige was not reversed.[41]

What seemed to be happening had been clearly heralded seven years
before by Judge J. Skelly Wright, of the United States Court of Appeals for
the District of Columbia, who said it was "inconceivable" the Supreme
Court would "long sit idly by, watching Negro children crowded into
inferior schools while whites flee to the suburbs to place their children in
vastly superior, predominantly white schools." He saw the Supreme Court
acting "if the problem persists and the states fail to correct the evil."[42] It was
not to be.

The first indication of what lay ahead came in a 5 to 1 opinion of the
Fourth Circuit Court of Appeals striking down Merhige's consolidation
order as an "excessive" extension of the Fourteenth Amendment. "If the
District Court's theory was that the counties [Henrico and Chesterfield]
were thus keeping blacks in Richmond schools while allowing whites to flee
to relatively white sanctuaries, the facts do not support the theory," the
court ruled.[43]

We think that the root causes of the concentration of blacks in the inner cities of
America are simply not known and that the district court could not realistically place
on the counties the responsibility for the effect that inner city decay had on the
public schools of Richmond. We are convinced that what little action, if any, the
counties may seem to have taken to keep blacks out is slight indeed compared to the
myriad of reasons, economic, political and social, for the concentration of blacks in
Richmond and does not support the conclusion that it has been invidious state action
which has resulted in the racial composition of the three school districts.[44]

The court went on to note parallels between the situation in Richmond
and other metropolitan areas such as New York, Chicago, Detroit, Los
Angeles, and Atlanta. "Typical of all these cities," said the court, "is a
growing black population in the central city and a growing white population in the surrounding suburban and rural areas. Whatever the basic
causes, it has not been school assignments, and school assignments cannot
reverse the trend."[45]

Of the six appellate justices, only Harrison L. Winter, a former Baltimore district judge, disagreed. Recalling "the sordid history of Virginia's and Richmond's attempts to circumvent, defeat and nullify" the desegregation rulings of the High Court,[46] he found the majority's opinion a "manifest frustration of the teaching of *Brown I.*"[47]

A month after the Fourth Circuit decided the Richmond case, the nation learned it no longer had a united Supreme Court that favored the incremental approach to school desegregation. The Court's long-standing unanimity ended when Nixon's four appointees dissented in a 5 to 4 decision involving the Town of Emporia in Virginia. Originally, the NAACP had sued Greenville County, of which Emporia was a part, charging that free-choice had not eliminated school segregation. In the midst of the litigation, the town of Emporia broke away from the county, and the *City* of Emporia, located within the town, decided to establish its own free-choice school system. The NAACP objected, as it had with Greenville, and Judge Merhige upheld the plaintiff.[48] Again, the Fourth Circuit reversed Merhige,[49] but when the case went to the Supreme Court on appeal, the majority upheld the district court, stating that Emporia could not use the adoption of new political boundaries as an excuse to escape a ruling on school desegregation.[50]

This turning of the court's philosophy by the Nixon four received a more precise interpretation on March 21, 1973, when the court divided 5 to 4 over litigation involving public school financing. Demetrio Rodriguez, a forty-eight-year-old Mexican-American, had filed suit against the San Antonio school system because the Edgewood school district, where his three sons studied, had a small property base with high tax rates, while the Alamo Heights district across town had a large property base and lower taxes. The district court agreed with the plaintiff's contention and ordered the Texas legislature to remedy the inequity,[51] but when Rodriguez came before the High Court on appeal, the plaintiff lost.[52]

Writing for the majority, Powell gave four reasons for denying the contention that Texas's system of financing was discriminatory. First, he said, there was "reason to believe that the poorest families are not necessarily clustered in the poorest property districts."[53] For example, poor families are located in areas peripheral to large industrial firms which afford a large base for taxable real property.

Second, the Court ruled that Texas had not violated the Equal Protection Clause of the Fourteenth Amendment because the Constitution did not guarantee or "require absolute equality or precisely equal advantages."[54] Under what was called the Minimum Foundation Program, Texas provided each child with twelve years of free schooling which was enough to assuage the majority's doubts over possible inadequacy. If some school wished to speed the minimum level of expenditure, that fact could not be used to charge the state with intended discrimination.

Third, the Court rejected the allegation that an unchallenged relationship existed between the quality of education and the amount expended per pupil. In this framework, the fact that some schools spent more, some less, was not compelling.

Finally, Powell referred to a study of 110 Texas school districts which showed that median family income determined district spending in only 12 percent of those surveyed—the richest and the poorest. "We thus conclude," he wrote, "that the Texas system does not operate to the peculiar advantage of any suspect class."[55]

Besides the allegation of financial discrimination, Rodriguez contended public education was a fundamental right guaranteed by the Constitution. Not so, replied Powell. "It is not the province of this Court to create substantive constitutional rights in the name of guaranteeing equal protection of the laws. . . . Education . . . is not among the rights afforded explicit protection under our Federal Constitution."[56]

Nevertheless, the Court conceded imperfections in the Texas tax structure, and said that states may well have relied too long and too heavily on the property tax, "but," said Powell, the majority could not "assume for ourselves a level of wisdom superior to that of legislators, scholars and educational authorities in 50 states."[57]

Rodriguez cannot be read without detecting a change in the court's philosophy. By a rigid interpretation of the Constitution, the majority had, in the words of dissenter Thurgood Marshall, retreated from its "historic commitment to equality in educational opportunity."[58] Without changing direction, it was bestowing on a lower level of government responsibility for duties the Warren Court had imposed upon the Federal government.

The next milestone in the court's changing role occurred two months later on May 21, 1973, when it split 4 to 4 on Merhige's Richmond decision,[59] thus upholding the Fourth Circuit Court which had already reversed the district judge. Justice Powell disqualified himself because of his former membership on both the city's school board and the State Board of Education. Consequently, since the Court customarily did not reveal how the justices stood on a tie vote, there was no way of discovering how the eight members divided. Presumably, either White or Stewart joined forces with Burger, Blackmun, and Rehnquist. Whatever the head count, the result was heartening to those who sought to halt metropolitan desegregation plans. The White House had particular cause to rejoice since the Administration had argued against the Merhige decision, and in Henrico and Chesterfield, jubilation reigned supreme. "I don't know of any way they can beat us now," crowed Chesterfield's state senator.[60] In Richmond, where the brunt of the reversal would fall, a downcast school superintendent, Dr. Thomas C. Little, mused that more white families would now flee to the suburbs "unless the school system [could] find techniques to reverse the white flight."[61]

Naturally, much conjecture centered on Justice Powell's leanings, had he taken part in the decision. In Detroit, where similar litigation was edging its way to the High Court, William Saxton, attorney for thirty-one of fifty-two suburban districts involved in Roth's desegregation order, saw the Richmond decision as "highly significant."[62] He said he would anticipate a 5 to 4 ruling against cross-district busing with Powell providing the deciding vote, based on his *Rodriguez* opinion.[63] This conviction was amplified the following day by Eugene Krasicky, assistant state attorney general, who represented Michigan in the proceedings. "If they [the NAACP which initiated the action in Richmond and Detroit] can't win in Richmond, they can't win in Detroit," he predicted.[64] Despite these anticipatory statements, Powell remained an enigma. He undoubtedly empathized with minority problems. His nomination to the Supreme Court would not have received NAACP support, had he not. What happened in Richmond as a result of the white exodus to the suburbs clearly troubled him. In 1969, when he retired from an eight-year term on the board, Powell had written, "in our larger metropolitan areas, there are income deficiencies and a racial mix which results in serious educational disadvantages. There is no longer any debate as to the need for vigorous action to right this educational imbalance."[65] The question was which side did he now stand on: state rights or human rights?

A month afterwards, on June 21, 1973, Powell furnished further illumination on his views when the court reached a decision in *Keyes* v. *School District Number One, Denver, Colorado*.[66] This ruling, like so many landmark opinions, had a long history. Beginning shortly after Martin Luther King's assassination on April 4, 1968, more than 200 concerned Denver blacks and whites joined hands to prevent a "split society" in their city. They called themselves Citizens for One Community and quickly permuted the spark into an organization of some forty cooperating civic groups, known as Speak out on School Integration. Within two weeks, Mrs. Rachel Noel, a black member of the Denver School Board, was asking her colleagues to adopt a resolution that would establish an "integrated school population . . . [and] achieve equality of educational opportunity."[67] Uncertain and apprehensive, the majority responded by tabling the motion 5 to 2.

Unquestionably, Mrs. Noel had succeeded in tweaking the city's racial nose. During a mass meeting that excoriated the resolution, one white ethnic foresaw the "death of the community school" and expressed weariness over "beatniks, hippies and other minorities pushing the majorities around."[68] Nevertheless, in the face of rising opposition, the Board found new resolve. It reversed its position and following an explosive five-hour debate, ordered the school superintendent to develop an integration plan.

This effort to diminish racial acrimony proved useless, however, for neither side would yield. On the one hand, the co-chairman of the Citizens for One Community denigrated what the superintendent brought forth.

"Black schools for black children in black neighborhoods run by black people," he stormed.[69] On the other, the segregationists, terming themselves the "silent majority," (which they hardly were) complained that they were "being sold out to a loud and persistent minority . . . and racial-balance fanatics."[70] Caught between these two fires, the Board refused to go beyond a few modest steps. In early 1969, it adopted three resolutions to desegregate seven schools in the northeast section of Denver, the Park Hill area, site of the most blatant segregation.

With another school election only months away, it seemed best to let the voters decide. At issue were two seats, held by integrationists who had supported the Noel Resolution. Should the "silent majority" capture both, the Board majority would shift from a 5 to 3 *for* to a 4 to 3 *against* desegregation, thus rescinding the Board's action of the previous year.

Under normal conditions, the integrationists would have won. Both were Democrats, supported by the Democratic party, in a city with a heavy Democratic enrollment. Edgar Benton, forty-two, had been a Board member for eight years, and blamed segregation for the fact that Anglo students rated scholastically better than black or Hispanic pupils, ascribing the difference to the "negative attitude of the dominant society towards the minority group."[71] What seemed clearly evident to this Yale Law School graduate took on a different meaning when spoken to the man on the street. The words, coming from a man of education and position, sounded exalted if not arrogant.

His running mate, Monte Pascoe, thirty-four, was no less a symbol of the establishment. A graduate of Dartmouth College and Stanford University Law School, he ran on a platform espousing integrated education, and if that meant busing, "so be it," he said.[72] It was Pascoe's theme that segregationists exaggerated the issue, that even complete integration would require transportation for only one student in five and add about one in eight of those not currently bused.

Benton and Pascoe faced two conservative Republicans. James Perrill, forty-four, a former GOP state senator, and graduate of Kansas State University and the Denver University Law School, plumped for neighborhood schools. When Mrs. Noel had introduced her resolution a year earlier, almost alone among thirty-five speakers appearing at a public gathering, he condemned its provisions. "It's too fast," he declared heatedly. "The white Protestant—or whatever you want to call them—majority isn't going to go away."[73]

The second antibusing candidate was Frank Southworth, forty-three, a realtor with a degree in economics from the University of Kentucky. During the previous year, he had chaired Ronald Reagan's unsuccessful campaign for the presidency in Colorado. Southworth vehemently opposed what he called the Board's "massive forced transportation program," saying it had

completely divided the community "in every section, every facet, throughout business, churches, racial, ethnic and political parties. Any way you
look," he declared, "there is division." Asked "whether he'd . . . favor the
school district's actively encouraging voluntary busing for integration," he
replied, "The Board of Education's primary purpose for being in existence is
not social problems in the community."[74]

From the sidelines, the *Denver Post* editorially observed, " 'Massive
forced busing'—was and is a strangely fearful" campaign slogan. It kindles
"the people's fears of what it would do to their children."[75] In vain did
George E. Bardwell, a mathematics professor at the University of Denver
and chairman of the Speak Out on School Integration group, point out the
benefits of integrating Anglos, Hispanics, and blacks. Using figures compiled by the U.S. Civil Rights Commission, he demonstrated that desegregation was the single greatest factor in raising the scholastic achievement of
the "disadvantaged."[76] It accounted for 69 percent of the gain, far more than
any enrichment due to improved teaching, better libraries, equipment, or
buildings.

On election day Perrill and Southworth swamped their opponents 2½ to
1, in a showing of white strength. While Benton and Pascoe won by as
much as 10 to 1 in some black areas, they lost white districts 6 to 1.
Quickly, the victors moved in to claim their spoils. The Board voted 4 to 3
to rescind its three anti-bias resolutions and to replace them with a voluntary student transfer program. It was then that eight frustrated families—
five black, two Anglo, and one Hispanic—filed a class action suit, seeking
an injunction against the Board's reversal. The litigation bore the name of
the first petitioner, Wilfred Keyes, a black pupil in Hallett Elementary, one
of the so-called Park Hill schools, that was 84.4 percent black.

The man before whom the plaintiffs appeared was a Denver native,
William E. Doyle, with a shirttail record of public service that included
stints of deputy district attorney, Denver District Justice, Colorado
Supreme Court Judge, topped by a place on the U.S. District bench. A
strong personality, Doyle believed in the Constitution and like so many
of his colleagues, would follow its commands regardless of personal loss or
tribulation. The evidence convinced him that the Board had clearly
abridged the rights of the petitioners. In less than five weeks, he ordered the
Board to desegregate the seven Park Hill schools by implementing the three
cast-off resolutions. It had, he said, engaged over almost a decade after 1960
in an unconstitutional policy of deliberate racial segregation.[77] Emboldened
by this victory, the families broadened their charge the following year to
include all 119 schools in the system, particularly the fifteen segregated
institutions in the core city. "Although we have concluded," wrote Doyle,
"that there is not *de jure* segregation in the so-called core city schools, we
have found and concluded that there is a denial of equal opportunity for
education in these schools."[78] To Doyle, the situation was one of de facto

segregation, a case of separate educational facilities, requiring a *Plessy* v. *Ferguson* solution.[79] Under this doctrine, Doyle ruled "a school board was under no constitutional duty to abandon dual school systems created by law so long as all schools were equal in terms of the educational opportunity offered."[80]

On appeal to the Tenth Circuit Court of Appeals, the higher court agreed with Doyle on his determination of the seven de jure schools, but not his adjudication of the fifteen de facto schools.[81] On further appeal, the Supreme Court disagreed June 21, 1973, with both lower courts, arguing in a 7 to 1 decision that because the Denver Board was guilty of de jure segregation, the entire system must be considered dual, and therefore, unconstitutional.[82] In short, one bad apple contaminates the whole barrel. Still timid, however, over launching a frontal attack on de facto segregation, it refused to take a direct stand while indirectly broadening the scope in which discriminatory suits might be argued. For Jack Greenberg, director-counsel of the NAACP Legal Defense Fund, it was "the first time that the Supreme Court [had] embraced the principle that if you show some governmental involvement in creating segregation, you would then treat the system more or less as you would treat a Southern system where segregation had been created by state statute."[83]

Justice Powell, though joining the majority, filed a separate opinion which spoke to several motifs.

[S]ubstantial progress toward achieving integration has been made in southern states. No comparable progress has been made in many nonsouthern cities with large minority populations primarily because of the *de facto/de jure* distinction nurtured by the courts and accepted complacently by many of the same voices which denounced the evils of segregated schools in the South. But if our national concern is for those who attend such schools, rather than perpetuating a legalism rooted in history rather than present reality, we must recognize that the evil of operating separate schools is no less in Denver than in Atlanta.

In my view, we should abandon a distinction which long since has outlived its time, and formulate constitutional principles of national rather than merely regional application. . . ."[84]

Powell feared that in expanding the definition of de jure to include a school board's "segregative intent," as *Keyes* had, the court was opening a can of worms. "The intractable problems involved in litigating this issue," he said, "are obvious to any lawyer. The results of litigation—often arrived at subjectively by a court endeavoring to ascertain the subjective intent of school authorities with respect to action taken or not taken over many years—will be fortuitous, unpredictable and even capricious."[85]

Justice Brennan, writing for the majority, tried to meet the Powell argument by listing such examples of "segregative intent" as confining black students to selected schools through gerrymandering district lines, selecting school sites to produce a segregated school, and assigning faculty and staff on the basis of racial discrimination, to name a few.[86]

By sending *Keyes* back to the District Court with instructions for the Denver Board either to prove it had not acted with "segregative intent" or to desegregate the school system, the court tore from every Northern school district the protective cloak that de facto categorization previously furnished. Presumably, the majority, faced with the ultimate declaration against de facto segregation, refused to equate de facto with de jure for fear of opening the flood gates of litigation, a development not even Brennan, Douglas, and Marshall cared to endorse.

Justice Rehnquist produced the lone dissent, rejecting the call for a broader definition of de jure segregation. "The Court," he decried, "has taken a long leap . . . in equating the district-wide consequences of gerry-mandering individual attendance zones in a district where separation of the races was never required by law with statutes or ordinances in other juris-dictions which did so require."[87]

With *Keyes* decided, it was now clear the Court's majority would not countenance school segregation in a single school district whether de jure or de facto if it had occurred with the "segregative intent" of the school author-ities. However, the Court's reaction to a metropolitan situation in which the segregated district was a city surrounded by a white suburban noose remained unsettled. In the eyes of Robert Merhige, in Richmond, and Stephen Roth, in Detroit, the only solution to the inner city problem lay in uniting the predominantly black urban population with the peripheral white population.

By the fall of 1973, the first shoe had dropped. The Fourth Circuit Court of Appeals found Merhige's plan of combining Richmond with Henrico and Chesterfield Counties unacceptable. Merhige, said the court, had exceeded his authority in erasing duly constituted school boundaries, an opinion the Supreme Court allowed to stand.[88] The Roth litigation, however, posed a slightly different question, small perhaps, but nevertheless significant. Roth had not ordered the elimination of school lines, only that students be bused across district lines to achieve integration.

Contrary to Richmond, the Sixth Circuit Court of Appeals had ruled the previous spring in favor of Roth's contention that only a metropolitan plan could solve the problem of school segregation in the City of Detroit.[89] Michigan's Attorney General Frank J. Kelly confidently expected that Roth and the Sixth Circuit would now be reversed, based on the Richmond ruling. In a ninety-page brief, filed the first week of 1974, he told the Court that "a multischool district remedy is constitutionally impermissible," and then apparently oblivious to the dictum of *Brown I* that segregated education is inherently unequal,[90] Kelly went on, "Unless the court is to abandon the principles of racial equality it has enunicated over the past 20 years, and hold that majority black school systems are somehow intrinsically inferior to school systems with white majorities, it must conclude that a Detroit-only plan of desegregation satisfies constitutional requirements."[91]

Opposing the Attorney General, William T. Downs, attorney for a Detroit-based interfaith group, embracing the city's leading religious organizations, pled with the Court to uphold Roth. "A metropolitan solution is required by the evidence, compelled by the Constitution, and demanded by justice." To confine any desegregation plan to Detroit would produce a system 90 percent black, a cure "worse than the disease." To the question of whether the suburban districts, included in the Roth plan, had to be found guilty of segregating blacks, in order to be embodied in the solution, Downs said, "No." Once the state had been judged "guilty," as the Court had previously found, "the choice of schools to be involved in the remedy is determined by the remedial effect and not by the alleged guilt or innocence of the proposed school districts." Moreover, if evidence of discrimination in the suburbs were needed, it was easy to find. He singled out the "point" system, used by the Grosse Pointe (Real Estate) Brokers Association between 1943 and 1960, which barred Jews and Negroes. With such discriminatory methods, the "racially identifiable school districts surrounding the city of Detroit are not a coincidence."[92]

On February 27, 1974, the Court listened to ninety minutes of verbal arguments. Again, Michigan's Attorney General argued that the suburbs were not responsible for possible constitutional violations in Detroit. Should such a finding occur, only the Detroit School District should be ordered to convert to a unitary school system. On the opposite side, the NAACP's chief attorney, Louis R. Lucas, maintained that the "deliberate confinement of black children to a core of schools within a line separating them from reciprocally white schools—is not constitutionally different from gerrymandering school attendance zone lines around black neighborhoods."[93] The Sixth Circuit, sitting en banc, had made a similar complaint: "The conclusion . . . is inescapable [that desegregation of the Detroit schools] cannot be accomplished within the corporate geographical limits of the city. . . . School district lines are simply matters of political convenience and may not be used to deny constitutional rights."[94]

Tragically for the plaintiffs, they failed to analyze the High Court's evolving direction; the belief that school lines were inviolate could only be changed by a finding of proven discrimination within each. Within this meaning, even two juxtaposed districts would bear no responsibility for eliminating discrimination outside their borders.

While the Roth opinion was being anxiously awaited, fate removed on July 1 the man responsible for the district ruling. After suffering a third heart attack within twenty months, Stephen Roth died. Momentarily, the ire he had stirred up subsided, and critics saw only the man. No voice had previously excoriated Judge Roth in such strident terms as the *Detroit News*, yet in death, it had the grace to credit Roth with "authoring one of the most discussed questions of law in modern judicial history. . . . Perhaps those tensions and the criticism he received for authoring the concept of metropolitan cross-district busing contributed to the ill health preceding his death."[95]

As Carl Sandburg said of Lincoln, referring to the death of the President, "a tree is best measured when it's down."[96] Of Roth, men could bear witness to his character after his departure. Roth had been a firm adherent of the law and the law held school segregation to be unconstitutional. Roth did not champion busing to accomplish this; he had opposed its use when the trial began in 1970. However, putting aside his personal predilection, he had concluded the only way to comply with the law was to order busing even though it resulted in crossing district lines and stirring up immense controversy. In the words of Martin Luther King, "There comes a time when one must take a stand that is neither safe, nor public nor popular, but one must take it, because it is right."[97] This Roth had done.

On July 25, 1974, the Supreme Court finally announced its decision. In a 5 to 4 opinion, the Court reversed Roth and the Sixth Circuit Court of Appeals. Chief Justice Burger wrote the majority opinion, joined by Powell, Blackmun, and Rehnquist, with Potter Stewart concurring in a separate opinion. In opposition were the four Warren holdovers—Brennan, Douglas, Marshall, and White.

Burger's reasoning rested on two general assumptions—the right of state government to control public education, guaranteed by the Tenth Amendment, and limitation of the Equal Protection Clause of the Fourteenth Amendment to single school districts.

On the first point, Burger relied heavily upon *Wright*[98] and *Rodriguez*,[99] precedents to nail down the majority's contention that the judiciary should not intervene in school affairs that were properly the concern of the state and its particular creations (i.e., school districts). "No single tradition in public education is more deeply rooted than local control over the operation of schools," he wrote, and to conclude as the district court had, that school district lines were "no more than arbitrary lines on a map 'drawn for political convenience'," was simply inadmissible.[100] An analysis of Michigan's educational structure "indicates the extent to which the interdistrict remedies approved by the two courts could disrupt and alter the structure of public education."[101] The thought of fifty-four independent school districts consolidated into one metropolitan entity staggered the Chief Justice. What would be the fate of the "popularly elected school boards?" Who would levy taxes in the fifty-four districts so as to ensure equality? "Who would establish attendance zones, purchase school equipment, locate and construct new schools [for] potentially more than three-quarters of a million pupils?"

Without a total revision of Michigan statutes to cope with these complex problems, the majority predicted the district court would become "first a *de facto* 'legislative authority' " and eventually the "school superintendent" for the metropolitan district.[102]

The minority unsuccessfully challenged this view of the sanctity of individual districts. Douglas saw the argument as a dodge. "Metropolitan treatment of metropolitan problems," he wrote "is commonplace. If there were a sewage problem or an energy problem, there can be no doubt that Michigan would stay well within federal constitutional bounds if she sought a metropolitan remedy."[103] In a concurrent minority report, Justice White said, "Obviously, whatever difficulties there might be, they are surmountable; for the Court itself concedes that, had there been sufficient evidence of an interdistrict violation, the District Court could have fashioned a single remedy for the districts implicated rather than a different remedy for each district in which the violation had occurred or had an impact."[104]

However true, the chief difference between the majority and minority decisions centered on two interpretations of the Fourteenth Amendment. Burger refused to budge beyond the ground already plowed in previous decisions. Never had the court sanctioned a plan the parameters of which extended beyond the single school district. In Burger's view, it should not do so now, even though a metropolitan solution was needed. The problem arose in *Milliken*, he said, because the lower courts had emphasized "racial balance which they perceived as desirable,"[105] when they should have restricted their solution to the one area of proven segregation. "Disparate treatment of white and Negro students," he said, "occurred within the Detroit school system, and not elsewhere, and on this record, the remedy must be limited to the system."[106] Burger made it clear that the Court would "prescribe appropriate remedies" if it found that school district lines were drawn in a discriminatory fashion,[107] but said he, "The record before us, voluminous as it is, contains evidence of *de jure* segregated conditions only in the Detroit schools. . . ."[108] Accordingly, the majority ruled that without a showing of de jure segregation within the fifty-three suburban districts, the latter could not be ordered to aid in the solution of Detroit's segregation.

This narrow interpretation, in the face of a social problem crying out for a solution, understandably infuriated the Court's minority. Caustically, Douglas wrote that "there can be no doubt that as a matter of Michigan law the state itself has the final say as to where and how school district lines should be drawn. When we rule against the metropolitan area remedy we take a step that will likely put the problems of the blacks and our society back to the period that antedated the 'separate but equal' regime of *Plessy* v. *Ferguson.* . . . Today's decision, given *Rodriguez*, means that there is no violation of the Equal Protection Clause though the schools are segregated by race and though the black schools are not only 'separate' but 'inferior'."[109] Sharing the same critical view of the majority opinion, Justice White professed to be "mystified" as to how the Court could overlook the fact that "constitutional violations, even if occurring locally, were committed by governmental entities for which the State is responsible and that it is the State that must respond to the command of the Fourteenth Amendment . . . The unwavering decisions of this Court over the past 20 years support the assumption of the Court of Appeals that the District Court's remedial power does not cease at the school district line."[110]

Nevertheless, it fell to Thurgood Marshall, the principal plaintiff attorney in *Brown I*, to make the most poignant arguments against the majority. Marshall called the decision a "giant step backwards." In a separate opinion, he wrote, "Ironically, purporting to base its result on the principle that the scope of the remedy in a desegregation case should be determined by the nature and the extent of the constitutional violation, the Court's answer is to provide no remedy at all for the violation proved in this case, thereby guaranteeing that Negro children in Detroit will receive the same separate and inherent unequal education in the future as they have been unconstitutionally afforded in the past."[111]

Based on previous decisions of the High Court, Marshall saw it as Michigan's duty "to eliminate root and branch all vestiges of racial discrimination."[112] Without involving the outlying metropolitan school district, "this duty cannot be fulfilled. . . . We deal here with the right of all of our children, whatever their race, to an equal start in life and to an equal opportunity to reach their full potential as citizens. Those children who have been denied that right in the past deserve better than to see fences thrown up to deny them that right in the future. Our Nation, I fear, will be ill-served by the Court's refusal to remedy separate and unequal education, for unless our children begin to learn together, there is little hope that our people will ever learn to live together."[113]

Why did the majority hold back? Why would Burger, for instance, who orchestrated a unanimous decision in *Swann*[114] to open the busing floodgates, now sidestep *Brown's* logical implementation, one supported by the district judge and the Sixth Circuit? Since there is no peephole through which we might elicit Burger's inner thinking, the answer has to be subjective. The Chief Justice embraced the essence of *Brown*, but time's accretion had raised doubts about expanding its application. No sooner had the Court ruled in *Swann* than Burger was telling district judges, unusual for a Supreme Court Chief Justice, to read the opinion carefully so as not to go overboard with the obvious intent of placing a checkrein on their future school decisions. Also, Burger presumably agonized over the Court's declining position in American life. He himself had criticized the Warren Court for eroding the plateau on which the High Court stood. Its adherence to *Miranda*,[115] protecting the rights of the accused, appeared to a majority of Americans as preference for the criminal over the rights of the injured.

Burger, in all likelihood, feared further erosion, if the Court did not fall back to more temperate positions on school desegregation. When the choice finally came down to broadening the Constitution's definition of equality, or restoring the majority's faith in the Court, Burger opted for the latter. Blackmun apparently endorsed Burger's conclusions, and Rehnquist's acquiescence, given his position in *Keyes*,[116] was not unexpected.

Of the Nixon four, then, Powell's stand was the hardest to decipher. As previously stated, he was well aware of the severe handicaps imposed upon minority children living in the inner city. Unfortunately, the cure struck him as worse than the disease. In *Keyes*, he had written that courts "may have overlooked the fact that the rights and interests of children affected by a desegregation program also are entitled to consideration. Any child, white or black, who is compelled to leave his neighborhood and spend significant time each day being transported to a distant school suffers an impairment of his liberty and privacy."[117] Powell considered this "impairment" of greater significance than the fact that, as Marshall pointed out, "all our children, whatever their race [are entitled] to an equal start in life and an equal opportunity to reach their full potential as citizens."[118] Of course, other reasons figured in Powell's determination. He had made it clear in *Rodriguez* that since the right to an education was not afforded equal protection by the Federal Constitution, it became a state responsibility within the meaning of the Tenth Amendment which granted states those powers not held by the national government. Thus, Powell too, if not for the same reasons persuasive to Burger, joined the majority.

Only Potter Stewart, of the majority, hedged his concurrence. While Stewart agreed with Burger's basic thesis, he allowed that under certain conditions he would have joined the minority thus upholding Roth. "Were it to be shown, for example," he wrote, "that state officials had contributed to the separation of the races by drawing or redrawing school district lines . . . or by purposeful, racially discriminatory use of state housing or zoning laws, then a decree calling for transfer of pupils across district lines or for restructuring of district lines might well be appropriate. In this case, however, no such interdistrict violation was shown. Indeed, no evidence at all concerning the administration of schools outside the city of Detroit was presented other than the fact that these schools contained a higher proportion of white pupils than did the schools within the city. Since the mere fact of different racial compositions in contiguous districts does not itself imply or constitute a violation of the Equal Protection Clause in the absence of a showing that such disparity was imposed, fostered or encouraged by the state or its political subdivisions, it follows that no interdistrict violation was shown in this case."[119]

Possibly had Stewart been less of a pragmatist, a different ruling would have emerged. "What I think is basically irrelevant," he would say later, "It's what the law says that matters."[120] He would not concede—as others in the minority had—the need to fashion new remedies to fit a new situation, a metropolitan situation. Nor did he seek from the plaintiffs information on the suburbs that would prove discriminating practices, i.e., Warren township with 132 blacks out of a population of 179,000; Dearborn with thirteen blacks, population 104,000; two blacks in a student body of 13,000 in Grosse Pointe.

The plaintiffs had been lulled into a false sense of security after the three-judge panel of the Sixth Circuit unanimously upheld in December, 1972, Roth's insistence on a metropolitan plan, saying "it will not be necessary for the District Court to find discriminatory conduct, either *de jure* or *de facto* as a prerequisite to including such districts in a desegregation area."[121]

The die was cast, and in casting it, the Supreme Court had endorsed a ruling that greatly impeded the work of proving metropolitan school segregation. In both *Rodriguez* and *Milliken*, the Court had reached conclusions, via the Tenth Amendment, that provided little help to minorities, hungering for a better deal, first in school financing, and then in classroom equality. As Paul Hazelton pointed out in *Commonweal*, "The Detroit case turns, not on busing, but on the question of the state's power and responsibility in designing the local school districts. . . . it is evident that the prevailing majority view of the Court with its consequences for financing as well as for school district organization sustains inevitably a dual system of public education in this country."[122]

On the day the *Milliken* decision was handed down, Verda Bradley, mother of ten-year-old Ronald, whose name the suit bore, had taken her television set to work, hoping to hear a positive news flash from Washington. "My mouth just fell open in a state of shock for a few minutes," she cried.[123] Not all blacks, however, shared her disappointment. Mayor Coleman Young, of Detroit, for one, called a news conference to say he was shedding "no big tears for cross-district busing. I don't think that was ever the basic issue which is the problem of equal education opportunity . . . . I don't think there's any magic in putting little white kids alongside little black kids on a school bench if the little white kids and little black kids over here have half a dollar for their education and the little black and little white kids over there are getting a dollar." Young wanted "state educational fiscal reform . . . [to give] all school children throughout the state . . . equal amounts of money."[124]

For entirely different reasons, "no big tears for cross-district busing" were being shed in the suburbs. There, residents exuded joy from knowing the barrier that separated blacks from whites was legally secure. William K. Stevens, of the *New York Times*, journeying to Roseville in Warren, found that middle-class white community happy that "their children were now 'safe'." Stevens approached a group of six women who were discussing the decision. With school integration "stalled," would fair housing be the next civil rights thrust, he asked. "If so, how would people react to the prospect of black neighbors?"

"My husband would put a for-sale sign right away," one said.

"If it's a colored person buying the house with his own hard-earned money, and he wants better for his kids, that'd be o.k.," said another. "But you get that welfare and that Aid to Dependent Children bunch. . . ."[125]

Shockingly, those who had once supported school integration hastened to lay the issue to rest. Said "ex-liberal" Rep. O'Hara, "Now that the issue has been resolved, I hope we can return our attention to more positive aspects of schooling our children," as though anything could be more "positive" than children of all races learning to know each other.[126] Joined in O'Hara's fellow Congressman, John D. Dingell, "The best way to improve the education system is to increase the dollar totals in federal funding to ensure adequate and equal educational opportunities for every child, regardless of race, creed or color,"[127] which under *Milliken* meant returning to the *Plessy* v. *Ferguson* 'separate but equal' philosophy, which *Brown* had outlawed twenty years before.

Others could not so casually cast the verdict aside. "Inherent in the Court's rejection of inter-district relief are two messages," wrote General Counsel of the NAACP, Nathaniel R. Jones, "To whites it says that if discrimination against blacks is on a vast enough scale, remedies will prove too awesome to invoke and thus the evil can be perpetuated; and to Negro Americans it says that they have only those rights that the white majority finds convenient to concede."[128]

The *Detroit Free Press* seemed to agree editorially with Jones's analysis: "Is it possible to avoid that result?" the newspaper asked rhetorically. "Is the state interested in avoiding it? We question whether it can be done, and we doubt even more strongly whether there is a will to avoid and reverse the trend toward the ghettoization of the central city. That is a problem too difficult, too massive, too requiring of courage to get the kind of action needed."[129]

Sadly, Roth's solution was aborted. A week after the decision, author William Serrin wrote from Detroit, "No one was happy with the idea of busing. It would have been accompanied by great traumas. But busing would have forced suburban communities to become interested in Detroit's schools. White wealth and power could not have ignored Detroit's schools without ignoring white suburban children. Money would have been forced into Detroit."[130]

Notes

1. *Bradley* v. *Milliken*, 418 U.S. 717 (1974), at 783.
2. *New York Times*, April 15, 1970.
3. Ibid.
4. *Brown* v. *Board of Education*, 347 U.S. 483 (1954).
5. *Time*, November 1, 1971.

6. Ibid.

7. *New York Times*, October 22, 1971.

8. *Time*, November 1, 1971.

9. Alan Dershowitz, "Of Justices and 'Philosophies'," *New York Times*, October 24, 1971.

10. *Time*, November 1, 1971, p. 18.

11. *Newsweek*, November 1, 1971.

12. *Time*, November 1, 1971.

13. *Newsweek*, November 1, 1971, p. 19.

14. *New York Times*, October 22, 1971.

15. *Richmond Times-Dispatch*, August 1, 1971.

16. Ibid.

17. *New York Times*, June 20, 1972.

18. Martin Waldron, "Rehnquist Is Described . . . ," *New York Times*, October 28, 1971.

19. *Time*, November 1, 1971, p. 19.

20. Waldron, "Rehnquist Is Described."

21. *Time*, November 1, 1971, p. 19.

22. Ibid.

23. *New York Times*, October 22, 1971.

24. *Time*, November 1, 1971, p. 19.

25. U.S. Congress, Senate Committee on the Judiciary, *Subcommittee Hearings on Federal Data Banks, Computers, and the Bill of Rights*, 92d Cong., 1st sess., 1971, 603, 863.

26. *Newsweek*, November 1, 1971, p. 19.

27. *New York Times*, October 30, 1971.

28. *New York Times*, October 26, 1971.

29. *New York Times*, December 7, 1971.

30. *New York Times*, October 30, 1971.

31. Ibid.

32. *New York Times*, November 4, 1971.

33. *Time*, November 22, 1971.

34. "The Rehnquist Fight," *National Review*, December 3, 1971.

35. *Time*, November 22, 1971.

36. *New York Times*, December 11, 1971.

37. William V. Shannon, "A Question or Three . . . ," *New York Times*, November 7, 1971.

38. *Bradley* v. *School Board of the City of Richmond, Virginia*, 338 F. Supp. 67 (1972), at 101.

39. Ibid., at 83.

40. "No Place to Hide," *Time*, January 24, 1972.

41. Ben A. Franklin, "A Decision That . . . ," *New York Times*, January 16, 1972.

42. Ibid.

43. *Bradley* v. *School Board of City of Richmond, Virginia*, 462 F. 2d. 1058 (1972), at 1065.

44. Ibid., at 1066.

45. Ibid.

46. Ibid., at 1075.

47. Ibid., at 1078.

48. *Wright* v. *County School Board of Greenville County, Virginia,* 309 F. Supp. 671 (1970).

49. *Wright* v. *Council of the City of Emporia,* 442 F. 2d. 570 (1971).

50. *Wright* v. *Council of the City of Emporia,* 407 U.S. 451 (1972) [hereafter *Wright* (1972)].

51. *Rodriguez* v. *San Antonio Independent School District,* 337 F. Supp. 280 (1971).

52. *San Antonio School District* v. *Rodriguez,* 411 U.S. 1, (1973).

53. Ibid., at 23.

54. Ibid., at 24.

55. Ibid., at 28.

56. Ibid., at 33 and 35.

57. Ibid., at 55.

58. Ibid., at 71.

59. *Richmond School Board* v. *Board of Education,* 412 U.S. 92 (1973).

60. *New York Times,* May 22, 1973.

61. Ibid.

62. *Detroit News,* May 21, 1973.

63. *San Antonio School District* v. *Rodriguez.*

64. *Detroit News,* May 22, 1973.

65. *New York Times,* May 22, 1973.

66. *Keyes* v. *School District Number One, Denver, Colorado,* 413 U.S. 189 (1973) [hereafter *Keyes* (1973)].

67. Resolution presented to Denver School Board by Mrs. Rachel Noel on April 25, 1968.

68. *Denver Post,* May 10, 1968.

69. *Denver Post,* September 5, 1968.

70. *Denver Post,* January 17, 1969.

71. *Denver Post,* May 11, 1969.

72. *Denver Post,* May 12, 1969.

73. *Denver Post,* April 26, 1968.

74. *Denver Post,* May 15, 1969.

75. Editorial, *Denver Post,* May 21, 1969.

76. *Racial Isolation in the Public Schools,* U.S. Civil Rights Commission, (1967), p. 98, Table 5.

77. *Keyes* v. *School District Number One, Denver, Colorado,* 303 F. Supp. 279 (1969).

78. *Keyes* v. *School District Number One, Denver, Colorado,* 313 F. Supp. 61 (1970), at 84 [hereafter *Keyes* (1970)].

79. *Plessy* v. *Ferguson,* 163 U.S. 537 (1896).

80. *Keyes* (1970) at 83.

81. *Keyes* v. *School District Number One, Denver, Colorado,* 445 F. 2d 990 (1971).

82. *Keyes* (1973).

83. Evan Jenkins, "Race Ruling Called . . . ," *New York Times,* June 23, 1973.

84. *Keyes* (1973), at 218-19.

85. Ibid., at 233.

86. Ibid., at 201-2.

87. Ibid., at 265.

88. *Bradley* v. *School Board,* and *Richmond School Board* v. *Board.*

89. *Bradley* v. *Milliken,* 484 F. 2d 215 (1973).

90. Ibid., *Brown* v. *Board of Education.*

91. *Detroit News,* January 3, 1974.

92. *Detroit News,* March 5, 1974.

93. *Detroit News,* February 27, 1974.

94. *Bradley* v. *Milliken* (1973), at 244.

95. Editorial, "Roth's Ruling Made History," *Detroit News* July 14, 1974.

96. Carl Sandburg, *Abraham Lincoln: The War Years,* Vol. 4 (New York: Harcourt, Brace and Company, 1939), p. 357.

97. *Detroit News,* March 5, 1974.

98. *Wright* (1972).

99. *San Antonio School District* v. *Rodriguez.*

100. *Bradley* v. *Milliken* (1974), at 741.

101. Ibid., at 742-43.

102. Ibid., at 743-44.

103. Ibid., at 758.

104. Ibid., at 769-70.

105. Ibid., at 740.

106. Ibid., at 746.

107. Ibid., at 744.

108. Ibid., at 745.

109. *Bradley* v. *Milliken* (1974), at 761.

110. Ibid., at 770-72.

111. Ibid., at 782.

112. Ibid.

113. Ibid., at 783.

114. *Swann* v. *Charlotte-Mecklenburg Board of Education,* 402 U.S. 1 (1971).

115. *Miranda* v. *Arizona,* 384 U.S. 436 (1966).

116. *Keyes* (1973).

117. Ibid., at 247-8.

118. *Bradley* v. *Milliken* (1974).

119. Ibid., at 755-56.

120. *New York Times,* April 30, 1982.

121. *Detroit News,* December 12, 1972.

122. Paul Hazelton, "Choice and the School," *Commonweal,* October 4, 1974, p. 13.

123. *Detroit Free Press,* July 26, 1974.

124. Agis Salpukas, "Joy Is Expressed . . . ," *New York Times,* July 26, 1974.

125. William K. Stevens, "Many Whites Now See . . . ," *New York Times,* July 27, 1974.

126. *Detroit News,* July 26, 1974.

127. Ibid.

128. Letter to the *New York Times,* August 15, 1974.

129. Editorial, "Court Calms the Waters . . . ," *Detroit Free Press,* July 26, 1974.

130. William Serrin, "Detroit, Where Life Is Worth Living," *New York Times,* August 1, 1974.

19

AGONY IN THE CRADLE OF LIBERTY

"They're doing the work for the bankers, for the politicians, for the ministers and priests . . . for all the holier-than-thou sermons that have been delivered in Boston for the last 100 years. . . . The ultimate reality is the reality of class, having and not having, social and economic vulnerability versus social and economic power—that's where the issue is."

Robert Coles, Harvard Sociologist.[1]

In the years following World War II, the City of Boston added a new chapter to the long history of racial conflict. Despite its historic reputation as the cradle of liberty during the American Revolution, and as the citadel of abolitionism prior to the Civil War, Yankee descendents of these freedom fighters had little understanding of the plight millions of Irish immigrants endured. A seemingly endless stream landed in Boston during the nineteenth century, fresh from potato famine and British repression in their own land.

In some ways, the class struggle between the two white groups resembled the conflict that broke out when another wave—Southern blacks—struck the city. To make the transformation more difficult, Boston had become an urban entity of tightly knit white ethnics surrounding an expanding black core concentrated in the central Roxbury section. Their juxtaposition, like coils surrounding a magnetic field, had induced a current of opposition as they moved to vie with one another for jobs and housing.

To keep the two separate, the Boston School Committee isolated black students and by 1960, approximately 80 percent attended public elementary schools in which blacks constituted a majority. After the Commonwealth's Commissioner of Education, Owen Kiernan, realized what was afoot, he enlisted the aid of the State Board of Education in appointing an advisory committee to study the trend. Its report, issued in April, 1965, revealed that forty-five Boston schools had more than 50 percent minority students. Importuned by this fact and goaded by the civil rights revolution, then reaching its apogee, the Massachusetts legislature enacted the 1965 Racial Imbalance Act, which went beyond comparable statutes passed in other states. Under its provisions, the Commonwealth was forbidden to support school systems whose nonwhite enrollment exceeded 50 percent. While the statute covered the entire state, its chief thrust was Boston.

At first, the Boston School Committee denied the new law's legality by challenging its constitutionality. As the lengthy litigation between state and committee, initiated in 1967, continued to drag on, Neil Sullivan, Massachusetts Education Commissioner, grew frustrated. In desperation, during the summer of 1971, he ordered $21 million in state aid withheld. Finally capitulating to this economic shortfall, the Committee agreed to build two integrated elementary schools, an act that persuaded Sullivan to release $7 million. For a time, it appeared a new day had dawned, but after angry parents objected to the concession, the Committee reneged on its promise and challenged the Commissioner's right to hold back the remaining $14 million.

Meanwhile, the Committee was feeling new and unanticipated pressure. Senator John McClellan, the powerful Arkansas Democrat, seething over HEW's enforcement of Title VI in the South, demanded an investigation of the Boston school segregation. Appearing before Sen. Mondale's Select Committee on Equal Education Opportunity, McClellan referred to Boston's record as one of "monumental hypocrisy."[2]

The in-depth eighteen-month study by HEW that followed demonstrated that Boston's school duality was contrived through a feeder system which sent whites to selected high schools and blacks to others. White students attended junior high schools, grades seven to nine, and then went to high schools grades ten to twelve. Black pupils studied at intermediate schools, grades six to eight, and then entered high schools, grades nine to twelve. Moreover, HEW found that in spite of the state's 1965 Racial Imbalance Act, Boston's schools were becoming ever more segregated. The forty-six schools that the Kiernan Report had once found to be racially imbalanced now numbered sixty-five.[3]

When word reached City Hall that HEW might slash $10 million from the city's Federal aid as a penalty for violating Title VI, Mayor Kevin White was furious. Instead of acknowledging the School Committee's complicity, he countered by blaming the 1965 law. Establishing a 50 percent cut-off, White said, "makes the law unworkable. The true test should be whether a city or town is making a sincere effort to achieve racial balance in its schools, not whether it has any given percentage of non-white enrollment in a particular school."[4]

Disheartened by City Hall's response, and assuming the School Committee would never correct the system's duality, Boston's black population reacted by announcing its own corrective measure. Not for the first time, either, for in 1965, black parents had undertaken Operation Exodus which transported nearly 600 black pupils from Roxbury to predominantly white schools and a similar operation, begun a year later, known as the Metropolitan Council for Educational Opportunity (METCO), sending black students across city lines to attend schools in the white suburbs. Now, in the aftermath of the HEW indictment, they sought legal recourse. Boston's NAACP's chapter filed suit in Federal District Court in behalf of Tallulah Morgan and other plaintiffs representing "black parents and their children who attend Boston public schools."[5] Since the defendant in the litigation was School Committee Chairman James W. Hennigan, Jr., the case went to trial as *Tallulah Morgan* v. *James W. Hennigan*, or more simply, *Morgan*.[6]

Before the court could complete its work, the Commonwealth's Supreme Court in late 1973 ordered Boston's School Committee to formulate a plan that would take effect when school opened the following September. According to the ruling, the number of "imbalanced" schools had to be reduced from sixty-five to forty-two through redistricting; the notorious feeder system had to be eliminated; and provision made to bus 19,000 of the city's 83,000 school population. Consequently, during March, 1974, the Boston School Department began alerting families to their children's new school assignments, causing the city to rock with rancor and painful outcries. A harried state legislature quickly undertook hearings aimed at repealing the unpopular eight-year-old Racial Imbalance Act.

On April 3, a crowd numbering between 20,000 and 25,000 persons, led by Boston's inveterate busing opponent, City Councilwoman Louise Day Hicks, wound around the city Common, chanting objections to school integration. Various colored ribbons and armbands were used to identify the ethnic adversaries, green for South Boston, purple for Hyde Park, and so on. As they had in Pontiac, Michigan, the police sympathized with the white protestors. They flew "bunches of ribbons from their handlebars."[7] To fan the spirit of civil revolt, the School Committee asked teachers to distribute leaflets, calling for support of the demonstration.

The protest marked the high point of the segregationists' complaint. Whatever hopes they had of maintaining the status quo were within weeks dashed when Federal District Judge Wendell Arthur Garrity, Jr., handed down his judgement. Like McMillan, of Charlotte, and Roth, of Detroit, Garrity had a profound respect for the law, and like them, knew little about school desegregation until assigned the litigation.

This was due, in part at least, to Garrity's upper class background. His father was a prominent attorney in nearby Worcester, who could afford the demands of gracious living. Thus shielded, young Garrity never experienced the abrasive existence of his Irish cousins in Boston.

Upon graduation from Holy Cross in 1941, he collected a law degree at Harvard, and following a short career as Assistant U.S. Attorney, entered private practice. His interest in elective politics only matured gradually. Not until 1958 did he take an active part, supporting John Kennedy's successful bid for the U.S. Senate. Two years later, he again aided Kennedy, this time taking over the candidate's Milwaukee headquarters and sparking the decisive victory that went far to assure the Bay Stater's nomination for the presidency. From the White House, a grateful Kennedy appointed Garrity U.S. Attorney for Boston, a post he held until 1965 when the President's younger brother, Senator Edward M. Kennedy, approved Garrity's nomination for Federal District Judge.

If Garrity had not become involved in the controversial school issue, it is safe to assume his tenure on the bench would have passed without flurry. He exuded courtesy and diplomacy. Describing this courtroom sensitivity, a correspondent for the Boston *Herald American* wrote, "Garrity is the most gentlemanly of men, quiet and informally courtly, exceedingly polite. He might be studying a court paper, then lift his balding head, fringed with white hair and enter the discussion with: 'Permit me if you will. . . .' Or, 'If you'll pardon me for saying it. . . .' "[8] Clearly, it was not Garrity's judicial bearing that led to community vilification, and eventually to his being hung in effigy. It was the fact that this man who lived in suburbia, secure from poverty, crime, and ghetto housing that plagued the city, could compel a reordering of the school system with the ease of a judicial pronouncement. Possessing top educational credentials and the professional skill to command a first-class income, Garrity had the unbounded freedom to do as he pleased, to live in a world denied Boston's white ethnics.

Although their aversion to the District Judge was understandable, the awful fact remained that they showed so little empathy for the plight of black parents and their children, or that Garrity, whatever his lifestyle, his place of residence, or his income, was sworn to uphold the law. Instead, the Irish, the Italians, and Boston's other ethnic groups only wanted to remain separate, to exclude others, to preserve their own enclaves, their own churches, their own schools, their own shops, their own mores. The Boston School Committee, pandering to these instincts, had sacrificed the rights of minority children as insurance to retain office.

On June 21, 1974, the timebomb that had been ticking in Courtroom Number Five, on the twelfth floor of the John W. McCormack Federal Building exploded. Judge Garrity, in a 152-page opinion loaded with statistics, ruled that the School Committee had been operating a dual school system, and ordered its termination. Carefully, almost tediously, the ruling followed the Denver *Keyes* reasoning so as not to overstep limitations established by the Supreme Court.[9] Already known as "painstaking and thorough," Garrity was determined not to be reversed by a higher authority.[10]

In his directive, he found the Boston system both overcrowded and underutilized. The all-white South Boston High, for instance, was over-enrolled by "676 students in the 1971-72 school year. In contrast, Girls High, 92 percent black, was underenrolled by 532 places. . . . In alleviating overcrowding at Cleveland Junior High, 91 percent white, students were assigned to the already overcrowded and relatively distant white South Boston High. There were closer schools with available seats but these schools were identifiably black."[11] When asked the reason for not filling the unused space, a deputy superintendent had answered that "he 'thought it would create a problem' of white parents protesting."[12]

Nor did Garrity stop there: the Boston School Committee had districted to preserve segregation. By arbitrarily drawing geographical boundaries, the racial composition of each school facility was controllable. "The elementary schools in a portion of Boston stretching just south of South Boston, through Roxbury and into Dorchester are districted" to achieve one result—to separate "the predominantly black areas . . . from the predominantly white areas."[13]

Garrity's third point was the one originally unmasked by HEW, the feeder pattern by which "a dual system of secondary education was created, one for each race. Black students generally entered high school upon completion of the eighth grade," the judge pointed out, "and white students upon completion of the ninth. High school education for black students was conducted by and large in citywide schools, and for white students in district schools. White students were generally given options enabling them to escape from predominantly black schools; black students were generally without such options."[14]

In fact, Garrity discovered, when black students tried to transfer to predominantly white schools under a policy of open enrollment, they "encountered locked doors, physical segregation in separate classrooms, auditoriums and corridors and placement in the rear of classrooms. Anticipating the arrival of black students, administrators of some transferee schools had desks unbolted from the floor and removed from classrooms."[15] Garrity lashed out at the open enrollment charade. During the school year 1970-71, more than one-sixth of all transfers (1,028) were "segregative: 324 non-white pupils transferred from majority white to majority non-white schools. . . . In sum, open enrollment as administered by the defendants became a device for separating the races and contributed significantly to the establishment of a dual school system."[16]

Garrity's fifth argument for upholding the plaintiffs' allegations was the Committee's policy of sending the "less qualified, less experienced and lower paid teachers" to the predominantly black schools.[17] In addition, black teachers were segregated. The court discovered that 75 percent of Boston's black teachers were in schools more than 50 percent black: ". . . as of 1972-73, no black classroom teacher, permanent or provisional, had *ever* been assigned to eighty-one of Boston's 201 schools; and an additional thirty-five had only had one black teacher in any year since 1967-68, the earliest year for which figures were put in evidence."[18] As to administrative

posts in the Boston school system, blacks filled only "3.5 percent of the positions. These percentages," declared Garrity, "may be contrasted with those
of black students in the system, approximately 33 percent, and of the city's
black population, approximately 16 percent."[19]

Finally, the court ruled that "a high degree of racial segregation also exists
in the city's specialized high schools and vocational programs. . . . The
question . . . is whether the racial segregation . . . is intentional and therefore unconstitutional."[20] *Keyes* provided the answer by declaring that a
"finding of segregative school board actions in a meaningful portion of a
school system . . . creates a presumption that other segregated schooling in
the system is not adventitious. It establishes . . . a *prima facie* case of
unlawful segregative design on the part of school authorities, and shifts to
those authorities the burden of proving that other segregated schools within
the system are not also the result of intentionally segregative actions. . . .
The burden of disproving unlawful intent thereupon falls upon the defendants, who in this case have failed to carry that burden."[21]

By following the Supreme Court's instructions to the letter, Garrity had
tightened a noose around the neck of the Boston School Committee. The
Committee tried to wriggle free by contending that other factors were
responsible for school segregation: housing segregation which occurred
regardless of school policies, and the Committee's adherence to the idea of
the neighborhood school which while conducive to segregation was not
necessarily unconstitutional. Garrity brushed the argument aside, writing
that "a school will cause the racial composition of the neighborhood to shift
and vice versa."[22] Then quoting *Swann,* he said, "People gravitate toward
school facilities, just as schools are located in response to the needs of
people."[23] ". . . In this respect," Garrity continued, "Boston is not unlike
other major urban areas [and the defendants] may not disclaim responsibility for segregated schools because of population shifts which they
themselves may have contributed [through] building relatively small
schools to serve defined racial groups."[24]

In view of the evidence, the court ruled that the Committee had "knowingly carried out a systematic program of segregation" and, accordingly,
the "entire school system of Boston is unconstitutionally segregated."
Defendants must "eliminate all vestiges of the dual system 'root and
branch'." Sensing what the future held, Garrity announced, "No amount of
public or parental opposition will excuse avoidance by school officials of
constitutionally imposed obligations."[25]

The court ordered a two-phase remedy: Phase 1, to take effect in
September, 1974, would implement the State Board of Education's Short-
Term Plan, promulgated in 1973, and forced upon the Boston School
Committee by order of the Commonwealth's Supreme Judicial Court in
January, 1974. Phase 2, fashioned by the School Committee, would expand

on Phase 1 and become operative in time for school opening in September, 1975.

Thus, within a six-month period, both the Federal and Commonwealth judiciary had thoroughly discredited the work of the Boston School Committee, leaving most Bostonians incredulous. In its wake came panic and hostility. "This is going to make law-breakers out of law abiding citizens," scoffed Joseph Timilty, an important local Democrat. Warned an Irish housewife, "Every parent I have talked to is preparing to go to jail" rather than comply with the ruling.[26]

As in Pontiac and Charlotte, white community leaders failed to speak out either on the need to conform with the court's ruling or to defend the constitution's morality. In June, 1975, Thomas Atkins, president of Boston's NAACP, told the U.S. Commission on Civil Rights that because of the white leadership vacuum, "the black community . . . had to bear the burden of leading the whole city. The mayor from time to time has refused to lead and has tried to hide. The Governor, this one and the last one, from time to time, has tried to say it's the mayor's problem, it's the judge's problem, it's anybody's problem, it's not my problem."[27]

Nevertheless, knowing the law had to be upheld, a reluctant City Hall took steps during the summer to counter violence. Mayor White tried to establish some form of communication with the disgruntled parents. Working without publicity, he visited the homes of antibusing leaders and attempted to soften their opposition. Unfortunately, he appeared to hold two views which he expressed the day before school opening in a thirty-minute television address. "I'm for integration," he frankly declared, "but against forced busing. They are not mutually exclusive."[28]

The mayor also appealed to the media to restrain its coverage of untoward incidents. It was widely believed that urban riots and campus demonstrations during the turbulent 1960s had been stimulated by on-the-scene coverage. At White's behest, a coterie of Boston's top news executives which included radio, television, and the city's two major dailies, the *Globe* and the *Herald American*, subscribed to a policy of self-censorship. "We went about it from the standpoint of our civic responsibility," Lamont Thompson, New England vice-president for Westinghouse Broadcasting, declared, "We made a very strong commitment to the mayor that although we would cover the totality of the news, there would be no inflammatory material, and unpleasant incidents would be written up judiciously."[29]

This determination to resist all fanfare was also reflected in the mayor's attitude toward the police. In early 1974, White ordered Deputy Mayor Robert Kiley to investigate the experience of other cities, forced to desegregate their schools. Following consultation with officials in Seattle, Washington, Pontiac, and Rochester, Kiley concluded that a low profile would work best. "There are occasions," he was told, "when police can be—the mere presence of police can be provocative. It simply adds an air of excitement and drama that one likes to avoid."[30] To accomplish this, he published Training Bulletin 74-1, which told how to cope with the problems of school desegregation. The idea was salutary enough, but because of differences between Boston's police management and the Boston Police Patrolmen's Association (BPPA), its collective bargaining agent, the manuals were never effectively used. As it turned out, the BPPA became a prime impediment to school desegregation. Through its publication *Pax Centurion*, BPPA openly opposed the implementation of Phase 1. Using its own treasury, the officers' agent proposed to mount a legal challenge to *Morgan*, and on August 30, less than two weeks before school opening, it had sent a letter to Judge Garrity requesting "clarification" of its role in the maintenance of law and order.[31] Members of the BPPA were, of course, Boston's first line of defense in case of violence, but by taking sides, they irretrievably cast themselves on the side of their tormentors. According to instructions contained in 74-1, ". . . the prime concern of the police must be the preservation of peace, the protection of life and property, and the avoidance of personal involvement in the issue,"[32] but the BPPA refused to heed this advice.

Nothwithstanding this liability, the biggest stumbling block to school desegregation remained the continued hostility of the Boston School Committee. From the time the *Morgan* decree was announced, its intransigence knew no bounds. Against the advice of William J. Leary, Superintendent, it refused to name a desegregatory coordinator, placing the burden on Leary who was already overwhelmed by administrative duties. The Committee simply would not cooperate and eventually the court had to step in and issue orders that were properly the Committee's responsibility.

When asked by the U.S. Commission on Civil Rights to give reasons for this behavior, Committee Chairman John J. Kerrigan replied, "If there were something I could do to stop it, I would. . . . There is nothing I can do to stop it," and a second member, John J. McDonough justified his conduct by saying, "For my part, I will not go any further than doing what Judge Garrity directly orders me to do. And I will not end up as a salesman for a plan which I do not believe in."[33]

This intractability was traceable to the Committee's past role in local politics. For years, a place on the School Committee had served as a launching pad for politicians seeking higher office. During the previous decade, the most cogent arguments for gaining admission to that select body were opposition to the Commonwealth's Racial Imbalance Act and a belief, openly expressed, that Boston schools would remain segregated. Having earned profiles of opposition, they could not reverse themselves without a face-lifting for which not one volunteered. Kerrigan, then campaigning for district attorney under the banner "Kerrigan the Fighter," hoped to capitalize on his hardline Committee reputation.

Even a former term on the Committee was enough to stimulate opposition to desegregation. Sensing the public mood, Louise Day Hicks responded by organizing an antibusing group dubbed ROAR (Return Our Alienated Rights). Its call for a school boycott became the rallying cry of angry white parents, abetted at one point by Leary himself, who announced, "If you are fearful of putting your children's lives in danger by putting them on a bus, be my guest down at the beach."[34]

Thus lacking positive leadership from the white community, handicapped by an ambivalent mayor, let down by politically motivated police officers, and betrayed by an obdurate School Committee, the City of Boston lurched toward its rendezvous with desegregation. As Harvard psychologist Thomas Pettigrew pointed out, "When a community senses that change is going to take place come hell or high water, you don't get the violence. In Boston more than in Little Rock, you have had people who have been told for years that busing is not inevitable, that it will not happen here."[35]

Inevitably, South Boston, the Irish bastion and home of School Committee members chiefly responsible for the city's dual system, became a tinderbox. In retrospect, one is hard put to explain the State Board of Education's insistence on including the area in Phase 1. Professor Louis L. Jaffe, of the Harvard Law School, who devised the plan, nevertheless advised against it. "Its people are intensely hostile to blacks," he warned.[36] However, the Board disregarded the warning.

The roots of South Boston's reputation were as much an accident of nature as a combination of religious, political, and economic forces. Isolated from the rest of the city, the area resembled a giant thumb planted in the waters of Boston Harbor and Dorchester Bay. Its population was 80 percent Catholic, mostly Irish, but sprinkled with Poles, Italians, and Lithuanians. Proportionately, it contained more churches than any comparable community in New England. Its stability was attested to by the reluctance of residents to move. Some had lived in the same house for generations. Yet, it was also a hard-bitten community with high unemployment and one in which 365 bars flourished alongside the many churches.

Nevertheless, by the fall of 1974, "Southie," as it was affectionately known to residents, had undergone a profound attitudinal change. Its people felt bitter and deserted. Describing the transformation, Pete Axthelm, of *Newsweek* magazine, wrote, "Southies have always loved their politicians, but now they hear only ineffectual slogans. The police, many of whom grew up in the community, were also local allies; now the local hangout, the Rabbit Inn, has been made a shambles by the Tactical Police Force. . . . Even the church has turned away: Catholic students boycotting the public schools have been refused admittance to the parochial system, and not a single priest has agreed to lead an anti-busing prayer meeting."[37]

According to *New York Times* correspondent Kifner, Southies with whom he had talked blamed "outsiders" for what was happening—"the suburbanites, the rich liberals who send their children to private schools, the liberal press and television and the politicians, even some of 'their own kind'."[38] Quick to commiserate, Harvard sociologist Robert Coles declared "working class people" were bearing the total burden when it rightly belonged to the total community—city and suburbs. "They're doing the work for the bankers, for the politicians, for the ministers and priests . . . for all the holier-than-thou sermons that have been delivered in Boston for the last 100 years. . . . The ultimate reality is the reality of class, having and not having, social and economic vulnerability versus social and economic power—that's where the real issue is."[39]

Yet, with all the talk and explanations about betrayal and injustice, nothing can adequately rationalize the vitriol that surfaced in Southie as soon as buses began exchanging white and black students between Roxbury and South Boston on opening day. It could only arise from a deeply rooted emotional fear, fear of a different ethnic group, different in color, in culture, in philosophy.

South Boston High School is situated atop historic Dorchester Heights, the same heights on which General Henry Knox planted cannons during the Revolutionary War to win Boston from the British. The first bus from Roxbury, carrying twenty black teenagers, arrived at eight o'clock on the morning of September 12, after passing through streets dotted with graffiti messages reading, "Niggers Go Home," "This is Klan Country," and "Go Home Mayor Black."[40] A mob of angry whites, mostly truant students, began throwing rocks and bottles and yelled, "Die, Niggers, Die!" Within seconds a phalanx of police pushed the crowd back before anyone could be severely injured. A dismayed Jesuit priest, looking on, exclaimed in unbelief, "If what I've been seeing isn't hate, then I don't know what hatred is."[41]

Out of a projected first-day attendance of 1,539, only 126 blacks, 57 whites, and 3 American Indians entered school. At Roxbury High, the other end of the transfer axis, where 525 whites had been assigned, only ten enrolled, proof of ROAR's initial effectiveness in curtailing attendance. Although only 66 percent of the school population turned out on opening day, compared with the previous average of 86 percent, there was no violence at seventy-nine of the eighty schools under court order. The *Globe* cheerfully headlined: "Boston Schools Desegregate, Opening Day Generally Peaceful."[42]

As Pontiac had already demonstrated, however, those bent on causing strife insisted on poisoning the atmosphere. On the fifth day of school, David Duke, head of the Knights of the Ku Klux Klan, could not resist visiting South Boston to give the Klan's ancient enemies, the Irish Catholics, the word on white supremacy. "We are going to win a great victory in South Boston for the white race," he cried to an enthusiastic crowd of

Southies. "The Federal government is taking little white children out of their homes and sending them into black jungles; the Federal government is taking money out of your pockets to finance the production of thousands of little black bastards. . . . We don't believe Negroes fit into modern society."[43]

Once fired, the racial pot continued to boil. On the day following Duke's address, a bullet crashed through the front door of the Jamaica Plain High School, and police had to break up student slugfests at Hyde Park High. Even when uniformed police, carrying nightsticks, stood guard in school corridors, fights erupted around them.

On October 2, eleven persons—students, teachers, and aides—were hurt in a racial fight at South Boston High. Within two days, the white attendance, which had risen to 121, plummeted to fourteen. Three hundred members of the Tactical Police Force were assigned to Southie to quell further uprisings. Despite these precautions, on the evening of October 4, a brick flew through the window of a cruising TPF patrol car and, when police attempted to apprehend the suspect, sympathetic onlookers intervened, indicating a dangerous anarchic climate.

Three days later, Southie again exploded when a gang of some thirty-five white toughs surrounded the car of a thirty-three-year-old black, a Haitian immigrant named Jean-Louis Yvon, as he turned into Dorchester Street. They rocked his car, broke the windshield, and dragged him from the car. Yvon broke loose and ran to a neighboring house where he grabbed the porch railing and held on long enough for police to break up the scuffle. "He would have been dead if I hadn't fired [a warning shot]," one distraught officer told the media.[44] The Yvon mugging quickly generated racial retaliation in Roxbury. The next day black students rampaged through the streets, stoning cars, beating occupants, and sending thirty-eight whites to hospitals for treatment.

A beleaguered Mayor White, in the face of the latest outbreak, asked Judge Garrity to send in at least 125 Federal marshals. "We can no longer maintain either the appearance or the reality of public safety. Violence which once focused on the schools and busing is now engulfing the entire community in racial confrontation."[45] The Judge refused. "The problems here," he told White, "are no different from those which have been solved in 200 other cities. It is just a question of how long, and how much heartache, it will take."[46] Garrity suggested White seek help within the Commonwealth, and in answer to White's second entreaty, Governor Francis W. Sargent assigned 300 state police and 100 riot-trained officers of the Metropolitan District Commission to prevent further violence in the city.

By coincidence, on the same day, October 9, a Washington correspondent asked President Ford to comment on Boston's ills. Understandably, the President deplored violence, but then went on to add that in his judgement, Garrity's decision was not the "best solution." He was against "forced busing to achieve racial balance as a solution to quality education."[47] Such a gratuitous remark had to overlook the fact that "forced busing" had not been ordered by Garrity to produce "quality education." It aimed at ending the dual school system. Once again, a President of the United States, choosing to misinterpret *Brown*, had refused to uphold the Constitution and the Supreme Court.[48]

Boston officials reacted predictably. The mayor angrily called in the press to flay Mr. Ford. "He is willing to taunt this city into becoming another Little Rock. . . ." The President's message was clear, he stormed. "You are on your own in the implementation of federal court orders, unless and until there is riot and rebellion in the streets of your city."[49] As a result, White threatened not to participate in Phase 2 of school desegregation unless Washington agreed to help with money and protection. Like the President, he undercut the very law he had taken an oath to uphold.

During the following week, trouble bubbled anew. On the same day that Mayor White asked Senators Kennedy and Brooke to confer with Governor Sargent at City Hall, a white youth was stabbed by a black student at Hyde Park High School. In the ensuing fracas seven other students received injuries, forcing the school to close. Sargent quickly sensed an opportunity for political gain. Without consulting either the mayor or the senators, he ordered 450 members of the Massachusetts National Guard to standby duty in Boston and chose the precise hour he was to have met in the mayor's office to announce his plan. "We cannot permit Roxbury to become another Watts," moaned White, recalling the Guard's role in previous racial outbursts. "We must not allow South Boston High to become another Kent State."[50] He needn't have worried. After sitting around the barracks for a day or two, the citizen soldiers quietly picked up their gear and left.

The fire, however, refused to die. On December 10, a black Hyde Park High School student knifed a white and, in desperation, the School Committee closed the system for a month. During the uneasy truce, the air was filled with myriad suggestions on how to cope with the latest crisis. Mayor White asked Garrity to end the trouble by closing the violence-prone schools and moving the students to "neutral" sites in the downtown area. He had, he said, support from city and Commonwealth police officials who claimed to possess "secret intelligence" reports of impending violence.[51]

Despite these warnings—real and imaginary—Garrity refused to budge. He again rebuked the School Committee for failing to formulate a Phase 2 program which he had called for by December 16. Indeed, by a 3 to 2 vote, the Committee had declined to submit a plan. In the aftermath of its default, the Committee counsel resigned, HEW announced a cut-off of Federal funds, and the U.S. Court of Appeals peremptorily turned down the appeal from Garrity's ruling. The infuriated judge meanwhile cited all five members for civil contempt. Reacting to these several stimulants, the members asked the court for permission to offer a new plan, one that did not provide for forced busing, and the judge, chary of stripping a duly elected official body of statutory powers, withdrew the contempt order.

Again, the Committee's offering, submitted January 7, 1975, turned out to be as unpromising as its predecessors. The schools simply could not be integrated without busing, and all along, Garrity had made it clear his primary objective was integration. Accordingly, the court now circumvented the Committee by appointing a board of six masters to design Phase 2. By April, their deliberations ended, Garrity began work on Phase 2, and using the board's conclusions as a starting point, he issued his order on May 10. It divided the city's school system into eight districts, each reflecting Boston's racial breakdown—51 percent white, 36 percent black, and 12 percent other minorities. Out of the city's school population of 72,000 a total of 24,000 would be bused, half for the first time, grades one to five, in order to desegregate 162 schools.

The so-called heart of the plan was a unique coupling of the public schools to twenty of the community's colleges and universities under which the resources of the latter would be used to lift the educational quality of the former. "The significance of this pairing effort," said the court, "is as a long-time commitment, a promise to the parents and students of Boston that these institutions, with their rich educational resources, are concerning themselves in a direct way with the quality of education in the public schools." For example, Garrity declared, the University of Massachusetts will work with troubled South Boston High, Harvard University with Roxbury High School, and so on. In addition, twenty businesses, including such influential firms as the First National Bank of Boston, Honeywell, IBM, and John Hancock Insurance, agreed to aid specific high schools by "supplementing academic theory with business practicability." Labor, too, offered to supplement technical and trade training, and the Metropolitan Cultural Alliance, a group of 110 institutions, promised to enlarge its role of promoting the arts within the public school system.

However promising these innovations, the primary strength of the Garrity plan lay in his idea for a "magnet school" district consisting of twelve high schools, four middle schools, nine elementary schools, and one special unit to give immigrant children instruction in English. These schools, designed to accommodate approximately one-quarter of Boston's school population, would be open to all pupils regardless of residence. Primarily, they would develop expertise in mathematics, science, and languages. Garrity summed it up: "The efforts of so many people to enrich public education in such diverse and promising ways will help ease the transition of Boston's school system from a dual system to one with no 'black' schools or 'white' schools, but just schools."[52]

Yet, even these hopeful creations made hardly a dent on a community opposed to change. On the day the court revealed the parameters of Phase 2, a crowd of 350 antibusing fanatics gathered on the steps of the Federal courthouse, shouting, "Southie's on warpath, OOH-AH!" and Mayor White helped not a bit by moaning it "has virtually guaranteed a continuation of the present level of tension and hostility throughout the city."[53] Two days later, the frustration was compounded when the U.S. Supreme Court voted to leave Garrity's Phase 1 ruling untouched.

Despite this new turn, members of the School Committee continued to sit on their hands, testing Judge Garrity's patience. Finally, as the time for school opening neared, he summoned them to a meeting in his chambers with representatives of the Citywide Coordinating Council (CCC), a forty-member body the judge had created under Phase 2 to help monitor the plan. Garrity instructed the CCC to file monthly reports with the court and look into resolved school problems without unsurping the Committee's responsibility. CCC would confer at least once a month in open session with the Committee to discuss the Phase 2 implementation.

The judge did not mince words. "The best way I know to frustrate the plan is delay, delay, delay, so that a shambles exists on opening day. That's not going to happen."[54] For once the mayor got the message and warned, "We will tolerate neither disruptions nor interference when school starts. Those who attempt trouble will face certain arrest and prosecution."[55] To back his threat, he called on 1,000 city policemen, 350 state troopers, 250 state park police, and 600 members of the Massachusetts National Guard. Even the Federal government made its presence felt when Assistant U.S. Attorney General, Stanley Pottinger, established a Boston command post, supported by Federal marshals.

Unlike the previous year, when all eyes turned to Southie, in the fall of 1975, Charlestown, another Irish bastion on the city's northern tip, seemed the most likely trouble spot. Like Southie, it was a peninsula, isolated from the rest of Boston by overhead highways and water surrounding three sides. Out of a population of 15,000, the 1970 census counted only seventy-six black residents. Prior to Phase 2, no attempt to desegregate its high school had been undertaken.

To prevent a recurrence of the violence of 1974, no stone remained unturned. The area crawled with police. Only a slight disturbance occurred when Louise Day Hicks led a mothers' march up Bunker Hill in a fruitless effort to pierce the high school perimeter. "We're asking God for relief because He's the only one that is listening," an anguished mother cried.[56]

That nothing more serious occurred to mar the peace indicated a more reflective public mood. While it continued to be deeply resentful, anger had given way to resignation. The thought was beginning to sink in that black and white children had to attend the same schools, regardless of parental objections. One Charlestown mother caught the shift and observed pragmatically, "They're going to get an education no matter what. It's the only way they will get anywhere."[57] However, the court's insistence that white children be bused into the black districts of Dorchester and Roxbury still rubbed a raw nerve. "They want to bus our kids out of Charlestown to the crummy schools that nobody ever worked to change," a community leader complained, absenting himself for responsibility in their condition.[58]

Painfully, haltingly, Bostonians were beginning to realize, however, that they had been misled by the School Committee, that the men and women they elected year after year were the architects of the inferior schools. Their decisions had interminably segregated their schools; their decisions had sent the inferior teachers to the black schools; they were the ones who decided Phase 1 should only be followed as minimally as possible. It did not have to follow that pattern either, as the U.S. Commission on Civil Rights pointed out, "Other desegregating school districts have utilized the retooling process that necessarily accompanies school desegregation as an opportunity to assess and improve the content and operation of their educational delivery systems. In Boston that opportunity was either missed or ignored by the school committee."[59] To make matters worse, just as Phase 2 was to start, the Committee fired Superintendent Lacy and replaced him with Marion J. Fahey. Under her jurisdiction, places were promptly found for deserving Committee satraps. She fired John Coakley, superintendent of the newly established magnet school program, who had, according to Joseph Feather-stone, of the *New Republic*, committed two offenses:". . . he worked hard and in good faith planning desegregation, and he publicly refused to go along with the custom of donating to the political campaigns of school committee members."[60] By November, the publicity that accompanied this mischief defeated two of the Committee's staunchest supporters, carrying to office Kathleen Sullivan, a moderate, whose topheavy victory was interpreted as a rebuke.

Despite this hopeful sign, little seemed to have changed at South Boston High. The atmosphere remained charged with racial tensions, and physical neglect was making a shambles of the structure. "When I graduated in 1940," a dejected Southie told the Civil Rights Commission, "South Boston High was a beautiful high school. You could eat off the floors. They had French doors going into the assembly hall . . . but when I went back in October and saw the appalling condition of that school, I could have cried. The filth, the paint peeling off the walls. The girls' gym hadn't been heated in three years . . . the doors on the ladies' room for girl students hadn't had doors on them for two years.[61] Queried why no repairs had been undertaken, South Boston's headmaster, William Reid, replied the school authorities simply had not responded to his requests. Its tiny library held no more than 4,500 volumes even after seven decades of operation. In the words of Harvard's Pettigrew, "If you want to go to college, you don't go to South Boston High, and if you go to South Boston High, you don't want to go to college."[62] In 1972, only 4 percent of its graduates entered college and of those, only 25 percent earned degrees. One student with a straight "A" average, after lasting one year at the University of Massachusetts, sighed, "I realized I couldn't read, write or even speak English well. I couldn't believe how smart the other kids were."[63]

With such a limited accent on scholastic achievement, sports became the school's major aim. "Sports mean an awful lot here," the school's football coach confided, "and getting on the team is what it's all about."[64] In early October, 1975, ninety-two black students, fed up by this parochial approach to education, boycotted classes, demanding "more black police, a black administrator, a black nurse's aide and 'sensitivity training' for Southie's white teachers."[65] Reid tried to meet their demands by agreeing to hire a black assistant football coach, by putting more black monitors in the hallways, and by enlisting a black nurse's aide. When the white students learned what had happened, they, too, submitted a list of requests. Fearful of losing their Southie inheritance, they demanded the American flag be displayed in all classrooms with an opening pledge of allegiance to the flag each day. As the bickering between black and white students continued, the time finally came when Judge Garrity concluded sterner measures were needed to avoid racial warfare. To accomplish this, he placed South Boston High in Federal "receivership" on December 9, 1975, after ousting Reid and seven other administrators.

To find Reid's successor, a search committee bypassed the Boston school system and picked Jerome Winegar, a thirty-eight-year-old assistant junior high principal from St. Paul, Minnesota. Predictably, his selection by Superintendent Fahey raised a storm of criticism. The Boston City Council condemned the appointment of an outsider; the chairman of the school committee, angered over not being consulted, complained, "No one from the administration on down to the teachers knows who is running the schools."[66] The sharpest rebuke of all came from James M. Kelly, president of the South Boston High School Home and School Association, who said he had talked to three parents and two teachers at the Woodrow Wilson Junior High School, St. Paul, where Winegar worked, and they alleged the school was in a state of chaos. "Education has taken a back seat to social programs, and because of the lack of discipline, there are still racial problems. One teacher classified Wilson Junior High as being a complete zoo."[67]

With such animadversions, when Winegar arrived in Boston on April 14, 1976, demonstrators met him carrying such signs as "Go Home, Jerome," "Winegar is a reject," and "Winegar is a member of the NAACP and the ACLU."[68] Three colleagues from St. Paul signed on as assistants and together the team immediately concentrated on the individual student, while avoiding the red tape that had engulfed the rest of the system. At the end of Winegar's first full year, student suspensions dropped by half. Noting the improvement, the new headmaster explained to Gail Jennes, of *People* magazine, "Desegregation is mechanically putting people in the same place. Integration means they can gain from a situation and learn about each other." However, he added, speaking empirically, "You can't mandate it."[69]

Another hopeful sign in Boston's ongoing desegregatory process was a strongly worded encomium from the head of the U.S. Civil Rights Commission. He commended the city for its compliance with Phase 2. Admittedly, a "rocky road," said Arthur S. Flemming. "But we feel that it is moving. . . . Constitutional rights are being protected, and children are having an educational experience they wouldn't have received if the judge hadn't issued his orders."[70]

In the afterglow of this praise, the city unexpectedly suffered a new burst of racial violence. It occurred after a group of one hundred Charlestown High School students visited a meeting of the City Council to explain why they were boycotting the system. Their presentation finished, they gave a pledge of allegiance to the American flag and filed out. Leaving City Hall, the unit happened to spot Theodore Landsmark, twenty-nine, a black Yale Law School graduate, and assaulted him. Landsmark's nose was broken, his face bloodied, and as he agonized on the ground, the bearer of a U.S. flag furiously thrust the pole into his side. There was no concealing the motive. An act of "racism, pure and simple," exclaimed an angry mayor who saw the whole incident from his office high above the street.[71] Fourteen days later, Richard Poleet, thirty-four, a white auto mechanic, was dragged from his car in Roxbury by a gang of twenty to twenty-five black youths and beaten so severely on the face with rocks and pieces of pavement that it required six hours of surgery at Boston City Hospital to save his life. After two years in a coma, he died.

As expiation for these two episodes, a vast crowd of 30,000 people, including the Commonwealth's two U.S. senators, the governor, and the presidents of Harvard and M.I.T., joined the mayor in a "march against violence" which wound through downtown Boston. "If you are against violence, come," pleaded Mayor White. "If you are for violence, you are not wanted."[72]

To allay community anxiety, White appointed a Committee on Violence to study the "causes of racial violence and tension" in Boston. Encouragingly, it reported that under Phase 2, 150 of the city's 165 schools were functioning well, that less than 10 percent had suffered racial upheavals. Nevertheless, there was a feeling among members of the committee, as expressed by Edward J. McCormack, Jr., former Massachusetts Attorney General, that trouble would continue until Boston residents found ways to narrow their differences. "To a very large degree," he said, "the cause of unrest and bitterness and frustration and anger in the city go beyond the question of educating young people. It really relates to housing and jobs and the environment in which people are living. . . . The facts are that there is unemployment in South Boston and East Boston and Charlestown and other sections of the city that are identifiably white, but there's twice as much unemployment in the black community."[73] In short, the visceral problems affecting the two races were so indigenous that any progress in their elimination would have to precede progress in school desegregation.

While McCormack's argument for joining black and white in a common struggle against unemployment and bad housing contained a certain rationale, it raised the question of whether he had confused the cart with the horse. How, for instance, could such problems be successfully attacked if their solution was impaired by feelings of discrimination and prejudice, learned in childhood? To delay the integration of schools until such time as blacks and whites found common ground on problems of jobs and housing would be to delay cooperation indefinitely. Either McCormack could not see this or preferred to overlook it.

Meanwhile, on May 4, 1976, Judge Garrity handed down his third desegregation order, scheduled to take effect the following September. Known as Phase 2B, it retained the basic outline of the previous directive. The number of children bused would remain unchanged, the number reassigned, minimal. Eight schools would close, four get major repairs, and construction would begin on five additional buildings. By now, Garrity's establishment of the magnet school district was being heralded far and wide. The country's sole school district with a magnet program, it was receiving queries about its operation from such distant points as Paris. It enrolled approximately 23 percent of Boston's school population and was the city's only district with more students (seventy-four) at the end of the previous school year than at the beginning. An indirect benefit, everyone agreed, was that in emphasizing curriculum, busing received less attention.

Garrity's chief problem now lay in sorting out the difficulties black students experienced at Boston's three highly prestigious schools—Boston Latin, Boston Academy, and Boston Technical—which historically prepared graduates for the nation's top colleges and universities. Rather than declare their eligibility to these "examination schools" through uniform test scores, blacks were admitted on the basis of high grades, whether or not their records deserved the superior rating. "These students," said Dr. Marvin Scott, an educational expert who served as a professional adviser to Judge Garrity, "were not prepared for the stress and the extreme discipline that they would face at these schools."[74] Accordingly, in Phase 2B, Garrity rescinded his earlier order and insisted that those entering the exam schools score above the median of those taking the entrance tests.

Despite this effort to strike a compromise between scholastic attainment and black opportunity, given the handicap of wretched elementary training, elements of the white power structure criticized Garrity for not going further. Robert C. Bergenheim, publisher of the *Herald American*, for one, complained that "in the name of equality, in certain key schools, we have lowered the standards instead of raising them. Instead of diluting differences of race, we have emphasized them."[75] Bergenheim ignored the fact that for the first time in Boston's history, white students were not getting the advantage. Theoretically, of course, black students of the pre-Garrity era could have entered Boston Latin, Boston Academy, or Boston Technical, but given the inferior quality of elementary and secondary education they received, precious few qualified.

Shortly thereafter, on June 14, Judge Garrity's cap attained a new feather when the U.S. Supreme Court upheld Phase 2 refusing to review an appeal of the School Committee, Mayor White, the Boston Home and School's Association, and the Boston Teachers Union. The legality of Garrity's opinion was now assured. Since the decision was unanimous, it had, as the *Christian Science Monitor* noted, ended "any doubt about the judicial validity of the basic court rulings permitting busing as a remedy for desegregating schools."[76]

Yet, even this action failed to deflate the diehards. They took encouragement from a 900-page report prepared by the Boston School Department and published in January, 1977 which showed serious reading deficiencies in the school system. Of 21,077 blacks in all grades who took the Metropolitan Achievement Test the preceding May, 63.8 percent scored below the national average, compared with a white percentage of 34.4 percent. Although the discrepancies had already been reported to Judge Garrity before the Phase 2B ruling, their publication in the Boston media released a new wave of antibusing sentiment. State Representative Raymond L. Flynn, of South Boston, acidly commented it was too late to rectify "the two-year tragedy [that had] virtually destroyed public education" in Boston, but the time was at hand for those who were "marching to a different drummer" to begin the painful assessment of the "folly called forced busing."[77] Providentially for desegregation, not everyone shared his view. For NAACP's Atkins, it verified the organization's fourteen-year contention that "black children were not getting the same education as white students, that the Boston school system operated a dual system and the education it provided minority students was separate and unequal."[78]

Although the test scores were mathematically correct, they were taken out of context, as Robert A. Dentler, a desegregation expert, demonstrated because they "did not include data on test scores taken before 1974 or substantiate any relationship between the latest scores and those occurring before desegregation."[79] Indeed, it was known for years that deficiency in reading scores afflicted the Boston system. As a matter of fact, some twenty months before Judge Garrity's ruling, a study by then Superintendent of Schools William J. Leary revealed that Boston's reading scores from 1969 to 1972 were below the national norm, especially in the black schools.

Moreover, those persons who adamantly tried to prove desegregation a failure consistently disregarded the fact that ending the dual system was not undertaken to cure educational deficiencies. Time and again Judge Garrity

emphasized the point that *Morgan* concerned itself with race, not education. Only the School Committee's unalterable opposition to change
induced him to assume responsibilities that he knew properly belonged to
the Committee. According to Garrity, the sine qua non was integration. If
the results boosted the system's scholastic achievement, fine; he sincerely
hoped they would, but his primary interest was elsewhere. Consequently,
Garrity would not monitor *Morgan* on the basis of test scores. That must
involve Fahey and her School Committee; in fact, by mid-summer, she was
announcing that tests administered citywide in the spring of 1977 demonstrated that black pupils were "closing the gap on their white peers."[80] It
proved, commented a spokesman for the system, the existence of "a continuing pattern of slow but steady improvement in reading which began in
1975" with the introduction of the Garrity plan.[81]

All in all, by the fall of 1977, remarkable changes had occurred in the
Boston school system. By placing full responsibility for school desegregation in one agency—the Department of Implementation—the way was
finally cleared for a comprehensive attack on racial isolation and ethnic
prejudice. Indeed, the city itself was accepting desegregation as a fact of life.
After sixteen years of steady campaigning for public office, Louise Day
Hicks, the arch opponent of change, was finally routed. She finished tenth
in a nine-winner race for City Council. In one six-year period, this ambitious personality had twice run for mayor against White losing both times,
had won and lost a seat in Congress, and been twice elected to the City
Council. Her meteoric career began in 1961 when she became a member of
the School Committee on a platform to "keep politics out" of its operation,
a curious statement for one totally permeated in the art.[82]

Within two years of taking office, she and the Boston branch of the
NAACP were in open opposition. Spokesmen for the civil rights organization who appeared before the School Committee, urging desegregation of
the city's schools, found her unyielding. "There is no *de facto* segregation in
Boston's schools," she announced, terminating the confrontation. "Kindly
proceed to educational matters."[83]

That single comment earned her the lasting loyalty of Boston's white
ethnics. The same fall her vote skyrocketed to 128,000, one of the highest
margins ever given a city official. It brought also the undying animosity of
the city's blacks. "The best thing that ever happened to us was Mrs. Hicks,"
quipped one black caustically. "She woke us up."[84] Then came the Commonwealth's 1965 Racial Imbalance Act. She attacked the "social experi-
menters" who, she claimed, would "deprive us of our neighborhood
schools," and when challenged, retorted, "In every major city, the civil
rights leaders have found a scapegoat. If it has to be me, so be it. My conscience is clear."[85]

This was heady stuff, especially when Mrs. Hicks went on to attack busing, promising there would be no forced transportation of schoolchildren

When Garrity handed down his opinion, she assured her adherents that higher judicial authorities would reverse the district ruling. As one promise after another failed, she resorted to a boycott in defiance of the law. Finally, the career that had soared on flouting desegregation came to an end.

Nor was Mrs. Hicks the lone victim of changing times. On November 8, 1977, three incumbent members, all known for their antibusing stands, lost their posts and for the first time, a black, John O'Bryant, was elected. "At long last," exalted the *Globe*, "Boston is free to debate issues that affect its people without having them distorted by racial fears."[86]

Despite these encouraging omens, 22,027 white students left the school system between 1973 and 1977, reducing their percentage from 55 to 42 percent. Only two of the city's eight community school districts were more than 50 percent white and one—East Boston—had never been desegregated.

While the figures did not lie, they needed an interpretive reading. Of the 22,027, a quarter had left the state. Another quarter had not left the city. Nor did the inference that desegregation caused the loss take into account the fact that white enrollment in Boston's public schools had been declining long before Garrity's opinion—17,110 for the decade beginning in 1963, and 8,421 more for the three years prior to the court decision. Nor did the allegation make allowance for the drop in Boston's birth rate from 20.0 births per 1,000 families in 1965 to 11.5 per 1,000 in 1975.

In February, 1977, a Boston University political scientist, Christine H. Rossell, entered the "white flight" controversy by arguing that the loss in white enrollment attributable to desegregation lay somewhere between 5,000 and 10,000, not the 20,000 cited by school officials and the media. Dr. Rossell, who had previously studied the social and political impact of school desegregation between 1973 and 1976 on 113 U.S. cities, had, at the request of Northwestern University, undertaken a similar analysis of Boston. She predicted that white enrollments would stabilize regardless of "prolonged defiance" by city officials to court-ordered busing and that white students would come "trickling back" to the Boston school system from parochial schools whose percentage of the city's school population had risen from 35 to 50 percent after Cardinal Madeiros reversed his original interdiction against transfer.[87]

Yet, whether desegregation would in the end succeed or fail depended upon the people's will. The court, through Garrity, could erect a temporary wall to hold back the sea of opposition, but eventually, the waters would have their way, to consume the barrier or leave it standing.

Notes

1. *Christian Century*, November 6, 1974, p. 1029.
2. *New York Times*, December 1, 1971.
3. Ibid.

4. Ibid.

5. *Tallulah Morgan* v. *James W. Hennigan*, 379 F. Supp. 410 (1974).

6. Ibid.

7. John Kifner, "Busing Opponents . . . ," *New York Times*, April 4, 1974.

8. Earl Marchand, "Garrity the Man . . . ," *Boston Herald American*, November 6, 1977.

9. *Keyes* v. *School District Number One, Denver, Colorado*, 413 U.S. 189 (1973).

10. John Kifner, "Judge Who Advocates Busing," *New York Times*, December 19, 1974.

11. *Tallulah Morgan*, at 426.

12. Ibid., at 427.

13. Ibid., at 435.

14. Ibid., at 448.

15. Ibid., at 450.

16. Ibid., at 452-53.

17. Ibid., at 456.

18. Ibid., at 459.

19. Ibid., at 463.

20. Ibid., at 466-67.

21. *Tallulah Morgan*, at 467.

22. Ibid., at 470.

23. *Swann* v. *Charlotte-Mecklenburg Board of Education*, 402 U.S. 1 (1971), at 20-21.

24. *Tallulah Morgan*, at 470.

25. Ibid., at 482.

26. *Progressive*, June 1974, p. 38.

27. Testimony of Thomas Atkins, President, NAACP, Boston Chapter, before U.S. Commission on Civil Rights, "Desegregating the Boston Public Schools: A Crisis in Civic Responsibility," *Report of the U.S. Commission on Civil Rights* (1975), p. 56.

28. Press release, Office of the Mayor, September 9, 1975.

29. *Time*, September 30, 1974, p. 76.

30. Testimony of Robert Kiley, Executive Director, Massachusetts Bay Authority (Mr. Kiley resigned the office of Deputy Mayor, May, 1975), before U.S. Commission on Civil Rights, "Desegregating the Boston Public Schools: A Crisis in Civic Responsibility," *Report of the U.S. Commission on Civil Rights* (1975), p. 83.

31. Boston Police Patrolmen's Association letter of August 3, 1974 to Judge Garrity.

32. Training Bulletin 74-1, Boston Police Department, "Implementation of School Desegregation," (1974), p. 1.

33. Testimony of John J. McDonough and John J. Kerrigan before the U.S. Commission on Civil Rights, "Desegregating the Boston Public Schools: A Crisis in Civic Responsibility," *Report of the U.S. Commission on Civil Rights* (1975), p. 1057.

34. *Time*, October 7, 1974.

35. *Time*, October 21, 1974.

36. John Kifner, "South Boston . . . ," *New York Times*, September 23, 1974.

37. Pete Axthelm, "Bad Times in Southie," *Newsweek*, October 21, 1974, p. 39.

38. Kifner, "South Boston."

39. *Christian Century*, November 6, 1974.

40. *Time*, October 21, 1974.

41. *Newsweek*, September 23, 1974, p. 48.

42. *Boston Globe*, September 13, 1974.

43. David Brudnoy, "Fear and Loathing in Boston," *National Review*, October 25, 1974, p. 1231.

44. *Time*, October 21, 1974, p. 22.

45. Ibid.

46. *U.S. News & World Report*, October 21, 1974.

47. Ibid.

48. *Brown* v. *Board of Education*, 347 U.S. 483 (1954).

49. *U.S. News & World Report*, October 21, 1974.

50. *U.S. News & World Report*, October 28, 1974.

51. *Newsweek*, January 20, 1975, p. 25.

52. Judge W. Arthur Garrity, Jr., "Memorandum of Decisions and Remedial Orders," U.S. District Court, District of Massachusetts, June 5, 1975.

53. *Newsweek*, May 26, 1975.

54. *Time*, September 1, 1975, p. 28.

55. *Newsweek*, September 15, 1975.

56. *Newsweek*, September 22, 1975.

57. Ibid.

58. *Time*, September 15, 1975.

59. "Desegregating the Boston Public Schools: A Crisis in Civic Responsibility," *Report of the U.S. Commission on Civil Rights* (1975), p. 56.

60. Joseph Featherstone, "Boston Desegregation," *New Republic*, January 17, 1976, p. 23.

61. "Desegregating the Boston Public Schools," pp. 706-7.

62. *Time, December 23, 1974.*

63. Ibid.

64. Ibid.

65. *Time*, November 10, 1975.

66. *Boston Herald American*, April 1, 1976.

67. *Boston Herald American*, April 2, 1976.

68. *Boston Herald American*, April 14, 1976.

69. Gail Jennes, "Teacher," *People*, October 3, 1977, p. 83.

70. *Boston Herald American*, February 11, 1976.

71. Edward Zucherman, "Beaten Up in Boston," *New Republic*, May 22, 1976, p. 11.

72. *Time*, May 3, 1976, p. 12.

73. James Worsham, "A Way out for Boston," *Boston Globe*, August 1, 1976.

74. Luix Overbea, "Education for Boston . . . ," *Christian Science Monitor*, June 16, 1976.

75. *Boston Herald American*, June 14, 1976.

76. Editorial, "Supreme Court and Busing," *Christian Science Monitor*, June 16, 1976.

77. *Boston Herald American*, January 17, 1977.

78. Ibid.

79. Marguerite Del Giudice, "School Report . . . ," *Boston Globe*, January 31, 1977.

80. *Boston Globe*, July 8, 1977.

81. Ibid.

82. *Boston Globe*, November 10, 1977.

83. Ibid.

84. Ibid.

85. Ibid.

86. Editorial, "A New Day in Boston," *Boston Globe*, November 10, 1977.

87. *Boston Herald American*, February 6, 1977.

20

BROWN III

"This is the fifth time now that HEW has been told by the courts to enforce Title VI. You would expect they would have gotten the message."

Joseph L. Rauh, Jr., Civil Rights Attorney.[1]

About six weeks after the Detroit decision, with civil rights activists still shaken by the direction the High Court had taken, a new judicial undertaking in Washington did much to lift their spirits.

It began when the Center for National Policy Review, a public interest law group affiliated with the city's Catholic University Law School, issued a "sweeping indictment" against HEW for its "abysmal failure" to end racial segregation in the thirty-three Northern and Western states outside the South.[2] A 117-page report, compiled by law students and professors using HEW files, contended that "bureaucratic caution, needless delays, administrative inefficiency and sloppy investigations" had prevented the Department from performing its statutory duty under Title VI of the 1964 Civil Rights Act, the law that interdicted payment of Federal funds to any agency that discriminated on the basis of race, color, or creed.[3]

According to William L. Taylor, Center director and former chief of the U.S. Civil Rights Commission, school desegregation in the North and West was now more pronounced than in the South because of HEW's lassitude. From 1964 to 1972, the percentage of black students attending segregated schools in the eleven states of the Old Confederacy dropped from 98 to 9 percent. In contrast, 57 percent of the black pupils in the North and West remained in schools at least 80 percent black.

Although Taylor blamed the Nixon Administration for slowing Northern and Western desegregation, he realized that his mischief alone did not explain the increasing bureaucratization of HEW's civil rights enforcement program. He pointed to the Department's failure to set goals and priorities, its inability to arrange deadlines and to resolve matters that had been pending for many years, a symptom of "hardening agency arteries."[4]

Not to be humiliated by this charge, Caspar Weinberger, HEW's new secretary, bristled. On the following day, he declared the Department should not be faulted for failing to enforce the law in the face of "very strong, bitter opposition" and in view of the wide gulf that "existed between what the law says and what the public wants." Moreover, said Weinberger, in answer to the allegation of noncompliance with Title VI, "We are enforcing the civil rights laws. . . . There are frequently many ways you can accomplish a great deal more by persuasion and discussion and negotiations to produce desegregation. . . . There are many situations in which withdrawal of funds promotes more segregation."[5]

Center architects of the polemic found Weinberger's rebuttal "shocking."[6] They could scarcely believe a cabinet officer, sworn to uphold the Constitution, would so easily forswear the "constitutional rights of children. If constitutional rights are not to be enforced by public officials in the face of local opposition," reminded a Center spokesman, "then respect for law is bound to be eroded," adding pointedly, "some of Mr. Weinberger's predecessors did not hesitate to enforce the law when the spotlight was on the South, despite public opposition there."[7] The thesis that school integration could be delayed because of adverse publicity must be rejected "*emphatically* and *unanimously.*"[8] Almost two decades before, the Supreme Court had ruled in *Cooper* v. *Aaron* that regardless of local opposition, Central High School in Little Rock, Arkansas, must be desegregated without delay.[9]

Finally, they condemned Weinberger for mentioning busing while totally neglecting other criticisms in the report. They singled out "HEW's continuing failure to end unequal programs and facilities in minority schools . . . , pupil segregation *within* schools . . . , discrimination in the hiring and assignment of teachers . . . , [desegregation] *without* busing . . . [and] HEW's constantly expanding civil rights enforcement staff and budget [on the one hand, and its] constantly declining enforcement efforts [on the other]."[10]

For its part, the NAACP's National Board of Directors was equally "outraged" that Weinberger would use such reasons to excuse his Department's failure.[11] "To accept strong resistance of residents, largely white, to desegregation as a valid reason for governmental inaction is as shocking as it is illegal." HEW's position is "untenable and we resoundingly reject it."[12] The staff was directed to meet with other civil rights organizations to work out plans for appropriate legal action.

Within weeks, the same legal strategies that had succeeded in *Adams* v. *Richardson*[13] were being used to goad HEW. On November 13, 1974, Joseph L. Rauh, Jr., the Washington-based civil rights lawyer, was writing Jack Greenberg, Director-Counsel, NAACP Legal Defense Fund, Nathaniel Jones, General Counsel, NAACP; and William Taylor, enclosing the outline for a suit that he referred to as the Northern *Adams* case. Our purpose,

Rauh told them, should be "to show up HEW's renunciation of Title VI enforcement . . . to identify the several aspects of its cop-out methodology."[14]

For eight months, these groups worked closely, conferring often, writing draft after draft. Eventually, on July 3, 1975—the sixth anniversary of the crippling Finch-Mitchell document emasculating HEW's enforcement powers—a class action suit was filed in the U.S. District Court for the District of Columbia, naming Weinberger and Peter E. Holmes, now director of the Department's Office for Civil Rights, as defendants. Plaintiffs were twenty-two black children in eight cities (suing through their parents). Since the first names to appear on the brief were Darryl W. and David Brown, thirteen- and fifteen-year-old sons of Jo Ann Brown of San Diego, California, the case appeared on the docket as *Brown* v. *Weinberger,* [15] or more simply *Brown III* in deference to *Brown I*[16] (1954) desegregating statutorily segregated schools and *Brown II*[17] (1955) calling for desegregation "with all deliberate speed."

"Defendants," charged the plaintiffs, "have deliberately renounced and abandoned their Title VI duty . . . in Northern-Western public school systems receiving HEW financial assistance. In large part as a result of this policy . . . in the 50 largest majority white Northern-Western public school districts, two out of every three black students attended schools with 50 percent or more [black and other minority] enrollment, one out of every two black students attended schools with 80 percent or more minority enrollment and one out of every 20 black students attended 100 percent minority schools."[18]

Until April, 1968, when HEW established a separate branch for Northern-Western schools in the Office for Civil Rights, it had paid scant attention to school segregation in the thirty-three states cited in the suit. In the following fifteen months, twenty-seven compliance investigations took place, but "even the promise of this modest start," said the plaintiffs, ground to a halt after the Finch-Mitchell announcement. "In the 11 years since the enactment of the statute, only five isolated school districts have been noticed for administrative enforcement proceedings . . . and only a single school district [Ferndale with 676 minority students, see Chapter Sixteen] had HEW funds terminated."[19]

Unquestionably, HEW's enforcement record had been seriously hobbled by Nixon's insistence that busing be held to the absolute "minimum required by law."[20] In fact, argued the plaintiffs understandably, the Administration's quietus "immobilized [HEW's] Title VI enforcement in major Northern-Western localities, where desegregation would plainly require resort to student transportation."[21]

Another bone in the plaintiffs' throats was their allegation that Secretary Weinberger had deliberately violated the Emergency School Aid Act of 1972 (ESAA) enacted by Congress to aid the process of desegregation.

Although HEW cited Los Angeles, Detroit, Rochester, and Richmond, California, in 1973 for operating segregated school facilities, making them ineligible for ESAA assistance, Weinberger had paid out millions of dollars until the District of Columbia's Court of Appeals ordered the Secretary to stop circumventing the law. More alarmingly, the Department had lost sight of its primary goal to end school desegregation. Instead, HEW sought to solve the nation's turmoil on the subject by substituting a quest for "quality education" as though the two goals were synonymous.

HEW's neglect also extended, said the plaintiffs, to its failure to establish standards that would broaden the interpretation of de jure segregation. Not even the enlarged scope of the *Keyes* ruling of 1973[22] had prompted the department to write new guidelines.

Consequently, in total HEW had merely scratched the surface in the Northern-Western territory. After eleven years, it could take credit for integrating only relatively small districts, those having a minority population of 98,181, which contrasted sharply with the 771,639 in medium-sized and larger segregated schools the Department had failed even to investigate; or with the 323,478 minority students in forty-two school districts with investigations pending from three to seven years; or with the 554,622 minority pupils in districts where HEW had found evidence of discriminatory faculty assignments, but had taken no action to halt the payment of ESAA funds, as required by Title VI.

Moreover, plaintiffs reminded the court, even on those occasions when HEW began action, it has been frightfully slow in completing its investigations. Of one-hundred inquiries initiated since 1964, fifty-eight remained unresolved; twenty-four were six to seven years old; eighteen three to five years, with the average forty-four months.

In view of HEW's record, the filing of *Brown III* should have produced little response in the Department. Instead bureaucratic shock set in, with HEW officials frankly admitting their distress as they gathered in Cleveland to plan counteraction. "In response to the lawsuit," was how Department spokesman Louis E. Mathis put it.[23] Learning this, plaintiff attorney John Silard exulted, ". . . to bring the pending cases to a head after so many years of delay, [is gratifying]. If we win nothing more, it would still have been worth the while."[24] Judge John J. Sirica, of Watergate renown, was assigned the case.

On October 31, 1975, Justice filed its papers in defense of Weinberger and Holmes, denying the applicability of *Adams*.[25] Defendants argued that *Adams* related only to school districts in the Southern and Border states with a history of dual systems. HEW officials now admitted they had "abused [the Department's] statutory discretion by engaging in negotiations for voluntary compliance too long before commencing enforcement proceedings."[26] Not so in *Brown III*.[27] Yet, plaintiffs were seeking an "order compelling HEW . . . 'to commence enforcement proceedings' within 60 days against some 58 school districts," regardless of proof of a Title VI violation.[28]

Secondarily, the defendants argued that since *Adams* concerned only schools with a history of de jure segregation, and since Northern and Western schools were not legally separated, *Brown III* could not be considered an extension of *Adams.*

Justice also had a third line of defense. Northern and Western schools, free of de jure segregation, required a more comprehensive investigation to establish Title VI violations. Therefore, the Secretary should not be rushed into enforcement proceedings until he had had time to negotiate voluntary agreements. This argument, however, did not explain why the Secretary waited eleven years after the enactment of the 1964 statute to take action nor why defendant Holmes admitted in an affidavit that the Department had discovered Title VI violations and was on the point of issuing findings in all but five of the "delay" school districts mentioned in the case.

Thus, when the plaintiffs replied on November 11 to HEW's opposition, they referred to the Holmes affidavit to refute the argument that *Adams* did not apply. It was "largely academic."[29] To allege, as HEW did, that *Adams* was limited "only to districts formally out of compliance" was to misread the opinion.[30] Judge Pratt had warned that if HEW failed to initiate enforcement proceedings within one to two years of finding a presumptive violation, the Department had "unlawfully defaulted upon its Title VI duty."[31] Admittedly, it had some "discretion" prior to taking action, but the Judge reminded, such "discretion is not unlimited."[32]

By its failure, plaintiffs argued, HEW had relinquished "its only effective statutory power in favor of ineffectual negotiations."[33] In contrast, by threatening fund termination, 400 of 600 Southern school districts found in violation of Title VI between 1964 and 1974 had agreed to desegregate rather than have their funds cut off. Of the remaining 200 recalcitrants, all but four eventually capitulated rather than lose Federal assistance. Caught on the horns of this argument, defendants countered that the solution was too burdensome to contemplate. It would require almost a total HEW effort too enforce Title VI within the thirty-three Northern and Western states.

To aid the court in reaching its decision, both parties appeared before Judge Sirica on December 5. Elliott C. Lichtman, arguing for the plaintiffs, pointed out that HEW's refusal to abide by Title VI had provoked an exasperated Judge Pratt to hand down his *Adams'* order: "90 days to make findings, 90 more days to get corrective action if the findings show merit, and 30 more days to get enforcement machinery going."[34]

Robert M. Rader, Justice defense attorney, told Sirica that simply because HEW had not taken action for four, five, or six years did not mean that it necessarily "should have. . . . it is like saying in a criminal case simply because you have been investigating someone's activities for a number of years that you should have the evidence to prosecute."[35]

At that, Sirica broke in, "Don't you think after four or five years you should have come up with a final answer one way or the other?

"If the law required that, your Honor. . . .

". . . you're saying the law doesn't require that?

"No, the law says HEW shall investigate these matters. The law doesn't contemplate within a specified period you must make a finding one way or the other . . . , [leaving] it to the discretion of HEW to determine whether or not a violation exists."[36]

Rader's casual attitude toward HEW's statutory responsibility so incensed Lichtman that he asked the court for time to reply:

Adams is very significant. . . . when there is a chance of fund cut-off, the people sit down and start negotiating. . . . The reason these things dragged out for years and years is they only started one or two, or four or five in the entire history of the North and West. These districts know darn well they have no incentive to give in because the agency never begins the proceedings. There is no credibility in their threat. Their system doesn't work in the North because they never begin proceeding. It has worked in the South. . . . It is a salutary process. It is an extremely effective statute. All we are asking you to do is what the courts did in *Adams*— force the agency to finally decide, fish or cut bait, begin proceedings if they can't get enforcement proceedings in the next two months.[37]

To HEW's counter argument that it still lacked the personnel to accomplish the job, plaintiffs replied that "in 1966 the Office for Civil Rights' staff was 100. In 1970, there were 400. By 1975, its professional and clerical employees numbered 850, with an authorization [for 1976] of 906. . . . During the summer of 1975, there were 59 unfilled positions at OCR, and in June, OCR returned $2.5 million of its 1975 appropriations to the Treasury [which represented more than 10 percent of its total appropriations]. The 'resources' contention is thus a sham."[38]

On July 20, 1976, Judge Sirica tersely dismissed the defendants' objection to a class action certification as "without merit."[39] His ruling consisted of three parts: The first gave HEW sixty days in which to decide whether the fourteen schools whose investigation had dragged on from one and one-half to eight years were in compliance with Title VI. If not, proceedings were to be undertaken within 120 days. Part two permitted twenty-six additional schools, already on notice of noncompliance, sixty days to comply with Title VI. The court made a special point of faulting Justice on its argument that *Adams* did not apply because Northern and Western schools were not historically dual systems. "Discrimination is discrimination," he wrote, "no matter where it exists in the country, and HEW's affirmative enforcement duty exists in all areas of the country. Congress made no such distinction as the defendants propose anywhere in the statute."[40]

Part three involved the six school districts that had received ESAA assistance despite evidence of discriminatory practices. Sirica ordered HEW to undertake enforcement proceedings within sixty days. Altogether, the court saw *Brown III*, and *Adams* as coterminous and complementary. Henceforth, their protective wings would enfold all fifty states. Quipped Rauh, at hearing the result, "This is the fifth time now that HEW has been told by the courts to enforce Title VI. You would expect they would have gotten the message."[41]

Unfortunately, the Department wanted to pretend otherwise. Within twenty-four hours, Martin H. Gerry, HEW's new OCR director, was challenging the "many erroneous factual findings" on which the decision rested.[42] Of the fourteen schools affected by part one, six, he said, "had already filed acceptable compliance plans and voluntary compliance was being sought with four."[43] Only New York City, of the fourteen listed, was still being investigated and this consisted of a massive study begun in September, 1974. The twenty-six schools, mentioned in part two, had been investigated. Thirteen had already prepared acceptable compliance plans and four more were expected to follow suit. Of the remaining nine, HEW was preparing to initiate enforcement proceedings against five. The six schools in part three were being similarly pursued.

Gerry's declaration gave no explanation of the long delay in commencing Title VI enforcement or the reasons for the Department's steady refusal to evaluate its own printouts showing discrimination in the thousands of school systems in the North and West. Moreover, regardless of departmental statements, doubts remained about HEW intentions. Would it, for instance, investigate all forms of discrimination?

Skeptic William Taylor, whose investigative work as head of the Center for National Policy Review had led to *Brown III*, wondered how HEW could already clear Fort Wayne and South Bend, Indiana; Sweetwater and Pomona, California; and New Britain, Connecticut—all cited in the Sirica ruling—of discriminatory practices in view of contrary evidence in the files. With the end of the Ford Administration only months away, Taylor held his fire, hopeful the Carter Administration, soon to take office, would prove more aggressive in enforcing Title VI. On June 15, 1977, he wrote the new OCR Director, David S. Tatel, formally requesting a reopening of the above cases. The latest OCR head, unlike his immediate predecessors, evidenced a willingness and desire to accomplish HEW objectives. A 1966 graduate of the University of Chicago Law School, Tatel taught law briefly at Michigan, with time out for service with the Lawyers' Committee for Civil Rights Under Law, becoming its national director from 1972 to 1974. His reply to Taylor touched all bases.

With regard to New Britain, a new investigation by HEW's Director of Region I failed to confirm a violation of Title VI. The existence of four segregated schools was not, according to Tatel, "the result of intentional state action," but "attributable to changes in residential patterns."[44] As to Pomona, the Director of Region IX had informed Tatel that his staff felt the evidence would not sustain a "viable student assignment case."[45]

On the question of Fort Wayne, South Bend, and Sweetwater, Tatel informed Taylor, "We have asked the Regional Directors to notify you as soon as a decision of compliance or noncompliance has been made. . . ."[46] For the first time in eight years, the Department of Health, Education, and Welfare demonstrated a willingness to enforce Title VI of its own volition.

Following this encouraging development, the United States District Court for the District of Columbia handed down in December, 1977, its latest ruling in the enforcement of *Adams*.[47] It was the fifth order since Judge Pratt's Declaratory Judgement and Injunction Order of February 16, 1973. The scope of its provisions were so broad as to be unique in specificity of its direction to HEW's new Secretary Joseph Califano, Jr. The court modified requirements for the seventeen Southern and Border states "to cover all educational institutions in the United States. . . ."[48] In an effort to unveil the secrecy hiding HEW operations during the Nixon and Ford Administrations, the Department was ordered to provide the plaintiffs every six months with computer printouts, "showing its enforcement activities under the applicable laws."[49] Such information should include the total number of complaints received, the number unresolved, the total closed for lack of evidence, those in which violations were found, the files closed due to corrective action, and the total number in which enforcement proceedings were initiated.

Besides this numerical sorting out, each complaint received or unresolved was to be tightly held by identifying pincers, (i.e., log number, date received, accused institution, allegations, whether backlogged, carryover, or current, and finally the date enforcement proceedings were undertaken, corrective action secured, or negotiations terminated). Should HEW fail to comply within the court-mandated time frame, the plaintiffs were to receive "an explanation of the specific reasons for the failure."[50] In the event the latter wished a closer look at HEW files, the court granted them the privilege of examining a "closed complaint and/or compliance review with confidential material deleted."[51]

On a practical note, it was surely the most heartening sign up to that point that school desegregation in the United States had finally tipped. Not only were all school systems now under one desegregatory umbrella, but for the first time the plaintiffs had an entree into HEW, guaranteed by the Federal judiciary. No longer could their complaints be brushed aside by a politically motivated HEW Secretary, as they had been for the previous eight years. It was no longer a question of when the fetid pools of segregation would be emptied, but when the action would start. The mandates of *Adams* and *Brown III*, ending in the comprehensive ruling of December, 1977, had retrieved much of the ground lost during the Nixon and Ford Administrations.

Notes

1. *New York Times*, July 22, 1976.
2. Bart Barnes, "Rights Program Seen . . . ," *Washington Post*, September 6, 1974.
3. Ibid.
4. Ibid.
5. *New York Times*, September 7, 1974.
6. William L. Taylor, Director, The Center for National Policy Review, School of Law, the Catholic University of America, "News Release," September 5, 1974.
7. Ibid.
8. Ibid.
9. *Cooper* v. *Aaron*, 358 U.S. 1, (1958).
10. Taylor, "News Release."
11. Roy Wilkins, Executive Director, NAACP, "News Release," September 13, 1974.
12. Ibid.
13. *Adams* v. *Richardson*, 351 F. Supp. 636 (1972).
14. Letter of Joseph L. Rauh, Jr., to Jack Greenberg and Nathaniel Jones, dated November 13, 1974.
15. *Brown* v. *Weinberger*, 417 F. Supp. 1215 (D.D.C. 1976) [hereafter *Brown* (1976)].
16. *Brown* v. *Board of Education*, 347 U.S. 483 (1954).
17. *Brown* v. *Board of Education*, 349 U.S. 294 (1955).
18. *Brown* v. *Weinberger*, D.D.C. Civ. A No. 75-1068, Plaintiffs' Complaint for Declaratory and Other Relief, (July 3, 1975), pp. 4-5.
19. Ibid., p. 7.
20. Ibid., p. 9.
21. Ibid.
22. *Keyes* v. *School District Number One, Denver, Colorado*, 413 U.S. 189 (1973).
23. *Brown* (1976).
24. Letter of John Silard, of the Rauh firm, to Jack Greenberg, Nathaniel R. Jones and William L. Taylor, September 2, 1975.
25. *Adams* v. *Richardson*.
26. *Brown* v. *Weinberger*, D.D.C. Civ. A No. 75-1068, Memorandum of Points and Authorities in Opposition to Plaintiffs' Motion for Preliminary Injunction or, in the Alternative for Partial Summary Judgment, (October 31, 1975), p. 4.
27. *Brown* (1976).
28. *Brown* v. *Weinberger*, Plaintiffs' Complaint, p. 5.

29. *Brown* v. *Weinberger*, D.D.C. Civ. A No. 75-1068, Plaintiffs' Reply in Support of Motion for Preliminary Injunction or, in the Alternative, for Partial Summary Judgment, (November 11, 1975), p. 3.

30. *Brown* v. *Weinberger*, Plaintiffs' Reply, p. 4.

31. Ibid.

32. *Adams* v. *Richardson*, at 641.

33. *Brown* v. *Weinberger*, Plaintiffs' Reply, p. 5.

34. *Brown* v. *Weinberger*, D.D.C. Civ. A No. 75-1068, Hearing Transcript, (December 5, 1975), p. 8.

35. Ibid., p. 18.

36. Ibid., p. 19.

37. *Brown* v. *Weinberger*, Hearing Transcript, pp. 29-30.

38. *Brown* v. *Weinberger*, D.D.C. Civ. A No. 75-1068, Reply to Defendants' Post-Argument Submission, (December 17, 1975), p. 2.

39. *Brown* (1976), at 1218.

40. Ibid., at 1222.

41. *New York Times*, July 22, 1976.

42. *Washington Star*, July 22, 1976.

43. *Washington Post*, July 22, 1976.

44. Letter of David S. Tatel, Director, Office for Civil Rights, to William L. Taylor, December 16, 1977.

45. Ibid.

46. Ibid.

47. *Adams* v. *Califano*, D.D.C. Civ. A No. 3095-70, Order of District Court (December 29, 1977).

48. Ibid., p. 10.

49. Ibid., p. 22.

50. Ibid., p. 24.

51. Ibid.

21

ESCH—BYRD—EAGLETON-BIDEN

"It ain't going to stop one bus that is court ordered."

Rep. David R. Obey, Wisconsin Democrat.[1]

The history of school desegregation in the United States has invariably produced a seesaw struggle between upholding and defying the law. During the Johnson Administration, herculean efforts by HEW ensured prodigious Southern desegregation. Then came the calculated efforts of the Nixon forces to ignore Title VI of the 1964 Civil Rights Act. In the judiciary, the Warren court's effort to enlarge the scope of *Brown I*[2] were seriously compromised when President Nixon appointed four conservatives to the High Court. The same swing of the pendulum occurred in Congress where Civil Rights activists engineered passage of Title VI, only to flee pell-mell when cries against busing were raised. In such a dichotomous atmosphere, Congress plunged ahead in the spring of 1974 with fresh attempts to curb *Adams*[3] and *Brown III*.[4]

Fall elections afforded the catalyst. Not since the Quie proposal failed to pass the Senate in October, 1972, had anything happened to stir up a busing controversy. To be sure, President Nixon had renewed his pledge to curb busing in a second State of the Union message the previous fall, but Congress paid scant attention to his entreaty, surmising the President had acted largely to divert attention from Watergate.

All this changed, however, with the approach of spring. On March 23, 1974, the Chief Executive delivered a nationwide radio address, calling for antibusing legislation. Like a hungry trout in search of flies, Congress leaped for the bait. First to take the lure was Marvin Esch, a Michigan Republican, who was anxiously awaiting the outcome of *Bradley* v. *Milliken*[5] and, like other Michigan Congressmen, under considerable pressure to halt busing for purposes of desegregation.

While the House debated a $25.2 billion education bill, Esch added an amendment that stated: "No court, department or agency of the United

States shall . . . order the implementation of a plan that would require the transportation of any student to a school other than the school closest or next closest to the place of residence. . . ."[6] The amendment quickly gained House approval 293 to 117, and on March 28, the educational aid bill, with the Esch Amendment, sailed through, 380 to 26.

Not to be upstaged, the Senate added its imprimatur to the antibusing movement. On April 10, Senator Sam Ervin, Jr., of North Carolina, the inveterate segregationist, opened hearings before the Senate Judiciary's Subcommittee on Constitutional Rights by declaring, "All across America, thousands of little schoolchildren have been ordered to board countless numbers of buses to be carried across neighborhood, city and county lines . . . to achieve some magical, racial mixing of bodies which satisfies the arbitrary and absurd sociological notions of misguided Federal judges and bureaucrats."[7]

Ervin's solution, S 1737, would prevent the government from moving against any school district as long as it operated under a "freedom-of-choice" system open to students of all races, the same scheme outlawed by the High Court six years earlier in *Green*.[8]

To this, Stephen Horn, Vice-Chairman of the U.S. Commission on Civil Rights, appearing before Ervin's Subcommittee, commented, "No matter how much choice is permitted in selecting the location of the place of one's education, it avails nothing if our children—black, brown, yellow, red and white—are educated in isolation from each other. . . . [Should S 1737 be adopted, it] would, in essence, repeal Title VI . . . [and] can only be viewed as a deliberative effort to condemn minority children to segregated education and as a step backward toward a racially separate society."[9]

Nonsense, argued Senator James B. Allen, Alabama Democrat, co-sponsor of S 1737. "I sincerely believe that Congressional inaction in the face of overwhelming sentiment against forced busing is a tremendously important factor in the erosion of confidence in Congress. The hostility of the people to the idea that the Federal Government has the power to yank up children and transport them to distant schools in conformity with half-baked sociological theories is illustrated by poll results."[10]

The conflicting points of view expressed before the Ervin Subcommittee characterized the arguments heard in the Senate, once debate began on the education bill already adopted by the House. Senator Edward J. Gurney, Florida Republican, moved to amend the proposal by adding language substantially similar to Esch's and, on May 15, after six hours of emotional appeals, the amendment finally lost by one vote, 47 to 46.

Gurney had argued that *Brown I* permitted free-choice, but was perverted through rulings of the Supreme Court which assigned "students to a particular school solely on the basis of race." As he correctly pointed out, "*Brown I* enunciated the principle that no child should be involuntarily assigned by State authorities to a certain school because of his race,"[11] but forgot to say the South had already twisted the thrust of the decision to mean the freedom to choose was the freedom to segregate. Thus, it had become not only a checkmate to desegregation, but a powerful weapon in maintaining a dual public school system. No one was better versed in this game of delay than Gurney.

Concerned that the Gurney-Esch Amendment might still be adopted, Majority and Minority Leaders, Mansfield and Scott, offered a compromise in the hope of cooling passions. Their proposal would allow the Federal courts to order busing if necessary to comply with the Fifth and Fourteenth Amendments. Yet, so fixed were the positions of the two adversaries that the compromise survived by only one vote, 47 to 46.

In the drawn out Senate-House conference that followed, sentiment remained sharply divided, made worse when President Nixon announced he would veto any measure containing the Mansfield-Scott language instead of the more restrictive Esch Amendment. On June 28, the House ordered its conferees to hold out for Esch, but neither the possibility of a veto nor an order to the House surrogates proved compelling. Mansfield-Scott won. True, HEW had had its wings clipped, but the Federal courts were still supreme. The Senate approved the conference report 81 to 15, the House, 323 to 83, and President Ford, who by now had displaced the disgraced Nixon, signed the bill on August 21, 1974. In one of those ironic twists of legislative history, the man whose name would be forever linked to the anti-busing amendment refused to vote for the conference report because the conferees had not excised the courts.

Thereafter, for more than a year, Congress paid scant heed to the alarms of the busing antagonists. Then, on September 19, 1975, Senator Robert C. Byrd, the West Virginia Democrat, proposed an amendment to the $36 billion 1976 Labor-HEW Appropriation Act that would strengthen Esch by limiting busing to the "school which is nearest the student's home."[12] In defense of his proposal, Byrd said the American people were tired of a "foolish social experiment" that "is inordinately costly."[13]

Like Sen. Gurney, he believed the High Court had "turned the original meaning [of *Brown I*] on its head . . . in the use of court-ordered busing to effect racial balance in the schools."[14] According to Byrd, "the first departure was the 1966 case of *U.S. v. Jefferson County Board of Education*[15] "where the Court read the landmark decision in such a way so as not simply to condemn segregation, but to require integration." Then the *Jefferson* idea trickled into the *Green* case of 1968 with its ruling that a "violation may exist when the segregation is not the result of racial assignments. This approach," he said, "was reaffirmed and extended"[16] in *Swann* and *Keyes*[17].

"To require the dismantling of "dual" school systems by not allowing the assignment of children to particular schools on the basis of race is one thing," he went on. "But to require schools to act affirmatively to achieve racial balance in schools by the assignment of children to particular schools solely on the basis of race is quite another thing."[18] What troubled Byrd particularly was that those who make the decisions on "arbitrary balance," as he termed it, be they a Federal judge or "a Federal bureaucrat in the Department of HEW," did "not have to stand for election" to test the fact that a majority of the American people, both black and white, oppose forced busing to accomplish an arbitrary racial balance in the public schools. "He simply lays down an arbitrary ratio and seeks to justify it on the overall demographic ratios of populations in the school district or city or county, and that is it."[19]

On September 24, by a 51 to 45 margin, the Byrd Amendment passed, and on December 4, following lengthy conference discussions over the Senate and House versions of the Labor-HEW Appropriations Act, the House approved a compromise that included the Byrd Amendment 260 to 14. Four days later, the Senate added its blessing and the measure went to the White House to be signed by President Ford.

By now the only hope civil rights protagonists had of stemming the congressional onrush lay in a judicial action. This the plaintiffs in the *Adams* and *Brown III* litigation undertook in May, 1977. Joe Rauh wrote Joseph A. Califano, Jr., the new HEW Secretary, urging him to counter "the ill effect of both the Byrd and Esch amendments, [which his predecessors had] interpreted in a manner damaging to school desegregation."[20] Rauh recalled that on October 1, 1974, just a few weeks after Esch became law, HEW's then General Counsel, John B. Rhinelander, had interpreted the statute "to bar HEW from requiring transportation of students beyond the next nearest school . . . including those cases where such busing is the only means of correcting Title VI or constitutional violation."[21]

"The effect of the Rhinelander opinion," Rauh argued, "is to require the HEW grant of funds to a district even where the district uses those funds to violate the Fourteenth Amendment. [Congress] recognized that the statute could not diminish a Court's authority to order busing where enforcing the constitutional rights of aggrieved students requires that remedy, [but] Congress could hardly have intended to require the Judicial Branch to act within the Constitution and leave the Executive Branch to violate it."[22]

As to the Byrd Amendment, HEW's reaction followed the same line, wrote Rauh. On December 13, 1976, Martin Gerry, former OCR director, defined the rider "as preventing HEW from requiring busing to paired or clustered schools where such remedy is the sole feasible means for desegregating a high school. . . . In short, even where pairing alone can achieve compliance, OCR has now construed the Byrd Amendment as barring that remedy—thereby requiring HEW to subsidize the segregating district in violation of the Constitution."[23]

To demonstrate his meaning, Rauh cited the conflict in Kansas City, Missouri, where HEW had conducted long negotiations with the Board of Education over school desegregation. According to the *St. Louis Post-Dis-*

patch, of May 1, 1977, the Department was even then "preparing a 'definitive' opinion on the reach of the Byrd Amendment to 'paired' schools."[24]

"It would be a substantial blow to school desegregation," continued Rauh, "if HEW were to deny itself the tools of pairing and clustering (and busing to paired and clustered schools) by an unnecessary interpretation of Byrd."[25]

Rauh was fortunate to find in Califano a kindred spirit. Carter's HEW Secretary had already written Attorney General Griffin B. Bell, asking whether in view of the Kansas City situation, pairing and clustering were legal under Byrd. The answer, written by Bell's Assistant Attorney General, Drew Days, declared that pairing and clustering did not violate Byrd even though their use in any desegregation plan might require the use of buses. To this interpretation, Congress reacted swiftly and explosively. Within ten days, angry members of the House had closed the "loophole" in Byrd. By a 225 to 157 margin, they approved a rider to the $61.3 billion 1978 Labor-HEW Appropriations measure which prohibited HEW from withholding aid to districts that barred busing in order to achieve pairing and clustering.

Rep. Ronald M. Mottl, an Ohio Democrat, sponsor of the amendment, explained it was "necessary because once again the powers-that-be over at HEW are doing legalistic somersaults to invent a new position that would permit HEW to use Federal funds to promote the pairing or clustering of local schools as a way of getting around the prohibitions of the Byrd Amendment. . . . Section 208 of that legislation . . . was an express, clear, and open statement of congressional intent to prohibit HEW from using Federal funds to require local school districts to bus their students away from their neighborhood schools."[26] In vain did Mottl's opponents point out that his amendment would not prevent the Federal courts from ordering busing, and that to obstruct HEW's role would merely force the school district to foot transportation costs out of its own pocket. "It ain't going to stop one bus that is court ordered," disgustedly cried Rep. David R. Obey, a Wisconsin Democrat.[27]

Rage over the Days memorandum was no less strident in the Senate. Thomas F. Eagleton, a Missouri Democrat, was incensed because it impacted on his own constituency in Kansas City. Under pressure from Washington, the Kansas City Board of Education had already filed suit in Federal District Court to permit formation of a metropolitan district containing thirteen Missouri and five Kansas districts. This would formalize interstate desegregation for the first time, and while the participants in the litigation were anxiously awaiting the outcome, Days announced his ruling.

A second angry senator was Joseph R. Biden, Jr., a Delaware Democrat, whose white constituency in metropolitan Wilmington was openly bitter over a series of court rulings involving the area's schools. The case of *Evans v. Buchanan* originally went to trial in 1957 with plaintiffs charging the existence of de jure segregation in Delaware schools.[28] Although a favorable decision and continued judicial prodding created plans designed to end school desegregation, by 1974 the Court found in renewed litigation evidence that "many schools in Wilmington which were black [before *Brown I*] remained identifiably black. . . ."[29] Then came the Supreme Court's *Milliken* decision with its restrictions on metropolitan integration,[30] and the District Court delayed action to give suburbia an opportunity to enter the litigation. Testimony showed a clear pattern of housing discrimination in that area: "Racially restrictive covenants . . . continued to be recorded in the New Castle County real estate deeds until 1973." The Delaware Real Estate Commission still abided by the Code of Ethics of the National Association of Real Estate Boards, cautioning realtors against "introducing into a neighborhood . . . members of any race or nationality . . . whose presence will clearly be detrimental to property values . . . in that neighborhood." Apart from private housing, evidence showed that "while the Wilmington Housing Authority operates over 2,000 public housing units within the City of Wilmington, fewer than 40 units were established in the suburbs."[31] In addition, the Court found the Delaware legislature guilty of intentionally keeping Wilmington's schools segregated. It had acted unconstitutionally by excluding the city from the Delaware Educational Advancement Act of 1968. Citing these points, the District Court called for alternative plans— intradistrict and interdistrict—to remedy the segregation, and in an extension of the suit a year later, restricted the solution to some sort of "consolidation or reorganization."[32]

Worried as Eagleton and Biden now were over the effect of Days's memorandum on their white constituencies, the two offered an amendment to the 1978 Labor-HEW Appropriations Act. Like Mottl's in the House, it barred "HEW from requiring transportation beyond the student's nearest school even if necessary for 'the reorganization of the grade structure of schools, the pairing of schools, or the clustering of schools. . . .' "[33] By adding this language to the previously enacted Byrd Amendment, the two hoped to emasculate HEW's authority. With a majority of the Appropriations Committee accepting the rider, the measure went to the Senate floor.

During the debate, Sen. Eagleton explained that the amendment would clarify congressional opposition to busing to achieve pairing and clustering. He carefully emphasized that it applied only to HEW's administrative authority, not to weakening the outreach of the Justice Department. "[We] are not talking," he soothed his colleagues, "about a case in Federal court where the judge finds a violation of the Equal Protection Clause of the Constitution and enters a busing order to remedy such violation. . . . I would not support a law which attempted to restrict the authority of federal courts to pass appropriate and targeted remedies to redress such constitutional violations."[34]

Sen. Biden spoke with equal emphasis in asserting that the amendment was an administrative matter that did not involve the courts. He even went so far as to deny the controversy had anything to do with school desegregation. "That is not the issue," he told his colleagues heatedly. "The issue is, can an administrative agency, the Department of Health, Education and Welfare, . . . absent a court ruling that there is a constitutional violation . . . make a determination that in their judgment there is in effect a constitutional violation; and that therefore, unless a school district . . . entered into a plan suggested by or sanctioned by HEW, that district . . . will have their federal funds withheld?"

"Joe Biden," he went on, "is not standing here and saying we should not have busing under any circumstances. If a court finds a violation, and decides the only remedy under the Constitution is busing, so be it. But that has nothing to do with what is happening here, nothing whatever."[35]

Others disagreed. Sen. Brooke, the Massachusetts Republican and only black member of the Upper House, scored the amendment as a "dismantling" of Title VI,[36] and Sen. Javits, New York's liberal Republican, argued the Eagleton-Biden Amendment was nothing but a "rear-guard action against human decency."[37] However, the mood of the Senate ran counter to their arguments and the rider passed 51 to 42. Shortly afterward, emboldened by the fact Congress had now hamstrung HEW, Biden, contrary to his floor avowal, proposed legislation that would restrain court-ordered busing to achieve pairing, clustering, or whatever. This measure, reminiscent of Esch's attempt to control the judiciary, was only narrowly defeated. Tom Eagleton himself cast the deciding vote after being reminded that his justification for Eagleton-Biden had rested on the Justice Department and the Judiciary's freedom to act.

Three weeks after Eagleton-Biden hurdled the Senate, the case to test its constitutionality along with Esch and Byrd began in earnest. Elliott C. Lichtman, thirty-eight, a Rauh firm partner, asked David S. Tatel, HEW's new director of the Office for Civil Rights, to identify those schools districts whose desegregation was being curtailed by antibusing legislation. Although young, Lichtman was already an experienced hand in the ongoing struggle for civil rights. A Phi Beta Kappa graduate of Yale, class of 1961, he had earned his law degree at Harvard. After a three-year stint with the National Labor Relations Board, Lichtman spent twenty months in Jackson, Mississippi, with the Lawyers' Committee for Civil Rights Under Law, then returned to Washington to join the Rauh firm.

In a deposition, taken July 28, Tatel admitted that "some school districts receiving federal funds are violating the Fourteenth Amendment because the student bodies of one or more schools are segregated on the basis of race where the desegregation requires transportation of students beyond the nearest or the second nearest school."[38] Asked for a list of such districts, Tatel informed Lichtman there were seventeen.

Throughout the summer and autumn of 1977, attorneys for the plaintiffs prepared their case. On December 9, the day Eagleton-Biden became law, they filed suit in Washington's Federal District Court.[39] Plaintiffs' motion

for Declaratory and Injunctive Relief rested on two premises: that by "inhibiting busing or other methods of desegregating school systems,"[40] Congress had prevented the implementation of the Fourteenth Amendment's
Equal Protection Clause, and that by continuing to pay Federal aid to
schools that remained segregated, HEW was violating Title VI.

To prove their first contention, plaintiffs relied heavily on *Swann* that
"desegregation plans cannot be limited to the walk-in school."[41] As one way
to accomplish desegregation, the justices sanctioned "pairing, 'clustering',
or 'grouping' of schools with attendance assignments made deliberately to
accomplish the transfer of Negro students out of formerly segregated Negro
schools and transfer of white students to formerly all-Negro schools," precisely what the antibusing amendments were designed to prevent.[42]

Beyond that, plaintiffs cited a companion ruling, *North Carolina State
Board of Education* v. *Swann*,[43] in which the Supreme Court struck down a
1969 state statute that sought to prevent forced busing for racial balance of
school populations. "[I]f a state-imposed limitation on a school authority's
discretion operates to inhibit or obstruct the operation of a unitary school
system to impede the disestablishing of a dual school system, it must fall,"
proclaimed a unanimous court.[44] In like fashion, because the three antibusing measures enacted by Congress tried to inhibit desegregation, they
too must fall, the plaintiffs argued.

As to the second issue that HEW was funding segregated schools in violation of the Constitution, the suit listed the seventeen Northern and Southern
school districts cited by Tatel. In eight, HEW had " 'settled or dismissed'
Title VI compliance efforts" as a result of congressional action even though
the schools were judged to be segregated.[45] In the other nine, de jure segregation could not be eliminated without additional busing, a remedy now
voided by Congress. Yet, argued the plaintiffs, "HEW intends to continue
providing financial assistance even if the districts do not choose to desegregate to comply with the Constitution."[46]

From the beginning of the litigation, top officials in HEW endorsed the
adversary move, but in the Justice Department a split existed. Assistant
Attorneys General Days and Barbara Allen Babcock, the two lawyers most
intimately associated with school desegregation suits, favored testing the
constitutionality of Esch, Byrd, and Eagleton-Biden. In a letter to Days,
copy to Babcock, written January 13, 1978, John Silard, a third Rauh
partner, reviewed the plaintiffs' "constitutional objections" to the antibusing amendments and said, "I believe [we] . . . will win [the suit] unless
the Department of Justice overrides the interests of HEW and of the Federal
Constitution by defending these indefensible measures."[47]

Judging by what eventuated, one can theorize that President Carter shied
from battling Congress and so informed Bell, or that Bell wanted a handle
on HEW's operation, as Mitchell had before him, or that Bell's fifteen years
as a Southern Federal judge had convinced him school desegregation was

better left to the courts—whatever the reason, he overruled Days and Babcock and ordered the Department to oppose the plaintiffs' motion.

Justice filed its opposition papers on the last day of February. An unenthusiastic Babcock frankly informed the court at the outset, "If the issue . . . were whether this legislation is good policy, we could not defend it. However, the appropriate forum for the executive branch to raise the policy issue is not this court, but the Congress. In this case, the issue is the constitutionality of legislation which, if it is constitutional, the executive branch is bound to enforce, like it or not."[48]

According to Justice, Esch, Byrd, and Eagleton-Biden were constitutional measures because Congress had not "altered the mandate of the 1964 Civil Rights Act," it had only regulated "the means by which that mandate is carried out."[49] HEW, said Babcock, was still empowered to call upon Justice to enforce Title VI, and nothing in the legislation limited "in any way the authority or ability of the Department of Justice to seek, or of the federal courts to order busing to remedy any *de jure* segregation found to exist."[50] Congress had "acted only to require an individualized court proceeding before the imposition of a transportation remedy."[51] Moreover, she argued, "Congressional authority . . . gave HEW and other agencies the choice between administrative and judicial enforcement of Title VI. . . . it would be anomalous to conclude that it was permissible for Congress to have given the agencies a choice between administrative and judicial enforcement, but that Congress may not constitutionally make that choice regarding a particular category of cases. . . . Congress was clearly acting within its authority when it embodied that preference in law."[52]

Babcock also contended that plaintiffs' argument about the amendments being a "desegregation-defeating effect" was simply "premature."[53] Had not the motion been filed on the same day that Eagleton-Biden became law? Consequently, the challenge was "based upon a set of facts plaintiffs, at most, speculate will exist at some future time."[54]

Despite her statement, HEW's attitude remained unchanged. Indeed, on February 28, 1978, Secretary Califano complained to the House Labor-HEW Subcommittee about congressional interference. "I think it does take away the last vestige of Title VI impact in terms of elementary and secondary education as far as student desegregation is concerned."[55]

Six weeks later, the plaintiffs replied by contending that what appeared to be "a choice between administrative and judicial enforcement" of Title VI was not a valid alternative.[56] OCR Director Tatel in a March 17 deposition said HEW would refer cases to Justice, but only when the latter agreed that civil action was necessary. This reluctance to act had already occurred when HEW concluded Kansas City's plan was unsatisfactory, yet could not persuade Justice to commence action.

In addition, plaintiffs noted that a "major uncertainty" existed as to whether Justice had sufficient manpower to undertake such actions.[57] A

240 FROM LITTLE ROCK TO BOSTON

letter from Days to Tatel, dated June 15, 1977, revealed "an undermanned division already concerned over the disproportionate use of Justice Department resources for existing Title VI duties."[58] Yet, Justice's Civil Rights Division had not requested more personnel "to prosecute HEW referrals arising from the anti-transportation laws" when it asked Congress for increased appropriations on January 23, 1978.[59] In short, the Department seemed eager to convince the court on the one hand that it stood ready to ask for Title VI enforcements while on the other it refused to lift the hand that would make it possible.

As to the strength of HEW's authority, plaintiffs reminded the court that in the past five years only one school district preferred losing its Federal assistance to complying with Title VI. In the same period, 1,025 districts complied rather than lose funds, "a fair reflection," Tatel had declared, "of the efficacy of the fund termination threat."[60] Indeed, only because of the "judicial orders issued in *Adams*" and *Brown III* in 1973, 1975, and 1976 had "Congress moved into the nullification business with Esch, then Byrd and now Eagleton-Biden."[61] What should be kept in mind, the plaintiffs declared, is that "instead of a bias against school desegregation these Congressional enactments [demonstrate] a legislative preference for litigation over fund termination.[62] HEW's fund cut-off power has been eliminated by the Congress *only* with respect to school desegregation; it remains intact for HEW's Title VI enforcement concerning all other instances of racial discrimination,"[63] and in fact since 1964, twenty other congressional antidiscrimination statutes were written with that provision.

Despite these contentions, on July 18, 1978, Judge Sirica ruled against the plaintiffs.[64] In a thirteen-page opinion, he accepted the constitutionality of Esch, Byrd, and Eagleton-Biden. Congress, he said, could express preference for Justice's litigation, over HEW's fund termination in the discharge of Title VI. He said the plaintiffs had "read their worst fears" into the amendments, and had asked "the Court to declare them unlawful regardless of what may actually come to pass."[65]

Sirica objected to plaintiffs' reference to *North Carolina State Board of Education* v. *Swann* to prove the unconstitutionality of the antibusing amendments. *Swann* had no bearing on the case, the judge also ruled, because Esch, Byrd, and Eagleton-Biden did not prevent local school officials from ordering busing when they believed it "necessary to insure equality of treatment. . . . Nor do these amendments bar federal authorities [from doing the same] to effectuate federal guarantees." The fact is nothing has changed the authority of "the Civil Rights Division of the Department of Justice, upon referral of a case from HEW, [to get] appropriate relief," not excluding busing. While the amendments "remove one setting out of which busing orders may originate, they quite clearly preserve student transportation as an available method of insuring equality in education."[66]

The alternative, the judge stated, also "undercut" plaintiffs' second argument that defendants had violated the principle established in *Cooper* v.

Aaron[67] of no government funds going "to support illegal discrimination. . . . the referral and litigation option remains an available enforcement technique that carries as much promise from the standpoint of assuring aid only to proper recipients as the fund cut-off procedure."[68] Consequently, "the enactments at issue in this case must survive plaintiffs' constitutional attack . . . , [but] should further proceedings . . . reveal that the
litigation option . . . cannot, *or will not*, be made into a workable instrument for effecting equal educational opportunities, the court will entertain a
renewed challenge by plaintiffs on an *as applied basis.*"[69]

Notes

1. *New York Times*, July 17, 1977.

2. *Brown* v. *Board of Education*, 347 U.S. 483 (1954).

3. *Adams* v. *Richardson*, 356 F. Supp. 92 (D.D.C. 1973).

4. *Brown* v. *Weinberger*, 417 F. Supp 1212 (D.D.C. 1976).

5. *Bradley* v. *Milliken*, 418 U.S. 717 (1974).

6. 20 U.S.C., §1714a (1974).

7. Sam J. Ervin, Jr., *Congressional Digest*, April 1974, p. 108.

8. *Green* v. *County School Board of New Kent County*, 391 U.S. 430 (1968).

9. Ervin, *Congressional Digest*, pp. 109, 111.

10. Ibid., p. 112.

11. U.S. Congress, Senate, *Congressional Record*, 93d Cong., 2d sess., 1974, Vol. 120, Part 11, p. 14820.

12. U.S. Congress, Senate, *Congressional Record*, 94th Cong., 1st sess., 1975, Vol. 121, Part 23, p. 29551.

13. Ibid., p. 29815.

14. Ibid., p. 30035.

15. *U.S.* v. *Jefferson County Board of Education*, 372 F 2d 836 5th Cir (1966).

16. *Congressional Record*, 94th Cong., 1st sess., p. 30035.

17. *Swann* v. *Charlotte-Mecklenburg Board of Education*, 402 U.S. 1 (1971); *Keyes* v. *School District Number One, Denver, Colorado*, 413 U.S. 189 (1973).

18. *Congressional Record*, 94th Cong., 1st sess., pp. 30035-6.

19. Ibid., pp. 29814-15.

20. Letter of Joseph L. Rauh, Jr., to HEW Secretary Joseph A. Califano, Jr., May 18, 1977.

21. Ibid.

22. Ibid.

23. Ibid.

24. Ibid.

25. Ibid.

26. U.S. Congress, House, *Congressional Record*, 123rd. Cong., daily ed., June 16, 1977, p. H6045.

27. *New York Times*, July 17, 1977.

28. *Evans* v. *Buchanan* 152 F. Supp. 886 (D. Del. 1957).

29. *Evans* v. *Buchanan* 393 F. Supp. 428 (1975), at 430.

30. *Milliken* v. *Bradley*, 418 U.S. 717 (1974).

31. *Evans* v. *Buchanan* (1975), at 434-35.

32. *Evans* v. *Buchanan*, 416 F. Supp. 328 (1976), at 350.

33. *Brown* v. *Califano*, D.D.C. Civ. A. No. 75-1068, Motion for Declaratory and Injunctive Relief, December 9, 1977, p. 9.

34. *Brown* v. *Califano*, D.D.C. Civ. A No. 75-1068, Defendant's Opposition to Plaintiffs' Motion for Declaratory and Injunctive Relief, February 28, 1978, p. 15.

35. Ibid., p. 16.

36. *New York Times*, June 29, 1977.

37. Ibid.

38. *Brown* v. *Califano*, D.D.C. Civ. A No. 75-1068, Deposition Transcript July 28, 1977, p. 3.

39. *Brown* v. *Califano*, Motion for Declaratory.

40. Ibid., p. 3.

41. *Swann* v. *Charlotte-Mecklenburg Board of Education*, at 30.

42. Ibid., at 27.

43. *North Carolina State Board of Education* v. *Swann*, 402 U.S. 43 (1971).

44. Ibid., at 45

45. *Brown* v. *Califano*, Motion for Declaratory, p. 17.

46. Ibid., p. 18.

47. Letter of John Silard to Drew Days, Assistant Attorney General, Civil Rights Division, January 13, 1978.

48. *Brown* v. *Califano*, D.D.C. Civ. A. No. 75-1068, Defendant's Opposition to Plaintiffs' Motion for Declaratory and Injunctive Relief, (February 28, 1978), p. 1.

49. Ibid., p. 19.

50. Ibid., p. 20.

51. Ibid., p. 26.

52. Ibid., pp. 28, 29, 31.

53. Ibid., p. 37.

54. Ibid., p. 42.

55. Testimony before the House Labor-HEW Subcommittee on Appropriations, February 21, 1978.

56. *Brown* v. *Califano*, Defendants' Opposition, pp. 28, 29, and 31.

57. *Brown* v. *Califano*, D.D.C. Civ. A. No. 75-1068, Reply Memorandum for Plaintiffs (April 7, 1978), p. 3.

58. Ibid.

59. Ibid.

60. Ibid., p. 7.

61. *Brown* v. *Califano*, Defendants' Opposition, p. 8.

62. Ibid., p. 10.

63. Ibid., pp. 10-11.

64. *Brown* v. *Califano*, 455 F. Supp. 837 (1978).

65. Ibid., at 840.

66. *Brown* v. *Califano* (1978), at 841.

67. *Cooper* v. *Aaron*, 358 U.S. 1 (1958).

68. *Brown* v. *Califano* (1978), at 842.

69. Ibid., at 843.

22

WHITE FEAR—BLACK HOPE

"When people like me, they tell me it is in spite of my color. When they dislike me, they point out that it is not because of my color. Either way, I am locked into the infernal circle."

Frantz Fanon, *Black Skin, White Masks.*[1]

"If you read the papers or listen to the media in Boston," Andrew Kopkind has written, "that would have been the first time you would have discovered that 'race' was an issue in the busing controversy. For years, the racists of Southie and the liberals in city government and the media have adopted or accepted the Nixonian convention that the issues in busing were 'neighborhood schools' and 'quality education.' It's true enough that those issues are important, but they are secondary to what anyone with common sense knows, despite an inane refusal to admit it. It's a matter of whites against blacks. When the mothers and fathers and kids of Southie threw stones and bricks and cursed out the black pupils in the buses from Roxbury, they were not arguing the merits of neighborhood schools or quality education."[2]

Such Negrophobic prejudice clearly derives from the white conviction, unspoken to be sure, that the black person is by nature inferior to the white and, accordingly, not to be measured with the same yardstick. Blacks are denied full membership on America's corporate boards, barred from white social clubs, and prevented from living in white neighborhoods despite Federal and state antibias laws. While certain whites—and blacks—like to divorce this exclusionary phenomenon from race, citing instead class and income, this hardly squares with the record.

Nowhere, perhaps, can the pernicious effect of such institutional racism be seen as in the operation of U.S. public schools. It was not merely the historical separation of black and white students, as undemocratic as it was, but the fact that such isolation made black pupils feel at once inferior, as pointed out by the Warren Court in *Brown I.*[3] What this does to an individual's self-esteem was aptly demonstrated in 1968 by an experiment conducted within an elementary classroom in Riceville, a tiny community in northeast Iowa. Teacher Jane Elliott wanted to instill in her children the incremental trauma that prejudice inflicts upon its victim. On April 5, 1968, the day after Martin Luther King, Jr., was assassinated, she divided her class into blue- and brown-eyed children. As reported by the media:

She gave the brown-eyed children special privileges during a Friday "Discrimination Day." The following Monday the blue-eyed youngsters were given the superior role.

Though they knew it was just a lesson, . . . the "inferior" group reacted with real anger, frustration and despair while their "superior" classes lorded it over them.

The people with blue eyes would not do the things the people with brown eyes did. One youngster wrote, "I felt left out. . . . I felt like giving them all black eyes."

. . . As to the effect of the two-day experiment on the 28 children, aged 8 and 9, one said, "Discrimination is not fun at all. I am glad I am not a Negro and being judged by my skin."

". . . "I think these children walked in a colored child's moccasins for a day," said the teacher, herself a white native of Riceville, which has no Negroes in its 1,000 population.[4]

Although not as clear cut as Jane Elliott's experiment, American school authorities still tend to follow procedures that produce similar emotions of inferiority among minority students. One such is to assign new or less experienced teachers to their schools. As Kenneth Clark, black psychologist, has written in *Dark Ghetto*, "Schools in deprived communities have a disproportionately high number of substitute and unlicensed teachers. Some of the classes in these schools have as many as ten or more different teachers in a single school year."[5]

White teachers at times display callousness to black sensitivity. A nationwide survey, undertaken in 1972 by *Phi Delta Kappan*, a writer's publication, revealed that 53 percent of the teachers questioned said that "when a school system reassigns teachers to secure better racial balance, the privilege of remaining" should be based, insofar as possible, on "seniority."[6] Of course, seniority has its perquisites, but choosing not to teach minorities is hardly one; its usage indelibly affects the heart of the black community.

A second fuel firing black inferiority is the attitude of rejection that white teachers often impart to minority children within the classroom. Children quickly learn the meaning of color prejudice through neglect.

Black students are further impeded scholastically by the penchant of many white teachers to classify their students on the basis of IQ test standings. The unfairness of rating students from minority and low income families with examinations prepared by those with middle class backgrounds has been well stated by Samuel Brodbelt, " . . . perhaps one of the great hoaxes perpetrated upon the poor, Negroes and some minority groups such as the Spanish Americans and Indians [is the IQ test, because] when one is economically poor in the dominant culture, one is apt to do poorly in a culturally determined IQ test." Having taken a result unfairly arrived at, the error is compounded by syphoning off minority pupils into "noncollege, occupational, and vocational courses. . . . Thus, the student in vocational programs soon learns that he is a second-class student in the school program."[7]

A final debilitating act is the actual separation under one roof of black and white students. This may occur because of teacher preference, academic standing, or administrative action, something the black community views as evidence of the majority's insistence on a better education for *their* children.

The distance separating black and white was given an unexpected push in the spring of 1975 by the man who had once tried so hard so bring them together. James S. Coleman, now professor of sociology at the University of Chicago, whose 1966 report had heralded the benefits of biracial learning, suddenly changed course. Addressing an April gathering of the American Educational Research Association, he reported the results of a statistical study of America's twenty largest central-city school districts which showed a substantial exodus of white families to the suburbs. Undertaken at the request of the Urban Institute, Coleman's report indicated that court-ordered integration had actually produced segregation, particularly when busing was involved. This convinced the sociologist the courts had gone too far in attempting to square integration with the Fourteenth Amendment, an effort better left to the executive and legislative branches of government.

Dubbed Coleman II, the thesis, as well as its author, came under immediate fire. He was castigated as another white liberal who had deserted the desegregation cause. Psychologists, Dr. Robert L. Green, of Michigan State University, and Dr. Thomas F. Pettigrew, of Harvard, argued that Coleman's figures did not explain the discrepancy between large cities losing whites and small cities remaining largely unaffected by busing, or why in reaching his conclusions, he left out such adverse factors as the impact of pollution, crime, or the departure of industry to the suburbs.

In time, the severest criticism came from the author himself. He admitted under questioning from Robert Reinhold, of the *New York Times*, to having gone beyond the "scientific data" in his public statements. His study had not dealt with busing and his contentions applied only to trends in two or three cities. Nevertheless, he insisted that the "over-all implications" of his argument had validity and that school integration could not work without the people's willingness to be integrated. There was further reason to suspect that Coleman had in fact tripped over his political conceptions in trying to make points as a sociologist. As Reinhold discovered, he had used as examples of white flight, cities that had "no court-ordered busing, rezoning or any other kind of coerced integration" during the first two years of the base period with which to measure white flight in the following three years 1970-73.

If there was "massive and rapid" desegregation, as Dr. Coleman said, it could not have been due to court-imposed remedies. Crosstown busing as a remedy for segregation caused by residential patterns became widespread only after [the *Swann* ruling of April 1971[8]] nearly a full year after Dr. Coleman's 1968-1970 integration study ended. Suburbanization began long before school desegregation. The white middle class—possibly fleeing inferior housing, poor schools, crime, dirt or black neighbors—had largely abandoned Boston long before busing started there [in 1974]. In Atlanta, where black enrollments have risen from 47 to 85 percent in the public schools in 15 years, no white child has ever been bused against his will.[9]

Once the shortcomings of Coleman's second report were made known, he attempted to clarify his position and only succeeded in confusing the issue further. First came an admission in July that his first conclusion on the white-loss ratio had been unduly influenced by fluctuations in the loss rates of the chosen cities. Atlanta, for instance, had suffered a 52 percent loss of whites between 1970 and 1973, but apart from Memphis and Houston, there had been little school integration in the other seventeen cities.

During August, he announced in a third paper that white erosion was continuing at an accelerated pace regardless of school desegregation in those urban centers with large black enclaves surrounded by a white suburban noose. This posed the question of what came first. Was it black in-migration or white departure for the suburbs or perhaps both that eventually disgorged itself in white flight, so disturbing to Coleman?

Finally, in October, writing in *Phi Delta Kappan*, he made a fourth revision, reverting now to his original thesis that "desegregation in some large cities is certainly not solving the problem of segregation. Ironically, 'desegregation' may be increasing resegregation." He had not lost his earlier belief in the achievement benefits of school integration, but admitted that subsequent studies had shaken his faith. In any event, he added, the benefits "are not so substantial that in themselves they demand school desegregation, whatever the other consequences. And particularly when desegregation occurs through bringing together for the school day students from several different neighborhoods, it is questionable whether the same achievement benefits arise."

Apart from any dialogue concerning "achievement benefits," Coleman remained convinced that busing on the scale needed to desegregate large urban schools violated "the rights of individuals" to select a "child's school through choice of residence." Donning the policy robe of the public man, Coleman now said each child in a metropolitan area should have the right "to attend any school in that area so long as the school to which he chose to go had a higher proportion of his race than his neighborhood school. This is the right to attend one's own neighborhood school, but it adds the right to choose a school unconstrained by residence. This right would be most important both to blacks and to the economically disadvantaged. For it is first of all blacks, and second the economically disadvantaged of all races, whose residential location has been most constrained."[10]

In arguing for free-choice, Coleman dusted off the now-discredited formula for circumventing *Brown I*. Passage of the 1964 Civil Rights Act and the cutting decisions of the Supreme Court had outlawed the doctrine, but the sociologist, whose research at one time had figured so prominently in the outcome, now advised his countrymen to return to square one. Along with other liberals who had lost their faith in the overriding value of school integration, he now saw the issue, not primarily as pluralism versus racial segregation, but as busing versus personal right. That perception and the call for free-choice overlooked the empirical fact that the majority of Americans only enjoy the constitutional guarantees of freedom and equality through judicial ukase. Coleman's suggestion of voluntary constraints would not only condemn school desegregation to the scrap heap, it would drastically undermine the claim of all minorities to constitutional protection.

Controversy stalked the Coleman update because of its emphasis on voluntarism and free-choice. Several researchers, using the same data, failed to replicate his findings. Not only the difference in statistical interpretation, but the very structure of Coleman's methodology figured in the discrepancies, his impersonal collection of data, aimed at predicting the rate of white urban attrition rather than the reasons behind white flight. White parents had not been asked why they left the city for suburbia. The "survey" assumed school desegregation, but as Gary Orfield took pains to show, "Reaching any kind of firm conclusions on these issues turns out to be an enormously difficult and complex process. . . . All we have now are preliminary studies, some national, some local, employing very different kinds of data and based on different analytic assumptions. Though the evidence raises important questions, it is impossible to demonstrate that school integration, in itself, causes substantial white flight."[11]

He listed no less than ten reasons for white flight in addition to school desegregation. Weighing their impact, he wrote "is exceedingly difficult but vitally important if one is to draw any valid policy conclusions." For example, "a family that leaves Detroit when a school integration plan is implemented will also be aware of the city's income tax, its 1967 riot, the extremely high level of violent crime, cutbacks in the police force, the city's controversial black mayor, the massive housing abandonment in the city, the recent loss of more than a fifth of the city's job base. . . . While the school crisis might be the final factor that determines the family to move *now*, the general condition of the city virtually guarantees that the family would move eventually and that it would not be replaced by a similar white family."

And even if these were not the "real issues," Orfield hypothesized, "If the changing racial composition of the public schools was the central problem . . . one could expect a heavy increase in the enrollment of whites in relatively inexpensive Catholic schools, schools which are heavily concentrated in central cities. They are real alternatives for many of the Catholic ethnic concentrations directly threatened by racial change. These schools, however, have declined sharply in enrollment in recent years."[12]

Besides, one would be clearly mistaken not to recognize that suburbia has its own charms for magnetizing white city dwellers. The availability of single residences, purchased on attractive terms, offers a great incentive. Federal laws permit income tax deductions for interest paid on residential mortgages, in contrast to the urban tenant with nondeductible rental payments. Indeed, from the passage of the original Federal Housing Act of 1950, a whole series of laws, all designed to aid suburbia, have seriously eroded white urban populations.

Once Washington had weaned suburbia, these satellite children became white sanctuaries, isolated from the inner city. Even though local and state fair housing laws, culminating in the Federal government's 1968 statute, attempted to obliterate these racist walls, they still remained largely impenetrable to suburbia's hastily drawn zoning restrictions such as minimum building lot sizes and minimum construction costs. At the same time, the refusal of municipal bodies to place public housing developments outside the city served to contain the minority groups within the urban core, thus maintaining black and white polarization.

In 1966, Congress amended the Federal Housing Act, adding Sections 235 and 236 which permitted unscrupulous contractors to take advantage of generous construction and rental subsidies to swindle big-city residents. Once the equities in these substandard homes receiving federally guaranteed mortgages dropped below the purchase price, their owners either perpetrated a similar hoax on the next buyer or simply abandoned the properties. In Detroit, where FHA was left with 11,000 vacant properties, a HUD official commented ruefully," [W]hite flight from the city was facilitated by FHA to the nth degree. Not only did the readily available FHA insured mortgages facilitate somebody selling and leaving the city, but of course we insured the other end of the transaction, when he bought a new house in the suburbs. We greased the skids the whole way. It's no wonder that Detroit lost 190,000 people from 1962 through 1970. The system was like a greased runway."[13]

More recently, the flight from the cities has even included minority families. Understandably, they raise the same objections as whites to urban crime, poor housing, and increased real estate taxes. From 1970 to 1974, Washington's black population declined 5 percent while it increased 61 percent in the periphery. According to the Washington Center for Metropolitan Studies, the city's loss in black population during this period doubled the white flight rate to the suburbs and accounted for almost three-fifths of the total suburban growth. As to demographic changes in metropolitan Washington's school population, by 1972 a third of the area's black children attended suburban schools, while inside the city, with a 97 percent black public school population, dissatisfied parents sent 10,000 of their off-spring to private schools. As a result, the capital is "experiencing 'massive black flight', and its public schools are becoming not simply black institutions, but black lower class institutions."[14]

The significance of this new development, at a time when black parents increasingly call for separate but equal scholastic institutions, has to be faced. Today's problems in desegregation cannot be understood without a comprehension of this harsh reality, born of frustration and anger over white racism. Black separation has enjoyed a long heritage. More than a century and a half ago, the American Colonization Society spent $2.5 million to transport 12,000 free blacks to Africa. The movement fell flat when no serious back-to-Africa agitation materialized. A second separatist attempt, this one led by Jamaica-born Marcus Garvey, got under way in the 1920s, but this, too, died. Although Garvey succeeded in enrolling a half million members in his Universal Negro Improvement Association, making it the black's largest organization in American history, his back-to-Africa call failed, and his following quickly dwindled after he was imprisoned for defrauding the mails and deported in 1925.

The third consequential effort to separate blacks from whites occurred in the mid-1960s with the birth of the black power movement. Once again, its basic thrust rejected white America and its majority culture. One of the most ardent spokesmen, Julius Lester, explained it this way, "The social, political, cultural and economic institutions of white America are designed to tell whites that they are superior and to tell blacks that they are inferior. Either those institutions (and the attitudes which created them) must be changed or blacks must remove themselves from them and create their own social, political, cultural and economic institutions which will give them the opportunity to live their lives feeling that they are, indeed, 'somebody'."[15]

The growing influence of this credo has substantially slowed the desegregation process in the large metropolitan areas. Black parents, originally gladdened by the *Brown I* victory and entertaining visions of a new society, were deeply hurt and then resentful to discover that white racism had not disappeared, particularly in the operation and administration of the schools. Overtly and covertly, the black community began to sympathize with appeals to black pride and independence. In calling for separation from white dominance, black educator Vincent Harding said the existence of all-black schools was not as much an impediment to black progress as the fact "that whites who were patently hostile to the fullest development of black people controlled those schools and the content of their curriculum . . . . That such people [are] in charge of *any* children's education [is] a tragedy. That they [attempt] to control the education of black children [is] almost disastrous."[16]

Out of this separatist gestation, aided by forces inside and outside the ghetto, came a black demand for community control of its schools. White apathy toward finding a solution to black grievances contributed heavily. Writing in May, 1974, Roger Wilkins, of the *New York Times*, concluded that white America was by now surfeited with black appeals. "Incessant civil rights demands by the 'responsible' Negro leaders," he wrote, "the specter of white school children being bused into ghetto schools; fiery rebellions in the cities; black rhetoricians screaming at 'whitey' all over the country, and blacks withdrawing from whites on college campuses, and from old alliances, was too much for white America to ingest."[17]

Also, the Federal government added its stimulation by stressing compensatory education in preference to desegregation, especially if the latter involved busing as it generally did. Back in 1965 when Congress enacted Title I of the Elementary and Secondary Education Act, it aimed at removing the discrepancy between expenditures for black and white education. Then came the initial Coleman report of 1966 which found only a remote correlation between scholastic achievement and fiscal input. With the outbreak of the busing furor in 1971 following *Swann*, Title I took on new meaning. It became the refuge of jittery white senators and representatives who feared public retaliation to busing, yet eagerly sought an opportunity to show their black constituencies their devotion to black improvement. The result was to increase black interest in the perpetuation of segregated schools.

A final outside force causing the ghetto to look inward was the *Milliken* decision that raised mountainous obstacles to metropolitan desegregation.[18] Indeed, any barrier to consolidation with suburbia inevitably cemented black community control in the cities.

Inside the ghetto, black separatism received a boost from the revelation that black pupils were scoring less than their white peers on achievement tests. While this fact troubled white-dominated school administrations, it infuriated black parents. To them, the results offered further proof of what happens when whites controlled their children's education.

The predictable black desire to wrest control from white school officials got a tremendous boost in the late 1960s from expanding political pressure. In the large urban enclaves as blacks began to exert political muscle, their influence if not their direct control, was felt in all the basic governmental services. They began to fill positions in the police, fire, and welfare departments and elect representatives to their municipal governing bodies. Concomitantly, the identical pressures that changed the face of big city government worked on the school systems, producing requests for decentralization with blacks taking over control of local school boards. Often, this led to a fierce struggle to occupy the teaching and administrative posts indigenous to the black community.

Whites, being longer in service and, therefore, protected by tenure and union seniority, deeply resented the challenge, as New York City witnessed

in the spring of 1978. The central Board of Education tried to comply with
an HEW agreement integrating the city's teaching personnel. The staff was
historically white, largely Jewish, and as the black student percentage continued to rise, so too did the ratio of white teachers instructing black pupils.
Finally, threatened by a loss of $35 million in Federal funds for violating
Title VI, the board capitulated and agreed to establish the same proportion
of minority teachers (within 5 percent) in each of the city's thirty-two school
districts as the minority school population in the whole system.

The decision so rankled the heavily white borough of Queens that a number of community school boards, led by Board 26 in the borough's north-
eastern section, filed suit to halt the agreement. Ranged against each other
in the proceedings were the United Federation of Teachers and the American Jewish Congress for the plaintiffs, the NAACP and the New York Civil
Liberties Union for the defendants. In an opinion, handed down April 7,
1978, Federal District Judge Jack B. Weinstein invalidated the agreement,
ruling that there had been insufficient public hearings prior to the accord.
Whereupon instead of attempting to cooperate with Weinstein's instructions, the Board of Education caved in to white pressures and voted to
abandon the plan, an act, said Horace Morris, of the New York Urban
League, that could "only be interpreted by the black community as a further
indication that these people who make decisions just don't care, or even
worse, that they work against our progress."[19]

Five years earlier, this precise feeling of rejection had led Atlanta blacks
to negotiate a compromise with the white Board of Education by which they
gained partial control of the city's school system. In the decade and a half
preceding the agreement, Atlantans had seen their school population shift
from 60 percent white to 80 percent black. The prospect of meaningful integration, despite fifteen years of litigation by the NAACP Legal Defense
Fund, appeared more and more remote. "You've got to have some white
kids to integrate with," quipped Lonnie King, black Atlanta businessman,
the plan's chief architect.

For giving up on desegregation, King received a commitment that blacks
would fill half the administrative posts, including the superintendency.
However, a total of 60 percent of the city's schools would remain entirely
black, only 5 percent would integrate, and a mere 3,000 of the city's 95,000
students (2,200 black, 800 white) would bus to school. "What we needed
down here," King told *Newsweek* magazine, "was to get more soul into the
top school positions—people who understand something about the black
life-style."[20]

Those favoring black community control were happy. "What," asked
Vincent Harding rhetorically, "is desegregation in places like Atlanta where
white parents have effectively abandoned the public schools of the central
city? . . . We want to help create a school system where no black or white

students will have to leave their own community to read. We want a school system where whites will be able to find cultural and spiritual enrichment in predominantly black settings. . . ."[21]

Predictably, Roy Wilkins took exception by pronouncing the compromise "an unholy mess of hopes and fears."[22] The NAACP's Executive Director, furious that his chief Atlanta spokesman (King was president of the local NAACP chapter) would negotiate such an agreement, had him suspended and when he and his board refused to recant, they were summarily dumped. Wilkins saw in this latest Atlanta compromise something similar to its famed 1895 predecessor when Booker T. Washington, the head of Tuskegee Institute, offered to renounce the battle for political equality to gain economic favor. To white clapping, he had consented to second-class black citizenship. "In all things that are purely social, we can be as separate as the five fingers, yet one as the hand in all things essential to mutual progress," he thundered. "To those of my race . . . I would say, 'Cast down your bucket where you are, . . . Cast it down in agriculture, mechanics, in commerce, in domestic service, and in the professions.'"[23] Within a year, the United States Supreme Court added its seal of approval to black inferiority by legalizing the separate but equal philosophy in *Plessy* v. *Ferguson*.[24] It had taken more than half a century to overturn that decision, yet thirty years later a deal was being cut to compromise what had been won. As one member, who was party to the agreement, put it, "Lonnie King and his group wanted more control and they got it through jobs. For its part, the board wanted stability and an absence of turmoil."[25]

The result was a major retreat from racial pluralism in the school system. The principle had been bartered away. Harvard's Derrick Bell told it as it was. "Because white resistance to integrated schools is symbolic—and represents the core of the philosophy that America is a white man's country —it must be fought by blacks who are convinced that the educational merits of integrated schools are overstated, misconceived, or simply nonexistent. The right of black children to attend integrated public schools—quite literally whether exercised or not—is a right that is crucial not only to black success, but to black survival in this country."[26]

Moreover, by bargaining jobs for maintenance of a cosmetic front, King was playing the white man's game. Atlanta's white power structure had coined the slogan "too busy to hate" on the way to industrial preeminence, and feared racial turmoil.[27] Too, with 80 percent of the school population black, King had won a black shortfall in getting half the administrative jobs, not a bargain.

Both King and Harding suffered from demographic myopia. Instead of abiding with the concept of American pluralism, both sought ways to constrict the effort. Instead of insisting on full participation in the mainstream, they would settle for full control over a tributary. Again, as Bell pointed out, "Education is more than achievement scores and standardized tests.

Education should prepare students for living. In integrated schools, what-ever the *academic* value of blacks learning with whites or vice versa, the two groups are forced to cope with the problems of racial hostility and ignorance which have been imposed on them by the society in which they will soon take their places. It may not even be too extreme to say that, to the extent education lacks racial conflict, it is insufficient preparation for living in America as it is and it is likely to be for a long time."[28]

Politics is an excellent example. In no state of the Union do blacks have a higher registration than whites. Legislative control at the state and Federal levels of government will, in all likelihood, continue under white domination. Thus, black demands for educational funds, welfare pay-ments, and adequate housing, to name three needs, will have to be weighed by a white majority. While it is true that this political relationship (black vis-à-vis white) has undergone profound upheavals at the local level, as America's cities have become increasingly black, it is also true that no large U.S. city can survive without huge appropriations from the state and Federal governments. In such a milieu, the folly of insistence on separatism is self-evident.

The same prognosis applies to the marketplace. Always, there will be a certain number of so-called black jobs. However, it would violate one's common sense to think that black America can exist on such a diet. The black sector would have to create jobs for the 50 to 60 percent of the black labor force that currently works outside the neighborhood, would require enormous investment capital, a commodity blacks lack, and a substantial market on the outside. In short, a pluralistic society cannot function with-out working together.

This togetherness has particular significance in the field of education. If schools train only the black teacher, the black grocer, the black funeral director, how are their graduates to compete apart from their limited clientele? "American economic life," warned Nobel economist Sir W. Arthur Lewis, some years ago, "is dominated by a few large corporations which do the greater part of the country's business; indeed, in manufactur-ing, half the assets of the entire country are owned by just 100 corporations. The world of these big corporations is an integrated world. There will be black grocery shops in black neighborhoods, but in your lifetime and mine there isn't going to be a black General Motors, a black Union Carbide, a black Penn-Central Railroad, or a black Standard Oil Company. These great corporations serve all ethnic groups and employ all ethnic groups. American economic life is inconceivable except on an integrated basis."[29]

Notes

1. Frantz Fanon, *Black Skin, White Masks* (New York: Grove Press, 1967), p. 116.

2. Andrew Kopkind, "Busing into Southie" *Ramparts,* December, 1974, p. 35.

3. *Brown* v. *Board of Education,* 347 U.S. 483 (1954).

4. *New York Times,* July 14, 1968, p. 55.

5. Kenneth Clark, *Dark Ghetto* (New York: Harper & Row, 1965), p. 138.

6. Harold Spears, "Kappans Ponder Racial . . . ," *Phi Delta Kappan,* December, 1972, p. 245.

7. Samuel Brodbelt, "Disguised Racism in Public Schools," *Educational Leadership,* May, 1972, pp. 700-701.

8. *Swann* v. *Charlotte-Mecklenburg Board of Education,* 402 U.S. 1 (1971).

9. Robert Reinhold, "Coleman Concedes . . . ," *New York Times,* July 11, 1975.

10. James S. Coleman, "Racial Segregation in the Schools . . . ," *Phi Delta Kappan,* October, 1975, pp. 77-78.

11. Gary Orfield, "White Flight Research," *Educational Forum,* May, 1976, p. 525.

12. Ibid., p. 528.

13. Ibid., p. 534.

14. Ibid., p. 529.

15. Julius Lester, "The Necessity for Separation," *Ebony,* August, 1970, p. 168.

16. Letter of Vincent Harding, "The Atlanta Compromise . . . ," *Christian Century,* October 3, 1973, p. 988.

17. Roger Wilkins, "The Sound of One Hand Clapping," *New York Times Magazine,* May 12, 1974, p. 48.

18. *Milliken* v. *Bradley,* 418 U.S. 717 (1974).

19. *New York Times,* April 15, 1978.

20. *Newsweek,* July 30, 1973, p. 42.

21. Harding letter, "The Atlanta Compromise . . . ," p. 989.

22. *Newsweek,* July 30, 1973.

23. John Hope Franklin, *From Slavery to Freedom,* 2nd edition (New York, Alfred A. Knopf, 1960), p. 385.

24. *Plessy* v. *Ferguson,* 163 U.S. 537 (1896).

25. *Newsweek,* July 30, 1973.

26. Derrick A. Bell, Jr., "Integration: A No Win Policy for Blacks?," *Inequality in Education,* March, 1972, p. 42.

27. *Newsweek,* July 30, 1973.

28. Bell, "Integration," pp. 40-41.

29. Sir W. Arthur Lewis, "The Road to the Top . . . ," *New York Times Magazine,* May 11, 1969, pp. 40 and 42.

23

THE TURN OF THE SCREW

"A contrary ruling might have undermined desegregation orders involving more than five million students in about 200 school districts throughout the nation.

Robert Reinhold, *New York Times* reporter commenting on the Supreme Court's decision in the *Dayton* case.[1]

Unquestionably, the Supreme Court's 5 to 4 ruling in *Milliken* dramatically arrested the Federal judiciary's effort to achieve metropolitan area school desegregation.[2] Like a watershed, it stood as the dividing line between what had transpired since *Brown I* and what followed.[3] From 1954 to 1974, the court had continuously enlarged its interpretation of de jure segregation to the point Northern de facto segregation was being voided.

With *Milliken* however, the bastions of metropolitan school segregation in the North and West took on an impregnable cast. Chief Justice Burger had delivered the summation by declaring, "it must be shown that racially discriminatory acts of the state or local districts, or a single school district have been a substantial cause of interdistrict segregation [to prove a] constitutional wrong."[4] That, as the majority knew, would entail mountains of documentation with no guarantee of success. Even the most dedicated civil rights organization blanched at the thought of the effort and money needed to undertake such massive litigation. The NAACP, for instance, estimated it would cost some $750,000 to sue the Chicago School Board, with costs added if the decision went against the plaintiff. In losing *Milliken*, NAACP had had to pay a $20,000 court assessment.

In the days following *Milliken*, to underscore its directional change, the Supreme Court went afield to define in more explicit terms its new understanding of unconstitutional school segregation.

The first case, decided April 20, 1976, involved angry black families who had sued the Chicago Housing Authority (CHA) and the national HUD administration, charging CHA with having deliberately selected "public housing sites in Chicago to avoid the placement of Negro families in white neighborhoods," and HUD with providing financial assistance to support

"CHA's discriminatory housing projects."[5] Despite the clear segregative action, the district court in *Hills* v. *Gautreaux*, denied the plaintiffs' motion for metropolitan relief, arguing the *Milliken* concept that since "wrongs were committed within the limits of Chicago and solely against residents of the City," the alleged violation was not subject to prosecution.[6]

On appeal, however, the Seventh Circuit reversed the lower court. "[W]e can but conclude," it said in remanding the opinion, "that the District Court's [decision to forego a metropolitan solution] was clearly erroneous."[7]

Taken to the Supreme Court, the justices unanimously backed the Appeals' decision. "We reject the contention," said Potter Stewart, "that, since HUD's constitutional and statutory violations were committed in Chicago, *Milliken* precludes an order against HUD that will affect its conduct in the greater metropolitan area. The critical distinction between HUD and the suburban school districts in *Milliken* is that HUD has been found to have violated the Constitution. . . . Here, unlike the desegregation remedy found erroneous in *Milliken*, a judicial order directing relief beyond the boundary lines of Chicago will not necessarily entail coercion of uninvolved governmental units, because both CHA and HUD have the authority to operate outside the Chicago city limits."[8] In short, the High Court was saying a cross-district remedy was allowable provided the authority in question possessed the legal right to correct constitutional violations in tangential districts.

Seven weeks later, the Supreme Court made a second interpretive ruling in *Washington* v. *Davis.*[9] The litigation involved a complaint by two black men rejected by the Washington, D.C., police force. Both men had failed the so-called Test 21, administered to prospective governmental employees to test their verbal skills. Reacting angrily, they sued the city's top executive, Mayor Washington. In the ensuing legal battle, the plaintiffs contended the examination bore no relationship to job performance and was distinctly discriminatory because a disproportionately high number of black applicants failed.

Despite this contention, the District Court ruled in favor of Mayor Washington, but the Court of Appeals reversed. Then the Supreme Court joined the argument. On March 11, 1976, the justices heard further arguments by the litigants and by a 6 to 2 vote, upheld the District Court. Writing for the majority, Justice Byron White said the court had not held a law "invalid under the Equal Protection Clause simply because it may affect a greater proportion of one race than of another." The proof of "invalidity," he said, must rest on intent. In school cases, for instance, the test had been whether a "racially discriminatory purpose" existed.[10] Without veering from the trail, the court was chipping branches from the trees along the way.

A third significant decision, *Village of Arlington Heights* v. *Metropolitan Housing Development Corporation* came down on January 11, 1977.[11] As in *Milliken* three years before, the same five justices—Burger, Blackmun, Powell, Rehnquist, and Stewart—formed the majority with Lewis Powell writing the opinion. The case arose over a housing dispute in the village of Arlington Heights, a Chicago suburb about twenty-six miles northeast of the downtown loop area. The 1970 census had tallied only twenty-seven blacks among the village's 64,000 residents. Situated near the center of the village was an eighty-acre plot, owned by the Clerics of St. Viator, a religious groups that wanted to use part of the tract for low- and moderate-income housing. Casting about for assistance, the churchmen engaged a nonprofit developer, knowledgeable in the art of getting housing subsidies under the Federal Housing Act (FHA). They chose the Chicago-based Metropolitan Housing Development Corporation (MHDC).

The following year, 1971, MHDC petitioned the village to rezone fifteen acres of the Viatorian property from single-family to multiple residence so as to build 190 clustered townhouse units. A dozen years before, the Village Board had adopted a zoning ordinance, giving all the properties surrounding the contested area an R-3 single-family classification. Before passing judgement on the question of a zoning change to permit building Lincoln Green, as the project was to be known, the village's Plan Commission held three public hearings.

They revealed a surface reason for keeping the areas R-3. Residents had purchased single-family homes on the assurance there would be no adjoining multiple residences to lower their property values. Only a few witnesses possessed the audacity to hint that racial antagonism might have stirred the overwhelming interest in the hearings, and so supported by the majority, the Commission turned down the petition while conceding the possible "need for low and moderate income housing . . . in Arlington Heights or its environs, [but not] at the proposed location."[12]

Nine months afterwards, three blacks filed suit against the village seeking declaratory and injunctive relief. The District Court took note that racial fears had been expressed during the Commission hearings, but brushed them aside stating "the petitioners were not motivated by racial discrimination . . . [but rather] by a desire to protect property values and the integrity of the Village's zoning plan."[13] Accordingly, it found in favor of Arlington Heights.

On appeal, the Seventh Circuit reversed the lower court in a split vote. While agreeing the defendants had not acted with discriminatory intent, it found the decision adversely affecting black families in search of housing. Minorities, the testimony showed, made up 18 percent of the Chicago metropolitan population and 40 percent of those eligible to occupy Lincoln Green. In addition, the court continued, rezoning had to be evaluated in its "historical context and ultimate effect." There was the indisputable fact of large-scale residential segregation in northwest Cook County combined with proof that the village had "exploited" its whiteness. Judged in this light, to deny Lincoln Green's application could only be countenanced if it served a compelling interest. Since the desire to maintain the Viatorian property as R-3 did not meet this exacting standard, the majority concluded that the defendant village board had violated the Equal Protection Clause of the Fourteenth Amendment.[14]

Not so, said the Supreme Court. Its majority, wrote Lewis Powell, was not concerned with the "ultimate effect" of the decision. That was "without independent constitutional significance." What mattered was a finding of "invidious discriminatory purpose," which demanded "a sensitive inquiry into such circumstantial and direct evidence of intent as may be available.[15] He then went on to list possible determinants. Citing *Washington* v. *Davis*, Powell said one might be "the impact of the official action—whether it 'bears more heavily on one race than another'." A second could revolve on whether the decision reflected a historical pattern of "official actions taken for invidious purposes" such as had occurred in *Keyes*.[16] Still a third criterion was the possibility the board had suddenly changed course, faced by the MHDC petition. Had the property, for instance, been rezoned out of fear it would be used for integrated housing? Finally, Powell declared, there was the question of "contemporary statements by members of the decision making body, minutes of its meetings, or reports" shedding light on the presence or absence of invidious discriminatory purpose.[17]

Pointedly, Powell declared that MHDC had failed to prove, by any of the above guidelines, a case of intended discrimination. "The statements by the Plan Commission and Village Board members, as reflected in the official minutes, focused almost exclusively on the zoning aspects of the MHDC petition, and the zoning factors on which they relied are not novel criteria in the Village's rezoning decisions. There is no reason to doubt that there has been reliance by some neighboring property owners on the maintenance of single-family zoning in the vicinity. The Village originally adopted its buffer-policy long before MHDC entered the picture and has applied the policy too consistently for us to infer discriminatory purpose from its application in this case. Respondents simply failed to carry their burden of proving that discriminatory purpose was a motivating factor in the Village's decision," he wrote.[18]

Arlington failed to change the court's direction, but it did encounter the search for proof of intentional discrimination.[19] By simply following the rules, by denying the existence of antiminority motivation, offending whites could now expect to sidestep charges of constitutional violation. However deleterious the effect of a public decision might be for minorities, judicial relief would be unobtainable unless the plaintiffs adduced evidence of discriminatory intent. Within this reasoning, a community like Arlington, in which whites outnumbered blacks more than 2,000 to one, could legally close its doors to multi-family housing built with Federal money, thus excluding blacks who were too poor to purchase single residences.

Moreover, by authorizing such exclusionary tactics, the court was gaffing the growth of integrated housing, the one development that could make busing unnecessary.

The full impact of the decisions in *Hills* v. *Gautreaux, Washington* v. *Davis,* and the *Village of Arlington Heights* v. *Metropolitan Housing Development Corporation* began to emerge in December, 1976, when the High Court handed down a series of decisions on school desegregation. It started with *U.S.* v. *Austin Independent School District,*[20] in which a District Court, supported by the Fifth Circuit, ordered a sweeping program to achieve in the words of Justice Powell, "a degree of racial balance in *every* school in Austin."[21] In the process, 18,600 to 25,000 students, ranging from 32 to 42 percent of the total school population would be transported. "[T]he remedy ordered," he wrote for the majority in remanding the ruling, "appears to exceed that necessary to eliminate the effect of any official acts or omissions. . . . the extent of an equitable remedy is determined by and may not properly exceed the effect of the constitutional violation. . . . A remedy is not equitable if it is disproportionate to the wrong."[22]

On June 27, 1977, the problem of fitting the "remedy to the wrong" received further interpretation in *Dayton Board of Education* v. *Brinkman.*[23] This litigation, originally filed in April, 1972, had twice been before the District Court for the Southern District of Ohio, and once before the Court of Appeals for the Sixth Circuit before reaching the U.S. Supreme Court.

Testimony showed that, although Ohio had enacted legislation in 1887 outlawing separate public schools for black and white children, the Dayton school system, like other Northern communities governed by similar laws, was permeated with a history of de jure segregation. Pupils and teachers had been separated in the early 1920s. During the 1930s and 1940s, black students were refused the use of the high school swimming pools, nor were black high school teams allowed to compete in the city athletic conference until 1948. In 1969, after reviewing the record of the Dayton school system, HUD announced, "[A]ll Negro principals are assigned to predominantly Negro schools, as are 11 of the 14 Negro assistant principals; 156 out of 181 Negro high school teachers are assigned to schools where Negroes constitute 92 percent of the total enrollment."[24] From this evidence, the District Court could hardly help but find the "great majority" of Dayton schools "racially unbalanced."[25]

Additionally, the court found evidence of unconstitutional action on two other fronts. One was the board's adherence to optional high school attendance zones which gave white students the choice of bypassing predominantly black schools in their neighborhoods. The other was the decision of the board, elected January 3, 1972, to rescind its predecessor's plan for eliminating segregative racial patterns. Because this behavior was "cumulatively in violation of the Equal Protection Clause," to use the court's phrase,

District Judge Carl B. Rubin ordered the Dayton Board to submit a plan abolishing all optional zones and assigning teachers to each school to reflect "the approximate ratio of the total black-to-white faculty in the Dayton system."[26]

When the case eventually reached the Supreme Court, Justice Rehnquist, writing for the majority, dismissed the evidence as too slender to confirm the ruling of the lower courts.

First, reasoned Rehnquist, "The finding that the pupil population in the various Dayton schools is not homogenous, standing by itself, is not a violation of the Fourteenth Amendment in the absence of a showing that this condition resulted from intentionally segregative actions on the part of the Board."[27] As to optional attendance zones, Rehnquist noted this applied only to three of the system's eleven high schools. Also, to the charge that the board's recision of "previously adopted School Board resolutions" was a constitutional violation, he found this of questionable validity. "The Board had not acted," he wrote, "to undo operative regulations affecting the assignment of pupils." Consequently, he went on, the "findings of constitutional violations did not, under our cases, suffice to justify the remedy imposed."[28]

Nevertheless, Rehnquist admitted the difficulty of measuring the extent of constitutional violation. [F]actfinding in such a case as this," he commented, "is a good deal more difficult than is typically the case in a more orthodox lawsuit. . . . the question of whether demographic changes resulting in racial concentration occurred from purely neutral public actions or were instead the intended result of actions which appeared neutral on their face but were in fact invidiously discriminatory is not an easy one to resolve . . . . Nonetheless, that is what the Constitution and our cases call for, and that is what must be done in this case."[29]

In permitting the plan of the District Court to remain in effect for the coming school year while remanding the case for further study, Rehnquist took pains to point out how *Dayton*[30] differed from *Keyes*. In the former, isolated violations had admittedly had their "incremental segregative effect,"[31] and the appropriate remedy must be designed to correct these violations and no more. With the latter, there had been a systemwide violation that could only be cured with a systemwide remedy.

The Court had once more, without changing direction, made it more difficult to find a cure for invidious discrimination. In *Keyes*, it held that a systemwide cure is permissible if it is determined that "school authorities have effectuated an intentionally segregative policy in a meaningful portion of the school system. . . ."[32] The key phrase was "meaningful portion." Unless the plaintiffs could prove the "incremental segregative effect" of constitutional violations occurred in a "meaningful portion," the remedy had to be curtailed, how severely time would tell.[33] As the United States Commission on Civil Rights now commented, "[T]he untangling of many complicated and interwoven chains of cause and effect to measure that degree of segregation . . . must of necessity be costly and time-consuming to litigants and to the courts, and the degree of desegregation that follows may not, in many instances, be substantial."[34] One encouraging fact, however, did spring from this judicial ruling: the High Court's refusal to consider remedies for segregative actions in terms of what effect it might have—positive or deleterious—on educational quality, since this had nothing to do with constitutional violations. In this context, the argument that busing interfered with the learning process became totally irrelevant in determining whether a child's constitutional rights had been violated.

As it turned out in *Dayton*, the litigation took an unexpected turn after remanding to the District Court for further hearings and investigation. This time, the District Judge cleared the school board of intentional resegregation, and on a third appeal, the Sixth Circuit overruled the lower court, reinstating once more the previously approved systemwide desegregation plan. However, now, by digging deeper into Dayton's history, the Circuit Court discovered evidence of greater offenses. Not only had the Board failed to eliminate the dual system, it had actually "exacerbated the racial separation" which existed in 1954 at the time of *Brown I*.[35] "Enrollment data . . . ," noted the Court, "reveals the substantial lack of progress that has been made over the past 23 years in integrating the Dayton School System. In 1951-52, of 47 schools, 38 had student enrollments 90 percent or more one race [4 black, 34 white] . . . . In 1963-64, of 64 schools, 57 had student enrollments 90 percent or more one race [13 black, 44 white]. . . . In 1971-72 [the year the complaint was filed], of 69 schools, 49 had student enrollments 90 percent or more one race [21 black, 28 white]. . . . *Every* school which was 90 percent or more black in 1951-52 *or* 1963-64 *or* 1971-72 and which is still in use today remains 90 percent or more black. Of the 25 white schools in 1972-73, *all* opened 90 percent or more white and, if open, were 90 percent or more white in 1971-72, 1963-64 and 1951-52."[36]

Consequently, the Circuit Court argued it was not a case for finding a remedy for isolated instances of debatable validity, as Rehnquist had suggested, but one involving systemwide violations over many years. In the Court's words, "[D]efendants' intentional segregative practices . . . infected the entire Dayton public school system."[37]

This additional evidence profoundly affected four members of the High Court who had previously voted to reverse the Sixth Circuit and, when the case again came before them, they changed position. Justices White, Brennan, Blackmun, and Stevens, joined by Marshall who had taken no part in the decision two years earlier, now supported the Sixth Circuit in a 5 to 4 majority.

To explain their changed stance, Byron White wrote that new evidence demonstrated the Dayton Board had maintained segregative practices dating back to 1954, continuing "intentional faculty segregation" into the

1970s. This, he said, constituted no isolated violation. This "was a system-wide practice," requiring a systemwide solution.[38] As in *Keyes*, a violation in "a meaningful portion of a school system . . . creates a presumption that other segregated schooling within the system is not adventitious."[39]

"A contrary ruling," commented Robert Reinhold, of the *New York Times*, "might have undermined desegregation orders involving more than five million students in about two hundred school districts throughout the nation."[40]

Reinhold knew whereof he spoke. Hardly a city in the North and West could escape the indictment of pre-1954 segregation. To draw the line and to absolve cities that showed no intentional segregation post-1954 would be to weaken Title VI. Sensing well the implications on the afternoon of decision day, Assistant Attorney General Drew Days immediately called a news conference to announce that ten school districts in communities similar to Dayton were being investigated.

Equally important to the decision was the dramatic shift of Harry Black-mun, ex-President Nixon's second appointee. Up to then, he had most often joined Burger, Powell, and Rehnquist, to curtail the Supreme Court's authority over school desegregation. With his changed stance on *Dayton II*, it was conceivable the Court might halt its drift to the right.

Meanwhile, new ground was about to be broken on the subject of metro-politan school segregation. In 1968, long before the Detroit ruling,[41] the United States government filed suit against the Indianapolis Board of School Commissioners (IPS), charging racial segregation in the city's public schools.[42] District Judge S. Hugh Dillin, on the testimony offered, found de jure segregation.[43] IPS had engaged in purposeful discrimination, gerry-mandering of school attendance zones, and faculty segregation. In addition, the State of Indiana, like Delaware, schemed to prevent metropolitan school consolidation involving Indianapolis and its suburbs, all lying within Marion County. In 1959, when the state's General Assembly enacted legislation to consolidate the state's school districts, under which the num-ber was reduced from 905 to 305, the only lines left untouched were those within Marion County.

The Marion County Reorganization Committee, established by the pro-visions of the statute, had recommended merger of all the county's districts into one school system, but suburbia objected, saying a consolidated dis-trict, as the suburbanites in Detroit had argued, would be too large, school taxes too high, and citizen participation in school affairs too little.

However, with the filing of the Federal suit, things began to happen. The General Assembly, prodded by Indianapolis's dynamic Mayor Richard Lugar, adopted in 1969 the so-called Uni-Gov legislation which transformed Marion County into a consolidated metropolitan government. Yet, fearing the new authority might expand IPS's boundaries to make them coterminous with Marion County, the legislature, a mere sixteen days before the Uni-Gov vote, amended the proposal to omit IPS from its jurisdiction.

Dillin ordered the United States to add other school districts in the metropolitan area as defendants to pave the way for a possible metropolitan remedy. A plaintiff's expert from the Office of Education had testified "that when the percentage of Negro pupils in a given school approaches 40, more or less, the white exodus becomes accelerated and irreversible."[44]

After appeal and affirmation of the facts, the Seventh Circuit remanded the case, ordering Dillin to fashion a plan.[45] In *Indianapolis II*, the court decided "the only feasible desegregation plan" involved the unification of IPS with "adjacent or nearby school districts," bringing the black population in each elementary school to approximately 15 percent.[46]

In a supplementary opinion, termed *Indianapolis III*, Dillin recommended to the State of Indiana legislative revisions for implementing his decision that were adopted in 1974.

Then came *Milliken* in July of the same year, and the Seventh Circuit, on a second appeal, affirmed the lower court's findings, but reversed the inter-district remedy, writing, the "District Court should determine whether the establishment of the Uni-Gov boundaries without a reestablishment of IPS boundaries warrants an inter-district remedy within Uni-Gov in accordance with *Milliken*."[47]

When Dillin began to take testimony anew on March 18, 1975, the suit involved two new defendants, the Metropolitan Development Commission of Marion County (Commission) and the Housing Authority of the City of Indianapolis (HACI). Evidence showed that HACI had selected its public housing sites in a way to ensure segregation. Under state law, it could construct its developments inside Indianapolis or up to five miles outside the city's boundaries with the permission of the affected municipalities. The fact that HACI projects, except for the elderly, were 98 percent black spoke for itself. Wrote Dillin, "Suburban Marion County . . . resisted the erection of public housing projects outside IPS territory, suburban Marion County officials . . . refused to cooperate with HUD on the location of such projects, and the customs and usages of both the officials and inhabitants of such areas has been to discourage blacks from seeking to purchase or rent homes. . . ."[48]

On the subject of schools, court testimony showed that "the suburban Marion County units of government, including the added school defendant corporation, [had] consistently resisted the movement of black citizens or black pupils into their territory. They have resisted school consolidation, they resisted civil annexation so long as civil annexation carried school annexation with it, they ceased resisting civil annexation only when the Uni-Gov Act made it clear that the schools would not be involved."[49] Dillin went on to say that because the State of Indiana shouldered ultimate responsibility for the operation of the public schools, it had a responsibility "to alleviate the segregated condition then existing in IPS." Instead, the "General Assembly expressly eliminated the schools from consideration under Uni-Gov," thereby signaling "its lack of concern with the whole problem." It warrants a limited "interdistrict remedy," he concluded.[50]

Accordingly, the Court ordered the transfer of 6,533 students (grades one to nine) transported during the 1975-76 school year, raising the percentage of black students outside Indianapolis to approximately 15 percent. In addition, to shrink the black core inside the city, he ordered HACI to cease building housing projects within the boundaries of IPS.[51]

Once more, the defendants appealed. In behalf of the majority, Judge Luther M. Swygert held that Uni-Gov standing alone was neutral, that its impact was to be "clearly perceived" only by weighing such correlative evidence as the hastily enacted 1961 Annexation Act. This, he said, indicated a "legislative intent [from which] a court is entitled to draw reasonable and logical inferences. . . . The record fails to show any compelling state interest that would have justified the failure to include IPS in the Uni-Gov legislation." Summarizing the court's stand, he said, "We are convinced that the essential findings for an interdistrict remedy found lacking in *Milliken* are supplied by the record in the instant case. . . . Indianapolis presents an entirely different situation. . . . The . . . Legislature acted directly in passing Uni-Gov, thereby creating the existing situation which confines black students within IPS."[52]

As to the housing issue, Swygert conceded many factors may have contributed to the concentration of 95 percent of Marion County's blacks inside the inner city. However, he shared Dillin's conviction that the principal cause was "racial discrimination in housing which has prevented them [blacks] from living any place else."[53]

On yet another appeal, the U.S. Supreme Court remanded the litigation for further consideration in light of *Washington* and *Arlington Heights*.[54] The court's majority evidently believed that the plaintiffs had not yet proven intentional discrimination to the point of triggering systemwide interdistrict relief. They simply would not concede, absent further proof, that passage of Uni-Gov and the selection of inner city sites by HACI had confirmed segregative intent. As the justices had previously observed, any action that produced a disproportionate effect on minorities was not by itself a constitutional violation.

Thus reversed, the Seventh Circuit called on Judge Dillin to make further findings.[55] In response, Dillin for the fifth time ruled the evidence showed intentional discrimination. After *Brown I*, he wrote, ". . . it became the duty of every member of the General Assembly, under his oath to support and defend the Constitution of the United States, to assist in desegregating the Indianapolis School system. The necessity of obtaining a wide dispersal

of Negro schoolchildren in order to secure a stable plan was obvious in
1969, as a result of the dreary experience of resegregation in such places as
Atlanta, Georgia, Washington, D.C., and elsewhere, which was widely
known at that time. However, the General Assembly reversed its forward
progress and departed from its long established boundary policy
by . . . eliminating the schools from Uni-Gov."[56] As to HACI, he now
wrote, "When faced with the choice of locating a public housing project on
the west side of Emerson Avenue [IPS territory] or across the street on the
east side of such avenue [Warren Township territory], HACI chose the IPS
side of the street. This deliberate choice was intended to, and did,
perpetuate Warren Township as a segregated community and IPS as a
heavily black community."[57]

On July 11, 1978, he ordered the reinstatement of his ruling of August 1,
1975, with its transfer of more than 6,000 black students to peripheral
schools. Again, the Seventh Circuit affirmed his judgement.[58] Finally, on
August 17, 1981, buses carried 387 black children across the IPS line to
schools in Franklin Township.[59]

It had now taken thirteen years to terminate a case of desegregation. A
child born at the time the original suit was filed would have completed
elementary school. Nevertheless, the evidence indicated the High Court's
sanction of interdistrict relief as long as the impermissible act showed intent
to discriminate. The key question in each case was still the *Keyes* question:
did discrimination occur "in a meaningful portion of a school system?"[60] If
yes, a systemwide solution; if no, a reduced order.

Notes

1. Robert Reinhold, "Top Court Backs . . . ," *New York Times*, July 3, 1979.
2. *Milliken* v. *Bradley*, 418 U.S. 717 (1974).
3. *Brown* v. *Board of Education*, 347 U.S. 483 (1954).
4. *Milliken* v. *Bradley*, at 745.
5. *Hills, Secretary of Housing and Urban Development* v. *Gautreaux*, 425 U.S.
284 (1976), at 284.
6. *Gautreaux* v. *Romney*, 363 F. Supp. 690 (1973), at 691.
7. *Gautreaux* v. *Chicago Housing Authority*, 503 F 2d 930 (1974), at 939.
8. *Hills* v. *Gautreaux*, at 297-98.
9. *Washington, Mayor of Washington, D.C.* v. *Davis*, 426 U.S. 229 (1976).
10. Ibid., at 240, 242.
11. *Village of Arlington Heights* v. *Metropolitan Housing Development Corp.*,
429 U.S. 252 (1977).
12. Ibid., at 258.
13. Ibid., at 259.
14. Ibid., at 260.
15. Ibid., at 266, 271.
16. *Keyes* v. *School District Number One, Denver, Colorado*, 413 U.S. 189
(1973).

17. *Village of Arlington Heights*, at 266-68.

18. Ibid., at 270.

19. Ibid.

20. *U.S. v. Austin Independent School District*, 532 F. 2d 380 (1976).

21. No. 76-200 *Austin Independent School District* v. *U.S.*, 429 U.S. 990 (1976) at 992.

22. Ibid., at 994-95.

23. *Dayton Board of Education* v. *Brinkman*, 443 U.S. 526 (1979).

24. *Brinkman* v. *Gilligan*, 503 F 2d 684 (1974) at 689.

25. Ibid.

26. Ibid., at 686.

27. *Dayton Board of Education* v. *Brinkman*, 443 U.S. 406 (1977), at 413.

28. Ibid., at 413-14.

29. Ibid., at 414-20.

30. *Brinkman* v. *Gilligan*, 518 F 2d 853 (1975).

31. *Dayton* v. *Brinkman*, at 420.

32. *Keyes* v. *School District*, at 208.

33. *Dayton* v. *Brinkman*, at 420.

34. *Desegregation of the Nation's Public Schools: A Status Report* (Washington, D.C.: U.S. Commission on Civil Rights, 1979), p. 5.

35. *Brown* v. *Board of Education*, 347 U.S. 483 (1954).

36. *Brinkman* v. *Gilligan*, 583 F 2d 243 (1978) at 253-54.

37. Ibid., at 252.

38. *Dayton* v. *Brinkman*, at 539.

39. *Keyes* v. *School District*, at 208.

40. Reinhold, "Top Court Backs."

41. *Milliken* v. *Bradley*.

42. *U.S.* v. *Board of School Commissioners of the City of Indianapolis, Indiana*, 332 F. Supp. 655 (1971).

43. Ibid., at 678.

44. Ibid., at 676.

45. *U.S.* v. *Board of School Commissioners*, 474 F 2d 81 (1973), at 89.

46. *U.S.* v. *Board of School Commissioners*, 368 F. Supp. 1191 (1973), at 1205.

47. *U.S.* v. *Board of School Commissioners*, 503 F. 2d 68, 86 (7th Cir. 1974).

48. *U.S.* v. *Board of School Commissioners*, 419 F. Supp. 180 (1975), at 183.

49. Ibid., at 182-83.

50. Ibid., at 183.

51. Ibid., at 185-86.

52. *U.S.* v. *Board of School Commissioners*, 541 F. 2d 1211 (1976), at 1220-21.

53. *U.S.* v. *Board of School Commissioners*, 368 F. Supp. 1191, at 1204.

54. *U.S.* v. *Board of School Commissioners*, 429 U.S. 1068 (1977), at 1068-9; *Washington* v. *Davis*, 426 U.S. 229 (1976); and *Village of Arlington Heights* v. *Metropolitan Housing Development Corp.*, 429 U.S. 252, (1977).

55. *U.S.* v. *Board of School Commissioners*, 573 F. 2d 400 (1978).

56. *U.S.* v. *Board of School Commissioners*, 456 F. Supp. 183 (1978), at 188.

57. Ibid., at 189.

58. *U.S.* v. *Board of School Commissioners*, 637 F. 2d 1101 (1980).

59. *New York Times*, August 18, 1981.

60. *Keyes* v. *School District*, at 208.

24

CONCLUSION

"The U.S. Commission on Civil Rights believes that school desegregation is the single most important task confronting the Nation today in the field of civil rights. . . . Either we are for desegregation and a system of education that provides equality of opportunity, or we are for a system of education that makes a mockery of our Constitution."

U.S. Commission on Civil Rights.[1]

Looking back over the quarter century since *Brown I*,[2] a believer in school integration is buoyed by the vast number of black children who now sit in desegregated schools, tempered, to be sure, by the realization that millions are still denied this opportunity through white fear, prejudice, and bigotry.

The history of this demographic distribution has been filled with victories, defeats, and what might have been if. . . . All three branches of the Federal government have played major roles, at times courageously, at times pusillanimously.

Swept along by the civil rights revolution of the mid-1960s, Lyndon Johnson gave historical dedication to desegregating the South. Had this momentum continued beyond the 1968 election, with continuing support from the White House, the nation's public school system would be fully integrated. Lamentably, the election of Richard M. Nixon, stained as it was from the beginning with pandering to the worst instincts of American intolerance, signaled retreat. After promising to close the wounds left by Vietnam, the President proceeded to set American against American in still another confrontation. Nixon's determination to undercut the enforcement of Title VI of the 1964 Civil Rights Act slowed the pace of integration in the South, and his opposition to busing, despite its authorization in the Charlotte case by a unanimous Supreme Court ruling,[3] so aroused the nation that public opinion quickly equated busing with integration and hating the one, decried the other.

Congress, reflecting this sentiment, gladly followed the White House lead as it shifted from pole to pole. During the Johnson tenure, it passed wide-ranging statutes to outlaw discrimination in education, voting, and housing. For many Northern Congressmen, preserving the constitutional rights of black people outside their own constituencies was simply pro bono publico and they luxuriated in the praise lavished on them for their outspoken liberalism. However, as Nixon fueled the busing controversy, and the Southern birds flew North to roost, they began to tremble. The same institution that enacted the 1964 statute now proceeded to pull its teeth.

Only the Supreme Court held firm. It chastised the South for dragging its feet, rejected "free-choice" plans when they proved futile, countermanded *Brown II's* "all deliberate speed" opinion for being too slow,[4] approved busing, and finally defined de jure segregation in such a way as to apply to the North. Its one failure to stand up lay in blocking the road to metropolitan desegregation. *Milliken* effectively crippled desegregation in such large centers as New York, Chicago, Los Angeles, Philadelphia, and Detroit when there was still time to act.[5]

Behind this, of course, stood Nixon's four appointees. All held strict constructionist views and, therefore, read the Constitution in narrower terms than their immediate predecessors.

Throughout the period, pressure from Richard Nixon went unabated. Whether a supine HEW, a feckless Congress, or a Supreme Court, fearful of losing prestige, his was the malevolent catalyst determined to slow down desegregation. He seemed impervious to taking from millions of children their constitutional rights, leaving them inexorably scarred.

It is interesting to speculate what might have happened, had Abe Fortas not been forced into retirement. Fortas was as unchanging as Marshall or Brennan in his support of civil rights legislation. In all probability, his vote, not Burger's, would have decided the outcome of *Milliken* and Stephen Roth's decision would have stood.

As another example, consider the 1968 presidential campaign. Had the election taken place a few days later, Hubert Humphrey, in all likelihood, would have won. For two decades, his voice had supported civil rights.

Alas, history is not concerned with "ifs," nor what might have been. Consequently, our primary concern now is to locate today's coordinates on the map of school desegregation and then to plot how best we may progress to tomorrow's.

Significant figures released by HEW's Office for Civil Rights showed that in 1976, of six regions in the U.S., only two had "low" levels of segregation—the Southeast (0.16) and the West (0.18). (By HEW standards, up to 0.20 is considered low.) States above the Mason-Dixon line are now the most segregated.[6]

A second fact to keep in mind is that school segregation is most concentrated in the nation's twenty-six largest cities, where 36 percent of the black population now resides. Three out of four black children attend segregated schools with the percentages varying from city to city, rising as high as nine out of 10 in New York.[7] Moreover, this urban massing has a geometric effect on the racial imbalance of pupil populations within the metropolitan areas. Baltimore's 70 percent minority enrollment, for instance, is surrounded by a suburban school population 92 percent white; Wilmington's 85 percent black population by one 94 percent white.[8]

Writing of this latter juxtaposition, the United States Commission on Civil Rights commented, "Even if every school in the city of Wilmington perfectly reflected the racial composition of the district as a whole [85 percent black], these schools would still be regarded as racially identifiable in a metropolitan area whose public school enrollment is 79 percent white and whose suburbs are 94 percent white. . . . In short, we have come to a point where a substantial integration of public schools can be accomplished only if the area covered is larger than the city itself. If, on the other hand, the responsibility to desegregate ends at the city line, the decision in *Brown* v. *Board of Education* will provide little or no tangible benefit to many millions of children who live in large cities. For these children, racially isolated education will continue to be a reality for the forseeable future."[9]

This, then, marks the battle's current coordinates. In addition to the adverse decision in *Milliken*, what impedes metropolitan progress most is the invisible racial wall separating black from white—city from suburb. If the research, analysis, and study for this volume teaches one lesson above all others, it is the failure of white America to bear its responsibility for the welfare of all children regardless of color. This escapism shows itself in the parent who places his or her child in a private school rather than uniting with other citizens—neighbors—to build a better school for the entire community. It shows itself in the family who flees the city to get away from the school that is increasingly black. In both instances, the family is unconcerned over what happens to another's child through its action. It is their own, theirs alone, that counts. That pulling out reduces the quality level in the school left behind causes little regret.

As eloquently described by Gunnar Myrdal, the Swedish economist, in his classic *American Dilemma*, American whites have historically rejected blacks as equals.[10] By now the reader should be aware that school desegregation is not being retarded so much by administrative difficulties, though they bulk large and are often vexing, not by lack of money, though busing clearly adds to the expense of school operation, but by racial intolerance, the fact that white people set very narrow parameters on their association with blacks.

For this Uncle Sam bears a heavy cross. It was he who formerly insisted on separate housing for blacks and whites. To preserve the homogeneous character of housing built with Federal money, the FHA adopted stern guidelines, for prudent financial reasons, but clearly segregative. "Underwriting manuals not only adopted the phraseology of 'inharmonious races and classes,' but advocated racial restrictions, physical barriers, racial covenants as methods of excluding certain racial and national groups. Pigpens and unwelcome races were classed as equally objectionable."[11]

States, too, played their part. The code of ethics for real estate brokers in Michigan and Delaware, as revealed during the *Milliken* and *Buchanan*[12] litigation, told realtors, following the Code of Ethics of the National Association of Real Estate Boards, not to deal with "members of any race or nationality . . . whose presence will clearly be detrimental to property values in the neighborhood."[13]

Moreover, discriminatory practices by the so-called gatekeepers of the housing industry—the banks, the builders, and the brokers—succeeded in keeping the invisible wall intact, and where minority families hoped to pierce the veil, town boards and municipal governing bodies rushed in with zoning and building restrictions to waylay the "intruders" at the pass.

Despite these facts, some white Americans still contend that black families are kept out of white enclaves by differences of income and the herd instinct to remain together, and not from prejudice.

As to income, demographer Reynolds Farley has calculated that 43 percent of all black families in the New York City metropolitan area would live in the suburbs on the basis of their earnings instead of the 17 percent who actually do; 46 percent in the Chicago suburbs instead of the 8 percent who actually do.[14] Karl Taeuber, another demographer, notes that income variations account for not more than 20-25 percent of racial segregation in metropolitan areas.[15]

The contention that blacks segregate themselves by choice is another canard. Although it is true that a congenital associative longing exists within all social and ethnic groups, this hardly explains why blacks are the *most* segregated group. Their isolation cannot be interpreted solely as a result of choice. In fact, many in-depth studies disclose a marked preference for integrated living. Less than one black family in five expresses a choice for the all-black neighborhood.[16]

In a pluralistic nation such as the United States, such racial chasms cannot be allowed to persist. Not only do they adversely affect the nation's health, they create an atmosphere in which the desegregation of the school system encounters intolerable obstacles.

To be realistic, however, if the Federal government is surfeited with the problem, as appears likely, we must look in other directions for aid. In this connection, Gary Orfield reminds us that "although busing has been pictured in congressional debates as a grave national problem, most senators and congressmen represent constituencies where the minority population is so low that even total desegregation would be a minor operation."[17] Accordingly, by deduction, it would seem pressure should be exerted in those states whose school systems are still laced with segregation since each one has a constitutional obligation under *Brown* to desegregate. Indeed, in *Bradley* v. *Milliken* decided August 15, 1975, the District Court ruled that the State of Michigan could be compelled to share the financial burden of remedial reading, in-service teacher training, testing, and counseling to compensate for previous deeds of de jure segregation. Under the order of the Federal District Court, the state had to contribute $5.8 million—or 50 percent—of their cost, the Detroit School Board, the remaining half.[18]

This could herald a new chapter. Instead of Washington leading the procession, each state would bear its own standard, use its own resources. Such a shift in responsibility would seemingly open new avenues to metropolitan desegregation.

Ohio already offers one of the best examples. With the possible exception of California, Ohio has more urban centers and more desegregation problems than exist in any of the other forty-eight states. To find a path through this maze, the Ohio General Assembly created a study committee in 1977 to analyze what the "state's role in reducing racial imbalance" should be.[19] It became a case study for legislators who up to then equated desegregation with "forced busing" because of what they had seen in the media and on television. State Senator M. Morris Jackson, committee chairman, reported, "[We] devoted seven day-long hearings to taking testimony. We listened to numerous witnesses, each with their own experiences, perceptions and objectives. We heard from attorneys; plaintiffs and defendants in desegregation cases; local, state and federal officials; desegregation experts, civil rights activists, and anti-bussers; city planners and fair housing advocates; school officials, parents, lobbyists, ministers, teachers, students, university professors and concerned citizens."[20] Out of the verbal potpourri came the committee's final recommendations.

As a practical politician, Jackson saw "little chance" of a group of legislators responding positively to sole appeals for school desegregation. On the other hand, such issues as the protection of constitutional rights , law and order, grass roots control, fiscal savings, and quality education, all associated with desegregation could, if organized properly, generate support. To illustrate, Jackson pointed out that in Ohio, local governments are encouraged to provide joint governmental services at reduced costs. 'Providing desegregation programs across district lines is surely one, particularly during a time of declining student enrollments and empty school buildings. Thus can desegregation appeal to fiscal conservatives."[21]

Members of Jackson's committee, initially hostile, backed off once they heard the testimony. They eventually "urged the state to provide transportation dollars to school districts for whatever the reason—geographic distance, rural consolidation, suburban sprawl, urban transportation or *desegregation*."[22] (Italics added).

Next to busing, the committee's greatest discovery was the effect of residential segregation on school segregation. Research showed that (1) flagrant violation of Federal and state open housing laws had occurred, and (2) the only viable long-term "alternative to busing" was an integrated society with a mixture of minorities and majorities. Accordingly, they "spent a good deal of time formulating recommendations strengthening both the content and the enforcement of fair housing laws."[23]

The committee also found that the issue of school desegregation cut across the usual guidelines separating political bodies. It was not Republican against Democrat, liberal against conservative, or urban against suburban. "At the outset," Jackson recalls, "the committee was justifiably leery of school desegregation particularly during an election year. Yet none of the members sidestepped the subject. Neither did they play to the grand-stands. . . . And despite a variety of partisan, racial, residential, philosophical, professional and educational backgrounds, the committee was able to adopt a final report unanimously."[24]

This is not the first time that the nation has had to look to state government to find a solution to its ills. By adopting the carrot-and-stick approach used by the Federal government, states can reward those cities that desegregate their schools and penalize those that ignore the pattern of Title VI. In 1977, the State of Connecticut announced such a procedure by threatening to cut Bridgeport's school aid if it did not comply.

A further alternative lies in the use of the state courts. In the past, they have decided some of the most delicate subjects involving equity. In *Serrano* v. *Priest* (1971), the California Supreme Court initiated debate over the disparity in per-pupil spending within the state.[25] The present majority of the Supreme Court demonstrates a strong belief in states rights as evidenced in *Milliken II*, when it held the lower court's decision requiring the state of Michigan to share with the Detroit School Board the cost of school desegregation as not violating "the Tenth Amendment and general principles of federalism."[26] It is to be hoped that this may encourage state participation in metropolitan desegregation.

Finally, initiative at the local level is having a growing effect on the desegregative process. After the Louisville-Jefferson County court-ordered metropolitan school desegregation plan went into effect on September 4, 1975, the Kentucky Human Rights Commission encouraged whites to welcome blacks into their neighborhoods to avoid busing. The district court had ruled that in elementary schools with a 12 to 40 percent black student body (12.5 to 35 percent in secondary schools) there would be no busing.[27] In a pamphlet entitled *Six Ways to Avoid Busing,* the Commission listed twenty-nine schools in the two categories. One elementary school, the Commission went on, already had a pupil body 9 percent black and needed only twenty-five new students in the attendance zone to terminate busing; a high school, 7 percent black, needed only forty additional black children to qualify.[28] As a result of this effort, in three years, "the number of black pupils residing in traditionally all white suburban Jefferson County" increased more than during the previous dozen years (by 63 percent from 3,948 to 6,451).[29] The possibility of harnessing this love-hate relationship between the neighborhood school and busing offers one of the best hopes for a long-range solution to segregation, especially in the North where segregated housing patterns have primarily caused de facto school duality.

Indicative of this shift from Federal to state and local involvement has been the formation in 1977 of the National Task Force on Desegregation Strategies, appointed by Dr. Otis R. Bowen, then Governor of Indiana. The twenty-two member body, consisting of recognized authorities on school desegregation, is meticulously "birddogging" what happens in every state from its Denver headquarters. According to Chairperson Francis Keppel, President Johnson's one-time Commissioner of Education, the Task Force lists three goals: (1) Integrated housing to achieve integrated education; (2) School metropolitanization; and (3) Leadership in key states.[30] In the words of the National Task Force:

Some argue that we should forget about desegregation and concentrate on improving the quality of those city schools which are presently not adequately educating their students. This argument overlooks the fact that improvement in academic achievement is not the sole, nor perhaps even the most important, reason for desegregation. In a multicultural society, the only truly effective education, for both minority and majority group children, is an integrated education. Not only is an integrated education necessary to allow all children to learn to function competently as adults in a multicultural society; the ability of persons from diverse groups to work together in an atmosphere of mutual respect is essential to the preservation of our society. Thus, while we must strive to achieve the best education for all children, regardless of the racial or socioeconomic composition of the school, our goal must be an integrated educational experience for all children.[31]

Notes

1. *With All Deliberate Speed: 1954-19??* (Washington, D.C.: U.S. Commission on Civil Rights, 1981), 1.
2. *Brown* v. *Board of Education*, 347 U.S. 483 (1954).
3. *Swann* v. *Charlotte-Mecklenburg Board of Education*, 402 U.S. 1 (1971).
4. *Brown* v. *Board of Education*, 349 U.S. 294 (1955).
5. *Milliken* v. *Bradley*, 418 U.S. 717 (1974).
6. *Desegregation of the Nation's Public Schools: A Status Report* (Washington, D.C.: U.S. Commission on Civil Rights, 1979), p. 20.
7. *Statement on Metropolitan School Desegregation* (Washington, D.C.: U.S. Commission on Civil Rights, 1977), pp. 6-7.
8. Ibid., p. 10.
9. Ibid., pp. 10-12.
10. Gunnar Myrdal, *An American Dilemma, The Negro Problem and Modern Democracy* (New York: Harper & Row, 1944).
11. Charles Abrams, *Forbidden Neighbors* (New York: Harper & Row, 1955), p. 162.
12. *Evans* v. *Buchanan*, 416 F. Supp. 328 (1976).
13. *Evans* v. *Buchanan*, 393 F. Supp. 428 at 434.
14. Reynolds Farley, "Residential Segregation and Its Implications for School Integration," *Law and Contemporary Problems* 39 (Winter, 1975): 175-76.
15. *Swann* v. *Charlotte-Mecklenburg*, at 25.
16. Ibid., at 31.
17. Gary Orfield, Must We Bus? (Washington, D.C.: Brookings Institution, 1978), p. 64.
18. *Bradley* v. *Milliken*, 402 F. Supp. 1096 (1975).
19. Ohio State Senator M. Morris Jackson, "Ohio's Joint Select Committee on

School Desegregation: A Political Evaluation," *Progress* (Denver: National Project and Task Force on Desegregation Strategies, Winter, 1979), p. 2.

20. Ibid., p. 3.

21. Ibid., p. 4.

22. Ibid., p. 3.

23. Ibid., p. 5.

24. Ibid.

25. *Serrano* v. *Priest,* 5 Cal. 3d 584, 487 P. 2d 1241 (1971).

26. *Milliken* v. *Bradley,* 433 U.S. 267 (1977), at 291.

27. *Cunningham* v. *Grayson,* 541 F. 2d 538 (1976).

28. *Six Ways to Avoid Busing* (Louisville: Kentucky Human Rights Commission, 1975).

29. *Housing Desegregation Increases as Schools Desegregate in Jefferson County* (Louisville: Kentucky Human Rights Commission, 1977), p. 1.

30. Author's conversation with Francis Keppel, Chairperson, National Task Force on Desegregation Strategies, December 24, 1979.

31. *Metropolitan School Desegregation* (Denver: National Project and Task Force on Desegregation Strategies, 1979), pp. 12-13.

BIBLIOGRAPHY

Supreme Court Decisions

Brown v. *Board of Education,* 347 U.S. 483 (1954). Court unanimously rules that de jure segregation (established by state law) creates "inherently unequal" schools, thereby violating the Equal Protection Clause of the Fourteenth Amendment.

Brown v. *Board of Education,* 349 U.S. 294 (1955). Court orders school desegregation to proceed "with all deliberate speed."

Green v. *Board of Education of New Kent County, Virginia,* 391 U.S. 430 (1968). Court, now edgy about "with all deliberate speed," declares acceptable desegregation must promise "realistically to work *now.*"

Alexander v. *Holmes,* 396 U.S. 19 (1969). Angry court unanimously reverses the Fifth Circuit for allowing thirty Mississippi school districts to delay desegregation. They are ordered to convert "from dual to unitary" at once.

Swann v. *Charlotte-Mecklenburg Board of Education,* 402 U.S. 1 (1971). A unanimous court upholds busing as a legitimate tool for desegregation.

Wright v. *Council of the City of Emporia,* 407 U.S. 451 (1972). Four Nixon appointees break the court's previous unanimity in school desegregation cases, becoming the minority in a 5 to 4 decision.

San Antonio School District v. *Rodriguez,* 411 U.S. 1 (1973). In a 5 to 4 decision, the court refuses to declare unconstitutional a Texas law permitting unequal school reimbursements. Education, it says, "is not among the rights afforded explicit protection under our Federal Constitution."

Keyes v. *School District Number One, Denver, Colorado,* 413 U.S. 189 (1973). Court applies de jure criteria to de facto segregative situations in the North. Purposeful official segregation in one part of a school district is seen as contaminating the entire system, absent evidence to the contrary proving it was accidental.

Bradley v. *Milliken,* 418 U.S. 717 (1974). A landmark 5 to 4 decision, effectively delaying metropolitan desegregation. Court denies Detroit permission to join its school district to suburbia in order to relieve segregation without proof that school segregation exists on both sides of the city boundary line.

Hills, Secretary of Housing and Urban Development v. *Gautreaux*, 425 U.S. 284 (1976). First in a series of High Court decisions following *Milliken* that sift the power of the judiciary in discriminatory actions. Here, *Milliken* is said not to apply because the defendant had authority to operate inside and outside the Chicago jurisdiction.

Washington v. *Davis*, 426 U.S. 229 (1976). To the argument the City of Washington used a discriminatory qualifying examination, the court replies it was not necessarily discriminatory because it affected one race more than another. There has to be a "racially discriminatory purpose to prove 'invalidity.' "

Village of Arlington Heights v. *Metropolitan Housing Development Corp.*, 429 U.S. 252 (1977). Again, the court states that discrimination without intent has no constitutional significance. Regardless of the effect, it has to have an "invidious discriminatory purpose" to warrant action.

Austin Independent School District v. *U.S.*, 429 U.S. 990 (1977). Court continues to reduce the area of its application to cases involving school desegregation. It remands a lower court decision that called for extensive busing because the remedy exceeded the constitutional violation.

Dayton Board of Education v. *Brinkman*, 443 U.S. 526 (1979). Reference *Austin*, the court decides in 1977 not to go the more expansive route of *Keyes*, saying the violation did not require such an extensive remedy, but upon remanding the case and discovering more evidence, the court splits 5 to 4, saying uncorrected offenses, dating back to 1954, necessitate the larger solution, the *Keyes* solution.

Lower Court Decisions

U.S. v. *Jefferson County Board of Education*, 380 F. 2d 385 (1967). Fifth Circuit Court of Appeals, sitting *en banc*, orders six Southern states within its jurisdiction to create a "unitary school system," not black, not white "just schools."

Bradley v. *School Board of the City of Richmond, Virginia*, 338 F. Supp. 67 (1972). Court tries initially to solve Richmond's school desegregation by creating a metropolitan district involving suburbia. Fourth Circuit kills effort and is upheld by Supreme Court.

Adams v. *Richardson*, 356 F. Supp. 92 (D.D.C. 1973). John H. Pratt, United States District Judge for the District of Columbia, finds HEW guilty of not enforcing Title VI of the 1964 Civil Rights Act in the seventeen Southern and Border states.

U.S. Board of School Commissioners, 368 F. Supp. 1191 (1973). Court successfully adopts the *Milliken* formula of establishing evidence of discrimination inside and outside the city limits of Indianapolis in a lawsuit of appeal and counter appeal lasting thirteen years.

Tallulah Morgan v. *James W. Hennigan*, 379 F. Supp. 410 (1974). District Judge Wendell Arthur Garrity, Jr., initiates one of the longest and most bitter efforts to desegregate an American school system—in Boston.

Evans v. *Buchanan*, 393 F. Supp 428 (1975). Another example of using *Milliken's* formula to form a metropolitan district out of Wilmington and peripheral New

Castle County, the court having found evidence of continuing school segregation inside the city and housing discrimination to keep blacks from moving into suburbia.

Brown v. *Weinberger,* 417 F. Supp. 1215 (D.D.C. 1976). Federal District Judge John J. Sirica rules that HEW intentionally violated Title VI of the 1964 Civil Rights Act in the thirty-three Northern and Western states, thus enclosing with the help of *Adams* v. *Richardson* all fifty states in the federal judicial net.

Books

Abrams, Charles. *Forbidden Neighbors.* New York: Harper & Brothers, 1955.

Chester, Lewis; Hodgson, Godfrey; and Page, Bruce. *An American Melodrama: The Presidential Campaign of 1968.* New York: Viking Press, 1969.

Clark, Kenneth. *Dark Ghetto.* New York: Harper & Row, 1965.

Ellison, Ralph. *Invisible Man.* New York: Modern Library, 1947.

Fanon, Frantz. *Black Skin, White Masks.* New York: Grove Press, 1967.

Franklin, John Hope. *From Slavery to Freedom, a History of Negro Americans.* New York: Vintage Books, 1969.

Myrdal, Gunnar. *An American Dilemma: The Negro Problem and Modern Democracy.* 1944. Reprint. New York: Harper & Row, 1962.

Orfield, Gary. *Must We Bus? Segregated Schools and National Policy.* Washington, D.C.: The Brookings Institution, 1978.

Panetta, Leon E., and Gall, Peter. *Bring Us Together.* Philadelphia: J. B. Lippincott, 1971.

Report of the National Advisory Commission on Civil Disorders. New York: Bantam Books, 1968.

Sandburg, Carl. *Abraham Lincoln, The War Years,* Vol. 4. New York: Harcourt Brace, 1939.

Magazines

Atlantic Monthly
Barrows, Frank. "School Busing," November 1972, p. 20.
Christian Century
Harding, Vincent. "The Atlanta Compromise," October 3, 1973, p. 988.
Nelson, J. Robert. "Blacks and Whites and Yellow Buses," November 6, 1974, p. 1029.
Commonweal
Hazelton, Paul. "Choice and the School," October 4, 1974, p. 13.
Ebony
Lester, Julius. "The Necessity for Separation," August 1970, p. 168.
Poinsett, Alex. "The Dixie Schools Charade," August 1971.
Educational Leadership
Brodbelt, Samuel. "Disguised Racism in Public Schools," May 1972, pp. 700-701.
Educational Forum
Orfield, Gary. "White Flight Research," May 1976, p. 525.

Harper's
   Buchanan, Patrick J. "Memorandum to the President," June 1972.
Inequality in Education
   Bell, Derrick A., Jr. "Integration: A No Win Policy for Blacks?" March 1972, p. 42.
   Brown, Cynthia. "Busing: Leaving the Driving to U.S.," (December 1971), p. 6.
   Pottinger, J. Stanley. "HEW Enforcement of Swann," August 3, 1971, p. 8.
Integrated Education
   Allen, James E., Jr. "Integration Is Better Education," September-October, 1969.
Juris Doctor
   Gillers, Stephen. "Joe Rauh An Integrated Life," February, 1975, p. 37.
Life
   "How the Candidates Stand on Busing," March 3, 1972.
Nation
   Cleghorn, Reese. "Shooting An Elephant," March 30, 1970, pp. 358-61; "Betrayal in the House," November 22, 1971, pp. 515-17.
   Owens, Patrick. "A Jury of His Club Mates," November 3, 1969, p. 462.
National Journal
   Rabb, Charles. "Education Report," June 17, 1971, p. 1305.
National Review
   Brudnoy, David. "Fear and Loathing in Boston," October 25, 1974, p. 1231.
   "The Rehnquist Fight," December 3, 1971, p. 188.
Nation's Schools
   Steif, William. "Desegregation Rider Exposes Northern 'Guilt Feelings,' " April 1970, p. 26; "Softer Line Appears on Desegregation," June 1970, p. 81.
New Republic
   Bickel, Alexander M. "Does It Stand Up?" November 1, 1969, p. 14; "Desegregation: Where Do We Go From Here?" February 7, 1970, p. 20.
   Featherstone, Joseph. "Boston Desegregation," January 17, 1976, p. 23.
   Grant, William. "Integration's Last Hurrah, 'Where Did Everyone Go To?' " September 12, 1970, p. 20.
   James, J. C. "The Black Principal," September 26, 1970, p. 18.
   Osborne, John. "The Nixon Watch," April 4, 11, 1970, p. 13; "Austin Story," August 21, 1971, p. 15.
   Rilling, Paul M. "Desegregation: The South *Is* Different," May 16, 1970.
   Zucherman, Edward. "Beaten Up in Boston," May 22, 1976, p. 11.
Newsweek
New Yorker
   Harris, Richard. "Annals of Politics (Judge Carswell and the Senate—I),"
   December 5, 1970, p. 60; "(Judge Carswell and the Senate—II)," December 12, 1970, p. 53.
   "The Talk of the Town," March 11, 1972.
People
   Jennes, Gail. "Teacher," October 3, 1977, p. 83.
Phi Delta Kappan
   Coleman, James S. "Racial Segregation in the Schools," October 1975, pp. 77-78.
   Spears, Harold. "Kappans Ponder Racial . . . ," December 1972, p. 245.

Progressive
Chapman, William. "Uptight in Boston," June 1974, pp. 38-39.
Ramparts
Kopkind, Andrew. "Busing into Southie," December 1974, p. 35.
Saturday Review of Literature
Foster, G. W., Jr. "Title VI: Southern Education Faces the Facts," March 20, 1965, p. 60.
Orfield, Gary. "The Politics of Resegregation," September 20, 1969, p. 78.
Serrin, William. "They Don't Burn Buses Anymore in Pontiac," June 24, 1972, p. 8.
School Management
Beckler, John. "Desegregation: Congress Wrestles with Nixon," August, 1970, p. 2; "Will the Court Settle the Question of School Segregation?" December 1970, p. 4; "Try, Try Again," March 1971, p. 4.
Southern Education Report
Batten, James K. "The Nixonians and School Desegregation," June 1969, p. 24.
Steif, William. "The New Look in Civil Rights Enforcement," September 1967, p. 3.
Time
U.S. News & World Report

Monographs and Periodicals

Congressional Digest
"Congress and Federal School Racial Policy." April 1970, pp. 99-102.
"Controversy in Congress over 'School Busing.' " April 1974, pp. 99-128.
"Racial Distribution in Public Schools." April 1970, pp. 103-27.
"Senate Rejects Carswell Nomination." May 1970, p. 129.
"Should Congress Restrict . . . Federal 'School Desegregation Guidelines?' " February 1969, pp. 39-64.
Congressional Quarterly
"Busing Opponents: New Friends in the House." December 11, 1971, pp. 2559-2562.
Congressional Record
National Project and Task Force on Desegregation Strategies
Metropolitan School Desegregation, 1979.
Progress, Winter 1979.
Orfield, Gary. The Reconstruction of Southern Education. New York: John Wiley, 1969.
Southern Regional Council
"Lawlessness and Disorder—Fourteen Years of Failure in Southern School Desegregation," *Special Report III*, 1968.
"School Desegregation: Old Problems Under a New Law," *Special Report I*, (September 1965).
"School Desegregation 1966—The Slow Undoing," *Special Report II*, December 1966.

Watters, Pat. "Charlotte," *Special Report* (1964).
U.S. Civil Rights Commission
   "Desegregating the Boston Public Schools: A Crisis in Civic Responsibility."
   Washington, D.C.: August 1975.
   "Desegregation of the Nation's Public Schools: A Status Report." Washington,
   D.C.: February, 1979.
   "Racial Isolation in the Public Schools." Washington, D.C.: 1967.
   "Statement on Metropolitan School Desegregation." Washington, D.C.: February
   1977.
   "With All Deliberate Speed: 1954-19??" Washington, D.C.: November 1981.

Newspapers

Atlanta Constitution
Boston Globe
Boston Herald-American
Charlotte Observer
Christian Science Monitor
Columbia State
Denver Post
Detroit Free Press
Detroit News
New York Times
New York Times Magazine
Richmond Times-Dispatch
Wall Street Journal
Washington Daily News
Washington Post
Washington Star

INDEX

Mitchell, Parren J., 116-17
Mizell, Wilmer D., 139-40
Mondale, Walter, 75-76, 139, 198; opposi-
    tion to Nixon's school legislation, 93;
    and Stennis amendments, 77
Mondale-Javits Resolution, 78-79
Morgan. See *Tallulah Morgan* v. *James
    W. Hennigan*
Morgan, Edward L., 109
Morris, Horace, 251
Morse, Wayne, 11
Morton, Rogers, 29, 33, 83
Mottl, Ronald M., 235
Mottl Amendment, 235-36
Moynihan, Daniel Patrick, 58; calls for
    "benign neglect," 80
Muskie, Edmund S., in 1972 presidential
    campaign, 119; on busing, 136-37; in
    Chattanooga, 136; in Florida, 142; in
    Nashville, 137
Myrdal, Gunnar, 269

NAACP. *See* National Association for the
    Advancement of Colored People
NAACP Legal Defense and Educational
    Fund, 8, 42, 44, 47, 51, 67, 98, 123-24,
    179, 185, 251
NAG. *See* National Action Group
NAREB. *See* National Association of Real
    Estate Brokers
Nashville, Tenn., 111, 136
Nation, 68
National Action Group (NAG), 132-33
National Association for the Advancement
    of Colored People (NAACP), 11, 182,
    193, 251; *Brown III*, 222; in Arizona,
    176; in Boston, 199, 203, 216; in
    Chicago, 255; in Detroit, 159; and
    Emporia litigation, 180; in Florida, 141;
    in Pontiac, 132; in Virginia, 174;
    opposition to Finch compromise, 24;
    opposition to Haynsworth, 65
National Association of Real Estate Brokers
    (NAREB), 269-270
National Education Association, 53, 85
National Task Force on Desegregation
    Strategies, 272-73
National Urban Coalition, 14
National Urban League, 65
Nation's Schools, 79
Nedzi, Lucien N., 163; opposed antibusing
    legislation, 163; and Whitten ambiva-

lence, 163
New Republic, 80, 86, 111, 131, 211
Newsweek, 56, 75, 102, 106, 205, 251
New York City, 227, 250-51, 268, 270
New York Civil Liberties Union, 251
New Yorker, 143
New York Times, 20, 25, 30, 47, 49, 52,
    55-56, 67-68, 78-79, 99, 102, 118, 136,
    145, 164, 178, 192-93, 206, 245, 250,
    262
Nixon, Richard M., 7, 51, 57, 60, 101, 110,
    112, 117, 170-73, 221, 223, 228-29
    Administration of, 231, 267-68
    Austin Decision (opposed to), 112
    136
    Bradley v. *Milliken*, 165-66
    Broomfield letter, 166
    Carswell: defeat, 69; nomination, 66
    Civil Rights Act of 1964, Title VI
        (opposed to), 19
    Finch removal, 95
    Haynsworth: defeat, 66; nomination,
        64-65
    Inaugural statement, 20
    "Instant integration . . . segregation
        forever," 46-47
    Key Biscayne home, 38
    Labor-HEW Appropriations measure
        (1970, amended) signing, 79
    Letter to Clarence Mitchell, 21
    Mansfield-Scott Amendment, 233
    Miami nomination, 18
    Panetta firing, 84
    Potomac excursion, 32
    Powell nomination, 173
    Presidential campaign of 1972: busing,
        113, 117, 138, 142-45; Texas, 111;
        victory, 145
    Rehnquist nomination, 173
    School desegregation measure ($1.5
        billion) proposal: in House, 92; in
        Senate, 92; statement on, 88
    Stennis amendments, 42, 74, 77, 88
    Swann, reaction to, 106, 109
    Thurmond alliance, 18
    Wallace, threat to election, 19
    Whitten amendments, criticized for
        silence on, 72
Noel, Rachel, 182
Noel Resolution, 182-83
Nordheimer, Jon, 52
North Carolina State Board of Education

About the Author

GEORGE METCALF, now a columnist for the *Auburn* (New York) *Citizen*, was a New York State senator and president of the National Committee Against Discrimination in Housing. He is the author of *Black Profiles* and *Up From Within*.